Flash™ *Studio Secrets*®

GLENN THOMAS
CO-FOUNDER, SMASHING IDEAS

FLASH™ STUDIO SECRETS®

Hungry Minds™

New York, NY ▲ Cleveland, OH ◆ Indianapolis, IN ▼ Chicago, IL ◆ Foster City, CA ▲ San Francisco, CA

Flash™ Studio Secrets®

Published by
Hungry Minds, Inc.
909 Third Avenue
New York, NY 10022
www.hungryminds.com

ISBN: 0-7645-3548-X

Printed in the United States of America

10 9 8 7 6 5 4 3 2 1

1K/RU/QT/QR/IN

Distributed in the United States by Hungry Minds, Inc.

Distributed by CDG Books Canada Inc. for Canada; by Transworld Publishers Limited in the United Kingdom; by IDG Norge Books for Norway; by IDG Sweden Books for Sweden; by IDG Books Australia Publishing Corporation Pty. Ltd. for Australia and New Zealand; by TransQuest Publishers Pte Ltd. for Singapore, Malaysia, Thailand, Indonesia, and Hong Kong; by Gotop Information Inc. for Taiwan; by ICG Muse, Inc. for Japan; by Intersoft for South Africa; by Eyrolles for France; by International Thomson Publishing for Germany, Austria, and Switzerland; by Distribuidora Cuspide for Argentina; by LR International for Brazil; by Galileo Libros for Chile; by Ediciones ZETA S.C.R. Ltda. for Peru; by WS Computer Publishing Corporation, Inc., for the Philippines; by Contemporanea de Ediciones for Venezuela; by Express Computer Distributors for the Caribbean and West Indies; by Micronesia Media Distributor, Inc. for Micronesia; by Chips Computadoras S.A. de C.V. for Mexico; by Editorial Norma de Panama S.A. for Panama; by American Bookshops for Finland.

For general information on Hungry Minds' products and services please contact our Customer Care department within the U.S. at 800-762-2974, outside the U.S. at 317-572-3993 or fax 317-572-4002.

For sales inquiries and reseller information, including discounts, premium and bulk quantity sales, and foreign-language translations, please contact our Customer Care department at 800-434-3422, fax 317-572-4002 or write to Hungry Minds, Inc., Attn: Customer Care Department, 10475 Crosspoint Boulevard, Indianapolis, IN 46256.

For information on licensing foreign or domestic rights, please contact our Sub-Rights Customer Care department at 650-653-7098.

For information on using Hungry Minds' products and services in the classroom or for ordering examination copies, please contact our Educational Sales department at 800-434-2086 or fax 317-572-4005.

For press review copies, author interviews, or other publicity information, please contact our Public Relations department at 650-653-7000 or fax 650-653-7500.

For authorization to photocopy items for corporate, personal, or educational use, please contact Copyright Clearance Center, 222 Rosewood Drive, Danvers, MA 01923, or fax 978-750-4470.

Library of Congress Cataloging-in-Publication Data

Thomas, Glenn (Glenn E.)
   Flash studio secrets / Glenn Thomas.
      p. cm.
   Includes index.
   ISBN 0-7645-3548-X (alk. paper)
   1. Flash (Computer file) 2. Computer animation. 3. Multimedia systems. 4. Web sites--Authoring programs. 5. Web site development. I. Title.
TR897.7 .T55 2001
006.6'96--dc21
                                          2001016552

is a trademark of
Hungry Minds, Inc.

Hungry Minds™

FOREWORD

The community today using Macromedia Flash continues to thrive and flourish through a consistent method of interaction and communication. This behavior has enabled many developers to learn techniques to effectively convey ideas using Macromedia Flash through a medium that is often otherwise static, unintuitive, and boring. The community-driven evolution of Web design is being led by the Flash community and, with its current momentum, shows few signs of slowing down.

At Macromedia, our passion is embodied in the product we work so hard to deliver. Working directly with the community ensures that real problems are being solved through technology and authoring solutions to harness creative expression and deliver effective designs, animations, and applications throughout the World Wide Web. We are committed to aiding the development community through mechanisms such as Macromedia Exchange, Macromedia Dashboard, community-driven usability guidelines, the Accessi-bility Kit, and many other solutions to help streamline the production process. Together, we are evolving this medium to match our vision of what the Web can be.

Glenn Thomas has been an unwavering supporter of the technology since the inception of FutureSplash Animator. As one of the early pioneers, he has insights very few developers have. His book compiles effective techniques from his projects, the development community, and Macromedia, providing a superb handbook for every developer using Macromedia Flash.

Eric J. Wittman
Director of Product Management, Flash Products
Macromedia, Inc.

What a pleasure to see such a remarkable book on Macromedia Flash. Glenn Thomas is the perfect person to have written a book on Flash. He and his team at Smashing Ideas provide Internet solutions through humor and entertainment. Glenn has built a successful company using the animation strengths of Macromedia Flash. In this book, he has shared his knowledge and his excitement. What an extraordinary opportunity to learn from one of the best in the industry!

This book has given you a genuine feeling for the essence of Flash. Flash is not just another Web drawing, animation, and user-interface design tool. It has a zest and liveliness of its own that is derived from the wonderful personalities of the people who designed, programmed, and used it to create numerous Web sites.

Macromedia Flash has come a long way, both in functionality and industry awareness, since its initial release in August of 1996. Flash was first released under the name of FutureSplash Animator by FutureWave Software, Inc. Flash's early success can be directly attributed to the indescribably hard work of the FutureWave team and the developers who embraced it from the start. Macromedia acquired the Flash team and technology in January 1997; at the time of the acquisition, a team of eight ran our entire company.

Inspiration for Flash came about in August of 1995 at the West Coast SIGGRAPH tradeshow. FutureWave was at the show to demonstrate SmartSketch, our first consumer vector-based drawing product. An attendee watching the demo made a comment, "the technology in this product would be great for animation." The Web was at its infancy and had not even begun to reach the commercial status of today, so we were not sure what the market was like for an animation tool. After much thought about his comment, we decided this passer-by was absolutely right. The technology was perfect for animation, more specifically animation on the Web, due to the small K-byte size of the graphics found in this technology. Within a couple weeks, we began working on what was to become Flash — first by stripping features from SmartSketch that were targeted for the consumer market, and then adding features targeted for the Web design and animation market.

In case no one else has done it yet, I hereby officially proclaim my partner at FutureWave Software, Jonathan Gay, to be a true programming genius! I do not make this proclamation lightly. Jonathan pulled off programming feats in Flash that were virtually impossible. For example, I approached Jonathan with an industry first . . . adding an antialiasing feature to our vector-based product. The next morning Jonathan had the "impossible" feature completed. This single feature opened the door to professional-quality vector graphics for the Web. I truly admire this man's mastery in writing extraordinary code.

June 1996 saw our first public beta release of FutureSplash Animator. Due to the ingenuity of our "early adopter" developers, many of them had sites completed before FutureSplash Animator's official release. These developers had figured out the features and functionality of FutureSplash Animator even before the manual was completed. We created the tool and they ran with it, creating a diversity of stunning Web site designs. These masterpieces were inspiration to other developers, and the love of Flash snowballed from this point.

Macromedia Flash would never have attained the status of "standard in the industry" without the brilliance of Web developers such as Glenn Thomas, pushing Flash to the limit and inspiring innovative ways to use the tool. I hope that you will take the wealth of useful techniques and in-depth knowledge in this book and use them to dazzle the Web with your own talents and inspiration.

Michelle Welsh

Michelle Welsh
Co-founder, FutureWave Software, Inc. & Flash

To all of the amazing, talented and passionate people who make up the Flash community around the world. We hope that you find what we've done with this book both useful and inspirational.

PREFACE

In September 1996, a salesman at a computer graphics store introduced Ben Yenter, Evan Clarrissimeaux, and me, the three founders of Smashing Ideas, to a little Web program from FutureWave called FutureSplash that promised to bring vector animation and limited interactivity to the Web. Having already worked on the nascent commercial Internet for a couple of years, I snapped up the program. Although the features were limited, what the program could do was a revelation. Out of that purchase, Smashing Ideas was born to create digital media for the Web.

Since that time Smashing Ideas has been involved with the growth of animation and entertainment on the Web as well as the creation of seminal Web applications using Flash. We've animated properties such as *Dilbert*, *Peanuts*, *CatDog*, *South Park*, and *Zombie College*, while creating award-winning interactive content for Devo and Madonna. The LAUNCHcast Player, a personalized streaming radio station (highlighted in Chapter 10) won the first ever Bandie Award from the broadband industry for the "Best Broadband Music Service."

Smashing Ideas specializes in the creation of innovative Flash content for the Web, interactive television, networked devices, and the wireless arenas. We have watched the program evolve from that little tool called FutureSplash that could create small interactive Web sites and limited animation to this program called Flash that enables full Web application development and amazing interactive and narrative digital content. As we seek to continually push the edges of what can be done for clients on the Web, we've learned a great deal about the program and ways to use it effectively.

We base our approach to using Flash on a deep understanding of the integration of the artistic, design, and technical aspects of the medium with the goal of always creating great media and applications. We find that Flash is a great solution for most of our client's digital media challenges.

When Flash started, the Web was a really low-bandwidth place. The standard modem speed was 14.4K and life on the Web was lived at a snail's pace. The joke heard everywhere was about logging on for the "world wide wait."

Flash helped solve this problem by providing superior performance in low-bandwidth situations with its vector-based approach to Web multimedia. File sizes were small. Production values were high. It was rich media for the Web. Because almost the entire Web was low-bandwidth, this was a significant advantage.

Macromedia looked at Flash and decided that it could be better and it could be everywhere. Macromedia has focused on those two goals with each new version of the product and has made Flash the most ubiquitous multimedia player in the history of the Internet, while at the same time providing a powerful tool for creating rich media and applications for the Web.

This book shares a variety of those real-world projects with you, using techniques and approaches appropriate for creating great rich media projects with Flash 5 and 4, but also going back to explain how to do a few tricks in Flash 3. Although the focus is on Flash 5 in this book, we have found that our clients require us to deliver great projects that can work with all versions of the Flash player.

YOU WANT TO CREATE SUCCESSFUL PROJECTS

We expect that readers of this book have a solid working knowledge of Flash. Knowledge of the interface and basic principles of Flash are extremely well covered in *Flash 5 Bible* by Robert Reinhardt and Jon Warren Lentz (from Hungry Minds, formerly known as IDG Books Worldwide).

This book combines an explanation of time- and project-tested approaches to creating rich media with explanations of how real projects were done. Projects covered in the book include work for clients such as Lycos, Cameraworld, Eddie Bauer, the Game Show Network, Egreetings, Wakmail, Icebox.com, the Crab Broker, WhatCard, and Smashing Ideas' internal projects.

The book starts with descriptions of how to begin creating a full Flash Web site and then moves through the process of optimizing the files associated with that site. We then cover motion graphics and the new approach to ActionScript. We next investigate rich media experiences and applications employing databases and Generator for dynamic data integration. The basics of using sound within Flash are then described, as are the fundamentals of creating broadcast-quality animation.

The last seven chapters describe areas where these techniques can be used such as entertainment, edutainment, branding, marketing, and product display. These chapters also describe various techniques that you can use to extend Flash with video and 3D. The book closes with conversations about using Flash for personal expression.

Included throughout this book are interviews with leading lights in the Flash professional and creative community. These are people who live and breathe digital media and Flash. They all care deeply about what they do. Their thoughts on our wired world and explanations of their processes and techniques are a fascinating and illuminating read.

Rather than create a CD-ROM for this book, we have made various files associated with the chapters in this book available at `www.flashstudiosecrets.com`. Due to licensing restrictions, not all .fla files associated with our clients' projects are available on the Web site.

NOTE

There are many areas in this book where we provide code examples during the discussions. Unfortunately, this book's design does not allow for the length of the lines of code that you would normally see on screen. In order to help you identify where these lines of code really should not be breaking, we have inserted a symbol in the code. When you see the ¬ symbol, this means the line should not have broken.

YOU WANT TO CREATE THE DIGITAL WORLD OF TODAY AND TOMORROW

The future of Flash looks incredibly exciting from where we stand. We have been involved with this tool for an extremely long time and truly love the richness of experience that the program can deliver to the user. We want you to use Flash to its fullest potential so you can help create a world of innovative digital media experiences for the Web and beyond.

   With this book, we have tried to showcase the areas where we feel Flash has a real and significant purpose. We believe it is the most powerful and interactive multimedia technology to ever grace the Web digital media field. We believe that as more and more developers discover the power and joy of creating with this tool, Flash will drive the creation of the interactive digital media world.

ACKNOWLEDGMENTS

I would first like to thank Ben Yenter and Evan Clarrissimeaux, without whose energy, dedication, and creativity Smashing Ideas would not exist. Without our collective passion to build a studio based on imagination and innovation, we would never have become a part of the Flash revolution on the Web. We are lucky enough to have a phenomenal staff of talented people who share a passion for creating amazing interactive media for the digital era.

Many, many thanks go to Beth Kluender, pictured here. Without her this book would not have happened. She not only magnificently managed the production of this book at Smashing Ideas, but also got all of the signed client licenses so we could show real projects in these pages. Without her perseverance and willingness to take on multiple legal departments simultaneously, this book would be a mere shadow of what it is.

Troy Parke, with the help of Steve D'Amico, developed the fantastic chapter and part openings for this book. Their designs beautifully reflect the idea of the blueprint as the start for the creation of the various projects.

Many thanks to the chapter authors from within Smashing Ideas who worked many long and hard hours to make sure the projects they've worked on were properly explained in these pages. Troy Parke introduces the reader to motion graphics, Andreas Heim shows how to program with ActionScript, Russ Tarleton talks about programming rich media experiences and printing, and Matt Rodriguez goes into depth about how to create real character animation in Flash.

We also owe a monumental debt to the authors and contributors from outside of Smashing Ideas who freely shared their expertise and creativity with us. These authors took precious time out of their busy schedules to lend valuable insights into their approach to Flash and multimedia.

Phil Torrone wrote a masterful introduction to Generator charting, Phil Scott discusses why Juxt Interactive used Generator on their phenomenal Web homebuilding application for SheaHomes, Heather Perkins gives the reader the benefit of her years of experience creating sound for Flash and multimedia, and Mano provides insight into the genius behind his creation of 3D in a 2D medium. The subjects of the interviews in the book are all masters in their respective areas; many thanks to Jason Alan Snyder, Todd Purgason,

Joel Trussell, Matt Rodriguez, Natalie Zee, Josh Ulm, and Shannon Rankin for sharing their thoughts and ideas on a variety of topics.

Dawn Boughton made everybody at Smashing Ideas look good in the author photos, while Markus Neidermeier took shots of cameras.

Our colleagues at Hungry Minds have been a pleasure to work with while writing this book. Many thanks go to Sharon Eames for her consistent and elucidating editing throughout this project. She gave this book a common voice so that it would remain consistent and easy to read. Michael Roney, our acquisitions editor, has been a great help throughout. Thanks for calling us; we've really enjoyed doing this book. We'd also like to thank all of the other people at Hungry Minds who have been involved with the creation and production of this book.

Chrissy Rey did the technical edit on this book and without her this book would not be nearly as clear and useful as it is. Her many suggestions have made this a better book.

I would like to personally thank the Flash team for bringing out this amazing product and making it into a standard for rich media on the Web and everywhere else. The people developing this program have consistently amazed me with their high standards, their passion, their attention to detail, and their desire to create a great tool for designers and developers. I truly believe that Flash has become great because so many great people are helping create it.

Many, many thanks to Eric Wittman of Macromedia for his contribution of one of the forewords to this book, as well as for his friendship and excitement throughout this Flash revolution. Michelle Welsh, one of the founders of FutureWave, graciously took time away from her beautiful son to write the second foreword, telling us a bit about the background of the program.

I'd like to praise the whole Flash community for being so full of creative, engaging, and genuinely kind people. I never thought I would make so many good friends through a software program, but it's happened and I value all of your talents and passion. The folks on the coast who helped pull me through the last hard rewrites get a double dose of thank yous.

And last, but not least, I would like to thank Celina for her encouragement in writing this book, as well as my family and friends for accepting my disappearance from their lives throughout the long process of writing. Without all of your friendship, love, and support, I would never have started on this adventure called Smashing Ideas.

CONTENTS AT A GLANCE

CONTENTS

CHAPTER 3
MOTION GRAPHICS AND
TYPOGRAPHY   49

CHAPTER 4
OBJECT-ORIENTED PROGRAMMING
IN FLASH   71

CHAPTER 5
ADDING VALUE TO WEB SITES WITH
RICH MEDIA APPLICATIONS   99

CHAPTER 6
INTEGRATING DATABASE
CONNECTIVITY AND PRINTING   125

CHAPTER 7
MAKING SITES DYNAMIC USING
GENERATOR   141

CHAPTER 8
GETTING GREAT SOUND
IN FLASH   161

PART II: FLASH
EVERYWHERE   175

CHAPTER 9
BROADCAST QUALITY
ANIMATION   177

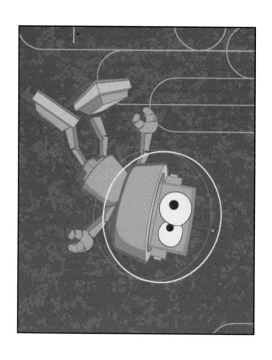

PART I
USING FLASH TO CREATE DYNAMIC WEB SITES

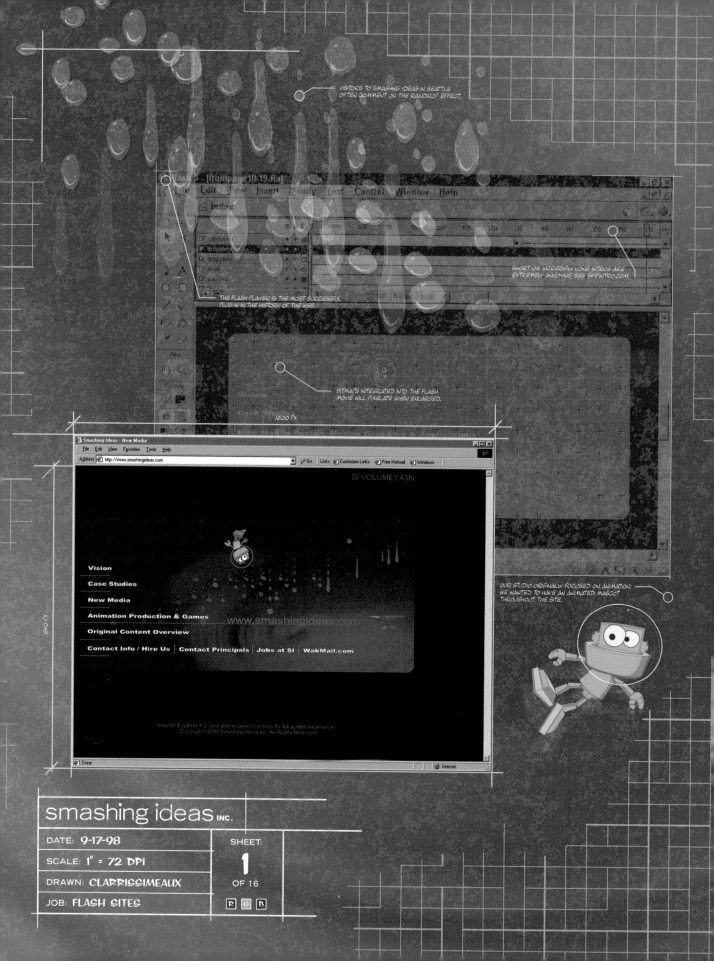

VISITORS TO SMASHING IDEAS IN SEATTLE
OFTEN COMMENT ON THE RAINDROP EFFECT.

Flash [frontpage10-19.fla]

File Edit View Insert Modify Text Control Window Help

index

SHORT OR INCREDIBLY LONG INTROS ARE
EXTREMELY ANNOYING. SEE SKIPINTRO.COM

robot
dropblet
droplets
stud
swashes

THE FLASH PLAYER IS THE MOST SUCCESSFUL
PLUG-IN IN THE HISTORY OF THE WEB.

BITMAPS INTEGRATED INTO THE FLASH
MOVIE WILL PIXELATE WHEN ENLARGED.

1200 PX

Smashing Ideas - New Media

File Edit View Favorites Tools Help

Address http://www.smashingideas.com   Go   Links   Customize Links   Free Hotmail   Windows

SI VOLUME3.43fs

OUR STUDIO ORIGINALLY FOCUSED ON ANIMATION.
WE WANTED TO HAVE AN ANIMATED MASCOT
THROUGHOUT THE SITE.

Vision

Case Studies

New Media

Animation Production & Games

www.smashingideas.com

Original Content Overview

Contact Info / Hire Us | Contact Principals | Jobs at SI | WakMail.com

Internet Explorer 4.0 and above users click here for full screen experience.
Copyright©2000 Smashing Ideas Inc. All Rights Reserved

Done   Internet

smashing ideas INC.

DATE: 9-17-98	SHEET:
SCALE: 1" = 72 DPI	**1**
DRAWN: CLARRISSIMEAUX	OF 16
JOB: FLASH SITES	F C B

CHAPTER 1
MAKING GREAT WEB SITES WITH FLASH

Web sites done completely in Flash have recently moved from the fringes of the Web into the mainstream. This is one of the most exciting developments with Flash. Previously, full Flash Web sites were created almost exclusively for films, television programs, and Web studios' portfolios (1.1). Now all of that is rapidly changing. Clearly, Flash is changing the face of the Web.

Flash has evolved from a simple tool used to create vector animation on the Web into a rich and complex medium used to produce full sites and applications. Because the production values in Web sites created with Flash can rival the production values found in established media such as television, film, and magazines, while adding the Web's own killer app of interactivity, Flash has become the medium of choice for great, creative Web site design.

Flash sites have geared themselves toward product marketing, branding, interactive advertising, banking, e-commerce and many other applications. Within the Macromedia Flash gallery, sites for companies such as Mercedes Benz, Volkswagen, Intel, and Disney demonstrate that Flash is the preferred solution in the rich media Web site design arena.

Nonetheless, a variety of specific problems must be taken into account when designing a complete Flash site. I'll address these issues by reviewing the strategy and creation of the Smashing Ideas studio site (1.2, 1.3). I'm one of the cofounders of Smashing Ideas, and have been involved with creating Flash-specific rich media entertainment experiences, applications, and Web sites for over four years.

> *... that which comes into the world and disturbs nothing deserves neither patience nor respect.*
>
> JEAN COCTEAU

1.1

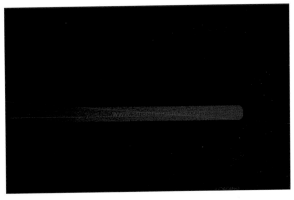

1.2

1.3

DECIDING TO USE FLASH

The first questions a Web designer needs to ask are what the client is trying to accomplish with a site and whether Flash offers the best possible way to achieve the client's goals. Flash offers a number of distinct benefits over regular HTML sites that often make it the preferred solution.

- **Player Ubiquity.** The Flash player is the most successful plug-in in the history of the Web. It has been downloaded more than 270 million times. It's also built into the major operating systems, comes with various browsers, is built into some set top boxes (for interactive television), comes with the RealPlayer, is part of QuickTime and is available for various PDA platforms. Flash penetration across

the Web reaches more than 96 percent for Flash 3 and currently stands at around 85 percent and moving higher for Flash 4. Predictions for Flash 5 are inexact at best, but 50 to 60 percent by late spring 2001 wouldn't surprise me. An independent research company undertakes a study of Flash player deployment on a regular basis and designers and developers should review those results periodially in the Flash section at Macromedia's site.

- **Rich Media Experience.** Flash offers the capability to create complete sites with high media production values combining complex interactivity and animation. As the Web moves from a mainly informational medium into one providing entertainment experiences along with information, users have come to expect richer media from Web sites. As broadband becomes a reality, users will expect even more. Currently, the reach and diversity that Flash offers developers can't be found with any other program.

- **Write Once, Play Everywhere.** Creators of non-Flash Web sites wanting to have similar media production values must rely on technologies such as DHTML and JavaScript. These technologies are supported differently by competing browsers, so developers have to spend extra time ensuring cross-browser compatibility. Flash enables Web developers to concentrate on creating one great experience that all Web users will see in the same way.

DESIGNING RICH, INTERACTIVE MEDIA

New York City–based creative director Jason Snyder has directed the creation of some of the most groundbreaking Flash work on the Web. He has developed and executed interactive branding and marketing strategies for clients such as Unilever, Coca-Cola Enterprises, General Motors, Microsoft, AltaVista, Lego, Launch, and Dell. Snyder also founded the Evil Robot Manufacturing Corporation in 1990 as a private fine-arts initiative focused on interactive development, and has been nominated for the Art Directors Club's Young Guns Award 2000.

Q: How do you approach your work on the Web?

A: The artist Jean Cocteau once said "that which comes into the world and disturbs nothing deserves neither patience or respect." This idea really impressed me and has affected my approach to creative development. Philosophically, it is important that everything I develop is impactful. Commercial interactive work tends either to lull its audience into complacency or it tries too hard and becomes too "fancy" to be usable. I have found my best solutions do not compromise func-

A Flash movie's layout and fonts display exactly the same wherever Flash is supported. (1.4, 1.5). Designers love to work with Flash because their work appears the way they created it without lots of difficult coding or browser testing. Designers should remember that colors and animation speed (frames per second) do vary on different computers.

■ **Seamless Experience.** With Flash, Web developers can load movies into and out of a base Flash movie. This ability lets designers create seamless transitions and gets rid of the page-to-page "blinking" of HTML Web sites. Developers can also reduce the download time for rich media content by using proper streaming design in Flash movies and intelligent preloading sequences. The goal is to create rich media that keeps users completely wrapped up in the experience without ever giving them a moment to pause or hesitate.

1.4

> **NOTE**
>
> The Flash 5 Player is available only for Windows 95/98/2000/NT, and Mac OS PowerPC. It's not available for Windows 3.1. Availability for other operating systems such as Linux is a question best left to Macromedia.

1.5

tion for design and I arrive there by pushing the medium to reveal the solution.

Q: How do you start thinking about a project?
A: I am very technology-focused and fundamentally believe that having an immersive understanding of the platform, distribution method and client device are fundamental to developing a successful interactive experience. As an example, IKEA's catalog and retail outlets are powerful things. IKEA has done what few corporations in the world can, which

is to bring a retail shopping experience to the level of art form. Its Web site really needed to provide an experience that the catalogs and outlets couldn't. Since there was not going to be e-commerce on the site, it needed to provide a unique and impactful, information-oriented, interactive experience for the consumer.

Q: How do you push the Web and interactive medium to reveal the solution?
A: It's about how I focus on the solution to develop the medium. I have had such a prolonged exposure to the tools avail-

able to a creative person in this industry that my exposure has me thinking a certain way. I understand the limitations of both the developer's toolset and the client-side technologies. Because I am so closely tied to both those influences I instinctively know what is and is not possible. I suppose, then, when I am thinking of how to develop a solution, and I want to do something fresh, it generally means I have to push the medium.

- **User Interactivity.** Flash enables extensive user interactivity within movies as well as the ability to interact with programs on backend servers. These abilities enable the user to create rich, immersive, user-directed experiences.

  Flash 5 adds the ability to read XML data (1.6) so Flash movies can tie into standard server-side data exchange as well as an XML socket connection (1.7) that enables an XML data connection to be kept open with a backend server.

- **Web Applications.** Flash 4 had limited programmatic abilities, but enabled creative Web developers to push the limits of interactivity and application

development. Flash 5 uses ActionScript, which is a JavaScript-like object-oriented programming language (1.8) that enables developers to create full and rich media applications. This new addition to Flash 5 makes it a significant tool for any Web developer who wants to reach the largest possible audience for rich media-interactive applications.

KNOWING WHEN NOT TO USE FLASH

Even though we want to create every Web site in Flash, it's not always the best solution for every client. Web designers need to consider the following potential

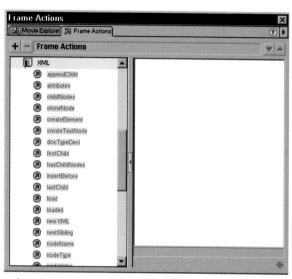

1.6

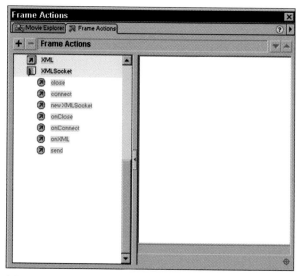

1.7

Q: Is your approach unique with each design question or do you have a standard thought process that you go through?

A: No — it's unique. Design solutions are very specific. Because so much of my work has been with huge brands, most clients get pretty touchy about how they are represented in the interactive space. Mostly, I consider my goal and then work backwards. I'm one of those people who can see the whole solution in my head in an instant. A client will ask for a product, a game, an identity, or a marketing cam-

paign, and instantly I see the solution pop into my head.

It then takes weeks or months working with my team and the technology (whatever it may be) to articulate the solution that pops into my head. It is largely an iterative process and almost instantly becomes a shared vision with my creative team. I am lucky that my team is extraordinarily talented and communicates really well, so they begin moving quickly toward the shared vision. But the process is actually very different each time.

Q: What aspects of the medium do you focus on most when you try to answer design questions?

A: That's a tricky one. I want the widest audience to see the solution, but I want to use the best technology available to develop it. So I suppose distribution — platform — is a huge aspect of my work. The tough thing about the medium is how disruptive it can be. I always enjoy when I get to do "traditional" broadcast work because the result is so smooth. But I also dislike it — because the product isn't interactive. So, interaction —

problems with using Flash and decide whether they are worth disregarding for any given project.

Not everybody in the world can see Flash movies. Although Flash is a ubiquitous plug-in, it's still not a 100-percent solution. If a client wants to create a Flash site but does not have the audience to fully support one, then a developer must push to create a simplified HTML version of the site that is accessible for this audience (1.9).

Older computers with bad graphics cards and low processor speeds don't play Flash movies well. Developers need to keep this in mind when defining the audience and create less motion-intensive Flash movies. Text readability can be a problem at smaller font sizes within Flash movies (1.10), but this is a

problem also shared to some degree when using smaller font sizes in regular Web pages. Other issues include a lack of easy disability access to Flash movies, and difficulties in doing robust searches within large Flash sites.

Although these concerns mean that Flash is not the right solution for every Web site in development, it is certainly the only reasonable solution to create amazingly rich media experiences for the average Web viewer. Anybody who wants to create ground-breaking, envelope-pushing work in rich, interactive media will find that Flash is the answer.

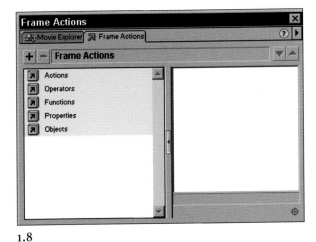

1.8

1.9

1.10

engaging the audience to respond and to think proactively about the content, to get them to respond in real time to the communication I design and develop — that's what's really tremendous about the medium.

Q: What other art forms or types of design influence your thinking on digital media the most?
A: Physical and industrial design has been a great influence on me. Looking at the interfaces I have designed — they are very appliance-oriented. Consumer elec-

tronics and packaged goods make excellent interactive design metaphors. You can communicate a great deal by examining industrial design and translating their subtleties to the screen. And as technology gets "better" the two are really becoming symbiotic. This merger of the physical and the virtual is making for some very interesting design examples.

CREATING AN EFFECTIVE FLASH-BASED WEB SITE

The Smashing Ideas Web site celebrates the use of Flash in all its forms. Created entirely in Flash, the site acts as a showcase of the studio's past projects for clients, original work, and experiments in pushing the limits of Flash (1.11). Because Smashing Ideas has been working almost solely in Flash since 1996, the studio had a wealth of innovative projects to display, and it needed a site design that would not distract from the work itself. In the case of Smashing Ideas' studio site, using Flash was never in question.

The first stage of the process was to define the audience for the site. In this case the audience was current and potential clients for Smashing Ideas' Flash services and original content. Because the audience was expected to have Flash installed and connect to the Web via a fast connection, Smashing Ideas felt that there was room to push the limits with both file size and a full Flash Web site.

The next step in our Web site project was to define the studio branding and figure out how that influenced the information architecture of the site. Creating a site in Flash is no different. Standard questions have to be answered, such as:

- What's the site trying to say to the audience?
- What's the content of the site going to be?
- How do the different parts of the site connect?

Smashing Ideas wanted to show its audience that we were experienced with rich media-interactive projects and had an established track record for innovative work. Because our studio originally focused on animation, we wanted to have an animated mascot throughout the site. We settled on an old-fashioned looking robot that moves throughout the site and spices up each section (1.12).

Because most of the studio's work communicates visually, we chose to focus on displaying the projects themselves rather than just writing about them. We chose a color palette based on a black background with blue text because the black background helped showcase all the different projects to the best effect.

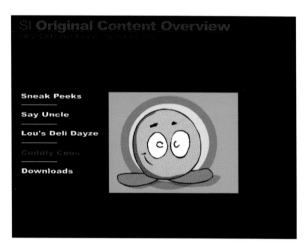

1.11

1.12

NOTE

If your target audience does have more advanced equipment, it is perfectly acceptable to take advantage of all Flash has to offer. However, developers should still view the project on an older monitor in order to know how bad the aesthetic degradation is on monitors with fewer colors.

Unless a designer has changed the default color palette, the standard 216-color Web-safe palette is the color palette that is loaded with each new Flash movie (1.13). This color palette already presents a serious challenge to any normal Web designer, but with Flash's capability to use gradients and partial transparencies, it is almost impossible to adhere to this set of colors. What tends to happen with some Flash Web sites is that designers, expecting that the target audience has new monitors and wants to see rich media, disregard the Web-safe color palette.

At the time the Smashing Ideas' site was designed, Flash still had not entirely entered the mainstream. Although it was turning the corner, with Flash 3 plug-in penetration passing 65 percent, Flash was still far from ubiquitous and we were even going to use Flash 4. Use of the technology still was confined mostly to entertainment and portfolio sites.

Taking this into account, Smashing Ideas created a Flash "Vision" piece that combined animation, motion typography, music, and a humorous attitude to help define the direction the studio wanted the Web to take. In the Vision piece, we told people that we saw a Web full of media, full of visual communication and interactivity. When the site launched, this was what we wanted viewers to see first. By defining our vision for the future of the Web (1.14–1.17), we hoped clients would give us the chance to create it.

Smashing Ideas wanted to highlight both the type of work that we had done with Flash as well as what we

1.14

1.15

1.16

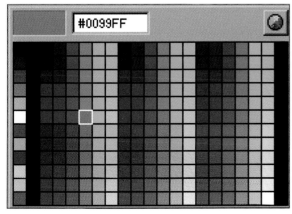

1.13

1.17

felt could be done using Flash. We created a "Case Studies" section to highlight these areas (1.18). Beyond that, Smashing Ideas provides services in the new media and entertainment field, so we added specific sections to showcase projects within those areas. The last main section of site content was dedicated to the original content Smashing Ideas creates and licenses. The last navigational line provided links to administrative and corporate areas.

Because the site does not have a lot of layers of content to drill through, the studio chose to create a simple "hub and spokes" navigation without any section-to-section navigation (1.19). No persistent navigation exists throughout the site; instead, users go down into a section, and then have to return to the front page before entering another section. We made this decision because we wanted to maximize the screen real estate for the projects, the core of the site, rather than taking up space with a persistent cross sectional navigation. Because a Web user can only go down three layers in the site, this navigation was reasonable.

The navigation and content are contained within a viewer area surrounded by a black mask that fills the browser (1.20). This visually implies that the viewer is experiencing something different from the standard HTML experience. This solution let us add supporting text about project goals and technical information and also let us solve the problem that many of our different projects had been done at different dimensions; placing them in a viewing window let us more easily display projects without completely modifying the original dimensions of the files.

Smashing Ideas chose to keep the front-page navigation and buttons of the site extremely simple in order to facilitate quick-and-easy access to the projects that make up Smashing Ideas' portfolio. The navigational buttons of the site are simple text buttons (1.21) that subtly change color when rolled over (1.22) and clicked (1.23).

No radical text effects occur during the button rollovers, nor does complicated transitional animation happen during the site navigation. We wanted to provide a clean informational design so it wouldn't take users long to move from section to section because the actual projects are much more important than the transitions.

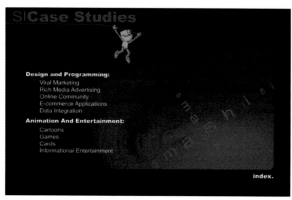

1.18

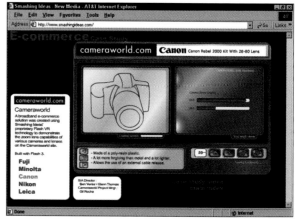

1.19

1.20

COMBINING NAVIGATION BUTTONS AND ANIMATED TRANSITIONS

One of the navigation design solutions for the site was to close each section with an animated screen and then reopen to a new layout that fits the specific content of that section of the site (1.24). The transition each time is an up and down closing of the viewer window that lasts approximately one second. Sometimes this is the only transition between sections, while at other times it is combined with the viewer window reopening on a new layout.

Our main recommendation on navigational transitions is to keep them economical. Always remember that the goal is to get viewers to the site content as easily as possible. As a designer, try to imagine what it would be like to have to sit through a transition not once, but a hundred times. If you can't imagine it, then sit down and do it. It quickly becomes apparent that gratuitous or long navigational transitions seriously impact the usability of a site.

KEEPING IT SMALL (OR, THOSE PESKY DOWNLOAD TIMES)

Although bandwidth and modem speeds continue to improve, the standard connection still remains mired between 28 and 56K in the United States. While the broadband audience is growing, the reality of the situation is that most consumers still have a low-speed connection. In other parts of the world, average speeds are even lower. Macromedia provides statistics on average connection speeds at the Macromedia Web site. This is important information for developers and designers to keep at hand (1.25).

1.21

1.22

1.23

1.24

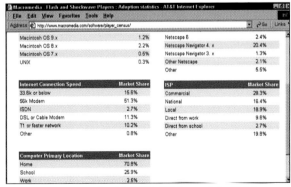

1.25

Flash was originally adopted by many designers to address download concerns, but more recently many designers have moved toward extremely complex sites with lots of large movies. There's nothing wrong in doing this if you have a broadband-only audience, but if you're after a more general audience then it's important to design Flash movies accordingly.

KNOWING THE IMPORTANCE OF THE FIRST FRAME

The way Flash displays movies is that whenever the first frame of the movie has been downloaded to a Web viewer's computer, that frame is displayed while the rest of the movie loads into the browser cache. The smart Flash developer uses this fact to create an intro or activity with a light footprint at the beginning of the file to keep the Web viewer occupied while the rest of the movie downloads in the background.

Designers always need to keep the user's experience in mind by trying to give viewers something to look at within six to eight seconds. Although this timeframe can be pushed somewhat higher at times, six to eight seconds is the generally accepted amount of time that Web users will wait before skipping to a new site.

The choices for a Flash Web site designer are to keep the first frame extremely simple so it downloads in a couple of seconds, provide the Web viewer with lots of feedback about how long they are going to have to wait, or create a diversion for the user to while away the time. Smashing Ideas chose the first solution by creating a first frame that loaded very quickly (1.26).

At the Smashing Ideas site, a small viewer bar opens and shows the text "www.smashingideas.com" with only 1.5 seconds of preload at 56.6 Kbps and under three seconds at 28.8 Kbps). The set of characters from the font family that are used in the text (about 5K) is the only item that needs to load for this text to show. After one or two more seconds, motion typography animates the text in a wave and then an anvil fades into the screen. A moment later the viewer bar opens vertically and reveals the entire front page.

As soon as the main navigation of the site is loaded, the "www.smashingideas.com" text becomes a button and the viewer can skip directly to the site without viewing the rest of the intro. Even if the viewer doesn't do this, the front page of the site opens within five seconds at 56 Kbps and ten seconds at 28.8 Kbps.

The Flash developer's best methods of figuring out preload times are the Bandwidth Profiler (1.27) and testing on a slow dial-up connection. Nobody ever wants to do real-world testing on projects, but it's extremely important to ensure a good user experience. The Bandwidth Profiler contained within the Flash authoring application provides a close-to-real-world way in which to test movie playback.

The other important consideration for streaming movies and download times lies in quick and easy navigation around the site. When the user moves between navigational sections, each area should load quickly

1.26

TIP

It's important for Web developers to understand how fonts work in order to choose fonts properly. Flash creates one copy of all the letters that are used in any font within the movie file. This means that file size can increase dramatically if a developer uses many different font styles, even if they're in the same font family. An "A" used as Arial, Arial Bold, and Arial Italic would each make a different symbol. This would rapidly increase the file size, so it's important to use as few fonts as are necessary. Font readability is also generally better with sans serif, although any fonts at small point sizes can be difficult to read. Using antialiased fonts can help if small point sizes are necessary.

and seamlessly. To do this, at the Smashing Ideas site each section is created as a distinct movie and loaded into a layer or movie clip within the main Flash movie. This strategy is covered in Chapter 2 about loading movies and creating intelligent preloaders.

INTRODUCING SPLASH SCREENS

Many sites have begun using Flash solely to create animated splash screens that act as short, or incredibly long, introductory commercials about the site. These can be extremely annoying to people and need to be used cautiously.

Splash screens should be kept short — a maximum of five to ten seconds. Rather than create one long splash screen that people will want to skip after seeing it for the first time, it's more viewer friendly and successful to create numerous short splash screens that appear randomly each time the user comes to the site.

If a client insists on a long splash screen, developers should always add a button that will enable a user to skip straight to the main navigation (1.28). Although the splash screen might seem interesting to viewers the first time, they're probably going to want to skip it after the first time. If they have no way to do that, then they might not wait through the splash screen to get into the site. This limitation radically affects the number of visits to a site. The Smashing Ideas site does not currently use a long splash screen for these exact reasons.

PLANNING SCREEN REAL ESTATE

Flash designers need to decide early on how to display the finished Flash movie within a Web page. Flash can fill the browser as a percentage of the browser size such as 100 percent (1.29), or it can be displayed at a fixed size such as 600×400 pixels.

Because Flash outputs a resolution-independent vector format, Flash movies can scale within the browser as a percentage of the screen real estate and still look good. This is not the case with any bitmaps integrated into the Flash movie as they will pixelate when enlarged.

In general, Flash movies that can fill the browser provide the best media experience. Although users

can make the browser small and the interface will shrink accordingly, it's more likely that the user will have the browser fill the whole screen. Displaying movies as a percentage of the browser screen also enables movies to be designed and displayed so that no browser scrolling occurs.

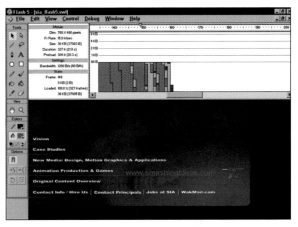

1.27

1.28

1.29

THE FULL SCREEN TRICK

Flash can even go beyond the browser in recent versions of Internet Explorer and completely fill the monitor without any browser controls being shown (1.30). The reason to provide a full-screen Flash movie is that it provides a full rich media experience without the distraction or branding of the browser.

The way to do this is to create a button within the Flash movie that triggers two JavaScript functions. These functions open another HTML page that "explodes" the Flash movie full screen.

The specific JavaScript functions that can be used to present movies at full screen are as follows:

```
function popup(url, features)
      {
    popWin = window.open(url, "Form",
features);
      }


function popfull()
      {
    popup( "sia_full.html" ,
"fullscreen=yes,toolbar=no,menubar=no
,location=no,status=no");
      }
```

This could also be done with one FSCommand that passes all of the URL and feature data out of Flash as arguments to a JavaScript function, but the process is more reliable with two separate JavaScript functions in the HTML page because some browser versions don't always send that information out of Flash.

The following code is added to the button within Flash (1.31):

```
on (press) {
getURL ("javascript:popfull()");
}
```

When the user releases the button, the popfull function runs which calls the popup function to open a new window with the defined URL and feature attributes. The Internet Explorer browser disappears because the attributes are set to full-screen without the toolbar or menu bar. The HTML page that "explodes" the Flash movie full screen, siafull.html, has the Flash movie added normally with the height and width attributes set to 100 percent.

The designer will then need to provide a way to return to the browser based version of the Flash movie. In fact, the standard browser is still around and is underneath the "exploded" Flash movie. It's easy enough to add another button to the Flash movie that triggers a JavaScript function that will close the "exploded" Flash movie completely to reveal the original HTML page in the browser.

The JavaScript code is:

```
function closefull()
      {
    top.close();
      }
```

On the button within Flash, the following code is added:

```
on (press) {
javascript: closefull()
}
```

Smashing Ideas has found that it's best to provide this functionality as a viewer choice. If full-screen movie presentations are done without first warning the Web viewer, it can be extremely disconcerting. Rather than doing this, the Smashing Ideas site enables the viewer to choose to make the site full screen each time he or she comes to the site. It is also fairly straightforward to enable users to set the full-screen mode as a preference by using cookies or a server-side script.

DETECTING PLUG-INS

Once the display size of the Flash movie within the browser has been determined, it's important to make sure as many people as possible can see it. Designers can improve these chances with a JavaScript plug-in detection scheme. As Flash has become ubiquitous within browsers and operating systems, JavaScript-based plug-in detection has become less important; however, it's still important to take steps to provide as painless an experience as possible for detecting and helping viewers get the necessary version of the plug-in (1.32).

JavaScript is the standard way to do this. The difficulties with JavaScript are that different versions of browsers on different operating systems need to have functions written differently and some don't even provide JavaScript compatibility. Macromedia provides a JavaScript detection routine with the publishing functionality of Flash, but this routine is not the most complete detection routine available.

Colin Moock has the best JavaScript/VBScript detection routine Smashing Ideas has seen anybody develop on the Web. The *moock fpi* (flash player inspector) is Colin's code to detect all possible Flash Player detection issues. Colin's code is available at `www.moock.org`.

The Smashing Ideas site also detects users who need Flash 4 from within the Flash movie itself. This is useful when somebody comes to the site with JavaScript turned off in the browser and the Flash 3 player installed. By using an action that didn't work in Flash 3 such as Call or by checking the version

> **NOTE**
>
> If a movie is set to a fixed size such as 600×400 and the user's monitor is set to a high resolution such as 1,024×768, the Flash movie will appear small to the user. If the monitor is set to a low resolution, such as 640×480, and the Flash movie is set to be bigger, then the user will have to scroll to see the entire movie.

1.30

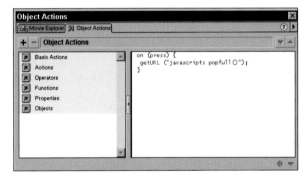

1.31

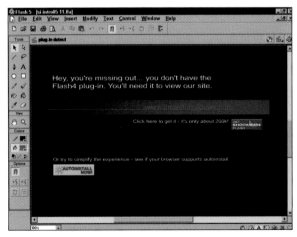

1.32

number of the player using $version (1.33), a Flash developer can direct a Web viewer to a separate HTML page or a frame within the Flash movie that instructs the viewer to download the latest version of the plug-in.

INTEGRATING ROLLOVER MOVIE CLIP EFFECTS

Even though Smashing Ideas chose to keep its site navigation simple, the studio wanted to add some luster to the site's front page. Smashing Ideas decided to surround the simple navigational scheme with the robot mascot character animation and interactivity to highlight the company's animation heritage while also introducing the company's other digital media capabilities.

Visitors to the Smashing Ideas home page often comment on the raindrop effect (1.34). As a user moves the cursor around the page, raindrops begin to slide down the page and disappear as if rain was hitting against a window pane. Because the mouse cursor never changes from an arrow to a hand to show that the user has actually rolled over a button, many visitors find the effect somewhat mysterious. It looks like the raindrops just appear when they move the cursor. So how does a developer create the raindrop cursor effect?

The invisible hand rollover effect is actually quite a simple technique and even works in Flash 3 movies. The key to this technique is to create "invisible" buttons

NAVIGATION CONCERNS

With the proliferation of Flash Web sites, a concern is growing over poorly conceived animated navigation sequences that confuse and disrupt the user's experience. Navigation schemes with long animated button transition sequences are extremely disruptive to the viewing experience. Most users want navigation buttons to come up quickly, so don't make users sit through long animated sequences just to bring up a new set of buttons.

Long animated sequences to move from one section to another are also a painful user experience. Keep these transitions to three seconds maximum or create multiple transitions that are randomly inserted to add variety.

Another navigation pitfall is not giving users a visual cue of where they are in a site. As an example, if a user clicks the Company section of a site and the navigation is persistent throughout the site, then the Company button should have a different state and be turned off. If the button for the current part of the site is active and unchanged, as is often the case, then when the user clicks the button, the current section pops up again.

Flash movies that are only useful for broadband users are another problem. Many sites with this problem don't tell lower bandwidth users about the possible wait times. Developers must provide an activity for users to do while they wait or provide information about how long the download will take.

If too many sites are created with these problems, Web users will begin to have negative reactions toward rich media Flash sites.

1.33

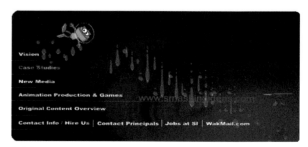

1.34

in a movie clip that trigger actions on the button's rollover state. The best part of this technique is that the hand that normally shows up with buttons never appears. This is because it uses the Go to Next Frame action and this causes actions to occur more quickly than the time it takes for the hand to appear.

Here are the steps for creating a rollover effect:

1. Insert a new button symbol and call it **rain-drops_bt**. You'll immediately be placed inside the symbol so you can begin editing it.

2. Leave the first three frames of the button symbol empty and then add a keyframe. Put a square in the Hit frame. This creates an "invisible" button that can cause actions without ever showing or changing graphics (1.35).

3. Return to the main movie (Edit ➤ Edit Movie). Create a new movie clip symbol (Insert ➤ New Symbol) and name it **raindrops_mc**.

4. Next, edit the movie clip to add the rollover functionality. Create two new layers (Insert ➤ Layer) and name the layers **labels**, **frame actions**, and **button**. Open the library (Window ➤ Library) and drag an instance of the **raindrops_bt** button onto the button layer (1.36). The light blue square shows the hit area of the button because no graphics or objects exist in the first frame. Make sure the button exists only in the first frame by selecting frame two of the button layer and inserting a blank keyframe (Insert ➤ Blank Keyframe).

5. Align the symbol to the center of the movie clip by bringing up the Align Palette (Window ➤ Panels ➤ Align). Select To Stage in the Align Palette and then, with the symbol selected, press Align horizontal center and Align vertical center (1.37).

6. Add three new layers, one for each of the different raindrops. Add new frames to the movie "clip by selecting frame 25 across all the layers and inserting new frames (Insert ➤ Frame). In frame 8 of the labels layer, insert a new keyframe and use the Frame panel (Window ➤ Panels ➤ Frame) to add a label to the keyframe called **fall**. While you're at it, go to the first frame in the timeline and add a label called **on**.

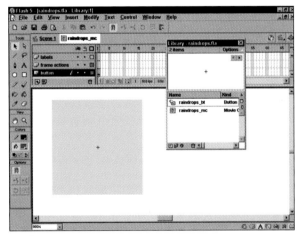

1.36

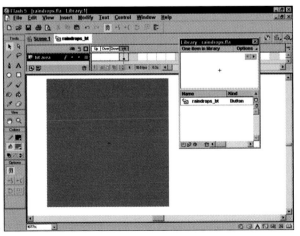

1.35

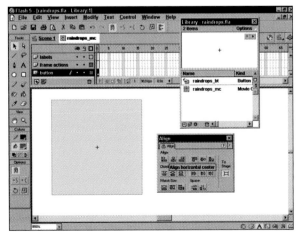

1.37

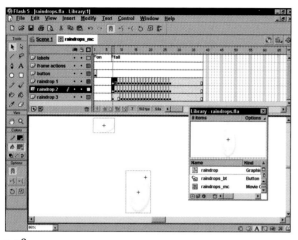

1.38

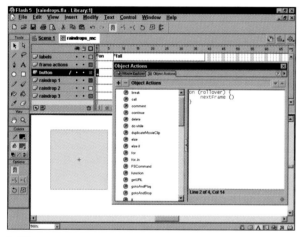

1.39

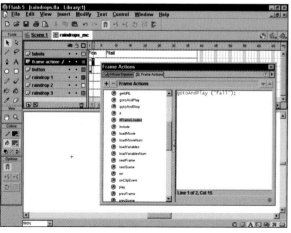

1.40

7. Now add the raindrops by creating a single partially transparent raindrop symbol. On the raindrop layers, add the raindrop symbol and animate the raindrops over the course of eight to ten frames (1.38). This is done by keyframe-animating each raindrop as if it has hit a window and is sliding down the glass pane. The principles of Flash animation are covered in more detail in Chapter 9.

8. The last step in the movie clip is to add functionality to the button. Return to the first frame of the movie clip and bring up the button's Action panel (Window ➤ Actions). Add an action to go to the next frame on rollover (1.39). This is the trick that keeps the cursor from changing to the hand when a user rolls over the button because the go-to-next-frame action happens faster than the cursor can change and, because the button is not in the next frame, the hand never appears.

9. In the *frame actions* layer, select the first frame and add a Stop action (Modify ➤ Frame). Next, add a blank keyframe (Insert ➤ Blank Keyframe) to the second frame of the *button* layer to get rid of the button. In the second frame of the *frame actions* layer, add a keyframe with an action to go to the label *fall* and play (1.40).

TIP

As Flash provides richer media experiences, viewers expect more and higher quality sound. Within full Flash Web sites, this has traditionally meant loops that play throughout a site. This is great, but remember to provide a way for viewers to turn sound off. Flash provides a Stop All Sounds action that should be used with some kind of interface scheme to enable visitors to turn musical loops off. Flash 5 also provides volume control so every developer has greater control over the richness of sound on Flash sites.

10. Go back to the main movie (Edit ➢ Movie). Open the library (1.41) and begin placing raindrops_mc symbols around the stage. In the Smashing Ideas site, symbols covers the entire interface. With the Buttons turned off (Control ➢ Enable Buttons should not be checked), the hit area of the button symbols should appear as a partially transparent blue square (1.42).

11. Test the movie (Control ➢ Test Movie). As the cursor moves over the main navigation interface, the background comes alive with raindrops (1.43).

Flash developers can use this "invisible" button trick to create surprises within Flash movies. The rollover does not have to cause raindrops to fall, instead it could cause objects to float or fly away, create characters that appear out of nowhere, change the look and feel of a site, or open navigation panels. The opportunities to use this effect in a clever manner are limited only by a developer's imagination.

MEETING WEB SITE OBJECTIVES WITH FLASH

The range of what can be done with complete Web sites created in Flash is immense. High media production values combined with interactivity enable dynamic, rich Web experiences. Many Web sites have goals and objectives that can only be met by using Flash to create a rich media experience. As the Web moves away from informational sites into more visually rich entertainment and interactive-based experiences, Flash will lead that revolution.

Smashing Ideas' site and work are at the forefront of this change. The company's vision is a Web that is rich, diverse, and interactive with extremely high media production values. By defining the site's audience as the potential clients who could help make that vision a reality, it was easy for Smashing Ideas to determine that a Flash site was the only proper solution. By understanding the audience and the site's objectives, the studio used Flash to create a successful rich media solution that best served both the user and the studio.

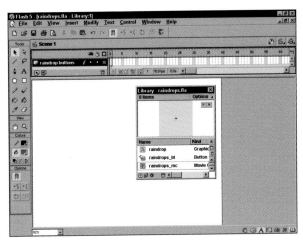

1.41

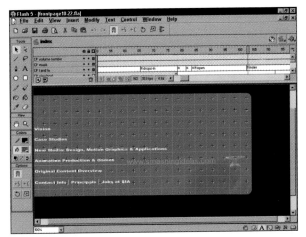

1.42

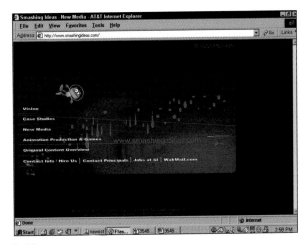

1.43

Flash 5 - [sia_flash5.swf]

File   Edit   View   Control   Debug   Window   Help

Tools

Zoom In   Ctrl+
Zoom Out
Magnification   ▶
✓ Bandwidth P...
✓ Show Streaming   Ctrl+Enter
✓ Streaming Graph   Ctrl+G
   Frame By Frame Graph   Ctrl+F
   Quality   ▶

SPECIFY: WHO IS THE AUDIENCE? WHAT IS THE STANDARD MODEM SPEED?

THE BANDWIDTH PROFILER SHOULD BE EVERY DEVELOPER'S BEST FRIEND.

Approximate Load

DSL/Cable   10-20 s
56K   1 minut
28K   2+ minu

SYMBOLS ARE KEY TO MINIMIZING FILE SIZE IN FLASH.

Vision

Case Studies

1200 PX

sia_flash5_end Report.txt - Notepad

File   Edit   Format   Help

Movie Report

Frame #   Frame Bytes   Total Bytes   Page
1   462   462   end
2   116   578   2
3   116   694   3
4   116   810   4
5   1030   5
6   1145   6
7   1262   7
8   1482   8
9   1598   9
10   1714   10
11   1830   11
12   2050   12
13   2166   13
14   2282   14
15   2502   15
16   2618   16
17   2734   17
18   18
19   3186   20
20   3302   21
21   3418   22
22   3638   23
23   3754   24
24   7118   25
25   7338   26
26   7454   27
27   7466   28
28   7468   29
29   7470   30

AT SMASHING IDEAS, WE BELIEVE THAT EVERY K COUNTS.

640 PX

Smashing Ideas

File   Edit   View   Favorites   Tools   Help

Address [●] http://www.smashingideas.com   [▼] ⟳ Go   Links ● Customize Links ● Free Hotmail ● Windows

SI Vision

LOADING

Approximate Load Times

DSL/Cable   10-20 seconds
56K   1 minute
28K   2+ minutes

index.

Copyright©2000 Smashing Ideas Inc. All Rights Reserved.

[●] Done   [●] Internet

MOST IMPORTANTLY, THROUGHOUT DEVELOPMENT YOU NEED TO CONTINUALLY TEST EVERY MOVIE ON A TARGET MACHINE.

Approxim
DSL/C
56K
28K

smashing ideas INC.

DATE: 2-20-00	SHEET:
SCALE: 1" = 72 DPI	**2**
DRAWN: THOMAS	OF 16
JOB: OPTIMIZATION / LOADING Ⓕ Ⓖ Ⓑ	

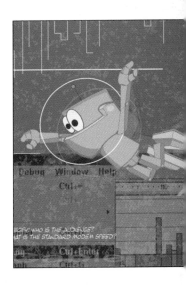

CHAPTER 2
OPTIMIZING, LOADING, AND PLAYBACK

O ne of the most important and least understood aspects of creating great Flash sites and content is knowing how to build movies that are properly optimized. In the case of Flash movies, this means that movies have a small file size, are set up to stream over the Web without making a user wait, and play back at the correct speed.

Developers must understand what can be done to minimize a Web user's download wait and to enhance the playback experience. This takes both planning at the start of a project and time near the end of a project to evaluate and optimize the final Flash files. Although doing this properly means long, hard, unglamorous work, it's well worth to improve the user's experience.

Flash originally gained support because its vector format could deliver great-looking graphics at a minimal file size. As Flash has become more widely accepted, designers and developers are pushing file sizes higher and higher. Although large file sizes may be acceptable when targeted at the right audience, it's important for all developers to work at creating a reasonable experience for all audiences. As developers and designers, we must be careful not to give Flash sites a bad reputation for having long wait times, the dreaded "loading" screen (2.1). On the Smashing Ideas site, users without high speed connections will come across loading bars with some regularity because the site was intended for broadband audiences (2.2).

At Smashing Ideas we believe that every byte counts. Consider that a 9K file takes almost eight seconds to

Our life is frittered away by detail....
Simplify, simplify.

HENRY DAVID THOREAU

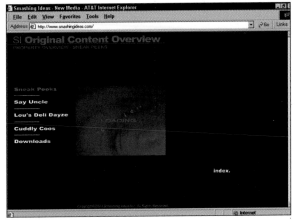

2.1

2.2

download at a 14.4 Kbps modem speed; at 56.6 Kbps it's almost two seconds. Because the average connection speed is still a bit under 56.6 Kbps, every extra byte of file size added to a site begins to seriously

impact the user experience. Even for broadband users, we still believe that striving for the smallest possible file size is the way to approach projects.

Developers also need to determine a site architecture (2.3) that allows for intelligent loading and preloading schemes in order to minimize the user's download wait times. Larger Flash movies need to be split into separate movies that can be loaded beside one another using Flash's Load Movie action (2.4).

Developers also need to be aware that, once the viewer has downloaded the movies, Flash's vector graphics can put an enormous strain on processors (2.5) and older graphics cards. Playback can be affected not only by the number of lines and shapes in Flash, but also by the area of the screen that must be redrawn. Playback concerns need to be addressed early in projects to ensure that a movie that plays back beautifully on a new, high-end computer doesn't crawl on older machines.

A processor-intensive Smashing Ideas Web site was created (2.6) to push the limits of what is feasible on current computers. The site combined 3D revolving letters with animation and gradient lighting effects (2.7). The site always had a draggable movie clip instance moving, while animated graphics continually changed transparency (2.8). While the site looks great on fast machines with new graphics cards; it barely moves on computers a couple of years old. Because it played back so poorly on so many machines, this site never went live.

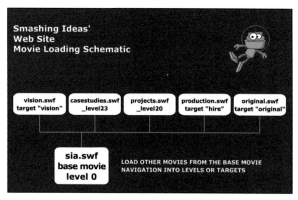

2.3

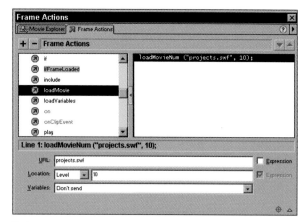

2.4

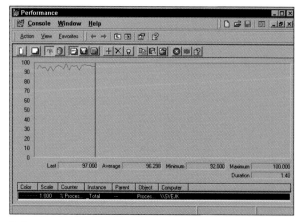

2.5

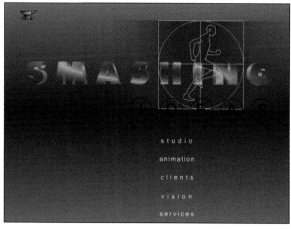

2.6

By deconstructing the current Smashing Ideas Web site, we can better understand the rationale and techniques behind the process of planning, executing, and implementing file-size optimization, playback, and loading schemes. The Smashing Ideas Web site consists of a small main navigation Flash movie that loads other areas of the site into itself. This is the standard technique Smashing Ideas uses to create seamless Flash Web sites.

DEFINING YOUR AUDIENCE

You need to ask a variety of questions about your audience when you begin planning a Web site.

- Who is the audience?
- What is the audience's standard modem speed?
- What kind of computers does the audience use?
- What is the audience's standard processor speed?
- What kind of browser does the audience use?
- What is the audience's standard monitor size and screen resolution?

Without considering these questions, a Flash developer can too easily create a site that is either too complex for a good playback experience or too large for a good download experience for the intended audience. The answers to these questions have to inform all of the design and development decisions that follow.

Smashing Ideas decided that our target audience consists of high bandwidth users connecting to our site from work using either PCs or Macs. The average computer used by our target audience is about two years old and the site needs to support all browsers that can install Flash. The audience's standard monitor size is 17 inches and the screen resolution is set to at least 800 × 600. What this means for the Smashing Ideas site is that we could aim high while still creating a site that would be serviceable for lower-end users.

OPTIMIZE, OPTIMIZE, OPTIMIZE

Consider how to create the smallest Flash movie possible within the context of the project. If the project is a single Flash cartoon, then the planning for this is much easier than if it is a complex Flash Web site with multiple movies preloading through an intelligent loading scenario. Regardless, the principles behind optimization remain the same.

USING SYMBOLS

Symbols enable developers to minimize file size in Flash. Any graphic that is used more than once should be turned into a symbol. The symbol can then be placed anywhere in the movie, but because the movie is showing a new instance of the original graphic the file size of the movie increases by only 12 to 14 bytes for static graphic symbols and movie clips. With this in mind, developers should rarely, if ever, use groups for graphics that are used more than once.

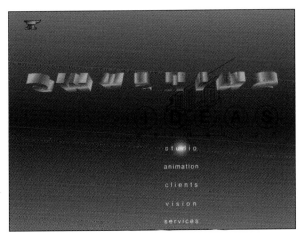

2.7

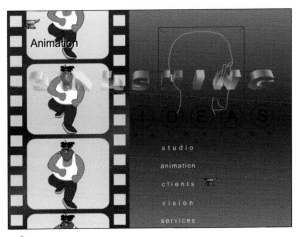

2.8

Developers need to keep symbol reuse in mind at all times while planning movies. As an example, Smashing Ideas' robot graphic is shown multiple times in two different movies (2.9, 2.10). In the first movie, it is a symbol that is placed as new instances multiple times on the stage. In the second movie, it is a group that is copied around the stage. The movies look exactly the same, but the first movie's file size is 2K, while the second movie's file size is 45K. Given these differences, it's easy to see why the intelligent use of symbols is the key to small file sizes in Flash.

USING GRAPHICS VERSUS MOVIE CLIPS

Animated symbols in Flash can have two distinct behaviors — Graphic and Movie Clip (2.11). A graphic

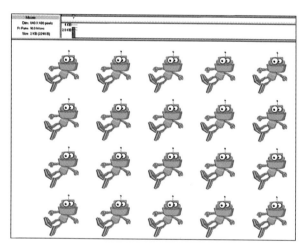

2.9

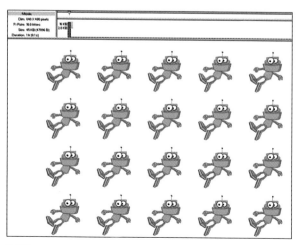

2.10

symbol's timeline is synchronized to the parent timeline, while movie clips play back independently of the parent timeline. This is important for file size because animated graphic symbols can add to the file size each time they are placed in a movie. This is because each frame in the animated graphic symbol is tied to a specific frame in the parent timeline, so more information has to be stored. Movie clips are independent of the parent timeline and only add to the file size the first time they are placed in the movie.

CREATING PENCIL AND PEN LINES

To achieve the smallest file size in Flash, use solid pencil lines. You can draw pencil lines in Smooth, Straighten, or Ink mode (2.12). If you're drawing directly into Flash, then it's important to use the smoothest possible line, because a smooth line has the fewest possible points. Flash 5 also has a Pen tool that, along with the Subselect tool, can create and modify Bézier curves (2.13) to help designers make curves with the smallest possible file size in mind.

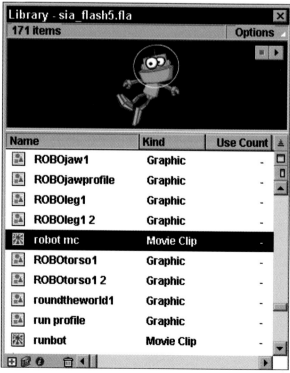

2.11

Flash includes optional pencil line styles such as dots, dashes, and ragged effects (2.14). When exported, each of these styles is broken into paint fills, so a greater number of points has to be saved by Flash to display these styles (2.15). They add significantly to a movie's file size because of this characteristic. Developers should use these types of lines sparingly, if at all.

BRUSH STROKES

Flash has a Brush tool that can add significantly to file size because brush strokes have many more points than pencil lines (2.16). To see the file size difference,

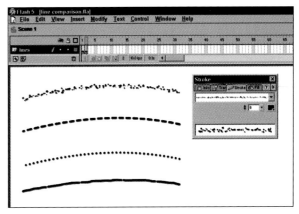

2.14

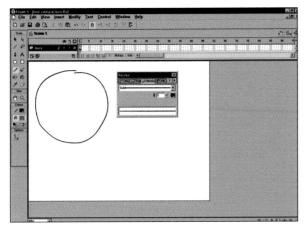

2.12

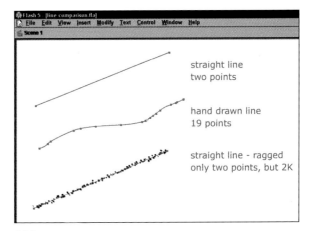

2.15

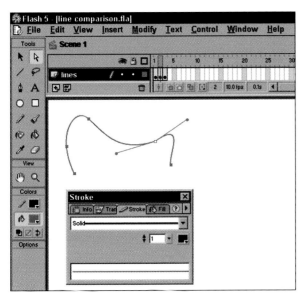

2.13

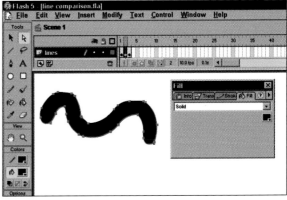

2.16

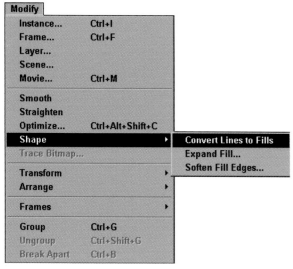

2.17

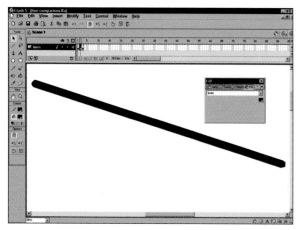

2.18

2.19

turn a pencil line into a brush stroke and compare the difference using the Convert Lines to Fills command in the Modify ➢ Shape menu (2.17, 2.18).

IMPORTED VECTOR ILLUSTRATIONS

You can use other vector illustration tools such as Macromedia FreeHand and Adobe Illustrator to create vector graphics that can then be imported into Flash. These files often need to be optimized in Flash to decrease the number of extra groups and shapes that are brought in on import. By selecting the illustration and ungrouping it or breaking it apart, the file size of the illustration can often be reduced by 20 to 50 percent. Graphics that are reused within the imported illustration should also made into symbols to further reduce the file size. Follow these steps to ungroup elements and create symbols in an illustration to reduce the overall file size:

1. Import a vector file into Flash (2.19, 2.20).
2. Select all of the pieces of the imported vector graphic (2.21).
3. Select either Ungroup or Break Apart from the Modify menu in order to take all the extra groups

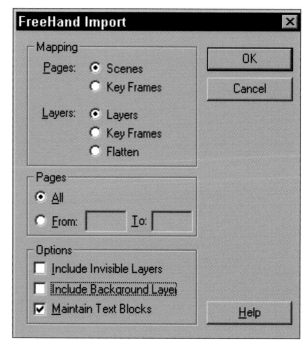

2.20

apart. You might need to repeat this step until all groups and items are broken apart (2.22).

4. During the ungrouping process, you can minimize file size by selecting parts of the illustration that are used more than once and making them into symbols. After an asset has been made into a symbol, you need to replace it throughout the illustration.

5. Depending on how the imported file was created, problems sometimes occur with ungrouping. Because ungrouped objects move underneath grouped objects in Flash, parts of the illustration can disappear depending on how they are grouped, such as the eyeballs in 2.23. If this happens, you

have to laboriously ungroup individual sections of the illustration and then regroup them in order to maintain the integrity of the graphic.

2.22

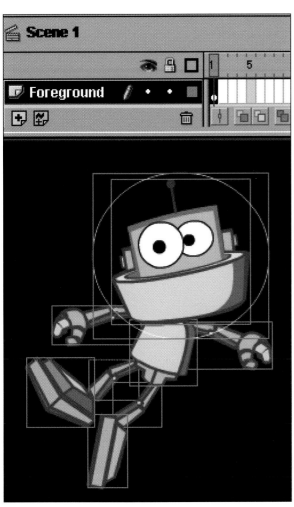

2.21

2.23

OPTIMIZING CURVES

In addition to enabling developers to select vector lines, brush strokes, and any other vector objects, Flash also enables developers to optimize curves in these vector objects (2.24). Flash optimizes curves by taking points out of lines and shapes. Fewer points means a smaller file size. Fewer points also means less complexity for the processor to deal with so playback is often improved.

Follow these steps to optimize curves:

1. Open the symbol to be optimized in symbol-editing mode
2. Select the area of the symbol to optimize, or select it all.

TIP

Smashing Ideas recommends using direct Free-Hand import in Flash 5. This new feature enables all of the attributes of your FreeHand files to import directly into Flash. Flash and FreeHand are tightly integrated and work well together as design, animation, and interactive tools.

3. Select Modify ➤ Curves, and then choose Optimize in the pop-up window
4. To reduce the number of curves it takes to display a symbol, drag the Smoothing slider to the right in the Optimize Curves dialog box. The farther to the right that you move the slider, the more curves are reduced. The results are not displayed in real time. Click OK to see percentile and new curve count (2.25). Click OK to close the alert window and view the results (2.26).
5. If the symbol is too distorted, undo the optimization and repeat the preceding steps. In the Optimize Curves dialog box, drag the Smoothing slider to the left, until you achieve acceptable results.

USING RASTER GRAPHICS WISELY

Flash imports raster graphic formats such as BMP, PICT, JPEG, GIF, and PNG (2.27). Smashing Ideas has had a lot of success using PNG files as our standard import for raster graphics. You can optimize PNGs in programs such as Macromedia Fireworks prior to importing them into Flash to get the best results.

We try never to bring JPEGs into Flash and then re-export with compression. The quality deteriorates

2.24

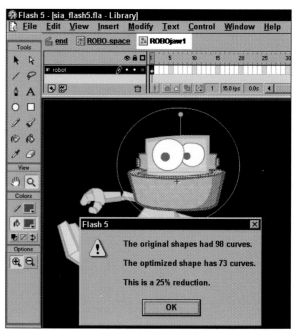

2.25

quickly because the JPEG is compressed twice. If you
have to import JPEGs and have already compressed
them in another program, set the Flash JPEG Quality
to 100 percent in the Publish Settings dialog box so as
not to recompress. We prefer to bring in the original
BMP or PICT file and then let Flash do the JPEG
compression on export.

It's important for developers to use as few raster
graphics as possible. The file size of raster graphics is
often much higher than vector graphics and, when
used excessively, can cause enormous download times.
Raster graphics also don't scale well so it's harder for
the Flash movie's dimensions to be changed as a percentage in the HTML page.

In other situations, designers might want to set the
JPEG Quality in the Flash Publish Settings dialog
box, but give individual raster graphics higher or
lower JPEG Quality settings. Designers can even force
the graphic to be compressed as *Lossless*, which is the
compression used for PNG and GIF images. Follow
these steps to adjust the JPEG Quality setting:

1. Open the Symbol Library and sort by Kind.
The raster graphics will move to the top of the
library (2.28).

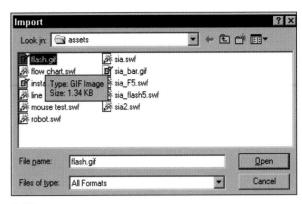

2.27

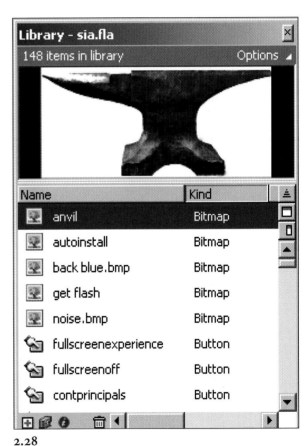

2.28

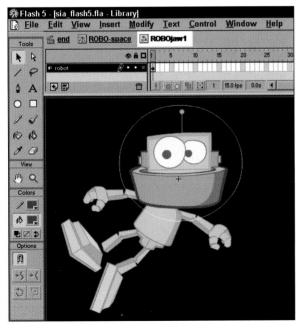

2.26

2. Double-click the anvil graphic. Doing so brings up the Bitmap Properties dialog box (2.29).

3. The raster graphic shows up at 100 percent in the viewing window in the upper-left corner of the dialog box. To see the entire graphic, right-click the image (Control-click on a Mac) and choose Show All (2.30). The entire graphic will be

---

NOTE

In the case of complex images such as photographs, the raster image is typically much smaller than the corresponding vector graphic. The Trace Bitmap feature enables raster images to be turned into vector graphics within Flash. This procedure generally can't capture the exact look of the raster image and is much larger than the raster image because so many vector points have to be added to the file.

---

shown in the window. You can also use this feature to zoom in and inspect the graphic more closely.

4. Because the anvil is a photograph, it is using JPEG compression. This could be changed to Lossless (PNG/GIF) in the Compression drop-down menu, but because we want it to be exported as a JPEG with different compression we just uncheck the "Use document default quality" box so we can specify a new Quality setting (2.31).

5. Type in a new Quality setting and click Test. The Quality setting, the original file size, the compressed file size within Flash, and the percentage of the original size are shown at the bottom of the dialog box (2.32). The graphic in the viewer window reflects the new quality setting.

6. Keep changing the quality values until you're satisfied with the results. You can treat each raster graphic in Flash the same way to maximize the graphic quality while minimizing the file size.

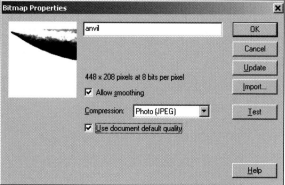

2.29

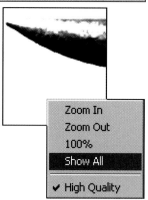

2.30

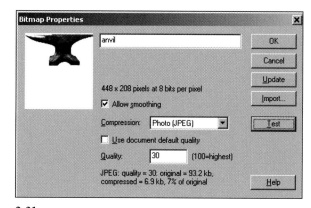

2.31

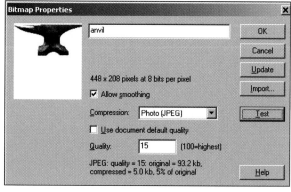

2.32

USING FONTS WISELY

Fonts can add significantly to file size because Flash includes graphic outlines for every letter of every font used. A full font family can range from 5K to more than 100K, so it's important to reduce the number of fonts used in a movie.

Avoiding decorative fonts

Developers should try not to use fonts that are too decorative because they can be much larger than less decorative fonts (2.33). As an example, the alphabet, numbers, and punctuation for most of the Arial font is only about 18K. The same characters in a decorative font, such as Rage Italic would be 30–40K.

Font families stick together

Fonts also download in a specific way in Flash. Characters in the font family are not downloaded individually when they are first used; instead, the entire font family is loaded the first time a character in the font family is used. This means that it's better for movie download times to start using font families with a large file size as late in a movie as possible.

Another strategy that can help work around this problem when only a few characters of a font are used at the start of the movie, and the bulk of the font occurs much later in the movie is actually to break the characters at the beginning of the movie into art-work. This is done by selecting the text field and then selecting Modify ➤ Break Apart. By doing this, the entire font family doesn't need to load right at the start of the movie.

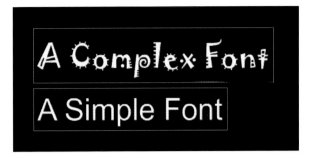

2.33

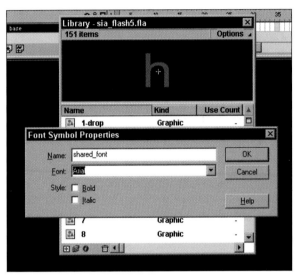

2.34

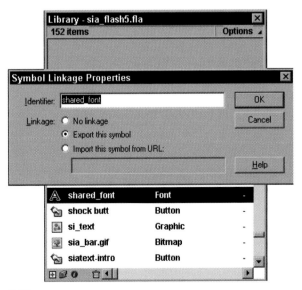

2.35

TIP

Flash 5 enables developers to share fonts and other assets throughout all the different Flash movies that make up a site. A font family can be defined as a shared library asset (2.34, 2.35) and then accessed by multiple movies using Static Text boxes. With a font, this capability could save 5–40K per movie, so the file size savings could be enormous depending on how many movies a site boasts.

TEXT BOXES VERSUS FONTS

Dynamic Text boxes enable users to input data directly into Flash movies. They also enable dynamic information to display in Flash from both external and internal sources (2.36). These text boxes use fonts differently than Static Text boxes and need to be approached accordingly. Because the Flash movie doesn't "know" which characters will be displayed from a chosen font in these fields, the designer has to designate what fonts will be included in the movie.

2.36

2.37

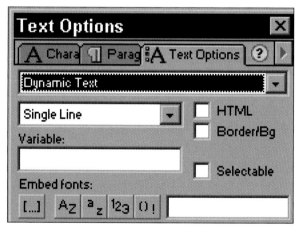

2.38

If characters are included in the movie that aren't used in the movie, then the movie's file size increases unnecessarily because the characters are still saved in the final SWF file. (2.37)Therefore, it's important for designers to use only one kind of font, use the default system font, or designate a specific range of characters when using Dynamic Text or Input Text boxes.

To choose specific parts of a font family, select the text box and open the Text Options panel. "Embed fonts" options appear at the bottom of the Text Options panel and you can select which parts of the font family you want to include (2.38). The entire font family, uppercase, lowercase, numbers, and punctuation are the possible selections. Unique combinations can be typed in the Include Outlines for Specific Characters text box.

It's important to use the minimum number of characters needed by the Flash movie so you can reduce the file size. Because file-size savings can be significant, check that only the characters necessary for Dynamic or Input text boxes are being exported.

Developers can also choose not to include any font outlines by leaving the [. . .] button in the lower left-hand corner of the panel unselected (2.39). In this case, the text box employs the user's default system font (2.40) and won't add anything to the final size of the Flash movie based on the font. Unfortunately, it doesn't let designers control the style of the text. This is usually a reasonable choice for form input fields because they are less likely to impact the overall aesthetics of a design.

2.39

Developers can choose to include all of the outlines from a font family. Doing so wraps absolutely everything into the Flash movie, including foreign and specialty characters, and can add significantly to the movie size, depending on the font family (2.41). This is often the only solution if a particular font must be used to display dynamic text. In these cases, it's important to choose a readable sans-serif font without too many extra characters that won't be used, such as foreign language characters. To keep the file size as small as possible, the Smashing Ideas Web site doesn't have Input or Dynamic Text boxes on the main part of the site.

STREAMING SOUNDS VERSUS EVENT SOUNDS

Sound is extremely important to the user experience, but even the current MP3 compression in Flash adds significantly to file size. Flash has two distinct modes of handling sound — Stream and Event (2.42). Each mode affects file size and playback differently.

WARNING

Choosing not to include font outlines can be a big space saver, but it also means that designers cannot control text design and that the text will not be antialiased. If control over design outweighs the need for a smaller file, you're better off not doing this.

■ **Stream.** Streaming sounds are flattened into each frame across the entire length of playback so they only add a little in terms of file size to each frame (2.43). Stream sounds download per frame, which helps for movie downloads, but because they are flattened into each frame, they can't be reused without adding to the file size.

■ **Event.** Event sounds start playing the moment the playhead comes to that frame. The entire event sound has to be loaded before it can play because the event sound isn't flattened into the timeline. The complete event sound exists as a discrete part of the Flash movie. This means that it can be reused and looped without adding to the movie's file size (2.44). Start and Stop are tied to event sounds in that Start begins a new instance of the event sound if that sound is already playing and Stop silences the chosen event sound.

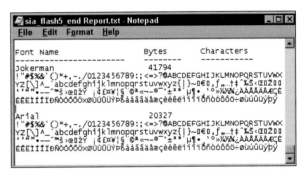

2.41

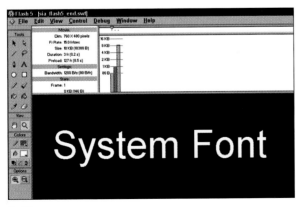

2.40

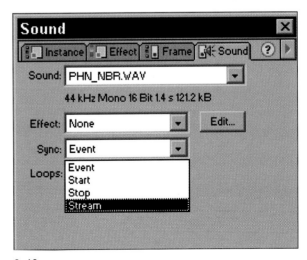

2.42

One good way to understand the difference between Event and Stream better is to look at a movie with a stream sound placed in the first 20 frames and the same sound placed as an event sound beginning in the 25th frame in the Bandwidth Profiler. The first 20 frames of the movie show a sound split across all of the frames, while the entire file size for the event sound occurs in the 25th frame (2.45).

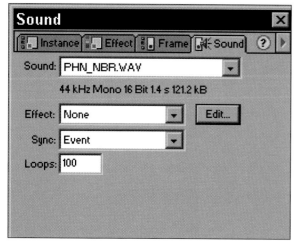

```
Movie Report
------------

Frame #    Frame Bytes    Total Bytes    Page
-------    -----------    -----------    ----
    1          462            462        end
    2          116            578         2
    3          116            694         3
    4          116            810         4
    5          220           1030         5
    6          116           1146         6
    7          116           1262         7
    8          220           1482         8
    9          116           1598         9
   10          116           1714        10
   11          116           1830        11
   12          220           2050        12
   13          116           2166        13
   14          116           2282        14
   15          220           2502        15
   16          116           2618        16
   17          116           2734        17
   18          116           2850        18
   19          220           3070        19
   20          116           3186        20
   21          116           3302        21
   22          116           3418        22
   23          220           3638        23
   24          116           3754        24
   25         3364           7118        25
   26          220           7338        26
   27          116           7454        27
   28           12           7466        28
   29            2           7468        29
   30            2           7470        30
```

2.43

Sound: PHN_NBR.WAV
44 kHz Mono 16 Bit 1.4 s 121.2 kB
Effect: None   Edit...
Sync: Event
Loops: 100

2.44

The best way to use sound in Flash from a file-size perspective is to use short looping files and sound effects to create a richly layered sound environment. Dialog and musical soundtracks are still very large, so use them with extreme care. Music with readily identifiable rhythms and beats work best with this layered approach.

LOADING MOVIES — SIZE AND STREAMING

The goal in developing a Flash Web site is to know the target audience's bandwidth and never make people wait for content. This is accomplished by providing intelligently loading movies. In practice this is often difficult, but developers need to do their best to reduce the amount of time the audience must wait for content to download.

Because Flash shows a movie as soon as the first frame is loaded, developers should be able to give the user some content almost immediately. Developers need to create introduction sequences, games, or other diversions related to the movie's content to occupy the audience while content downloads.

Flash comes with two tools that can help developers realize the size of a movie and determine how long it will take to download—the Bandwidth Profiler and the Size Report. The Bandwidth Profiler is part of the authoring tool, and developers can use it to test the streaming capabilities of the movie. The Size Report is created when a movie is published or exported, including when the movie is tested using the Test Movie command, and developers can use it to see a frame-by-frame analysis of file size, as well as the size of each symbol, event sound, and font family. By using both of these tools, a developer can find frames, symbols, fonts, and sounds in the movie that can be optimized to reduce the file size and enhance the streaming.

USING THE BANDWIDTH PROFILER

The Bandwidth Profiler should be every developer's best friend (2.46). Every developer should use it throughout the development phase to test whether the project conforms to the user's connection speed specifications.

While working within the Flash authoring environment, a developer can test the streaming capability of a Flash movie by using the Test Movie command, accessed in the Control menu (2.47). Flash creates a movie using the attributes selected on the File panel in the Publish Settings dialog box (2.48), and then plays the movie within the authoring environment.

While in the Test Movie window, choose View ➢ Show Streaming (2.49). You can see how long the movie will take to load at a specified modem speed. The modem speed can be changed in the Debug menu to predefined 14.4 Kbps, 28.8 Kbps, and 56.6 Kbps settings or one of three user-defined settings (2.50).

The Bandwidth Profiler contains a red line that shows what can be downloaded without preloading at the specified modem setting. Any spikes above the red line show where the Flash movie will have to stop playing and wait for more of the file to download before it can continue.

Every developer working on a high bandwidth connection should set streaming to 33.6 Kbps and review

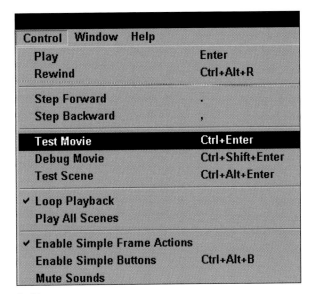

2.47

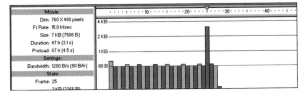

2.45

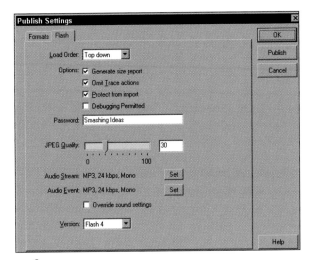

2.48

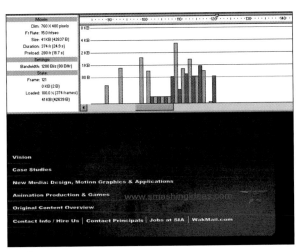

2.46

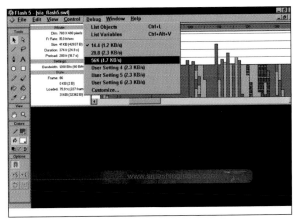

2.49

each project multiple times. This continuous testing ensures a better end-product by showing developers and designers how tedious and frustrating long waits can be. This keeps everybody in tune with the reality of the user as he or she waits for a multimedia experience to download. When multimedia designers won't even wait for their own work to download, they've begun to understand the problem of excessive file size.

If we put the Smashing Ideas site through the Bandwidth Profiler, the situation rapicly becomes clear. The wait on a 56 Kbps modem, our target audience, is short but acceptable at about 1.5 seconds, and 3.6 seconds at 33.6 Kbps (2.51), while the high-bandwidth target audience immediately gets the site experience. The Bandwidth Profiler shows that the site more than meets the target audience criteria.

CREATING A SIZE REPORT

Flash provides developers with the opportunity to create a Size Report when publishing or exporting a

Flash movie. This capability can be set individually on export in the Export Flash Player dialog box or in the Publish Settings panel (2.52). The Size Report is a text file that shows the frames in the movie, the number of bytes in each frame, the total bytes of the movie, and the frame numbers related to each scene.

The Size Report shows individual shape and text bytes for each scene before showing the shape and text bytes of each individual symbol. The Size Report then shows bitmap and event sound sizes. Stream sounds are not shown individually in the Size Report because they are flattened into individual frames throughout the movie. The last section of the Size Report shows all the fonts and characters associated with the file (2.53).

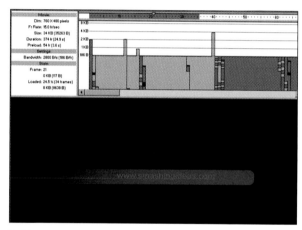

2.51

> **TIP**
>
> Although the Bandwidth Profiler is an extremely useful tool, we recommend that every studio maintain a slow dial-up connection in the neighborhood of 33.6 Kbps. There's nothing like the real thing to show what a true slow day on the Web can feel like.

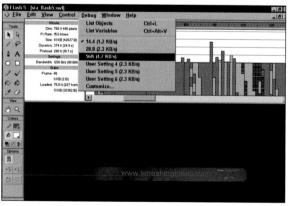

2.50

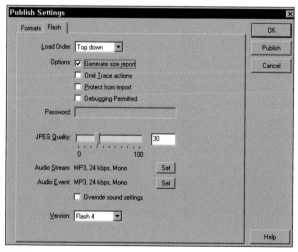

2.52

TABLE 2-1   MOVIE REPORT

FRAME	FRAME BYTES	TOTAL BYTES	PAGE
1	1956	1956	plug-in detect
2	15	1971	2
3	30	2001	3
4	36	2037	4
5	2	2039	5
6	2	2041	6
7	2	2043	7
8	2	2045	8
9	2	2047	9
10	107	2154	10
11	2	2156	11
12	3810	5966	12
13	2	5968	13
14	2	5970	14
15	2	5972	15
16	2	9990	16
17	1416	7388	index

FRAME-BY-FRAME ANALYSIS

The Smashing Ideas' main movie consists of two scenes — a plug-in detection scene and the main navigation scene. The first frame of the movie contains the text "www.smashingideas.com" and is less than 2K so users always see something very quickly. Table 2-1 shows the information from the Size Report for the main movie from the Smashing Ideas' site.

If a user does not have the Flash 4 plug-in, then the movie goes to a frame that tells the user how to download it (2.54). Otherwise, about 5K of more data needs to download before the site intro begins and enables the user to access the main navigation scene. The following is a frame-by-frame analysis of what happens to the file size in the eight seconds from the moment a user gets to the site until the main navigation is in place.

Table 2-2 contains the section of the Size Report that shows the start of the main scene of the movie, the index scene. The first six frames of the index scene (frame 16 in Table 2-2) are the opening of a window vertically around the "www.smashingideas.com" text. The 14 frames after that (frames 22–35) are static while other assets load.

```
sia_flash5 Report.txt - Notepad
File  Edit  Format  Help

Bitmap                     Compressed  Original
Compression
-------------------------  ----------  ----------
------------
anvil                            3131       93184    JPEG
Quality=5
back blue.bmp                    5164      739840    JPEG
Quality=30

Font Name                    Bytes     Characters
-------------------------  --------  ----------
Arial Black                      3030
&,./:ACDGHIJMNOPSUVWabcdefghiklmnoprstuvwx

Arial                            3514
.0234ACDEGILMNORSTUVabcdefghiklmnoprstuvwxy©
```

2.53

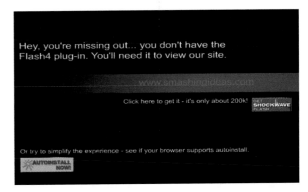

2.54

FRAME #	FRAME BYTES	TOTAL BYTES	PAGE
16	1416	7388	index
17	22	7410	2
18	22	7432	3
19	22	7454	4
20	22	7476	5
21	117	7593	6
22	2	7595	7
23	2	7597	8
24	2	7599	9
25	2	7601	10
26	2	7603	11
27	2	7605	12
28	2	7607	13
29	2	7609	14
30	2	7611	15
31	2	7613	16
32	2	7615	17
33	86	7701	18
34	2	7703	19
35	2	7705	20

Table 2-3 shows the section of the Size Report that details the next parts of the movie. A text wave effect occurs for the next two and a half seconds where each letter of "www.smashingideas.com" gets larger and then falls back into place (2.55). This text effect is a movie clip symbol (2.56) that is loaded in frame 36 so it must load entirely in the frame where it first occurs.

In frame 40, the background raster graphic (5K) is placed.

In the rest of the introduction, an anvil fades in from complete transparency over the next second and a half. This adds about 3K for the anvil the first time it appears and adds a minimal amount of file size over the time frame (2.57). Then, about one and

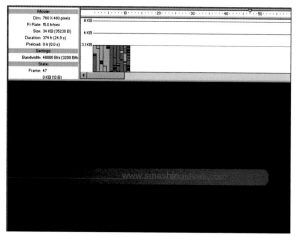

2.55

2.56

TABLE 2-3	MOVIE REPORT		
FRAME #	FRAME BYTES	TOTAL BYTES	PAGE
36	2575	10280	21
37	30	10310	22
38	2	10312	23
39	2	10314	24
40	5270	15584	25

a half seconds pass without motion before the window opens over one second to reveal the navigation space. About 3K is added to the file size here. The last event is that the navigation menu text buttons slide into the scene in different ways over one second, starting in frame 109, and adding about 5K.

All told, the introductory presentation to the Smashing Ideas site should play seamlessly and unobtrusively for each user every time he or she visits the site. No long wait should occur for anybody in the target audience.

During the loading sequence, the raindrops (2.58) and robot are loaded as separate movies. This enables every user to get to the navigation without having to download animation that adds to the file size.

In more complex movies, it's possible to test the specific size of various parts of a Flash movie using Test Scene. This generates a Size Report that shows the size of the individual scene and also plays it back in the Bandwidth Profiler. It's also useful to copy individual movie elements or sets of frames into a new Flash movie. This enables a developer to test the exact size of the elements and frames without any extra or extraneous numbers from other symbols or movements in the movie, which just confuse matters.

BREAK THE MOVIE APART

In larger Flash projects and full Web sites, the next step is to review the best possible manner in which to break the site content into smaller movies (2.59). These movies are then loaded into a base Flash navigation movie. Doing so provides the viewer with a seamless media experience. Unlike Web pages, no annoying blink occurs when "pages" are changed. The entire concept of intelligent loading is predicated on the

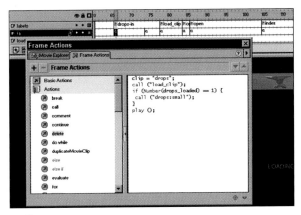

2.58

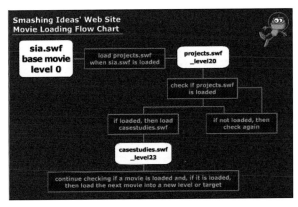

2.59

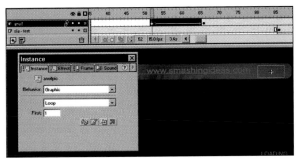

2.57

capability of Flash to load other Flash movies into levels or movie clip targets.

Imagine what would happen if loading movies was not possible and the Smashing Ideas' site was one single Flash movie. It would require 8 to 10MB to load before the user could access all of the content. By splitting up the navigation and content into separate movies and using the Load Movie action, the viewer only needs to load 32K to get to the main navigation. Each specific content file is loaded when requested from the Web site or as a preloaded item from the user's cache.

ANTICIPATING THE USER'S MOVES

To figure out the most intelligent preloading schemes, a developer must consider the order in which users will navigate the site. This enables the next navigation files to be loaded into the user's cache in the background so that the user has a seamless experience when moving through the site. The Smashing Ideas site has a first page with multiple navigation buttons. In the preloading scheme, the next navigational page that is loaded is the Case Studies page (2.60), which is accessed by clicking the second button from the top. The other navigational pages are then loaded one by one in descending order. This is a straightforward way to decide how users will go through the site, but it might not reflect how users actually navigate the site.

Developers should check Web logs to see which areas of the site are most popular with users. Although Web logs with Flash sites aren't always completely correct because of cacheing issues, they are good enough for this purpose. Whichever areas of the site users actually go to should then be preloaded first. In the case of Smashing Ideas, this means that we changed the order of preload so that the New Media section of the site is loaded first followed by Case Studies and then Animation Production & Games.

The Smashing Ideas site loads navigation movies into levels. The navigation levels are loaded above the main Flash movie. One problem with this approach is that the buttons in the main movie are sometimes underneath the navigation movies, and if those buttons remain active it is possible to accidentally hit a button in the underlying main navigation movie. To avoid this problem, it's necessary to send the main movie to a frame without the buttons when a navigation page is loaded. When the user wants to return to the main movie, the movie is then sent back to the frame containing the buttons.

> **LOADING MOVIES — LEVELS VERSUS TARGETS**
>
> You have two distinct ways to load one Flash movie into another Flash movie. The first method is to load a Flash movie into a level such as `_level10` using the Load Movie action. If that level already contains a movie, then the currently loaded movie is unloaded. Movies can also be removed from a level with the Unload Movie action. This loads and unloads navigation movies as necessary.
>
> The Flash movie that is embedded in the HTML page is `_level0` and controls the size, background color, and playback speed of all of the loaded Flash movies. When a Flash movie is loaded into a level, it is placed based on a registration point in the upper-left corner of the base Flash movie and occupies the same area.
>
> Flash movies can also be loaded into a target. A target can be more useful than loading into levels because the target is a movie clip instance that can be manipulated. The size and placement of the target can be changed as well any other symbol attribute; for example, navigation layers can be made visible and invisible.

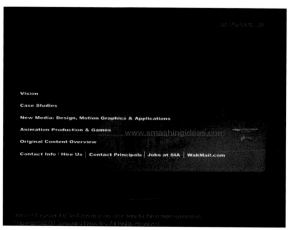

2.60

TESTING THE PLAYBACK

Once the file is fully optimized, you're able to begin testing the playback on various computers and processors. The factors that influence playback the most, regardless of platform, are the frame rate (2.61), the size and complexity of the movie (2.62), and the area of the screen that needs to be redrawn at any given moment (2.63).

Movies with high frame rates are more susceptible to problems with playback than movies with lower frame rates. The Smashing Ideas front screen movie is set at 15 frames per second (fps), which works well for properly designed motion graphics and text animation because it creates smoother movement and transitions. However, if the movie slows down for any reason, because of such factors as multiple tweening objects, moving gradients, and heavy alpha effects, it can be extremely tedious to watch. To design movies properly for playback, it's necessary to understand what causes problems on slower processors.

USING PANS AND ZOOMS

Full-screen pans and zooms with complex backgrounds and foregrounds are two of the most processor-intensive actions that you can do in Flash. Because Flash must redraw all of the graphics full-screen in each frame, slower processors show significant playback problems.

If pans and zooms are done in frames with streaming sound, multiple frames will be dropped because the sound playback controls the animation playback. If done without streaming sound, playback can be reduced to 2–3 frames per second as the computer slows down the playback. Refrain from full movie screen pans and zooms if at all possible. If they are necessary, then try to minimize the complexity in the areas being panned or zoomed.

The Smashing Ideas site does not use any pans and zooms in the intro to the site, but does use a simple window opening transition against a blue background. This transition is fairly easy on the processor, so it doesn't cause any problems.

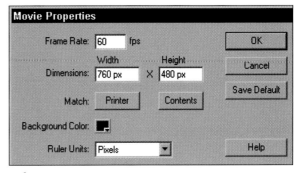

2.61

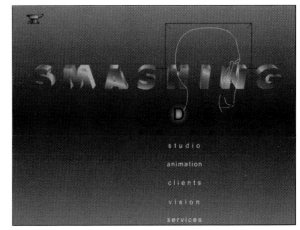

2.62

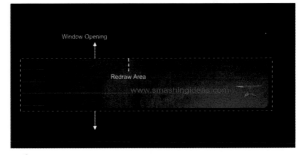

2.63

TIP

Flash redraws graphics based on a bounding box drawn around the elements that are moving at the same time. For example, if two moving objects are close to each other, Flash only redraws the area inside the box drawn around the two objects (2.64); if the two moving objects are placed in opposite corners of the movie, Flash still has to redraw the area in the box drawn around the two objects (2.65). In the latter case Flash has to redraw almost the entire screen and the movie will play back poorly because it's much more processor- and graphics-card-intensive.

TWEENING

Multiple tweening of complex objects increases the load on the processor as well. Flash supports two kinds of tweening (motion and shape) that affect the processor for different reasons (2.66).

Motion tweening is used to move objects around the screen, resize objects, change the color of objects, rotate objects, and change the transparency of objects. You can add motion guides to create more complex animation paths. Easing in and easing out when tweening also adds more complexity to the movie and uses more processor power (2.67). Easing in and out with complex symbols on motion guides can actually crash slower processors, so the technique should be used sparingly and tested thoroughly.

2.64

2.66

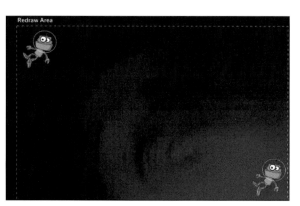

2.65

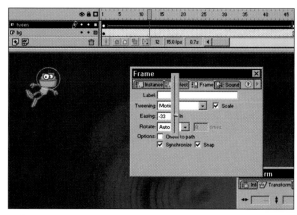

2.67

Shape tweening is used to force one shape to change into another (2.68). Flash will do this automatically or the developer can designate up to 26 Shape Hints to control the tween (2.69). The more Shape Hints designated by the developer, the more complex the shape tween is for the processor. Shape tweening can be extremely processor-intensive when used in this manner.

Tweening, especially motion tweening, is excellent for creating text animation and motion graphics. It's important to remember that many of the techniques used to create high production values with motion or shaped tweened animation are processor-intensive during Flash playback. The Smashing Ideas site uses a motion tween to bring in all the navigational text buttons after the window opening transition.

GRADIENT AND TRANSPARENCY EFFECTS

You can use multiple gradient and transparency effects within Flash to simulate lighting or artistic styles such as watercolor (2.70). Transparency especially adds the feeling of high production values to Flash movies. Developers can also move those gradients and transparencies with tweening across the entire movie or over specific objects (2.71).

NOTE

It's also possible to use shape tweens to change gradient colors. To do this, create a shape with a gradient color fill and then add a keyframe later in the timeline. Use Transform Fill to change the gradient color and then create a shape tween. This can create intriguing effects and is often not too processor-intensive.

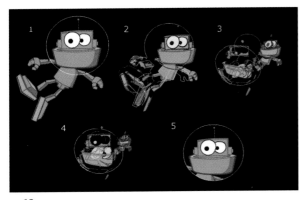

2.68

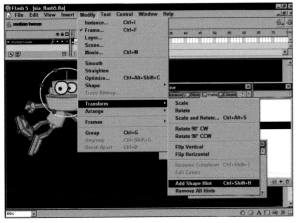

2.69

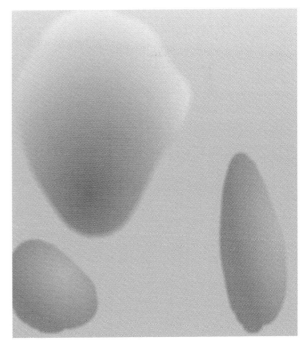

2.70

Gradients and transparency take more processor power to display, so a number of these effects occurring at the same time over large areas of the movie will cause the playback to drop significantly on many computers. The Smashing Ideas site uses one minor transparency effect on the anvil to the left of the "www.smashingideas.com" text. This minor effect won't affect playback on its own.

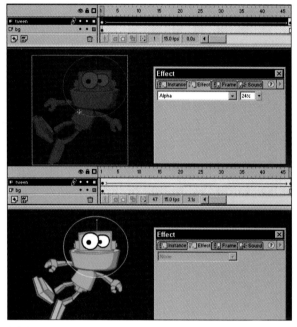

2.71

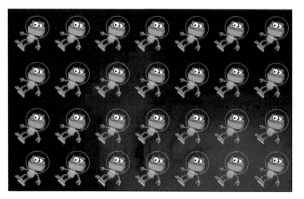

2.72

MULTIPLE MOVIE CLIPS

Developers should be careful about creating multiple animated movie clips or animated graphics and playing them back simultaneously all over the movie stage. The combination of screen redraw and multiple symbols can significantly slow playback. Multiple symbols can slow down playback even if there's no movement within the symbols from frame to frame (2.72). The sheer number of symbols placed on the stage does affect the playback of movies, although it would normally require hundreds of complex symbols to significantly alter the playback speed.

The Smashing Ideas site uses multiple movie clips to achieve the rollover raindrop effect (2.73). Because this effect is user-created and the movie clip contains only a small number of frames to play back, this has never been a problem for playback. If all the raindrops were set to play back simultaneously, then the movie would play more slowly.

ANIMATING COMPLEX VECTOR SHAPES

Animating complex vector shapes that have many jagged or unoptimized lines will result in slower playback because so many points continually need to be recalculated. The Smashing Ideas site uses no complex vector shapes. The animated robot has extremely clean lines so this isn't a problem.

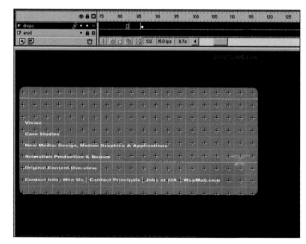

2.73

ANIMATING TEXT

Animating text that uses fonts with jagged edges will make a movie play back very slowly in Flash because too many points continually need to be redrawn. Tweened font blocks that go far off the movie stage, such as scrolling credits at the end of a cartoon, might play slowly and have jerky movement because the entire font block, not just what is being viewed, has to be redrawn in each frame (2.74, 2.75). The Smashing Ideas site uses two clean fonts, Arial and Arial Black, and only animates small font blocks at any specific time.

HAVING TOO MANY SYMBOLS AT A TIME

Some Flash animations contain hundreds, if not thousands, of symbols. It takes Flash time to place and redraw each of those symbols. If the symbols have been modified in any way, such as with an alpha transparency or color tint, then it takes even longer to place all of them each time they need to be redrawn. The Smashing Ideas site uses several simple animations with a minimum number of symbols in order to achieve proper playback.

INFLUENCING PLAYBACK WITH SOUND

You can set up sound files in Flash to stream in synchronization with the animation (Stream setting) or play independently of it (Event and Start settings). In the case of streaming sound, the sound file controls the playback of the movie. Frames of the movie will be dropped in order to keep up with the playback of the sound. Low- and high-end systems play the movie file back in the same amount of time, but high-end systems will drop fewer frames in a complex movie. Depending on the movie, the frame drop might not be noticeable, so frame dropping can be used to force the graphics to keep up with the sound. One problem with using this process in movies with a lot of ActionScript code is that frames with code can be dropped. If this happens, then those actions won't occur.

In the case of event sound, the sound plays at its correct speed and the animation plays back as quickly as it can based on processor speed. Exact synchronization is almost impossible to achieve using event sound even on high-end machines. Files with event sound will play back the animation at different frame rates based on what the processor is capable of handling.

PLAYBACK SETTINGS BASED ON HTML

The HTML for Flash movies can be created directly by using the Publish Settings dialog box. The main value that affects playback is the Quality setting (2.76). The Best Quality setting always plays the movie back in the highest quality possible, always antialiasing graphics and smoothing bitmaps, without considering playback speed. The High setting plays back graphics and text at the best quality possible and, if no animation exists, it smoothes bitmaps. Auto High degrades the quality of the graphics and text to try to maintain the frame rate. Low and Auto Low are also options that start the movie off at the lowest graphic quality and are therefore rarely used.

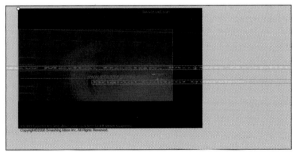

2.74

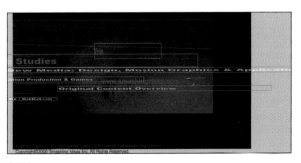

2.75

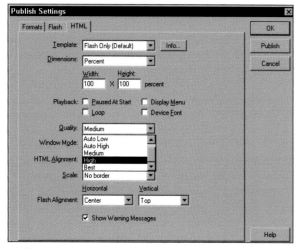

2.76

The Smashing Ideas site uses a High Quality setting because we prefer the quality of the lines and artwork, rather than the playback speed, to remain constant. We concentrate on creating movies that will play back at the proper speed no matter what. Depending on the project, we also use Auto High to enable the playback speed to remain more constant on slower machines.

GETTING IT RIGHT THE FIRST TIME

It's extremely important to put optimization, streaming, loading, and playback high on your list of concerns as you begin developing a project if you want the project to be a success. You also need to define who the target audience is and determine the standard bandwidth, processor speed, and monitor configurations.

As a developer you need to know all of the ways to optimize your Flash movies in order to minimize file size and create intelligent, seamless loading sequences for your sites. You need to understand what effect the processor speed has on movie playback and plan accordingly. Most important, you need to test every movie on a target machine throughout development.

If you plan your movies with these concerns in mind and then use the tools and the medium to your advantage, you'll create exciting, compelling, rich media experiences for Web users. If you don't take all of these potential problems into consideration, you may create rich media that is unusable for your audience and they won't return to your site.

WE ESTABLISHED THE VISUAL BRANDING
OF SMASHING IDEAS AS A PRIORITY.

THE SIMPLE IDEA BEHIND THE MOTION:
THE LETTERS 'SMASHING IDEAS' MOVING
IN A CONTINUOUS ELLIPTICAL ORBIT.

NOTE: UTILIZE TWEENING EFFECTIVELY IN A
MOTION TYPOGRAPHY PIECE. (トロイ リーグ)

PER SPECIFICATIONS:
STAGGER THE MOTIONS OF THE LETTERFORMS AND
ADJUST FRAME POSITIONS FOR LOOPING.

THE LETTERFORMS WOULD NEED TO MOVE IN AN
ELLIPTICAL PATH WHILE APPEARING TO MOVE CLOSER
AND FARTHER AWAY FROM THE USER.

smashing ideas INC.

DATE: 10-17-99	SHEET:
SCALE: 1″ = 72 DPI	**3**
DRAWN: YENTER	OF 16
JOB: TYPOGRAPHY	R G B

CHAPTER 3
MOTION GRAPHICS AND TYPOGRAPHY

BY TROY PARKE

Imagine a title sequence that sets the tone and mood of the story that is about to unfold. A glowing blue horizon shifts and rotates with a lone floating figure in space (3.1). A mysterious portal unlocks, grants access, and beckons the viewer to explore inside (3.2). Rapid-fire words blanket the screen to form a texture of thoughts, shapes, and colors (3.3). These are examples from the world of motion graphics and motion typography.

Motion graphics and motion typography are design-based solutions to time-based communication problems. Motion graphics employ dynamic shapes, and motion typography uses type in motion. Their goal is to communicate. Working with motion means more than simply moving shapes or type around. Instead, using motion graphics and motion typography means designing a dynamic message, not only in terms of what is being said, but also how it is said. Motion designers and animators consider arrangement and texture in addition to pacing, rhythm, storytelling, choreography, and sound design.

Motion graphics and motion typography have a rich history ranging from the precedent-setting pioneer Saul Bass (the creator of the film title sequences for *Psycho* and *The Man with the Golden Arm*) to modern masters such as Kyle Cooper (creator of the titles for *Seven* and *The Island of Dr. Moreau*). Television has also broken ground with its use of motion graphics and motion typography. MTV, in particular, established new approaches to both motion graphics and network identity by using raw and raucous bumpers and interstitials to intentionally target an audience known for it's decreasing attention span.

We are all astronauts.

R. BUCKMINSTER FULLER

3.1

3.2

49

Until recently, the field of motion typography and motion graphics has only been open to those who function as broadcast designers, film title designers, or animators. Today, cutting-edge digital technologies and Flash have placed the tools of motion design and motion typography in the hands of the masses.

Unquestionably, Flash has greatly contributed to the explosion of motion graphics and typography on the Web. The use of compact vector graphics coupled with compressed sound files and the widespread proliferation of the Flash Player all made Flash an ideal choice for Web-based motion typography and motion graphics. Even though the full potential of broadband technology and streaming video is still out on the horizon, today's solution for creating rich files with low file size is found in Flash. Examples of *trailblazers* and leading-edge sites currently developing the

language of Web motion graphics and motion typography include `www.hillmancurtis.com`, `www.juxtinteractive.com`, and `www.yugop.com`.

Motion graphics and motion typography are solutions employed in virtually every aspect of the Web environment. Examples range from the ubiquitous *loading . . .* indicator with blinking dots, to lavish, flowing page titles. Motion graphics and motion typography are most often employed to spotlight features, brand an identity (3.4), provide dynamic navigation, create site intros (3.5), previews (3.6), title sequences, advertising, and promotion, and as elements that enhance the user experience.

The solid use of motion graphics and motion typography can be a rapturous experience. Motion graphics and motion typography approach this level when the elements act in concert and flow together. To communicate a feeling to the viewer, motion designers use

3.3

3.4

AUTHOR PROFILE

Troy Parke

Troy Parke is an Art Director at Smashing Ideas. With an emphasis on design structure and process, Troy has been instrumental with Smashing Ideas projects for Eddie Bauer, WhatCard, and Shockwave.com. He co-directed the team that created Madonna's first interactive web music video for her hit single "Music." When Troy grows up, he wants to philosophize and produce books on the caliber of Edward Tufte's classics on the visual display of information.

techniques such as pairing visuals with sound, visually driven storytelling, and dynamically targeted visuals.

UNITING DISCIPLINES

The field of motion graphics and motion typography can be viewed as a union of many disciplines. Motion design requires an understanding and execution of filmmaking, advertising, brand strategy, graphic design, animation, and sound design. Knowing the rules and how to traditionally apply them enables you to better understand when and how to begin breaking them.

GRAPHIC DESIGN FUNDAMENTALS

Graphic design is visual problem-solving in two and three dimensions. A solid grasp on the fundamentals of graphic design is essential when taking the next step in creating designs for a motion- and time-based medium. A strong static design with energy translates into motion far better than sloppily arranged elements transformed into scattered shapes that simply slide around begging for attention.

A motion designer must understand the fundamentals of position, alignment, shape, color, repetition, and texture, and know how these fundamentals apply to a design. With a solid foundation, a sense of design can be nurtured from time and experience. Working hard to know a computer application inside and out

is valiant, but it does not substitute for the forethought that is fundamental to the design process. Those interested in working with motion graphics should take advantage of the wealth of college programs, classes, and Web communities that offer instruction in the basic principles of design.

The discussion of typography itself has already filled many books and can not be distilled down to a font name and size selected from a dialog box. Notable references on type include Robert Bringhurst's *The Elements of Typographic Style* (Point Roberts, WA: Hartley & Marks, 1996) and *Stop Stealing Sheep* by Erik Spiekermann and E. M. Ginger (Mountain View, California, Adobe Press 1993). Working with type requires a sensitivity to legibility, character, form, and an understanding of issues such as leading (space between lines of type) and kerning (the space between letters). The use of type in motion typography should appear to be effortlessly integrated into a piece, even though it's actually the element that can be the most difficult to shape (3.7–3.9).

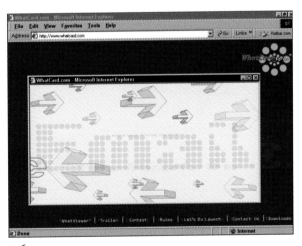

3.6

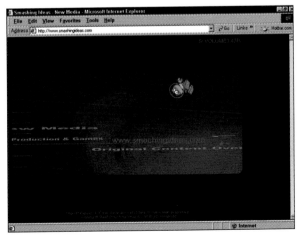

3.5   3.7

CREATING THE ILLUSION OF LIFE

The process of animation is perhaps best described as creating the illusion of life. The key word here is "illusion" because animation is not an exacting, mechanical refabrication of life movements. Understanding and correctly using the principles of animation is fundamental to creating motion graphics that appear alive and fluid. For more information, see Chapter 9, "Creating Broadcast-Quality Animation," which outlines Smashing Ideas' approach to applying the concepts of traditional character animation to Flash and to the Web.

Animation relies on exaggeration in applying the principles of squash, stretch, blurring, anticipation, and cushion to create the feeling of life. A ball does not merely move up and down as it bounces. The ball experiences an impact, a flattening out at the moment it strikes, and then it recoils, gaining energy to bounce in a motion that happens so fast that it appears only as a blur (3.10). Type that is stretched and squashed gives a sense of character and creates the feeling of fluid motion (3.11 and 3.12). Employing animation techniques when working with motion graphics and typography can create the sense that type or graphics are alive when they move, instead of just appearing to mechanically change positions.

Frame rate is another consideration in animation that plays a very large role in the development of motion graphics and motion typography. The higher the frame rate used, the smoother the motion appears. While film animation is viewed at 24 frames per second (fps), because of file size and playback considerations, character animation in Flash is typically displayed at 10 to 12 fps. Where possible, motion designers try to use higher frame rates in Flash than animators would because motion graphics typically require fewer symbols and elements.

3.8

3.9

USING TIME AND SOUND

Graphic designers and illustrators are accustomed to developing solutions for two- and three-dimensional spaces. Designing and animating motion graphics and dynamic typography means more than just considering the width and height of a page or the depth of a space; a motion designer must also consider time and sound.

The greatest consideration in the design and execution of motion graphics or motion typography is the passage of time. A motion designer must approach a

3.10

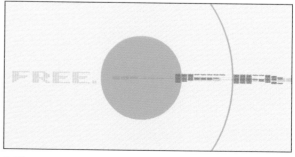

3.11

solution from a film director's perspective by employing both pacing and storytelling techniques to create a particular message or experience for the viewer. For instance, a slow zoom through trees opening in a forest was used to establish a sense of winter tranquility for Eddie Bauer's "Holiday Central" (3.13–3.15). A motion designer, like a filmmaker, can elicit feelings of peace, apprehension, or joy in the viewer simply by manipulating the speed, pacing, and rhythm of images.

Designing sound and establishing well-planned timing between the audio and visual portions of a piece is an extremely effective way of creating an immersive viewer experience. The opening winter scene for "Holiday Central," while visually rich, is a much fuller experience when accompanied by the "Winter Wonderland" score. As the symphonic sound swells, the forest trees part ways to reveal the snowy stage. Timing the visuals to match the tone of the music enhances the experience to a level that pictures or sound used alone could not reach.

APPROACHING PROCESS

With so much to understand and so many disciplines to draw from, where one should begin becomes a very daunting question, particularly when deadlines loom in the near future. Going from initial creation to the final execution of motion design and typography is a detailed process. The goal is to provide a time-based communication solution. By focusing on the role motion graphics and typography play in a piece, the designer can reduce the possibility of wasting precious time as a result of going down unnecessary roads during development.

> **NOTE**
>
> For additional reference, David Mamet's *On Directing Film* (New York: Penguin, 1991) is a concise resource that provides insight into the filmmaking perspective, while Karel Reisz and Gavin Millar's *Technique of Film Editing* (London, New York: Focal Press, 1968) is a must-have for any serious student of editing. Walter Murch's *In the Blink of an Eye: A Perspective on Film Editing* (Los Angeles: Silman-James Press, 1995) presents the ideas and process of the editor of such films as *Apocalypse Now*, *The English Patient*, and *The Unbearable Lightness of Being*.

3.13   © Eddie Bauer, Inc. 2000

3.14   © Eddie Bauer, Inc. 2000

3.12

3.15   © Eddie Bauer, Inc. 2000

Process is a tool, and the stages are not discrete; instead, they often flow into each other. It is a plan of attack that is inherently flexible in order to meet changes in a project's often fluctuating development. Process is not a method to curb experimentation or serendipity, but an approach to keep a project on schedule. A process approach enables you to take advantage of all the wonderful "mistakes" that happen along the way, instead of waiting for solutions to appear and present themselves.

The following is a process approach to motion graphics and typography illustrated by a recent Smashing Ideas project for WhatCard.com. As we discuss the various phases, keep in mind that the motion designer should continuously test his or her approach on others with a fresh perspective and incorporate their feedback into the continuing design process.

DEFINING THE PARAMETERS

The first phase of developing any solution is to define the purpose. What is the message and what are its desired results? Other issues to define include the needs of the client, the project's target audience, the target technical environment for the users, and any other technical constraints. Obviously, these issues are not very creative, but they should be some of the first items addressed on a project along with budget, scope, and responsibilities.

WhatCard.com was preparing a site and wanted Smashing Ideas to develop a piece that would generate a strong interest in the launch of the site—a similar task to creating a buzz before the release of a movie. The target audience was defined as tweens (from preteen through the teen years), and the target environment was defined as Windows/Mac, minimum 266 MHz machine with a 56 Kbps connection and Flash 4 Player. Given these technical constraints, bitmaps were not available for use because of their prohibitively large file size. Likewise, any sound would need to be highly compressed and streamed to account for file size and bandwidth limitations of the target audience.

IDENTIFYING THE FEELING

With the technical constraints defined and set aside, the motion designer needs to identify the project's soul and feeling. These impressions can be attitudes of the target audience, keywords that define the project vision, or the message the client wishes to convey. Through brainstorming, the motion designer will gravitate toward an idea or thought that will help identify the project's overall desired feeling. At this phase the focus is on identifying what the project feels like, not what it looks like.

Turning back to our example, the key feeling behind the WhatCard.com site was determined to be a bubble-gum pop and fanatical-teen sensation, fueled by celebrity-fascinated teens. We wanted the user to experience the feeling of watching a preview for an upcoming blockbuster event. The introduction would start slowly, but build to a fever pitch with glimpses of upcoming features, including the option to personalize the site. With a direction established, the process of writing the script and composing the score began.

FOCUS ON THE ESSENTIAL ELEMENTS

The floodgates are open, and feelings and ideas are flowing. Now is the phase for the motion designer to determine and focus on the essential message elements. Ideally, the graphic-based solution should emerge from the soul of the project and shape all of the project's elements. In this step, the problem of conveying the message should be addressed by structuring the delivery vehicle, storyboarding the motion graphics/typography, and choosing movie size, frame rate, color palette, typeface, and choreography.

The goal for the WhatCard.com project was to create a sense of anticipation and introduce an element, in this case a bouncing dot, from the WhatCard.com logo to be used as a guide throughout a trailer. This approach fit the pop-oriented audience and helped to further establish the character of the preview site. The essential elements for the WhatCard.com trailer were as follows:

- Using the dot as a guide
- Developing and working very closely with a pop-feel soundtrack to help reinforce the mood
- Highlighting only the most distinctive features through the use of motion typography
- Offering teaser snapshots of the content to be available at launch

From these core elements, we began to create the trailer for WhatCard.com, while taking audio loading time into consideration. First, storyboards and visuals were sketched by hand (3.16), and then translated into Flash (3.17, 3.18). The primary color palette of charcoal gray, green, crème, and red-orange was selected along with Terminus and Taser as the typefaces.

REFINING THE DETAILS

With major issues addressed, the motion designer next needs to flesh out the details and adjust positions, motions, and transitions. From the storyboard, the motion designer labors over finessing the movement of each design element to elicit the correct feel, synchronize to the audio, and add sound effects where necessary. At this phase, the piece should require no additional explanation from the designer: Either the design's message succeeds in reaching the viewer, or it does not.

This phase of the WhatCard.com trailer development absorbed the most time on the project. Details such as the number of frames used to stretch a word and the frame in which a sound effect should occur were addressed, including the time it takes for "WhatCard.com" to appear (3.19), and the wavy motion of the letters as they peel off the card (3.20). Even fine details were addressed, such as the exact order in which the letters that spelled "ACCESS"

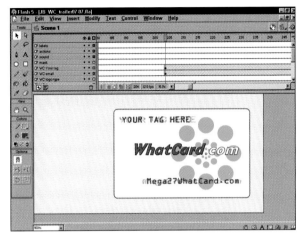

3.17

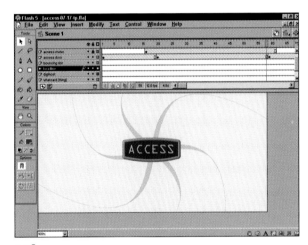

3.18

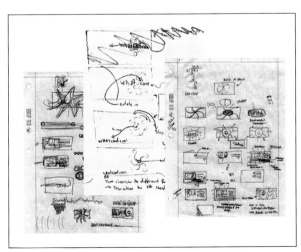

3.16

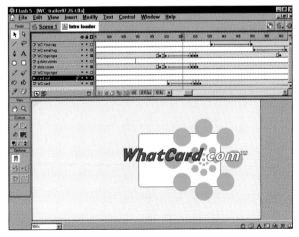

3.19

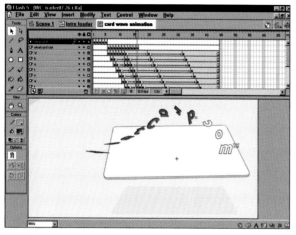

3.20

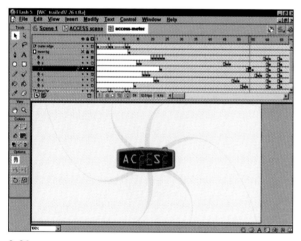

3.21

would appear (3.21). The motion designers tweaked and refined the trailer until every detail had been set.

EVALUATING THE WHOLE

With the details defined, the motion designer takes in the whole piece, evaluates which portions work or not, and begins the final phase of file-size optimization. If a sequence, or element, stands out as particularly weak, the sequence should be improved to uphold the integrity of the piece as a whole. Designers hardly need to be reminded that this is the version of your work that will be distributed (and judged) around the world.

When evaluating the WhatCard.com trailer, minor points in transitions were adjusted and overused sound effects were removed or replaced. The wave effect of the logo, letters, and card was adjusted to achieve smoother animation (3.22–3.24). Responses from the client and other viewers who saw the project for the first time were positive. As a whole, the piece incorporated strong pacing, a solid integration of sound with visuals, and felt complete, indicating that it was time to stop before it became overworked.

CASE STUDY TECHNIQUES

Now that we've addressed theory, let's turn our attention toward practice. The following case studies

TODD PURGASON ON TYPOGRAPHY AND DESIGN

Todd Purgason is the creative director for Juxt Interactive, a company specializing in Internet strategy and Flash-based interactive Web sites. His work has won numerous awards, including the Clio Award, *How Magazine*'s International Design Competition Award for Outstanding Design, the IPPA StudioONE Award, the *Communication Arts Magazine* Web Site of the Week, the High Five Award, and seven Macromedia "Site of the Day" awards. Todd was selected by Spain's leading news publication *El Pais* as one of the world's top six Web designers.

Q: Your work has a strong typographical focus. Where does that come from?
A: A love for type forms, I guess. My background is in architecture and in that medium design is often very structured. When I started doing graphic design, my layout concepts would often reflect this. But typography is so organic, I started juxtaposing structured layouts with the organic type forms in a way that produces a dialog between the two. I view the layout as the space or the "room" and the typography as the characters in that room. Each typeface has a tone of voice

deconstruct the steps behind generating segments of recent Smashing Ideas projects that incorporated motion graphics and motion typography. The following examples also illustrate two different approaches to generating motion in Flash — specifically, keyframing and tweening.

Keyframing refers to the process of creating motion by physically adjusting and controlling the contents of each individual frame. This method offers a more organic, lifelike feel, but is very labor- and time-intensive, especially when compared with tweening. By using separate layers for each element, the number of keyframes can be reduced and the workflow efficiency for adjusting keyframe to keyframe can be maximized. Keyframing is a technique often embraced by animators because it affords them the highest degree of control and provides the most realistic method to mimic life. The WhatCard.com typing dot is an example of

3.23

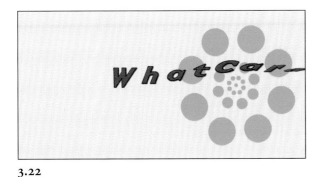

3.22

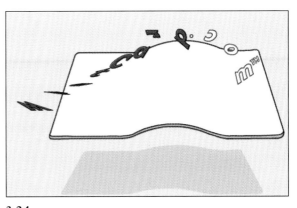

3.24

and I try to play with that — setting off different tones of voice, playing them against each other or playing with each other. Sometimes the tones are arguing, creating a dynamic that is very loud, and sometimes they are just conversations that are subtle and subdued.

Q: What role does motion typography play in your approach to projects? Is it the starting point for projects or does it come out of the larger site conceptualization and design?

A: A bit of both, actually. I first build a concept and a visual language around that concept and then, while I'm creating the visual language, I think about motion and interactivity. I don't believe in FX design for FX design. I believe that motion communicates the same way a font does, so I'm thinking about the nature of the motion while I'm doing layouts. I lay out keyframes of my motion graphics in FreeHand, studying how the design will be carried out with time and motion. I don't do this with every little piece but with the major pieces of the

project. I like to have substance — solid, interesting, and appropriate design that moves with purpose and reason.

Q: You've worked on a number of different sites for architecture or building firms. How does that discipline influence your approach to interactive media?

A: Interactive media and architecture have some notable similarities. I think the three primary areas would be visual communication, function, and circulation.

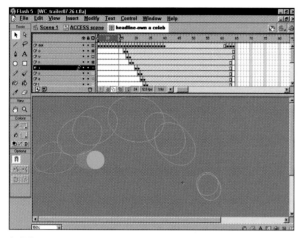

3.25

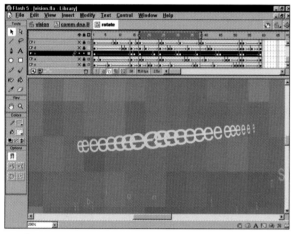

3.26

using the keyframing technique as the primary vehicle for motion (3.25).

In opposition to keyframing's time-intensive nature, *tweening* is a computed, mechanical translation of a symbol from one keyframe to another keyframe. In Flash, tweening is easier and faster to produce, but the ease and speed comes at the cost of quality and often processor-intensiveness. Tweened motion often appears very rigid and inorganic. Flash offers a few tools, such as Easing, to reduce the strictly mechanical feel of tweening. Depending upon the feeling identified for the piece, tweening may be an appropriate solution. With experience, designers and animators increase their understanding of how to use tweening effectively and how to reduce the mechanical sensation it can produce. The Smashing Ideas circle is a deconstruction of using tweening as the primary vehicle for animating motion. A snapshot from this motion typography piece demonstrates the use of tweening to generate the motion of the letterforms. (3.26).

USING KEYFRAMING — WHATCARD.COM TYPING DOT

Returning to the process of the WhatCard.com trailer, motion graphics and typography solutions were employed to highlight the most distinctive features of WhatCard.com. With the feeling already established, motion typography headlines were

Visual communication. As architects, 80 percent of our job is communication documentation, communicating a design to the client so that he is excited about it and could sleep knowing his $30 million is being well spent. Then we would have to develop the project doing visual studies for ourselves so we could better understand it. Finally, we have to build the instructions (plans) for a builder (usually the lowest bidder) to build the design and not destroy the design integrity in the process. In interactivity we do much of the same task for

our projects, but the plans are more for us and we call them specs.

Functionality. I have noticed that many designers seem to have a battle between their design and functionality. In architecture, functionality was 70 to 80 percent, while design was whatever was left. A building falling down and killing people is not too good for the architect's résumé. For me, design and functionality are all a part of the whole. They're so connected, especially today with Flash and interactivity becoming its own art form.

Circulation. In designing a building, first you study how a client needs to use the building. You develop key efficiencies so that the building will support all the necessary activities without wasting employees' time as they move around within the building to carry out their job functions. At the same time, we try to create a building to add quality to the life of the people working in the building through the design, without letting that design become a nuisance to them. The people who have to live and work in a building also demand a good design that geared around the concept of bouncing and a "typing dot" host. The technique behind the motion of the typing dot was used effectively throughout many sequences in the trailer.

The idea behind the motion is that the dot appears to type the letters of the headline and eagerly await the next sequence (3.27–3.29). Translating this motion into Flash meant using simulated stretches and squashes created by scaling symbols. The effect would need to occur very quickly, at near typing speed, and place emphasis on the entrance of each letterform. After presenting the headline, the dot host would need to loop through an animation that conveys a sense of anticipation and excitement about presenting the next message.

For a variety of reasons, this animation was employed very effectively. The motion makes an extremely effective use of keyframing by using the animation techniques of squash, stretch, and blur. The typing effect continues the theme of the dot acting as a host. The file size of the motion effect is extremely small; the following example yielded an exported file of 2K. Last, the motion works on not only a visual level, but is also choreographed with the flow of the audio soundtrack to ensure maximum emphasis.

Creating the typing dot

The approach to achieve this effect in Flash is to start by laying out the headline "Own a Celebrity!" to be

3.27

3.28

3.29

does not force tedious and unnecessary movement through the building to carry out their lives. This is very much like information architecture. It's always our goal to grab visitors to a site by the hand and guide them to the content they want in a dynamic and nontedious way.

Q: What influences your work?
A: I try to draw my designs out of the project itself. I like to have meaning in almost every element in my design. To do this I start by brainstorming about the particular project, always keeping in mind the target audience and the brand of the client. I try to dig deep into it and develop creative concepts that are totally unique to that project and avoid any clichés. Once I have a concept I evolve it, basing all my design decisions on that idea so that in the end I have a piece with several layers of meaning all interwoven together and connected in some way. I do have a style that is always evolving but I approach projects from a branding standpoint and I don't let my style fight a client's brand. My style is more prevalent when working on a more personal project or a Juxt project because my style greatly influenced the brand I created for Juxt.

Q: Whose work do you look to for inspiration?
A: I am inspired by lots of things around me, not just people's work. I am greatly inspired by nature. I see God as the master designer and all that we create in this lifetime is simple garage-sale fodder in comparison to the most simple structures that are all around us in nature. I get a lot of inspiration driving down the

revealed by the typing dot. Next, create each letter-form as a separate symbol. Then, create a symbol for the bouncing dot animation that will also be used in the typing effect. Create the punctuated keyframe motion for the entrance of each letterform. Finally, stagger the keyframe motions for the appearance of typing. Here are the steps:

1. Set up the movie. Choose File ➢ New (Ctrl+N / ⌘+N) to create a new file. Choose Modify ➢ Movie (Ctrl+M / ⌘+N) to open the Movie Properties dialog box and set the frame rate to 10 fps and the movie dimensions to 500 pixels in width by 200 pixels in height (3.30). Choose a dark gray color as the background. Click OK to close the Movie Properties dialog box and choose File ➢ Save to save the file. (The frame rate of this file was set at 10 fps because other sequences included character animation developed for 10 fps.)

2. Create the type for motion. Select the Text tool and in the Character panel (Window ➢ Panels ➢ Character) select a sans-serif font (in this example we used Terminus from T-26 Fonts, at www.t26.com). Set the font height to 50 and type **Own a**, the first portion of the motion typography message, on the stage. Continue to adjust the font size and color for the remainder of the message (**celebrity**) using separate text boxes as necessary. Finish the headline with an oversized exclamation point (3.31).

road seeing the dynamics of an urban environment juxtaposed with the daily life that takes place around it. I also love driving up the interstate here in California through rural areas seeing old farm equipment and landmarks that are eroding and becoming more a part of nature than a man-made structure, such as old faded billboards and signs. If I were a more patient person I would love to drive across the country and stop and photograph all the inspiration that is no doubt there.

3. Create symbols for each letter. Select all of the text boxes (Edit ➢ Select All) and choose Modify ➢ Break Apart (Ctrl+B / ⌘+B). The type is no longer text, just vector shapes. Carefully select the first letter and choose Insert ➢ Convert to Symbol (F8). Name the symbol **lett-1**, select the Movie Clip behavior, and click OK. Repeat this process for all remaining letterforms (3.32), making each letter a new symbol, *except* for the dot of the exclamation point, which is addressed in a subsequent step.

4. Create a layer for each letter. Create 15 layers (Insert ➢ Layer) for each letterform symbol and the dot. Select the letterform-symbol "lett-1" in the Library window (Window ➢ Library) and Cut (Ctrl+X / ⌘+X) and then Paste in Place (Ctrl+Shift+V / ⌘+Shift+V) in an empty layer. Repeat cutting and pasting until each letterform-

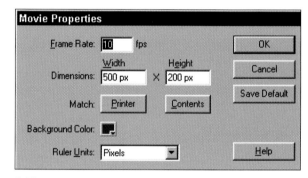

3.30

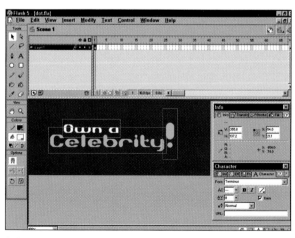

3.31

symbol is in its own layer. Arrange the order of the layers so that the first letterform is the top layer (3.33). Name the layer containing the dot of the exclamation point **bouncing dot**. Name the other layers for clarity and save the file.

5. Create the typing dot symbols. Select the dot, which should be in its own layer, and choose Insert ➢ Convert to Symbol. Name the symbol **bounce-dot**, select the Graphic behavior, and click OK. Double-click the newly created bounce-dot symbol to edit in place. Select the dot and choose Insert ➢ Convert to Symbol (F8). Name the symbol **dot**, choose the Movie Clip behavior, and click OK (3.34). Creating a symbol inside a symbol is called *nesting* and is a powerful technique for maximizing the benefit of symbol byte costs.

6. Animate the bouncing dot. From inside the "bounce-dot" symbol, select frame 2, and choose Insert ➢ Keyframe (F6). Repeat inserting keyframes through frame 5. Leave the first keyframe in the "bounce-dot" symbol unaltered. Select frame 2 and select the instance of the dot

movie clip on the stage. In the Transform panel (Window ➢ Panels ➢ Transform), set the Height to 80 percent and align the bottom of the dot to the bottom of the dot in frame 1 (3.35). Select frame 3 and select the instance of the dot movie clip on the stage. In the Transform panel, set the Height to 140 percent and align the bottom of the dot to the position of the dot in frame 2. Repeat this process for the instances of the dot movie clip in frames 4 and 5, setting the Height to 80 percent and 110 percent, respectively. Frames 2 and 4 act as squash while frames 3 and 5 act as stretch (3.36). Scrub through the timeline or use the controller to watch the animation and spot areas for adjustment.

7. Set up the typing dot effect. Return to the main timeline by clicking the Scene 1 tab. Select all layers and choose Insert ➢ Frame (F5). Continue to add frames until you reach frame 40. Outline all the letterform layers by clicking the Show All Layers as Outlines icon on the timeline. Lock every layer except the "bouncing dot" layer. Select frame 15 of the "bouncing dot" layer and choose Insert ➢ Keyframe (F6). Select the instance of the bounce-dot symbol in frame 1 of the "bouncing dot" layer and then, in the Instance panel, set the Animation to Loop in the drop-down menu below the Behavior setting. For the same frame, *not* frame 15, use the arrow keys to align the dot to the baseline of the first letterform character "O" (3.37).

3.32

3.33

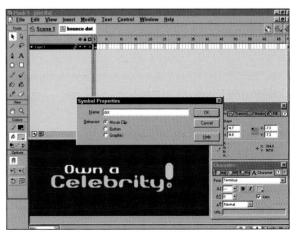

3.34

3.35

3.36

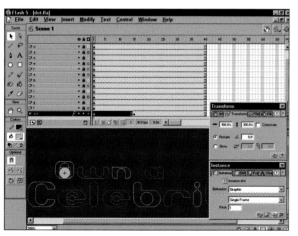

3.37

8. Create the dot typing effect. Select frame 2 of the "bouncing dot" layer and choose Insert ➤ Keyframe (F6). Align the instance of the bounce-dot symbol in frame 2 of the "bouncing dot" layer with the next letterform "w." Select frame 3 of the dot layer, choose Insert ➤ Keyframe (F6), and align the instance of the bounce-dot symbol with the next letterform "n." Continue this process for all the letterforms. When the dot moves from one line to the next in frame 5 (from "a" to the "C" of "Celebrity"), keyframe a position of the dot between the headlines and stretch the dot using Scale and Rotate to simulate the appearance of blurring (3.38). Because the dot in frame 15 was left in position under the exclamation symbol, it should not require adjustment. Scrub through the timeline to view the typing motion of the dot.

9. Create the letter typing effect. Lock the bouncing dot layer, unlock and change from Outline view to Solid view for the letterform

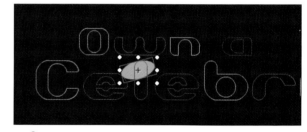

3.38

3.39

layers. Select frame 2 of all letterform layers and choose Insert ➤ Keyframe (F6). Select frame 1 of the top letterform layer and enter 130 percent horizontal and vertical in the Transform panel. Press Enter so that the change takes effect. For the same letterform symbol, select Alpha from the Effect panel, enter 70 percent, and press Enter so that the change takes effect (3.39). Select frame 1 of the next letterform layer and repeat this process for all the letterform symbols in frame 1. Frame 2 for each letterform should remain unaltered.

10. Stagger the individual letterforms. Select frames 1 to 40 of the top letterform layer. Drag the entire selection one frame to the right, so that the first keyframe is now in frame 2. Repeat this process for all the letterform layers, staggering the entire layer selection one frame to the right from the layer above it. When completed, the timeline should look like a descending staircase. Be sure to stagger an additional frame in the fifth layer to compensate for the dot leaving from one line of type to the next (3.40). Scrubbing through the selection, the letters should appear to pop in as the typing dot advances.

11. Remove frames. Select all frames in all layers from frame 41 on and choose Insert ➤ Remove Frames (Shift+F5). Playing the motion with the movie controller should yield the headline typing effect followed by the bouncing dot of the exclamation point (3.41).

12. Save the file. Choose Control ➤ Test Movie and view (3.42).

USING TWEENING

Early in the development of the third version of the Smashing Ideas Web site, visually branding Smashing Ideas was established as a priority. When the look and feel of the site (deep water blues and a sense of floating space) was established, we decided to incorporate motion typography as a solution to augment site branding. Originally designed only as part of a sequence in the vision statement, this versatile motion also became the site loading indicator when large files are downloading.

The simple idea behind the motion is the letters *s m a s h i n g i d e a s* moving in a continuous elliptical orbit (3.43–3.45). In Flash, this meant facing the challenge of using a two-dimensional tool to simulate the illusion of depth and dimension. The letterforms would need to move in an elliptical path while reversing and appearing to move closer and farther away from the user.

3.40

3.41

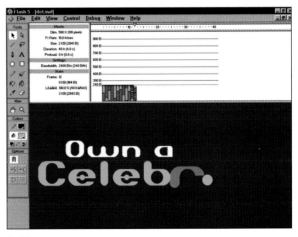

3.42

This motion is successful for a few different reasons. First, the animation uses tweening effectively in creating a motion typography piece. Second, the motion gives the illusion of depth and the feeling of dimension. The file size of the motion is also small; the following example yielded an exported file in the neighborhood of 12K. Finally, this motion takes advantage of seamless looping and symbol reuse for a very compact yet dynamic visual.

Smashing Ideas circle — step by step

The approach to creating this motion in Flash was as follows: Start with a line that outlines the motion path. Next, build each letterform as a symbol and place each one on a separate layer. To use tweening, keyframe extreme positions of the letterforms through the orbit. After creating a tween that computes movements between keyframes, adjust the motion by adding additional keyframe positions. Stagger the motions of the letterforms and adjust frame positions for looping. Here are the steps:

1. **Set up the movie.** Set the frame rate to 15 fps and the movie dimensions to 600 pixels in width by 200 pixels in height (3.46). The higher the frame rate, the smoother the motion, but at a cost of file size. The frame rate of this file was increased from 10 or 12 to 15 fps because the focus is smooth motion typography.

2. **Draw a line that represents the motion path** (a circle viewed from the side). Select the Line

tool. Use the Stroke panel to set the Stroke Color to Black and the Stroke Thickness to 0.25. Draw a line across the middle of the stage and use the Info panel to set its width to 550 pixels (3.47).

3. **Create a movie clip for the motion.** Select the line and choose Insert ➤ Convert to Symbol. Name the symbol **whole-circle**, select the Movie Clip behavior, and click OK. Double-click the "whole-circle" symbol on the stage to edit it in place. Change the name of the layer containing the line to **construction** (3.48).

4. **Create the type for motion.** Select the Text tool (T) and, in the Character panel (Window ➤ Panel ➤ Character), set the font to a sans-serif font. We used Trade Gothic LH Extended, and set the font height to 85. Create a new layer, select it as the current layer, and type **smashingideas** on the stage (3.49).

5. **Create symbols for each letter.** Select the type and break it apart. Carefully select the first letter

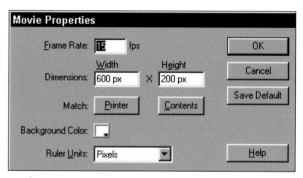

3.46

3.43

3.44

3.45

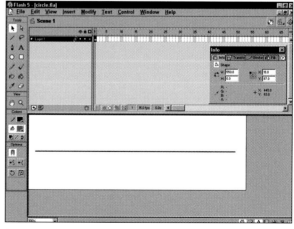

3.47

and choose Insert ➤ Convert to Symbol. Name the symbol **lett-s1** or something appropriate, select the Movie Clip behavior, and click OK (3.50). Repeat this process for all remaining letterforms. Make each letter a unique symbol so that the motion can be "recycled" to create a message different than "smashing ideas."

6. Create layers for each letter. Create 12 new layers. Select the letterform symbol "lett-s1," and choose Edit ➤ Cut. Select an open layer and choose Edit ➤ Paste in Place. Repeat cutting and pasting until each letterform symbol is in its own layer. Arrange the order of the layers so that the first letterform is the top layer (3.51). Name the layers for clarity and save the file.

7. Visually center the letters. Lock the "construction" layer and select a letter symbol. Center the letterform symbols on the lower curve of the oval using the align tool and arrow keys. Be sure to keep the baseline of the letters in alignment and use the Outline view to assist in arranging (3.52).

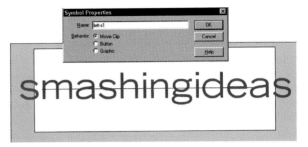

3.50

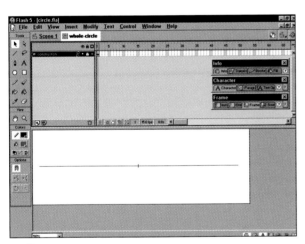

3.48

3.51

3.49

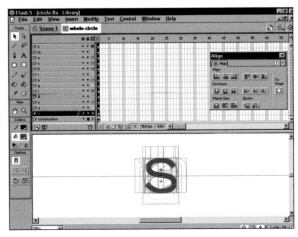

3.52

8. Add frames for the loop. Select the timeline and insert frames. Continue to add frames so that all layers have 61 frames (3.53). The finished loop will eventually be composed of 60 frames.

9. Keyframe the first portion of letterform motion. With the "construction" layer locked, select frame 14 of all the letterform layers and

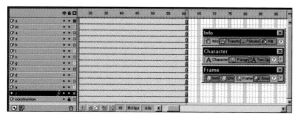

3·53

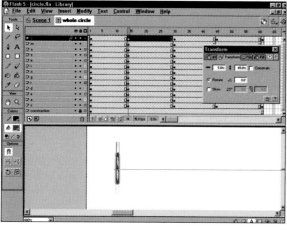

3·54

insert a keyframe. Repeat inserting a keyframe for frames 30, 45, and 61. Next, select keyframe 14 of all the letterform layers, enter 5 percent horizontal and 45 percent vertical in the Transform panel, and center the symbols on the left-most edge of the line (3.54). Save the file. When scrubbing back and forth from frame 1 to 14, the letterforms should appear to move to the left and back. Hide all layers except one to see this effect clearly.

10. Continue keyframing. Now select keyframe 30 for all layers, enter 20 percent horizontal and vertical in the Transform panel, choose Modify ➤ Transform ➤ Flip Horizontal, and center the symbols on the center of the line (3.55).

11. Keyframe the next position. Select keyframe 45 for all layers, enter 5 percent horizontal and 45 percent vertical in the Transform panel, choose Modify ➤ Transform ➤ Flip Horizontal, and center the symbols on the right-most edge of the oval symbol (3.56). When scrubbing, the letterforms should now appear to complete a clockwise circle.

12. Complete the first turn. Select frame 15 of all letterform layers, insert a keyframe, and flip it horizontally (3.57).

13. Complete the second turn. Select frame 46 of all letterform layers, insert a keyframe, and flip it horizontally (3.58). When scrubbing, the letterforms should appear to take quick turns at the edges of the line.

3·55

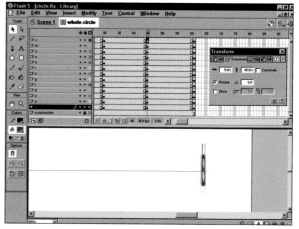

3·56

14. Create motion tweens. Select all letterform frames from 1 to 61. Select Motion from the Tween drop-down menu in the Frame panel. Set Easing to 0, Rotation to none, and check Scale (3.59). Save the file. When scrubbing, the motion should be complete with "in-between" states between keyframe positions.

15. Smooth the motion. For all letterform layers, create keyframes at frame 7 and 53. Select the keyframes at frame 7 and, using the arrow keys, adjust the *horizontal* position until it is about one-sixth of the way from the left-hand edge of the line. Repeat for frame 53, positioning the frames about one-sixth of the way from the right-hand edge of the line (3.60). These adjustments will give the appearance of a rounder motion.

16. Eliminate duplicate keyframes. Insert a keyframe at frame 60 for all layers. Select frame 61 and remove frames (3.61). Choose Control ➤ Loop Playback and play the motion with the Movie Controller. Frame 61 was used to help create tweens. In a looped playback the motion would appear to pause because frame 1 and 61 are identical.

17. Stagger the individual letterforms. Select frames 1 to 60 in the layer that is second from the top. Drag the entire selection three frames to the right, so that the first keyframe is now in frame 4. Repeat this process for the layer below, staggering the entire selection three frames to the right from the layer above it (3.62). Be sure to stagger more

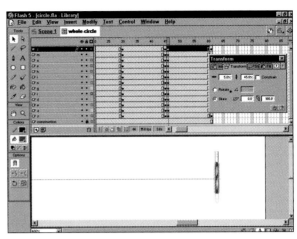

3.58

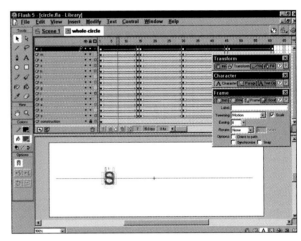

3.59

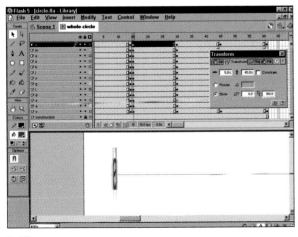

3.57

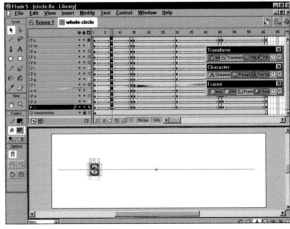

3.60

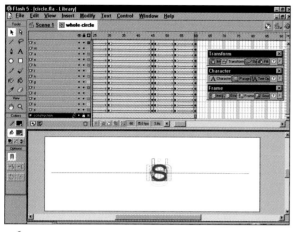

3.61

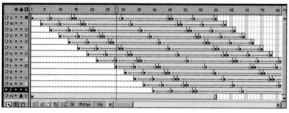

3.62

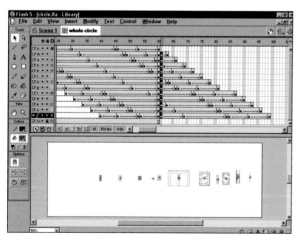

3.63

than three frames (about six) between the words "smashing" and "ideas." Save the file.

18. Keyframe again to position tweened frames. Select frame 60 for all letterform layers and insert a keyframe. Select frame 61 for all letterform layers and insert a keyframe (3.63).

19. Fill in the gap. In each letterform layer, either select or cut the frames from frame 61 on, and then move or paste them into the empty frame gap *on the same layer* created from staggering the letterforms (3.64).

20. Remove empty frames. Select all frames in all layers from frame 61 on and choose and remove frames (3.65).

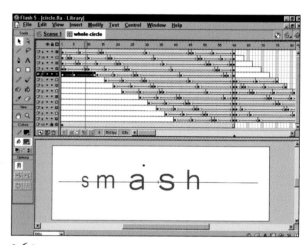

3.64

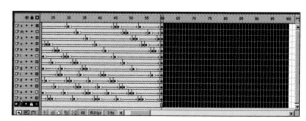

3.65

21. Convert the construction layer to a guide (3.66).

22. Click the Scene 1 tab. Save the file. Test the movie and view it (3.67).

MOVING FORWARD

Motion graphics and motion typography are extremely effective in conveying messages. The motion designer's first duty is to distill the essence of a message and then design a solution that connects with the viewer. Intended or not, every turn of an object or blur across a screen imparts a message to the viewer. Motion graphics and motion typography are multifaceted disciplines. Learn the governing principles of design, animation, and filmmaking first, and then understand how to effectively break the rules.

The ubiquity of Flash and the ever-increasing impact of the Internet on our daily lives will only continue to drive the evolution of high-impact messages. Even today, motion graphics and motion typography are being employed as solutions in the fifth dimension: interactivity. Sites such as `www.juxtinteractive.com` and `www.yugop.com` use motion graphics as a form of communication not only between the designer and the viewer, but rely on the user's active input to generate the motion and the message. Interactivity, the defining feature of the Web, appears to be the inevitable future of motion graphics and typography.

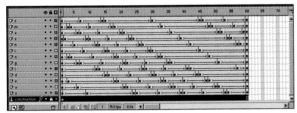

3.66

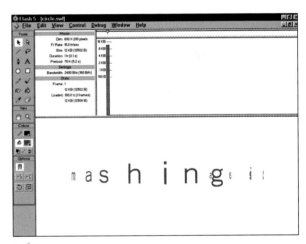

3.67

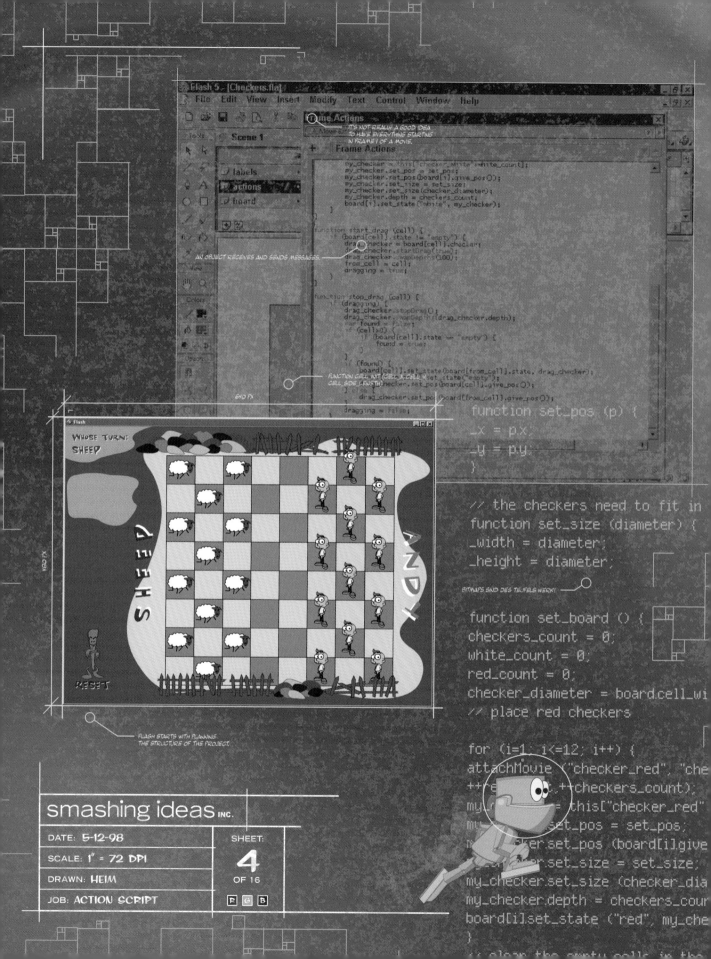

CHAPTER 4
OBJECT-ORIENTED PROGRAMMING IN FLASH

BY ANDREAS HEIM

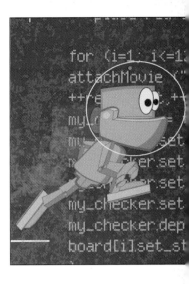

What is an *object?* If you try to define an object, your definition will probably begin with the qualifier, "It depends. . . ." However, in the world of programming, it is very important to differentiate between things out in the world and *objects*.

For the sake of argument, let's refer to something in the world as an object, something that we would not normally consider an object, for instance a dog. Our dog has many attributes that can be used to describe it. Our dog has a name, a breed, a size, a color, and attributes such as a personality. We can communicate with our dog by telling it to "Sit," "Fetch," and "Roll Over". In the case of the command "Fetch," our dog will retrieve something and return it to us. The dog will follow our commands, provided they are presented in a manner the dog can recognize.

The example of a dog following our commands provides an analogy of what objects do in our computers. They too have certain properties, or *attributes*. We, as programmers, have defined *methods* through which we can communicate with the objects. Some objects will even return a "result" to us.

Not all objects are complex, in that not all of them have methods. A good example of a simple object is a coin. It has properties, the most important of which is its value, but a coin also has a predefined size, weight, and consists of certain materials.

Flash 5's addition of an object-oriented style programming language allows for the programming of rich, deep, interactive applications.

ANDREAS HEIM

We can pass this coin into a soda machine by placing it into the coin slot. Eventually, after making a selection, the soda machine will give us a can of soda. This example demonstrates how we can pass one object to another one, in this case by using the first object (the coin) to communicate with the second object (the soda machine) to receive, in return, a third object (a can of soda).

Essentially, that is the gist of how object-oriented programming works.

INTRODUCING OBJECT-ORIENTED PROGRAMMING

Over the last few years Macromedia has continually added significant new features into Flash's programming capabilities. In the beginning, Flash and its predecessor FutureSplash could not do much more than have a button go to a frame in the movie timeline or open another Web page (4.1). As each release came out, a new and better feature was added to the program so that symbols could be controlled from other symbols (4.2) and from actions in the timeline (4.3). In Flash 5 this has culminated in the addition of an object-oriented style programming (OOP) language that enables rich, deep interactive applications to be programmed (4.4).

OOP AS A TERM

These days, almost everything is programmed in an object-oriented manner, but where does the term come from? For a long time, programming meant separating code from data. Code was stored in functions and procedures; data was stored in variables, arrays, and more complex structures.

With object-oriented programming, code and data are merged together to form one unit, the *object*. Sometimes the object is referred to as a black box that receives and sends messages. This is a good analogy, as an object has properties (*variables*), and methods (*functions*) to control these properties and to communicate with other objects (4.5).

Table 4-1 defines a number of terms associated with object-oriented programming.

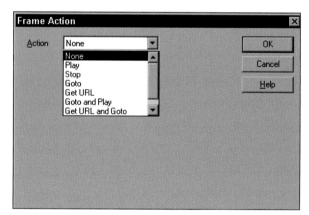

4.1

AUTHOR PROFILE
Andreas Heim

Andreas Heim is from the small town of Hattenhofen, close to Stuttgart, in Germany, a center of German car engineering. Originally intending to become a professional soccer player, his education took him into the area of media studies and programming. After Andreas created an edutainment CD-ROM, his focus shifted from film and video to interactive media. His school required a six-month internship, which brought him to Smashing Ideas, where being a soccer-playing-and-beer-drinking German intern was highly respected. He had so much fun with his work that he extended his stay at SI for one year, and then decided to stay permanently. Andreas currently works on all kinds of cutting edge digital media projects, while enjoying his time outside of work in Seattle snowboarding and playing soccer.

TABLE 4-1   OOP GENERAL TERMS

TERM	DEFINITION	EXAMPLE
Class	A blueprint to build objects. Defines properties and methods for object instances, but is not an object itself.	
Object	An instance of a class. Each object contains all of the properties and methods of the class, and can contain additional properties and methods not defined in the class.	`myObject = new Object();`

Variable	A container for a value. The value, which can be stored for later use, can have different data types, including number, string, Boolean.	`myCity = "Seattle";`
		`myLength = myCity.length;`
		`// myLength is now 7`

Function	Reusable code that processes the parameters you pass to it and returns a result.	`function myAdd (a,b) {`
		`    result = a + b;`
		`    return result;`
		`}`
		`a = 2;`
		`b = 3;`
		`c = myAdd (a,b);`
		`// c is now 5;`

Method	A function that is assigned to an object.	
Identifier	The name of an object, variable, property, function, or method.	

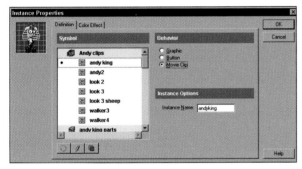

4.2

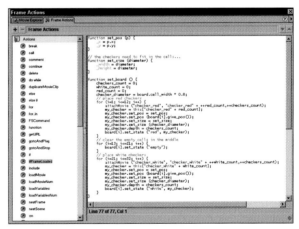

4.4

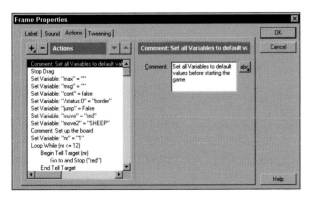

4.3

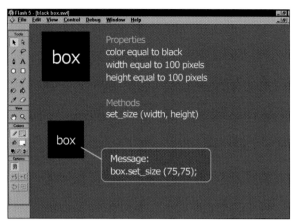

4.5

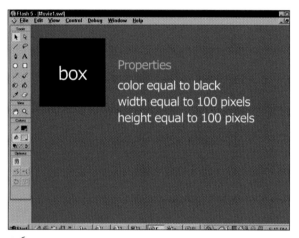

4.6

4.7

As an example, the properties of the black box (4.6) would be its color, width, and height. The methods to control these properties would be to change the color, change the height, and change the width. Other methods to control the properties of the object would be to rotate the box, make it transparent, and move it.

OOP IN FLASH 5

The previous versions of Flash did include object-orientation, just not the object-oriented programming. Flash programming has radically changed with Flash 5. ActionScript, the programming language in Flash, has been made ECMA-262-compliant, which means Flash is compliant with JavaScript 1.0. This eases the way the program exchanges code with JavaScript and other established languages such as Java or C++. Flash would not be Flash if it did not have its own idiosyncrasies. Movie clips are now objects, fully integrated in this true object-oriented model, and of course they have kept their unique behaviors. Macromedia also added a few more new toys to play with movie clips. The focus of this chapter is object-oriented programming with movie clips in Flash 5.

Table 4-2 defines more terms and concepts associated with programming.

CREATING CHECKERS IN FLASH 5

It's hard to explain these concepts in plain text, so let's use an example. We have chosen a checkers game originally created with animated characters from the Smashing Ideas cartoon "Say Uncle" in Flash 4 (4.7). We'll show you an approach to creating a nonanimated checkers game in Flash 5 using object-oriented programming (4.8).

Checkers is a game in which opponents use two different colored sets of checkers. The checkers move diagonally forward from square to square on a checkerboard. When a rival checker sits diagonally with an empty square behind the checker, it can be jumped and retired from the board. If a checker is moved to the opposite end of the board, then that checker is *crowned* and can move both forward and backward. The object of the game is to capture all of the opponent's checkers.

TABLE 4-2   PROGRAMMING TERMS

TERM	DEFINITION	EXAMPLE
Passing by value; passing by reference	When passing something to a method, variables and normal objects differ. Variables will be passed by value — inside the method no relation exists to the original variable anymore, whereas objects get passed by reference. This means the object itself does not get passed, but instead, a reference to it is passed. When the reference is modified, the original object is also modified. Only the simple variable types — number, string, and Boolean — will be passed by value; everything else gets passed by reference.	

Array	A structure to organize data. Usually contains several variables or even objects. They can be accessed and assigned by an index — whereas item 0 is actually the first item of an array.	`list = new Array("Andreas", "Glenn", "Russ");`
		`myName = array[0];`
		`// myName will now be "Andreas"`

Associative array	In an associative array, the items are not identified by a number, but rather by a "real" name. This makes sense when different kinds of data or objects are stored in the same container, where accessing them with a number doesn't seem very useful. In Flash, actually all variables and objects of an object (even the main timeline) are arranged in an associative array, and it works both ways, for reading and assigning.	`address = new Object();`
		`address.name = "Andreas";`
		`// address["name"] is now also "Andreas"`
		`address["city"] = "Seattle";`
		`// address.city is now also "Seattle"`

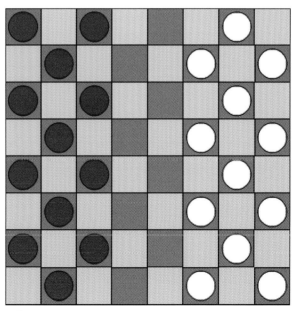

Programming in Flash starts with planning the structure of the project and deciding what is needed to complete the project. Here's an overview of the objects we will use:

- The main object, which will include everything else, is our game — or in other words, the Flash movie file we will be using. All of the other objects are inside this one.
- The board and the cells on the board.
- The two different colors of checkers.
- Players.
- Display areas for game information.
- Background artwork.

4.8

The board in checkers is a regular 8×8 chessboard. However, only the dark cells are used in checkers so only 32 cells are used during the game. These cells are numbered 1–32, beginning from the lower-right corner from the red player's point of view. We're looking at the board from the side, so red is to the left, white is to the right, and cell 1 is therefore in the lower-left corner. (4.9)

CREATING THE MOVIE AND GRAPHIC ASSETS

Once you've figured out what graphic assets you need for your game, it's useful to create them before you begin programming. This helps keep your programming structured and logical because you've thought out the direction of your programming before you start in Flash.

1. We start with a new movie — if you don't have an empty movie, choose File ➤ New to create a new one. Choose Modify ➤ Movie to open the Movie Properties panel (4.10) and set the dimensions of the movie to 400×300.

2. Create the board using the rectangle tool. Set the Stroke Color to #000000 and the Fill Color to #ADEBAD and draw a square on the Stage. Choose the size you would like the board to appear — we will take care of fitting the cells and checkers into it programmatically later on. Select the Arrow tool, and select the entire rectangle. Make it a movie clip by choosing Insert ➤ Convert to Symbol. When the Symbol Properties dialog box opens, set the Behavior to Movie Clip and set the Name to **board template** (4.11). This is just the name representing the symbol in the library, not the name of the instance on the stage. To name the instance, go to Window ➤ Panels ➤ Instance. Make sure the board is still selected and enter **board** in the Name setting in the Instance panel (4.12).

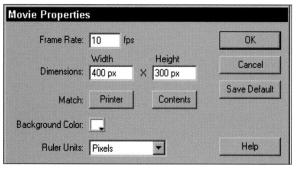

4.9

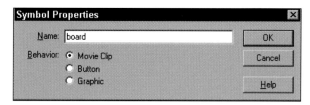

4.11

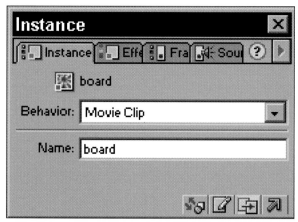

4.12

Movie Properties dialog

4.10

3. Now we need a dark cell for the cells on the board — create a square with the desired dark color as a filling. Don't worry about the size too much; we will take care of that later. Make it a movie clip named **cell**, and make sure the center point of this new symbol is at the upper-left corner of the square. To do so, double-click the cell, which leads you to the Edit in Place mode. Select the square, open the Align panel (using Window ➤ Panels ➤ Align), click Align to Stage, and then click Align Top Edge and Align Left Edge (4.13) Exit Edit in Place mode by double-clicking outside the cell square on the stage. Remove the cell movie clip from the stage by selecting it and deleting it.

4. Open the library (Window ➤ Library), locate the cell movie clip, and right-click (Windows) or Control+click (Mac) the clip. Select Linkage from the context menu (4.14). In the Linkage dialog box, select Export this Symbol, and enter **cell** in the Identifier text box (4.15). Click OK. The cell will now be part of your file when you export it, even if you don't use it in the timeline. This is a new feature in Flash 5 that enables you to place symbols directly on the stage without having to actually be in the timeline. This is more flexible and facilitates much more modular programming.

5. To finish the symbol library, we need checkers — a white checker and a red checker. Draw a white circle and make it a symbol. This time the center point has to be in the actual center. If it's not already there, use the align tool to adjust it. Again we don't need the checker directly on the board, so remove it from the stage. As with the cell, we need to set the linkage properties — choose Export this Symbol and enter **checker_white** as the identifier. Follow the same procedure for the red checker and name it **checker_red** (4.16).

BUILDING THE BOARD

In the case of the checkers game, the board is built with ActionScript. No graphical checkerboard exists in the movie; instead, all of the necessary cells are placed inside the static rectangular board movie clip. This is useful because it enables the game to be very modular both for programming and for graphics because only the one cell symbol exists.

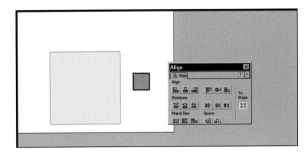

4.13

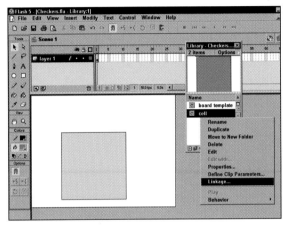

4.14

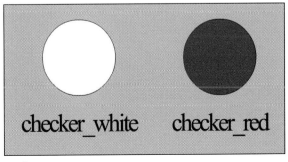

4.15

4.16

Select the board movie clip and open the ActionScript panel. You will find it if you choose Window ➤ Actions, or, by using the launch bar in the lower-right corner of the movie window, the diagonal arrow is the icon for ActionScript. The panel will read "object actions" on top — we will program code directly for an object, our board, in the ActionScript panel (4.17). You can also edit frame actions in the same panel.

The ActionScript panel offers various ways for creating and editing scripts. To the left you see the Toolbox list, which shows you all the ActionScript available. You can add them to your code by double-clicking an action. You will then be able to modify the

parameters for that action in the Parameters panel on the bottom. You can also use the plus button in the top-left corner of the Actions panel to open a menu to find the action that you need.

The minus (–) button, next to the plus (+) button, removes the current line of code. The ↑ and ↓ buttons to the right let you move the current line of code up and down in your script, so you can change the execution order.

In the upper-right corner of the Actions panel is a triangular button that opens the Options Panel (4.18). You'll find most of the options in this panel quite useful. One of the options, Expert Mode, changes the Actions list window to the right into a text editor where you can enter your scripts directly. Once you get familiar with writing code in ActionScript, you'll want to begin using this option.

The board is a movie clip, which is a predefined object. In the Actions category of the Toolbox list in the Actions panel you can see a list of actions to choose from (4.19). Certain events can occur to or in a movie clip, so let's have a look at onClipEvent — scroll down first if you can't see it yet in the list of actions. Double-click it to begin your script in the Actions list to the right. Keep Load selected in the Parameters pane — this event will be triggered when the object appears for the first time. Any movie clip actions have to be defined within these events. (4.20).

So far our code looks like this:

```
onClipEvent (load) {
}
```

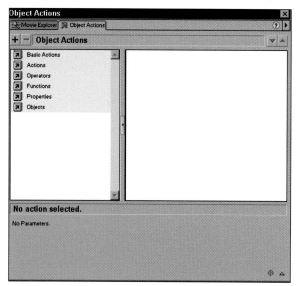

4.17

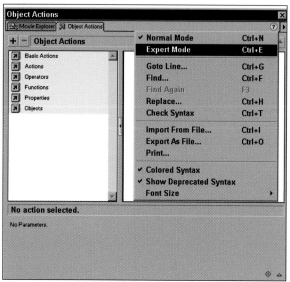

4.18

TIP

Through Edit ➢ Preferences, you can choose whether the ActionScript panel should default to Normal or Expert Mode. Once you're comfortable with programming in Flash, Expert Mode enables you to program more quickly.

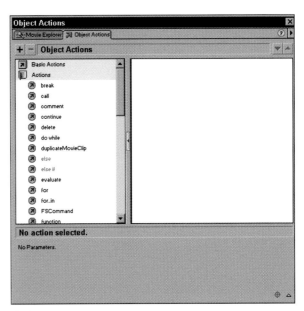

4.19

Now we need to define some variables that we will need to build the board, so add a Set Variable action (4.21). In the Variable text box type in **ROWS**, and **8** as the value. ROW is a constant that won't change through the whole game, and it is common to use uppercase only for constants. Please note that the 8 you typed in will show up as "8" in the code in your Actions list (4.22). By default, anything you type in will be regarded as a string. A *string* is a variable that is text only.

Because we want to have a number here we need to select the Expression checkbox next to the Value setting, and it will change to 8 without the quotation marks showing that it's a number (4.23). In Flash, you can set a value either to String or Expression. String means Flash keeps what you type exactly as it is, as a text string. If you use Expression, Flash checks if the text you typed refers to a variable, if it is a Boolean expression (true or false), or, as in our case, reads it as a number. You can switch back and forth between using a number as a number or as a string. However you should always be sure that Flash reads

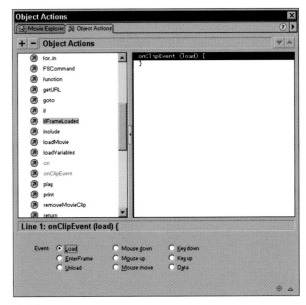

4.20

TIP

Many of the earlier Flash actions associated with movie clips such as `ifFrameLoaded` or `tellTarget` have been deprecated and are highlighted in green (4.26). This means that a new and better action or method exists for them in Flash 5.

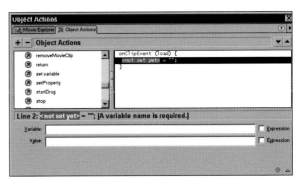

4.21

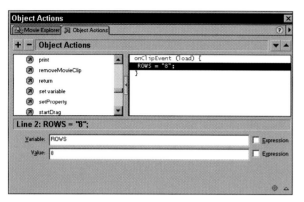

4.22

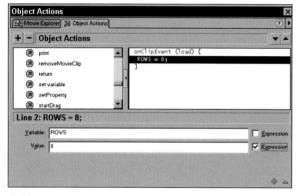

4.23

your variable as a number when you want it to be a number and a string when you want it to be a string.

Alternative ways to enter this variable are to choose an `evaluate` action (also in the Actions category of the Toolbox list) and then type **ROWS = 8** in the line. Or switch to Expert Mode and type **ROWS = 8;** in the text editor. A line of code needs to end with a semicolon. In Normal Mode you don't have to worry about it because it will be inserted automatically; in Expert Mode you need to type it yourself. Curly brackets — {} — embrace blocks of code that belong together. So, because **ROWS = 8;** is part of the "load" event, make sure it is inside the curly brackets. Your code should now look like this:

```
onClipEvent (load) {
    ROWS = 8;
}
```

NAMING CONVENTIONS IN FLASH 5

Flash 5 allows for great flexibility when naming variables, instances, and frame labels. The downside of this flexibility is that Flash lets you select naming conventions that will become problematic in terms of code.

For example, Flash will not prevent you from using spaces in instance names. However, if your instance names have spaces in them, you cannot address these instances using ActionScript because in ActionScript spaces work as separators. Other problems arise if you use special characters in your instance names because these characters may have predefined functions in ActionScript. As a general rule, do not use spaces and special characters in your instance names; use only letters, numbers and the underscore.

Try to use descriptive variable names whenever possible. Flash does not limit the length of variable names, so make these names as descriptive as possible. For example, names such as `current_article` or `next_picture` are helpful because they are self-explanatory. Often users select multiple-word variable names and separate the words with the underscore. I use this method in this chapter. Another very common method is to capitalize the first letter of each word. Reserved keywords in ActionScript are built this way, for example. By using the underscore you make an easy-to-remember distinction between the code you create, and what is built in. Either way, be sure to always type your variable name the same way; in other words, pay attention to which words you capitalize and be consistent throughout.

Currently, Flash is not case-sensitive in terms of variable names. However, keep in mind that you may be exchanging your code with other languages such as JavaScript and that these other languages may be case-sensitive. Remember that Flash is case-sensitive with its own identifiers, such as `loadVariables`.

A later version of Flash may become case-sensitive throughout. Establishing a proper naming convention now may prevent you from having to troubleshoot in the future.

Now add a variable that will track the width of the board:

```
side_length = _width;
```

If you enter this in Normal Mode, make sure to check Expression for the value. The `_width` property of our board movie clip is already defined in Flash — it tells us how many pixels wide our board is. Flash has a variety of these predefined properties of movie clips that you can access directly, such as `_width` and `_height`. Instead of typing `_`**width** you can also find it in Properties (4.24). To keep a distinction from the predefined movie clip properties in Flash, which all start with an underscore, I will only refer to the predefined movie clip properties as properties.

We can access this property directly because we create an object script for the board object, which acts and reacts as if it was inside the board object. We

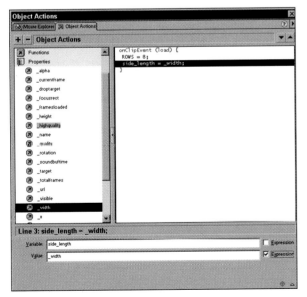

4.24

> **WARNING**
>
> To avoid serious trouble, try to choose variable names that do not interfere with Flash's reserved keywords. The ActionScript editor will, by default, highlight some of Flash's keywords (for example, Options menu, Colored Syntax). However, the ActionScript editor will not always highlight a name that will cause problems. For example, Flash has a built-in `Date` object (note the upper-case "D"). Now you might think that you could name an object `date` (all lowercase) as an instance name. If you use it, the ActionScript editor won't highlight it, so the name does not appear to be problematic. However, in actuality, because Flash is not case-sensitive, if you use *date* as a name, you have effectively overwritten the built-in `Date` object. This means that, after using `date` as an instance name, you will no longer be able to use the `Date` object in your movie. A general rule is to steer clear of using names that are close to Flash's reserved keywords. In this particular case, a better idea would have been to name your object **my_date**. When creating names, use unique names; otherwise, objects with the same names might conflict with, or be overwritten by, another.

could also use `this._width` where *this* is a self reference to the object we are currently in. By using the dot you can access variables, properties and methods (functions) and even child objects of other objects.

Set the following variable on the next line:

```
dim = new Object();
```

So what are we doing here? We defined a new object called `dim` in the board object. So far it isn't doing anything, so let's fill it with something by adding the next line:

```
dim = getBounds();
```

The predefined `getBounds()` method returns the boundaries of a movie clip. The returned value is an object containing the minimum and maximum *x* and *y* coordinate values (`xmin`, `xmax`, `ymin`, and `ymax`). These values are the placement values of the movie clip in pixels related to the top-left corner of either the main timeline or the timeline that the movie clip is nested inside of.

You can also pass another movie clip as a parameter, and it will return the values relative to that movie clip; for example, `this.getBounds(_root)` could return 20 as value for `xmin`, which then means the first pixel of this object is 20 pixels away from the left border of the stage. `_root` always refers to the main timeline, or the root movie clip. You will find `getBounds` in the **MovieClip** Object category in the Toolbox list (Objects ➤ **MovieClip**).

Add a comment to the code:

```
// get the boundaries of the field.
```

Now add two more lines:

```
x_start = dim.xmin;
y_start = dim.ymax;
```

We previously assigned the boundaries of the board to `dim`; now we grab the values we need at this point, using the dot syntax for accessing properties inside the object. Coordinates in Flash start from the center point of an object. The center point for the main timeline is the upper-left corner of the stage. `xmin` is how far left a movie clip extends from its center point, `ymax` how far down. Thus `x_start` and `y_start` now represent the coordinates of the lower-left corner of the board (4.25).

We want to have eight rows and eight columns, so we need to define the side length for one cell by dividing

the width by the number of rows. Add the following ActionScript:

```
cell_side_length = side_length / ROWS;
```

We don't have any cells yet so we create a variable that reflects that. This variable will enable us to track the number of cells we've placed on the board and let us stop when we reach 32. Add the following ActionScript:

```
cell_count = 0;
```

Our code now contains the initial settings that will be needed to build the checkerboard programmatically and looks like this (4.26):

```
onClipEvent (load) {
ROWS = 8;
   side_length = _width;
   dim = new object();
   dim = getBounds ();
// get the boundaries of the field.
   x_start = dim.xmin;
   y_start = dim.ymax;
   cell_side_length = side_length /
ROWS;
   cell_count = 0;
}
```

Now that we've set the initial variables, we can define our first function (you'll find `function` in the Actions category of the Toolbox list):

```
function cell_init (cell_x,¬
cell_y, cell_side_length) {
}
```

The identifier for your function is `cell_init`. In the parentheses we define the parameters that can be passed to the `cell_init` function—in this case

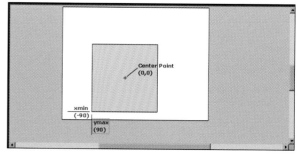

4.25

cell_x, cell_y, and cell_side_length, which are the *x* and *y* coordinates of the cell and the side length of the cell. Now we need to make the function do something, so add the following code between the curly braces of the function:

```
_x = cell_x;
_y = cell_y;
side_length = cell_side_length;
_width = side_length;
_height = side_length;
```

We set the _x and _y properties to the passed values for cell_x, and cell_y—that is where we want to place the cell. We specifically set side_length to cell_side_length; this way we will keep the variable around after the function has been executed, otherwise passed parameters perish and you would lose the variable value. Then we set _width and _height both to the same side_length—so we ensure it is a square.

The completed function looks like this (4.27):

```
function cell_init (cell_x, cell_y,
cell_side_length) {
    _x = cell_x;
    _y = cell_y;
    side_length = cell_side_length;
    _width = side_length;
    _height = side_length;
}
```

Now it's time to place the cells on the board. We will use two nested loops after the function for this. The first loop creates the columns:

```
for (i=1;i<=ROWS;i++) {
}
```

This means we use i as an index, the loop will go on while i is smaller than or equal to ROWS, and i will be increased by 1 in each iteration (i++ is the same as i=i+1, but shorter).

Now we need to pick an *x* position—move one column for each iteration. Place the following ActionScript between the curly braces of the first loop:

```
x = x_start + (i-1)¬
cell_side_length;
```

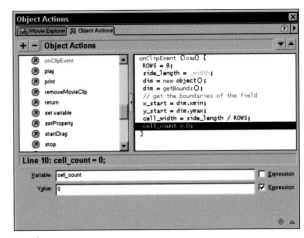

4.26

4.27

Now we determine whether i is even (we only need to place a cell every other field):

```
i_even = (i/2 == Math.round (i/2));
```

All mathematical functions are to be found in the Math object—so we make use of it here. In our first iteration, i will be equal to 1. i/2 equals 0.5. If you round this, it will be 1. This determines that 1 is not even. You compare values by using two equal signs (==)—one equal sign always assigns a value. As i/2 does not equal to Math.round (i/2), the expression will be false—and thus i_even will be false in this case.

Now we move on to the second loop for the rows. This loop should be placed inside of the first loop (after the last line of code you just added):

```
for (k=1;k<=ROWS;k++) {
}
```

It's the exact same loop definition, but now we use k as the index. Add the following ActionScript inside of the second loop (between the curly braces):

```
k_even = (k/2 == Math.round (k/2));
```

As we scan through the whole 8×8 grid, we need to find the spots where the dark cells are to be placed. Add the following ActionScript:

```
if ((k_even && !i_even) ||¬
(!k_even && i_even)) {
}
```

This means if k is even, but i is not, or if k is not even, but i is, then take action. The && operator is a Boolean AND comparison, which means that if both expressions are true, the expression as whole will be true. The ! is a NOT operator. You could also look at it as an inverter where !i_even will be TRUE if i_even is FALSE. And finally, || is a Boolean OR comparison. It will return TRUE if either the expression to the left or to the right is true. These comparisons replace the previous "and," "not," and "or" actions in Flash 4, all of which have been deprecated.

Each time the preceding expression is true, we have found a spot to add a new cell. First, we define the *y* position. Add the following ActionScript inside the if statement that you just added (between the curly braces):

```
y = y_start - (k) * cell_side_length;
```

And then we increment the cell count:

```
cell_count++;
```

Now we place the cell from the library on the board:

```
attachMovie ("cell",¬
cell_count, cell_count);
```

cell is the identifier we specified earlier in the Symbol Linkage Properties panel. The first cell_count is the name for it. Yes, it can be a number. The second cell_count defines the depth level of our movie clip—when attaching movie clips there can only be one movie clip per depth level. Using the cell_count for the depth level value is the most logical way to build the board.

We want to directly address the cell we attached, so add the following line:

```
my_cell = this[cell_count];
```

This is another way to access objects inside another object. All objects, variables, properties and functions inside an object are arranged in an associative array. This means you can get to their value by typing their name as a string inside the brackets. This string can also be represented by a variable (cell_count).

An array is an object. In this case we access the board object as an array, and the quickest way to access it is by using this here. this is a reference to an object itself.

An example follows, though this code is not part of the game:

```
ROWS = 8;
a = this["ROWS"] // is also 8
row_string = "ROWS";
b =this[row_string] // is also 8
```

So with this[cell_count] we don't want the value of cell_count, but our newly created movie

---

WARNING

All attached or duplicated movie clips placed in the main movie are in a layer on top of everything that you place directly in the timeline. If you're not careful, these movie clips will not appear in the correct place and will cover up your other graphics. If you need to use attached or duplicated movie clips, you may need to put all of your graphics into symbols and control the layer levels programmatically. The other way to achieve the same results is to add your attached or duplicated movie clips inside a specific movie clip that is placed on the desired layer in the main movie timeline.

clip. So please note that no quotes exist around `cell_count`. If this was the first time we found a place for a cell, you could also write `this["1"]` — which is the value of `cell_count` at the beginning.

If we used `this.cell_count` instead it would return 1. That's not what we want here; we want the movie clip or object that is behind it.

`my_cell` is now a reference to our object, and we can give it some more methods and make it do things with them:

```
my_cell.cell_init = cell_init;
```

`cell_init` is the function we defined before; now `my_cell` has its own `cell_init` method.

Now continue creating the script and add two new lines:

```
my_cell.cell_init(x,y,
cell_side_length);
```

Finally, we call the `cell_init` function, pass the x, y, and `cell_side_length` parameters to it, and it places itself in the correct spot, with the correct size!

Here is the finished code to create the board (4.28):

```
onClipEvent (load) {
// initialize variables
    ROWS = 8;
    side_length = _width;
    dim = new object();
    dim = getBounds ();
// get the boundaries of the field.
    x_start = dim.xmin;
    y_start = dim.ymax;
    cell_side_length = side_length /
ROWS;
    cell_count = 0;

// adjust place & size of a cell
function cell_init (cell_x, cell_y,
 cell_side_length) {
        _x = cell_x;
        _y = cell_y;
        side_length = cell_side_length;
        _width = side_length;
        _height = side_length;
}

// scan the grid and place cells
for (i=1;i<=ROWS;i++) {
        x = x_start + (i-1) *
cell_side_length;
        i_even = (i/2 == Math.round
(i/2));
for (k=1;k<=ROWS;k++) {
        k_even = (k/2 == Math.round
 (k/2));
if ((k_even && !i_even) || (!k_even &&
 i_even)) {
        y = y_start - (k) *
 cell_side_length;
        cell_count++;
        attachMovie ("cell", cell_count,
cell_count);
        my_cell = this[cell_count];
        my_cell.cell_init = cell_init;
```

```
      my_cell.cell_init
 (x,y,cell_side_length);
            }
        }
    }
}
```

Now save your movie, if you haven't done so already, and test it by choosing Control ➤ Test Movie. You will see the board for the checkers game, all created dynamically and object-oriented using ActionScript (4.29). This may seem to be a lot of work for a small visual result, but this is just the beginning. It needs to be done this way so that later, when we create our game code, everything will function properly.

GATHERING INFORMATION ABOUT THE BOARD

Now we want to place the checkers on the board. Before we can do that, we need to add a few more methods to the cell objects. These methods enable us to get the information we need about the different cells so we can place the correct checkers on them.

Because we want to place the checkers on the cells, we need to know the position of each cell. We create the following function `give_pos` to let the cells tell us

where they are. Add the code below the `cell_init` method, but above the cell placing loop (4.30):

```
function give_pos() {
   var p = new object ();
   p.x = _x + _width / 2;
   p.y = _y + _width / 2;
   _parent.localToGlobal(p);
   return p;
}
```

First we define `p` (point) as a new local object. `var` means that whatever we create exists only as long as this code exists. In this case, it will perish once the function is finished. Because we won't need it anywhere else in the code, this is useful.

```
p.x = _x + _width / 2;
```

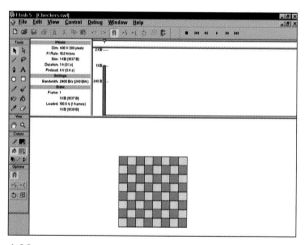

4.29

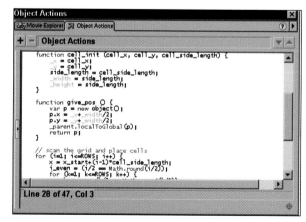

4.28

4.30

_x gives us the *x* position of the cell. We want the real center of the cell, but the center point of the cell is in the upper-left corner, so we must add half of the width to get the correct center point.

```
p.y = _y + _width / 2;
```

The same holds true for the vertical position.

Now we have a point object (p) with an *x* and *y* position. But these coordinates are relative to the movie clips own system. So we need to transform them:

```
_parent.localToGlobal(p);
```

localToGlobal converts an object with coordinates, as we defined p here, into the coordinate system one level above. We want to go up two levels, so we use _parent.

```
return p;
```

Now that we've converted the coordinates, we also want to make use of them so we return the p object with the converted coordinates to the caller, the function that wants to receive the position of this object. This also ends the execution of the function — code written afterwards won't be executed anymore.

We will also have to keep track of where we placed the checkers and which cells are empty so we create a function called set_state (4.31):

```
function set_state(color,¬
checker_obj) {
    state = color;
    if (color != "empty") {
        checker = checker_obj;
    }
    else {
        delete checker;
    }
}
```

First, we define the state the cell is in — white, red, empty:

```
state = color;
```

If the cell is not empty, we also store a reference to the checker — so we can easily access the checker later.

```
if (color != "empty") {
checker = checker_obj;
}
```

If the cell is empty, we make sure to remove an eventually existing reference:

```
else {
    delete checker;
}
```

We don't need the reference to checker any more, so we delete it.

Now we need to assign the new methods to the cells, so we need to add two lines to our cell-creating loop that we created earlier, after my_cell.cell_init(x,y,cell_side_length);::

```
my_cell.give_pos = give_pos;
my_cell.set_state = set_state;
```

Now the board is entirely initialized and we have all the information we need to place the checkers on it. First, we need to determine whether the checkers are part of the board movie clip or part of the main game timeline. Although they certainly interact a lot with the board, the checkers are part of the game, not part of the board, so I chose to have them become part of the main game. We add one more line almost at the end of the script, just before the last bracket (}):

```
_root.set_board();
```

We will define the function set_board() in a moment, but first the finished script (4.32):

```
onClipEvent (load) {
// initialize variables
    ROWS = 8;
    side_length = _width;
```

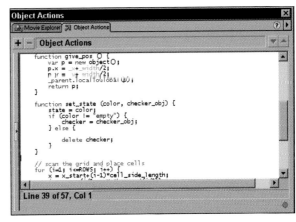

4.31

```
dim = new object();
dim = getBounds ();

cell_side_length = side_length / ROWS;
    x_start = dim.xmin;
    y_start = dim.ymax;
    cell_count = 0;

// adjust position and size of a cell
function cell_init (cell_x, cell_y,
width) {
        _x = cell_x;
        _y = cell_y;
        _width = width;
        _height = width;
    }


 // where is the cell located at?
function give_pos() {
        var p = new object ();
        p.x = _x + _width / 2;
        p.y = _y + _width / 2;
        _parent.localToGlobal(p);
        return p;
    }


 // red, white, empty - and which
checker is here if not empty
```

```
function set_state(color, checker_obj)
 {
        state = color;
        if (color != "empty") {
          checker = checker_obj;
        } else {
            delete checker;
        }
    }

for (i=1;i<=ROWS;i++) {
x = x_start + (i-1) *
cell_side_length;
    i_even = i/2 == Math.round(i/2);
for (k=1;k<=ROWS;k++) {
    k_even = k/2 == Math.round (k/2);
if ((k_even && !i_even)|| (!k_even &&
 i_even)) {
    cell_count++;
y = y_start - (k) * cell_side_length;
    attachMovie ("cell", cell_count,
 cell_count);
    my_cell = this[cell_count];
    my_cell.cell_init = cell_init;
my_cell.cell_init(x,y,cell_side_length
);
    my_cell.give_pos = give_pos;
    my_cell.set_state = set_state;
        }
    }
 }
_root.set_board();
}
```

4.32

So far we have created the checkerboard program-matically and we've gathered information about all of the cells. All of these actions are attached to the board object so they occur when the board object is first placed in the movie.

PLACING CHECKERS ON THE CHECKERBOARD

Let's organize the timeline of the main movie a bit. So far we have one layer with one keyframe in it—named the layer **board**. Although it would be possible to put all your code in the movie's first frame, it's not a good idea to have everything starting in frame 1 of a movie. Flash needs to initialize before it can run the actions and, although technically everything should work fine, it doesn't always do so.

We'll actually build our checkerboard further out on the timeline to avoid this hazard. Click frame 1 and drag it to frame 15 (4.33). Now add two more layers, one called **labels** and one called **actions** (4.34). Layer names don't have any influence on your code; they are for better orientation only. If you happen to have a syntax error in one of your scripts, Flash will tell you in which layer and frame it happened. It's really easier to locate them if you name them.

In frame 15 we want to create a "start" label: Click frame 15 of the label's layer and choose Insert ➤ Keyframe. Open the Frame panel — by default it is grouped with the instances panel. If you can't locate it or have closed it, choose Windows ➤ Panels ➤ Frame. Double-clicking the frame will also open it, but the sound panel, which also will be opened by this action, may hide it. Make sure the new empty keyframe is still selected and set the Label to start (4.35). As soon as you press enter or click anywhere outside the frame panel, the timeline updates and shows a red flag in the keyframe. However, you can't read the label yet because not enough frames exist to display it (4.36). To fix this situation, go to frame 20, select all three layers by dragging, and choose Insert ➤ Frame. Doing so adds enough frames so you can read the label (4.37).

Now we could start to write our code to place the checkers on the board, but first we need to create a little load check to make sure everything has been loaded when we get to that point. The purpose of this is to make sure that when the movie is streaming over the Web the code won't run before all of the necessary symbols have downloaded.

In the actions layer, click frame 5, insert a blank keyframe, and select the Actions panel (or open it again if you closed it). Please note that it will now be labeled "Frame Actions." Enter the following code (4.38):

```
if (getBytesLoaded() ==
 getBytesTotal()) {
    gotoAndStop ("start");
}
else {
    play ();
}
```

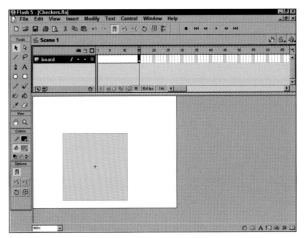

4.33

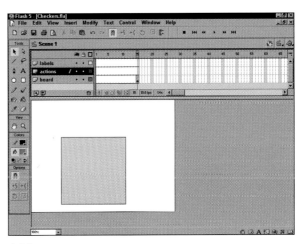

4.34

WARNING

Frame labels are needed for programming with Flash, and thus they will be exported with the final Flash movie. When naming labels, try to avoid spaces; use the underscore instead. Frame labels are similar to variable names, and so spaces in the label name may cause problems. If you just want to place a comment in your timeline, start the frame label with two slashes (//). This converts the label into a comment, which won't be exported.

getBytesLoaded() does just what it says—it returns how many bytes of the movie have been loaded so far. getBytesTotal() returns the size of the movie and, if they are equal, we're done with loading and can go to label "start." If this is not the case the movie will keep on playing.

Eventually it will also get to start without us checking it again. To prevent that, click frame 6 and insert

another blank keyframe. In the Actions panel enter the following:

```
prevFrame();
```

prevFrame() simply goes to the previous frame, or one frame back. There we will check again if the movie is fully loaded. We created a two-frame loop that will stop when our condition (movie loaded) is fulfilled.

Select frame 15 of the actions layer and choose Insert ➤ Keyframe. Now we can define the methods for the main timeline that will actually be the code that sets up the checkers and makes the game function.

Make sure you have the Actions panel still open. Add a function that will actually set the position of the checkers (4.39):

```
function set_pos (p) {
    _x = p.x;
    _y = p.y;
}
```

set_pos is the counterpart to the give_pos method of the cells; we will use it to place the checkers. A point object (p) will be passed, and we set the _x and _y properties accordingly.

Add a function to set the size of a checker (4.40):

```
function set_size (diameter) {
    _width = diameter;
    _height = diameter;
}
```

Similar to the cells, we'll need to adjust the size of the checkers.

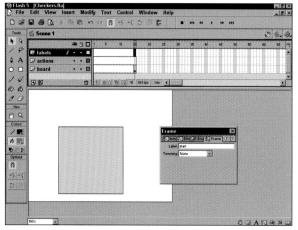

4.35

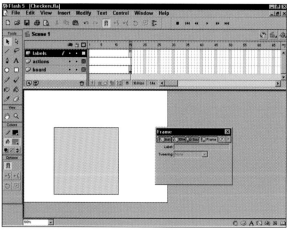

4.36

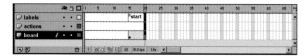

4.37

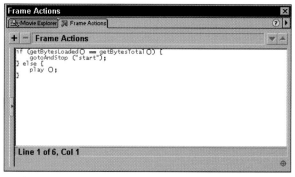

4.38

We already placed the call for the `set_board` method in the board script so it would occur after the checkerboard was created; now we need to define it. Add the following line:

```
function set_board () {
}
```

First we initialize some variables to count the number of checkers. Add the following ActionScript inside the function:

```
checkers_count = 0;
white_count = 0;
red_count = 0;
```

We then need to set the diameter for the checkers based on the cell width:

```
checker_diameter =
board.cell_side_length * 0.8;
```

In checkers, red goes first, so we start placing the red checkers next (each player has 12):

```
for (i=1; i<=12; i++) {
   attachMovie ("checker_red",
 "checker_red" + (++red_count),
 ++checkers_count);
   my_checker = this["checker_red" +
red_count];
   my_checker.set_pos = set_pos;
   my_checker.set_pos
(board[i].give_pos());
   my_checker.set_size = set_size;
   my_checker.set_size
(checker_diameter);
   my_checker.depth = checkers_count;
```

```
board[i].set_state ("red",
my_checker);
}
```

We used the `attachMovie` method previously, but "`checker_red`" + (`++red_count`) is new to us. This means we name the checker **checker_red** and concatenate the value of `red_count` to that name, but before we do that, we add 1 to the value of `red_count`. We also increment `checkers_count` by 1 before it is used to define the new checker's layer.

```
my_checker = this["checker_red" +
red_count];
```

`my_checker` is now set to be the checker we just created.

```
my_checker.set_pos = set_pos;
```

Attach the `set_pos` method to the checker:

```
my_checker.set_pos
(board[i].give_pos());
```

Then place it in the correct position. Inside the board we created cells 1–32. Any child objects of an object are arranged in an associative array that can be accessed with the brackets ([]). If *i* equals 1, `board[i]` gives us cell 1 inside the board because we named the cell **1**. `board[1].give_pos()` invokes the `give_pos` method of cell 1, and we directly pass it on to the checker's `set_pos` method.

```
my_checker.set_size = set_size;
my_checker.set_size
(checker_diameter);
```

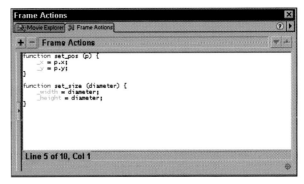

4.39

4.40

This attaches the `set_size` method to the checker and then calls it.

```
my_checker.depth = checkers_count;
```

The layer we created the checker in doesn't get saved as a property, so we need to remember it ourselves.

```
board[i].set_state ("red",
my_checker);
```

Now we tell the cell that we placed a red checker on it, and also let it know which checker it was. Add the following ActionScript to the `set_board` function:

```
for (i=13; i<=21; i++) {
   board[i].set_state ("empty");
}
```

The middle of the board is empty, so we set those cells to empty.

And finally, we place the white checkers on the board using the same procedure we used to place the red checkers. Add this ActionScript to the `set_board` function:

```
for (i=21; i<=32; i++) {
   attachMovie ("checker_white",
"checker_white" + (++white_count),
++checkers_count);
   my_checker = this["checker_white" +
white_count];
   my_checker.set_pos = set_pos;
   my_checker.set_pos
(board[i].give_pos());
   my_checker.set_size = set_size;
   my_checker.set_size
(checker_diameter);
   my_checker.depth = checkers_count;
   board[i].set_state ("white",
my_checker);
}
```

The entire script to place the checkers on the board looks like this (4.41):

```
function set_pos (p) {
   _x = p.x;
   _y = p.y;
}
```

```
// the checkers need to fit in the
cells...
function set_size (diameter) {
   _width = diameter;
   _height = diameter;
}
function set_board () {
   checkers_count = 0;
   white_count = 0;
   red_count = 0;
   checker_diameter =
board.cell_side_length * 0.8;
// place red checkers
for (i=1; i<=12; i++) {
   attachMovie ("checker_red",
 "checker_red" +
(++red_count), ++checkers_count);
   my_checker = this["checker_red" +
red_count];
   my_checker.set_pos = set_pos;
   my_checker.set_pos
(board[i].give_pos());
   my_checker.set_size = set_size;
   my_checker.set_size
(checker_diameter);
   my_checker.depth = checkers_count;
   board[i].set_state ("red",
 my_checker);
   }
// clear the empty cells in the middle
for (i=13; i<=21; i++) {
   board[i].set_state ("empty");
   }
// place white checkers
for (i=21; i<=32; i++) {
   attachMovie ("checker_white",
 "checker_white" +
(++white_count), ++checkers_count);
   my_checker = this["checker_white" +
white_count];
   my_checker.set_pos = set_pos;
   my_checker.set_pos
(board[i].give_pos());
   my_checker.set_size = set_size;
   my_checker.set_size
(checker_diameter);
```

```
  my_checker.depth = checkers_count;
  board[i].set_state ("white",
my_checker);
   }
}
```

It's time to save your work again — and you can test your movie. It will now show the board with the checkers on it (4.42).

4.41

DEFINING THE MOVEMENT OF THE CHECKERS

We now need to add some interactivity to the game because checkers need to be dragged and dropped. Select the script at the start label again, and open the ActionScript panel. We will add more methods here that enable us to drag the checkers. Add the following first method (4.43):

```
function start_drag (cell) {
  if (board[cell].state != "empty") {
     drag_checker =
board[cell].checker;
     drag_checker.startDrag (true);
     drag_checker.swapDepths (100);
     from_cell = cell;
     dragging = true;
   }
}
```

We will call this method when we start dragging a checker — and the cell that we start dragging from is being passed.

```
if (board[cell].state != "empty") {
}
```

The `if` statement code won't let the function be called if the cell is empty, because we can, of course, only drag a checker if one exists on the cell.

```
drag_checker = board[cell].checker;
```

The name of the chosen checker is stored as a reference in the cell.

```
drag_checker.startDrag (true);
```

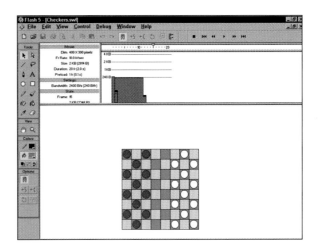

4.42

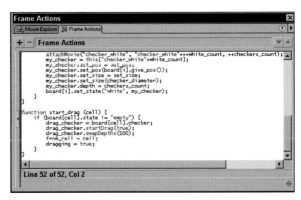

4.43

Now we start dragging the checker, and using `true` means that the checker will be dragged at the center point.

```
drag_checker.swapDepths (100);
```

While a player is dragging the checker, it needs to appear on top of all other checkers, so we use the `swapDepths` method to move it temporarily to layer 100. The `swapDepths` method can also be used to actually swap the depths of two movie clips.

```
from_cell = cell;
```

This variable remembers the cell we started dragging from so we can check if the move being made is a legal move.

```
dragging = true;
```

The preceding variable tells us we are in dragging mode. We'll use this later to find out if we're actually dragging a checker or not.

We also need a method to take action when we drop the checker. This method needs to know which cell the checker is dropped onto and calculate whether it's a legal move, so add the following method below the `start_drag` method (4.44):

```
function stop_drag (cell) {
   if (dragging) {
```

4.44

```
      drag_checker.stopDrag ();
      drag_checker.swapDepths
(drag_checker.depth);
      var found = false;
   if (cell > 0) {
      if (board[cell].state ==
"empty") {
         found = true;
         }
      }
      if (found) {
   board[cell].set_state
(board[from_cell].state,
   drag_checker);
      board[from_cell].set_state
("empty");
      drag_checker.set_pos
(board[cell].give_pos());
      } else {
   drag_checker.set_pos
(board[from_cell].give_pos());
      }
         dragging = false;
   }
}
```

With this simple bit of code, we're almost done with the game.

```
if (dragging) {
}
```

First we need an `if` statement to check to see whether we're actually dragging a checker.

```
drag_checker.stopDrag ();
```

If we are dragging a checker, then we stop dragging it.

```
drag_checker.swapDepths
(drag_checker.depth);
```

The preceding code then sends the dropped checker back to its original layer. It's good we saved the original layer before. Otherwise it would switch its layer depth with the next piece you drag, and it would be impossible to keep track of which checker is on which layer.

```
var found = false;
```

We want to verify if the move was legal. First assume that it was not legal. This enables us to check the ways in which a move could be illegal. If the move has no illegal aspects, then it must be a legal move. It's a programmatic approach to either assume everything is wrong and search for something correct or assume everything is right and search for something wrong. Assuming everything is wrong is usually more flexible in board games because the number of illegal aspects is easier to check than the number of legal aspects.

```
if (cell > 0) {
```

To make a legal move, the checker needs to be dropped on a cell between 1–32 so we check that the cell number is above 0.

```
if (board[cell].state == "empty") {
```

We can only drop a checker on an empty field, so we check the state of the field to make sure of that.

```
found = true;
```

If those two aspects are true, then we know it's a legal move. That's all the move verification we will do in this example, but feel free to expand on it later when you're comfortable programming in Flash. Rules to check whether a checker has been jumped, force a jump when it's available, remove checkers when they've been jumped, and crown a checker when it reaches the end of the board can all be created.

```
if (found) {
}
```

We now know that we have a legal move so we need to move the checker.

```
board[cell].set_state(board[from_cell]
.state, drag_checker);
```

This code transfers the board state from `from_cell`, the cell where the checker started, to the destination cell, the cell where the checker is being dropped. It also passes a reference to the checker so the destination cell knows which checker is now on the cell.

```
board[from_cell].sct_state ("empty");
```

The old cell is now empty, so set the state accordingly.

```
drag_checker.set_pos(board[cell].
give_pos());
```

And finally, we place the checker in the center of the destination cell.

```
else {
   drag_checker.set_pos(board[from_cel
l].give_pos());
}
```

In the preceding case, where we didn't make a legal move, we send the checker back to its original position.

```
dragging = false;
```

Because we've placed the checker, we need to set the dragging variable back to false. This way if a mouse release occurs before another checker is dragged, then none of the `stop_drag` function's code will be run.

MOVING THE CHECKERS

We now have methods to drag and drop a checker, but we haven't defined yet how to capture the actual mouse events — click, drag, release the mouse button. Flash 5 has built-in event handlers to capture them: `onClipEvent (mouseDown)` and `onClipEvent (mouseUp)`. However, these can only be placed as object actions, and the main timeline doesn't support this so we will place them on the board object.

Select the board. Open the ActionScript panel again if it's not already open. It will show the script again that we created in the beginning. Add the following method at the end of the existing script before the last }, but after `_root.set_board();` (4.45):

```
function get_cell (x,y) {
   found = false;
   for (i=1;i<=cell_count;i++) {
      var my_cell = this[i];
      var bounds =
my cell.getBounds(this);
      if (x >= bounds.xmin && x <=
bounds.xmax && y >= bounds.ymin && y
<= bounds.ymax) {
```

```
            found = true;
            break;
        }
    }
    if (found) {
        return i;
    } else {
        return -1;
    }
}
```

We will pass in *x* and *y* coordinates from the checker that is being dragged and this function will return the cell these coordinates are over — if they are over a cell at all.

```
found = false;
```

Because we just started checking for a cell and haven't found one, the variable found is false at the beginning of the function.

```
for (i=1;i<=cell_count;i++) {
}
```

Now we check each cell to see if it is the cell where the checker is located.

```
var my_cell = this[i];
```

Get the cell object that goes with the index (i).

```
var bounds = my_cell.getBounds(this);
```

We already used `getBounds` to determine the dimensions of the board; it is also a movie clip method that returns the boundaries of the movie clip as an object — just what we want. We save the result in the `bounds` variable.

```
if (x >= bounds.xmin && x <=
bounds.xmax && y >= bounds.ymin && y
<= bounds.ymax) {
```

Now we just check to see whether the *x* and *y* coordinates passed from the checker are inside the boundaries.

```
found = true;
```

When the coordinates fall inside a cell, we set the found variable to true so we don't keep looking for the correct cell — we've already found it.

```
break;
```

We don't have to continue the loop as we found what we were looking for and so we stop it with break.

```
if (found) {
    return i;
} else {
    return -1;
}
```

When the loop has gone through all of the cells and we've either found a matching cell or not, we return the cell's number or else we return -1 to signify that the checker isn't over a cell. The stop_drag method we wrote uses a positive cell number to check whether it's a legal move and so -1 always returns an illegal move.

Now it's time to create the event handlers for the mouse interaction. As we create new event handlers, we define the mouse handlers code below the existing onClipEvent (load) handler (4.46):

```
onClipEvent (mouseDown) {
    cell = get_cell (_xmouse, _ymouse);
    if (cell > 0) {
        _root.start_drag(cell);
    }
}
```

4·45

Here is the breakdown into its parts:

```
onClipEvent (mouseDown) {
}
```

This event handler will be invoked whenever you press the mouse button.

```
cell = get_cell (_xmouse, _ymouse);
```

_xmouse and _ymouse are the coordinates of the current mouse position — relative to the current time-line, which is fine. We pass them on to the get_cell method, and it will return us the right cell.

```
if (cell > 0) {
    _root.start_drag(cell);
}
```

If you really clicked a cell, we can start dragging a checker (4.47).

```
onClipEvent (mouseUp) {
    cell = get_cell (_xmouse, _ymouse);
    _root.stop_drag(cell);
}
```

That's the event handler for releasing he mouse button.

```
cell = get_cell (_xmouse, _ymouse);
```

Capture the cell again that we are over.

```
_root.stop_drag(cell);
```

And call the stop_drag method we defined earlier.

Save your file again and test the movie. You can now drag checkers onto empty cells. If you move them and don't drop them on an empty cell, they will bounce back to the original cell (4.48).

Of course this not a fully functional checkers game. That would be beyond this introduction to the object-oriented model used in Flash 5. Feel free to use this code and develop your own checkers game. Both the original Flash 4 animated checkers game and the Flash 5 game developed for this book are available at the Smashing Ideas' Web site.

And that's it — for your reference the completed scripts are located at www.FlashStudio Secrets.Com

4.46

4.47

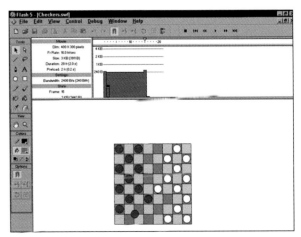

4.48

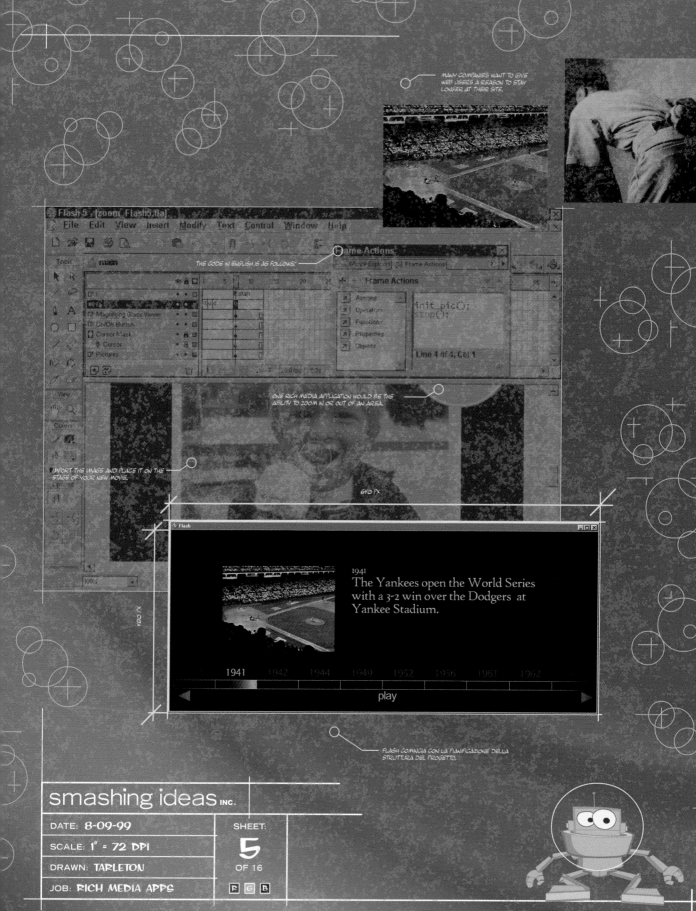

MANY COMPANIES WANT TO GIVE
WEB USERS A REASON TO STAY
LONGER AT THEIR SITE.

THE CODE IN ENGLISH IS AS FOLLOWS:

ONE RICH MEDIA APPLICATION WOULD BE THE
ABILITY TO ZOOM IN OR OUT OF AN AREA.

IMPORT THE IMAGE AND PLACE IT ON THE
STAGE OF YOUR NEW MOVIE.

1941
The Yankees open the World Series
with a 3-2 win over the Dodgers at
Yankee Stadium.

1941   1942   1944   1949   1952   1956   1961   1962

play

FLASH COMINCIA CON LA PIANIFICAZIONE DELLA
STRUTTURA DEL PROGETTO.

smashing ideas INC.

DATE: 8-09-99

SCALE: 1" = 72 DPI

DRAWN: TARLETON

JOB: RICH MEDIA APPS

SHEET:
5
OF 16

CHAPTER 5
ADDING VALUE TO WEB SITES
WITH RICH MEDIA APPLICATIONS

BY RUSS TARLETON AND GLENN THOMAS

Many companies don't want to create an entire Web site in Flash, but they do want to give visitors a reason to stay longer at their site. To hold user interest, rich media applications integrated into the overall Web site architecture are a perfect solution.

We define a rich media application on the Web as anything that goes beyond a standard HTML page to encompass animation, interactivity, sound, graphics, photos, and video in a standalone application. Many times these applications live in a pop-up browser separate from the main Web site to emphasize their media difference, while at other times the applications are integrated directly into the regular Web site.

Examples of rich media applications created in Flash include such things as foreign currency calculators, build-your-own-furniture applications, interactive product demos, learning tutorials, music mixers, create-your-own-cartoon programs, and visual chat applications. This chapter looks at another example — timelines.

Rich media applications give the Web user a reason to stay.

5.1

CREATING TIMELINES

We'll begin by looking at an example of how to use an interactive timeline in Flash. In this example, we create a baseball digital timeline and photo album that enables users to find out about baseball's past (5.1). To give more control to the user, the timeline enables viewers to watch the project as a linear slideshow or explore the history of baseball by using a navigable timeline (5.2).

5.2

99

Because the photo history was a separate and distinct component to the Web site, it was integrated as a pop-up Web page. This gave the rich media application a feeling that it was different and distinct from the rest of the Web site. It also enabled users to keep the photo history open while investigating other parts of the Web site.

USING POP-UP PAGES

Currently many of the rich media applications that are being created as components of normal Web sites are displayed in separate Web pages that pop up in a new browser window above the rest of the site. The JavaScript code for this is fairly straightforward, but you need to keep a few things in mind.

The first issue is that a visitor can accidentally enter a new URL into the pop-up browser. JavaScript code

NOTE

If you are not yet familiar or comfortable with JavaScript, try reading *Danny Goodman's JavaScript Bible, 3rd Edition* (from IDG Books Worldwide, now known as Hungry Minds, Inc.).

can be developed that alerts a user and requires a positive response before the new page loads. The other problem with a pop-up browser window is that whenever the viewer clicks the main Web page, the pop-up browser window moves behind it. Although most Web users are savvy about this, this needs to be kept in mind.

The JavaScript code used to pop up the new Web browser window defines what Web page will open in the window, the name of the browser window, and the features of the new browser window such as dimensions, scrollbars, and resizability. The following JavaScript code is placed after the header information in your HTML file:

```
popUp();

function popUp(){
   timeline =¬
window.open("timeline.html","time",¬
"toolbar=no,location=no,¬
directories=no,status=no,menubar=no,¬
width=640,height=240,scrollbars=no,¬
resizable=no");
}
```

COAUTHOR PROFILE
Russ Tarleton

Russ Tarleton is a Programmer at Smashing Ideas who focuses on Flash 5 and CGI scripting. He keeps many of the server-side computers and applications running while still getting to design and play games most of the day and keep up to speed on the latest Flash 5 happenings. He started programming in Pascal back in 1993 and moved on to C++ shortly after. He's now studying what he loves to do best by pursuing a degree in Computer Engineering at the University of Washington.

When he finds some free time in his busy schedule he enjoys playing tennis and can be found on the mountain slopes snowboarding.

PLANNING THE MOVIE

Before we start entering code in Flash, we need to have a good idea of what the Flash movie is to do. The baseball timeline needs to be designed so that it can run on its own or enable the user to interact with it at any time. It is helpful to draw a flow chart of how the timeline should work. Here's what needs to happen:

1. Display the loading graphics.
2. Wait until the movie is completely loaded.
3. Play the intro animation if it's added.
4. Show the interactive elements and begin playing the baseball timeline.
5. Check if the user interacts with the movie and process the input, if any.
6. Repeat Step 5 to check for user interaction.

We will be designing the baseball project in the same order as the flow chart. We will start with the layout, and then the loader, skip the intro animation, and then show the programming for the interactive elements and event handler.

DESIGNING THE LAYOUT

We've created a total of seven layers (5.3). It's easy to create a layer; just click the button with a "+" on it below all the layer names. To name a layer, double-click the layer you want to rename. I've labeled the layers as follows:

- **Layer 1: l (meaning labels).** It is a fairly standard convention in Flash to keep all the timeline labels on the top layer to keep the content organized.
- **Layer 2: fa (meaning frame actions).** I always keep frame actions on a layer of their own just below the frame labels to keep the ActionScript easy to find.
- **Layer 3: outer mask.** This layer is not a Flash mask layer but I've described it as such because it contains a black box that covers everything except for the stage. This guarantees that the viewer will never see any elements outside the boundaries of the movie.

- **Layer 4: side masks.** This layer contains graphics on the side of the movie that fade out to black, making the elements appear as if they are fading out as they leave the stage.
- **Layer 5: ticker and years.** The baseball timeline is put on a lower layer so that it won't be visible as it moves off of the stage.
- **Layer 6: world/ button next.** It doesn't matter what layers the buttons are put on. The arrow buttons will always stay in the same place and they don't overlap any of the other elements. "World" refers to the world graphic placed on this layer in the introduction.

PROGRAMMING THE FUNCTIONS

A simple way to make sure that the functions are loaded before we show the timeline is to put all the functions on frame 1. This way we know for sure that the functions are available to call by the time we get to the frame that holds the baseball timeline and other interactive elements. Another common approach is to make the Flash movie repeat on the first two frames until the desired frame is loaded. You can accomplish this by inserting the following code in the first two frames of any movie.

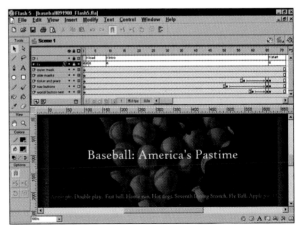

5.3

In frame 1 insert the following ActionScript:

```
// "start" is where the Baseball¬
timeline is.
ifFrameLoaded ("start") {// "begin" is
where the Intro animation begins.
  gotoAndPlay ("begin");
}
play ();
```

In frame 2 insert the following:

```
prevFrame ();
```

When the Flash movie arrives at the "start" frame that triggers the baseball timeline to begin playing. The baseball project uses a combination of the preceding methods. We placed all the functions on the first frame and then repeated between frames 2 and 3 until the "start" frame was loaded.

We decided to show a masked image of baseballs during the waiting period and brief intro animation (5.4, 5.5).

TIP

It is common to use frame labels instead of frame numbers in case you ever decide you need to lengthen the intro animation. Then you could easily insert the necessary frames without needing to change any of your code that points to a particular frame number.

When the Flash movie arrives at the "start" frame, we will cause the baseball timeline to begin playing. If the user interacts with the movie, then we will handle the event accordingly. But what are all the ways a user can interact with the timeline? As we decide on the ways, we'll implement empty functions or skeleton functions in the first frame. These functions will consist of a simple function declaration followed by empty brackets. Because they don't contain any code yet, these functions are sometimes referred to as *skeleton* functions. It's a good idea to start off by defining all of these empty functions so we can make sure the script works correctly from the beginning. You can also add a trace call in the function so you can be sure that the function was called.

A basic skeleton function consists of the following:

```
function function_name()
{
    trace ("function_name() was¬
called.");
}
```

CHECKING FOR USER INTERACTION

We know that this project will be event-driven so we will start be creating a function that handles all the possible events called event_handler.

```
function event_handler() {
}
```

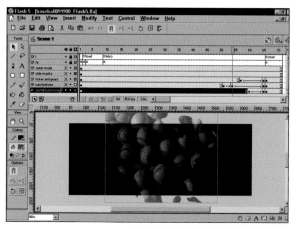

5.4

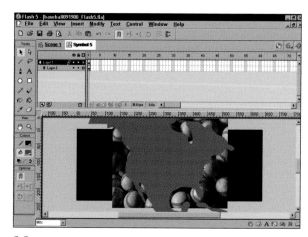

5.5

TABLE 5-1

EVENT	JUNCTION
Move the timeline to the left when the right button is rolled over	`move_timeline(target_x)`
Move the timeline to the right when the left button is rolled over	
Show the correct picture and stop the timeline when a year is clicked	`show_year(new_year)`
Stop the baseball timeline when stop is clicked	`stop_timeline()`
Play the baseball timeline on its own when play is clicked	`play_timeline()`
Move a time indicator along the baseball timeline by default or whenever the play button is selected	`move_ticker()`

You can then add a trace function to make sure the `event_handler` function is called (5.6).

We'll call the `event_handler` function repeatedly to test for user interaction with the movie and to move the time indicator — or *ticker*, as we call it. We could achieve this by looping on the main timeline as we did for the loader but this time we'll implement the looping using a new action in Flash 5 called `onClipEvent`. If we add the code directly to the baseball timeline movie clip, then as soon as the instance appears, whatever code is contained within the curly braces will be continually repeated.

At the "start" frame we put the sole action:

```
stop();
```

But contained right on the baseball timeline movie clip is the following code (5.7):

```
onClipEvent (enterFrame) {
   _root.event_handler();
}
```

The timeline should be able to handle several events at once. We will create empty functions in frame 1 to handle all of the scenarios. Table 5-1 lists these events and functions.

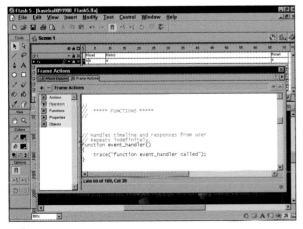

5.6

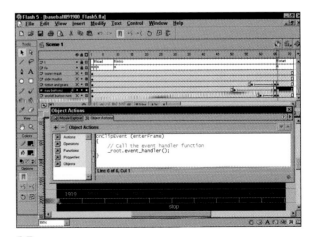

5.7

Frame 1 now contains the following:

```
// Handles timeline and responses¬
from user.
event_handler() {
}
// Slides the timeline in to the¬
desired "target_x"
move_timeline(target_x) {
}
// Shows the desired time clicked¬
on in the Baseball timeline.
show_year(new_year) {
}
// Stops the ticker from moving
stop_timeline() {}
// Starts the ticker playing at¬
the next time period.
play_timeline() {
}
// Move the "ticker" to the right.
move_ticker() {
}
```

Before filling in the code for the new functions, it would be a good idea to identify a few of the extremes the movie might encounter. We can define a few of the movie *constants* at this point, as follows:

```
// Total years I will be displaying
MAX_YEARS = 20;
// The Pixel width of each box on¬
the Baseball timeline
BOX_WIDTH = 63;
//  How long it will take to¬
travel one box. (In Frames)
// You can change this variable or¬
your Frames/Sec to adjust¬
ticker speed.
```

```
BOX_TIMEINTERVAL = 140;
// I set my movie to 15 frames a¬
second so the ticker travels
// 15 * TICKER_STEP per Second.¬
TICKER_STEP =¬
(BOX_WIDTH/BOX_TIMEINTERVAL);
// The width of the Baseball¬
scrolling timeline
SCROLL_WIDTH = MAX_YEARS*BOX_WIDTH;
// Where the Baseball timeline¬
starts - where X is the very
// left hand side of the Baseball¬
timeline (not the center!)
// Also where the Baseball¬
timeline is prohibited to move¬
left of.
SCROLL_STARTX = 6.9;
// Where the ticker will start¬
referenced to the Baseball timeline¬
X axis.
TICKER_STARTX = 0;
// This is the X coordinate where¬
the Baseball timeline is prohibited¬
to move right of.
SCROLL_ENDX = 637;
// SPEED_FACTOR can be set to adjust¬
the speed at which the Baseball¬
timeline scrolls to the right and¬
left.
SPEED_FACTOR = 6;
```

By defining these constants at the beginning of the programming process, we are enabling the project to be scalable. If we want to add another year on the timeline, the programming update will be as easy as changing MAX_YEARS from 20 to 21. We will still need to add another picture for the new year but fortunately, as we program with scalability in mind, most of the code should not need to be changed.

Now we will add a few global variables to frame 1 that we need during the movie:

```
// Is the ticker moving?¬
By default, yes.
ticker_moving = true;
// Did the ticker make it to the¬
next year? When we start, no.
```

TABLE 5-2

CONDITION	ACTION
If the timeline should be moved to the right . . .	Then move it to the right
Otherwise, if the timeline should be moved to the left . . .	Then move the time line to the left
Otherwise, if neither of the preceding conditions is true and the next year's picture should be shown . . .	Then move the baseball timeline to the next year and show the next picture
No matter what the preceding conditions are, if the ticker should move . . .	Then move it forward

```
show_next_year = false;
// current_year is the year that¬
the timeline is currently showing¬
and is updated when a new year is ¬
clicked on or the time passes to ¬
show the next year.
// By default the first "year" we¬
will show will be the
first.current_year = 1;
// The speed at which to move the¬
timeline left or right.
// The variables equal 0 to 9¬
allowing for varying speeds at¬
which the user can move the ¬
Baseball timeline.
// These are multiplied by¬
SPEED_FACTOR to scroll the¬
Baseball¬
Timeline that many pixels.
left_speed = 0;
right_speed = 0;
```

At this point you should be able to test your movie with no errors.

ESTABLISHING NAVIGATION

Now we'll go over the code for each of the skeleton functions in frame 1 and each of the Flash elements that will call those functions.

The `event_handler` function will be called repeatedly. To help program the code for this function, first write the basic logic that will happen each time the function is called (see Table 5-2).

Notice how the timeline has scrolled to the left because the right button was rolled over (5.8).

The code for the `event_handler` function is as follows:

```
// event_handler()  Repeats¬
indefinitely. Called from¬
onClipEvent() on Baseball¬
timeline movie clip
//
function event_handler()
{
   if (left_speed > 0)
   {
      // Right arrow is rolled¬
over. Slide the timeline to the¬
left.
move_timeline(scroll_nav._x -
(SPEED_FACTOR * left_speed));
```

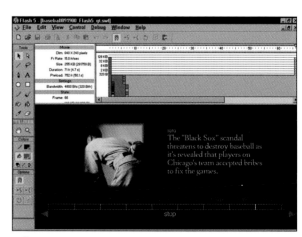

5.8

Table 5-3

CONDITION	ACTION
If the baseball timeline has scrolled too far to the left . . .	Then move it back to the furthest it should go to the left
Else if the baseball timeline has scrolled too far to the right . . .	Then move it back to the furthest it should go to the right
Else if we've gotten close enough to the target *x*-coordinate . . .	Then stop the `event_handler` function from calling the timeline (because as we continue to go ⅓ the distance to the target we'll never get there!)

```
    }
    else if (right_speed > 0)
    {
        // Left arrow is rolled¬
over, Slide the timeline to the¬
right.
        move_timeline(scroll_nav._x +
(SPEED_FACTOR * right_speed));
    }
    else if (show_next_year == true)
    {
        // Play is selected, Slide¬
the timeline to the next period of¬
time.
        // Note the "3" can be¬
changed to whatever position you¬
want the
        // default position to be for¬
the selected year.
        move_timeline(SCROLL_STARTX +
(3 * BOX_WIDTH) - (current_year *
BOX_WIDTH));
    }

    if (ticker_moving == true)
    {
        // Move the ticker along¬
nice and steady.
        move_ticker();
    }
}
```

The move_timeline function accepts parameters to move the baseball timeline to the right or the left. Only one parameter is sent: the target *x*-coordinate to which we want to move the timeline. It would seem easy enough to move the baseball timeline immediately to the new *x*-coordinate but we thought it would be fun to spruce up the program a little and *ease in* the baseball timeline to its new coordinate location. This is done using some basic math. Move the baseball timeline to a location a fifth of the distance between where it currently sits and the target coordinate to which we want to move the timeline (this creates the ease-in effect). The logic behind the code is demonstrated in Table 5-3.

The actual code for the move_timeline function is as follows:

```
// move_timeline(target_x)
// creates the visual effect of¬
sliding the
//   Baseball timeline to the¬
current selected year.
function move_timeline(target_x)
{
    // I usually use "Ox" to mean¬
Object X.
    Ox = scroll_nav._x;

    // The trick to the "easing in"¬
is here...
    // Move it 1/5th the distance to¬
the target each time.
    scroll_nav._x = Ox + ((target_x -
Ox)/5);

    if ((scroll_nav._x + SCROLL_WIDTH) <
SCROLL_ENDX)
    {
        // if adjusted too far left
        scroll_nav._x = SCROLL_ENDX -
SCROLL_WIDTH;
        show_next_year = false;
    }
```

Table 5-4

CONDITION	ACTION
When the left button is rolled over …	Set the variable `right_speed` to the speed at which the baseball timeline should move
When the left button is rolled off of …	Stop the baseball timeline from moving by setting the `right_speed` variable to 0
When the right button is rolled over …	Set the variable `left_speed` to the speed at which the baseball timeline should move
When the right button is rolled off of …	Stop the baseball timeline from moving by setting the `left_speed` variable to 0

```
else if (scroll_nav._x >
SCROLL_STARTX)
   {
       // if adjusted too far right
       scroll_nav._x = SCROLL_STARTX;
       show_next_year = false;
   }
   else if ((0x - target_x) < 3 && (0x
- target_x > -3))
   {
       // if we've reached the¬
target then stop moving the¬
timeline.
       show_next_year = false;
   }
}
```

ENABLING NAVIGATION

The two main elements of the Flash movie that call the `move_timeline` function are the right and left arrow buttons. Because the baseball timeline is longer than the width of the screen. we need these arrows to enable us to scroll the timeline. In the following examples, the buttons have been placed inside of movie clips because they contain an additional animation that is used for the variable-speed effect explained later on. Let's take a look at the meaning of the code that will be inserted into these buttons (see Table 5-4).

JUMPING THROUGH THE TIMELINE

The code is just as simple as the logic behind it:
  The code for the left button:

```
on (rollOver)
{
    _root.right_speed = 9;
}
on (rollOut, dragOut)
{
    _root.right_speed = 0;
}
```

  The code for the right button:

```
on (rollOver)
{
    _root.left_speed = 9;
}
on (rollOut, dragOut)
{
    _root.left_speed = 0;
}
```

If you wanted to enable the user to jump immediately to the beginning or end of the timeline, only one line of code is needed in each button. The timeline moves by changing its _x value, the x-coordinate property. When the left button is clicked, we want the timeline to jump all the way to its starting point (`SCROLL_STARTX`). And for the right button, when clicked, the timeline should jump to the farthest it can go to the left (`SCROLL_ENDX - SCROLL_WIDTH`).

The actions when the user releases the left button are (5.9):

```
on (release)
{
    _root.scroll_nav._x =
_root.SCROLL_STARTX;
}
```

The actions when the user releases the Right Button are (5.10):

```
on (release)
{
    _root.scroll_nav._x =
_root.SCROLL_ENDX -
_root.SCROLL_WIDTH;
}
```

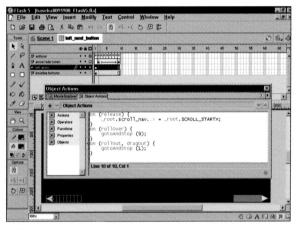

5.9

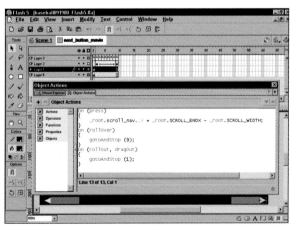

5.10

ADDING VARIABLE SPEED

Let's say we want to add the effect of variable speed. That is, the closer you move your mouse to the arrows, then the faster the baseball timeline moves. All we would need to do is add a few invisible buttons (buttons with an image in only the "hit" frame) next to the arrows and give them in the following code:

```
on (rollOver)
{
    //When this button gets rolled¬
over the speed of the Baseball¬
timeline will be 2 times the
    // _root.SPEED_FACTOR to the¬
left.
    _root.left_speed = 2;
}
on (rollOut, dragOut)
{
    _root.left_speed = 0;
}
```

In addition, if you wanted the image of the arrow to change the closer you moved the mouse to it, then the preceding code would be slightly different. On rollover each invisible button tells the arrow movie clip to go to a different frame, as follows:

```
on (rollOver)
{
    gotoAndStop(x);
}
on (rollOut, dragOut)
{
    gotoAndStop(1);
}
```

The preceding x should be replaced with the frame number that you wish the arrow movie to go to when that invisible movie clip is rolled over. In our baseball example, the arrow movie clip contains nine frames of a tween of the arrow. Eight invisible movie clips and one arrow exist. Fortunately, each frame contains the exact same code:

```
_root.right_speed = _currentframe-1;
stop();
```

SHOWING THE CORRECT YEAR

The next function we will look at is show_year. When called, we want to show the user the image that corresponds to the selected year. This function is called only when the user clicks one of the years on the baseball timeline (5.11).

When a year is clicked, the current_year variable should be set so we can pass it to the show_year function. We can make sure the current_year variable and all other necessary variables are getting updated at the right time by using the new debugging feature in Flash 5. Instead of just testing the movie by choosing Control ➢ Test Movie (Ctrl+Enter for the PC, ⌘+Return for the Mac), you can publish the movie with the debugger running by choosing Control ➢ Debug Movie (Ctrl+Shift+Enter for the PC, ⌘+Shift+Return for the Mac). As you can see from the screen shot, when the second year in the timeline is clicked, the variable current_year is changed from 1 to 2 (5.12, 5.13). This is the expected behavior.

In plain English, whenever a box on the timeline is clicked we want to do the following:

- Show the correct picture animation to the user
- Highlight the year that was selected on the baseball timeline (5.14)
- Change the stop/play button (we'll go over the stop/play button later) so the button displays "play" — that is, the timeline is currently stopped and the user can begin playing it by pressing play
- Call the stop_timeline function to make sure we stop everything

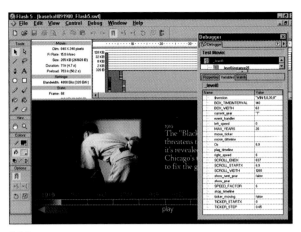

5.12

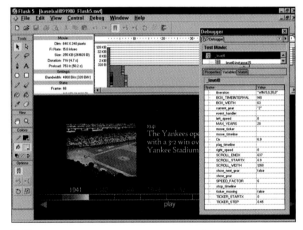

5.13

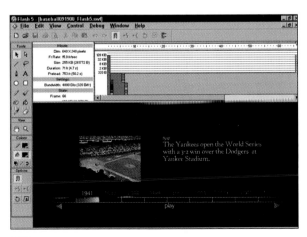

5.11

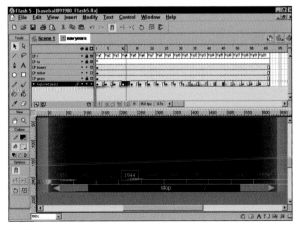

5.14

Here's the code to do so:

```
// show_year: This is called when¬
one of the sections of the timeline¬
is clicked on.
//
function show_year(new_year)
{
    current_year = new_year;

    years.gotoAndStop("y" + current_
year);
    scroll_nav.gotoAndStop("y" +
current_year);
    stop_play.gotoAndStop("stop");

    stop_timeline();
}
```

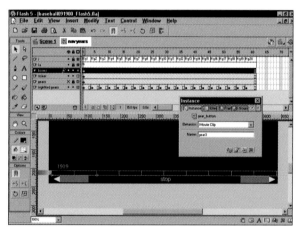

5.15

At any time, the user may interact with the baseball timeline by clicking a period to show the picture associated with that period. The baseball timeline is a movie clip that contains all of years that can be viewed. We've named the baseball timeline movie clip `scroll_nav`.

Programming the baseball timeline so it's scalable will make it easy to add more year entries in the future. To do this we will design each of the boxes to be nearly identical. The only difference will be the instance name of each box. We will name each box `yearX`, where X is the order it appears starting from the earliest on the timeline, such as "year1," "year2," "year3," and so on (5.15).

When clicked, the box should call the function `show_year` and pass the value of the year that corresponds to that box.

To create each period on the timeline, follow these steps:

1. Draw a square, make it a button, and embed the button in a movie clip.

2. Give the movie clip an instance name of **yearX**, where X is the order of the year on the timeline, starting with "year1".

3. Add the following ActionScript to the button embedded in the movie clip:

```
on (press)
{
    //Parsing the name to get the year.
    _root.show_year(_name.substr(4));
```

4. Now copy the movie clip and rename its instance name to the next position. For example, the first movie clip would be called "year1" so the next one would be called "year2."

5. Repeat Step 4 for as many times as there are years on the timeline and line up each movie clip next to each other. Remember, all of these movie clips reside in the movie clip `scroll_nav`.

TABLE 5-5

CONDITION	ACTION
Increment the current year variable by 1	
If the current year is now set to a value greater than the maximum number of years set on the baseball timeline . . .	Then set the current year variable back to 1 And start the ticker over again at its starting position
Set the `show_next_year` variable to `true` to cause the baseball timeline to move to the next year	Show the picture that corresponds to that year Highlight the next year on the baseball timeline
Start the ticker moving again by setting the `ticker_moving` variable to true	

STOPPING THE TIMELINE

The `stop_timeline` function should stop the ticker from moving and move it to the end of that current year. This function is called only if the user clicks one of the boxes on the timeline or clicks the "stop" button. Here's the code:

```
//
// stop_timeline
//
function stop_timeline()
{
    // Stop moving the ticker along¬
the Baseball timeline.
    ticker_moving = false;

    // Now move the ticker to the end¬
of the current year.
    // (which is the same as the¬
beginning of the next year)
    // Note: current_year starts at¬
1 not 0.
    scroll_nav.ticker._x = TICKER_STARTX
+ (current_year * BOX_WIDTH);

    // If the timeline was moving,¬
stop it.
    show_next_year = false;
}
```

PLAYING THE TIMELINE

The `play_timeline` function is not called at the beginning of the movie to get everything rolling. That happens by default. The `play_timeline` function will only be called when the play button is pressed.

The intention of the code is expressed in Table 5-5.

The code for the `play_timeline` function follows:

```
//
// play_timeline
//
function play_timeline()
{
    current_year ++;

    if (current_year > MAX_YEARS)
    {
        current_year = 1;
        scroll_nav.ticker._x = TICKER_
STARTX;
    }
    show_next_year = true;

    years.gotoAndStop("y" +
current_year);
    scroll_nav.gotoAndStop("y" +
current_year);

    ticker_moving = true;
}
```

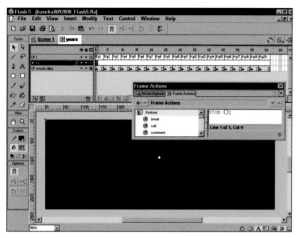

5.16

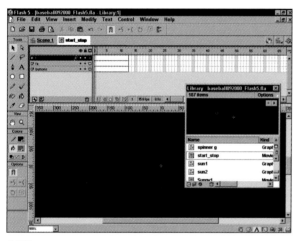

5.17

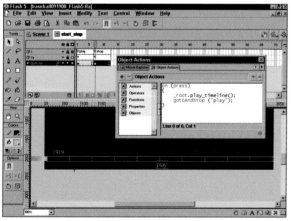

5.18

CREATING A TOGGLE BUTTON

We want to enable the user to stop the baseball time-line from moving automatically or continue playing the timeline after he or she has stopped the playback. If we create two buttons and place them at different frames inside a movie clip, we can switch between the two frames to achieve the visual effect of a toggle button. What we want is explained in Table 5-6.

To create the start/stop button, do the following:

1. Create two buttons, but do not place them on the stage. One should have the text "play" and the other "stop."
2. Create a new empty movie clip called `start_stop` (5.16).
3. Make two separate key frames in the movie. Label one "play" and the other "stop."
4. In the frame labeled "stop," place the play button on the stage, and in the frame labeled "play," place the stop button on the stage.
5. Under each label place the command: `stop();`.
6. On the start button place the actions `_root.start_timeline();` and `gotoAndStop ("play");` (5.17).
7. On the stop button place the actions: `_root.stop_timeline();` and `gotoAndStop ("stop");` (5.18).

TIMELINE POSITION

The "ticker," as we are calling it, is used on the baseball timeline to indicate what year we are viewing. The "ticker" movie clip is placed inside the `scroll_nav` movie clip so that it travels along with the timeline if it is moved. The `move_ticker` function is called by the `event_handler` function by default or anytime that the "play" button is selected to handle the movement of the ticker. In plain English, this function moves the ticker forward along the baseball timeline one `TICKER_STEP`.

If the ticker reaches the next period of time, then advance the baseball timeline by calling the `play_timeline` function.

TABLE 5-6

ACTION	RESULT
The stop button is clicked	Move the ticker to the next closest year on the timeline and stop it from moving
	Show the start button
The start button is clicked	Start moving the ticker forward
	Show the stop button

The ActionScript looks like this:

```
//
// move_ticker: Called by¬
handle_event to move the timeline¬
indicator forward.
//
function move_ticker()
{
   // Advance the ticker forward¬
one "TICKER_STEP"
   scroll_nav.ticker._x +=
TICKER_STEP;
   if (scroll_nav.ticker._x >
(current_year * BOX_WIDTH))
   {
      // If we've reached the¬
next period of time, advance ¬
timeline to next year.
      play_timeline();
   }
}
```

YEAR GRAPHICS

Because only one year on the timeline is shown at a time, the graphics for each year are all stored in one movie clip at different frames. This enables us to effectively hide all the other graphics and show the current graphic by simply moving to another frame in the movie clip. We've called this movie clip "years" and each frame is labeled yX where X represents the order that year appears on the timeline. Each frame that is labeled contains a movie clip of an animation for that year sliding to the center of the screen. Each

movie clip in the "years" movie clip appears empty at first because the first frame of each sliding animation is blank.

At this point we've entered all the necessary code for the baseball timeline to run on its own or facilitate any user interaction during the movie. All that's left is adding your custom graphics to the "year" movie clip by inserting graphics into the timeline.

FLASH 4 VERSUS FLASH 5

When programming in Flash it is helpful to know if the final project will need to be published in Flash 4 or Flash 5. The reason for this, as you probably already know, is that those people who come to your Web site with the Flash 4 plug-in installed will not be able to view your movie if it was published as a Flash 5 .swf file. This could be a concern for companies who expect thousands of visits to their Web site. Even though the Flash 5 plug-in is only about 200K and fairly easy to install, some Web site administrators feel that users won't want to wait for the download and will click away from their site.

Fortunately, in Flash 5 we are able to export to any previous version of Flash. The downside to this is that not all the ActionScript will be available for us to use because previous versions of Flash don't recognize much of Flash 5 ActionScript.

For example, the baseball project was originally designed in Flash 4. We converted many of the commands to Flash 5 syntax and made abundant use of the function capability. When we tried to publish it as a Flash 4 movie, the output window filled with errors. Let's take a look and see what we could do to increase the backward compatibility.

For every function declaration the following error appeared: "You must export your movie as Flash 5 to use this action." Each function call also resulted in almost the same error message.

The solution? Simply revert to the old style of "calling" functions. Place all the code for the function you wish to call in a single frame and give that frame the label of the name you wish to name that function. Then, whenever you want the code to be executed in that frame, you can use the Flash 4 command: `Call("label_name")`.

The following is another common error we received when we tried to publish my movie in Flash 4:

"You must export your movie as Flash 5 to use this action."

```
years.gotoAndStop("y" + current_year);
```

Using the new function `gotoAndStop();` was just fine. But when we tried to apply it to a movie clip using the new dot-syntax, we got an error. Fortunately this doesn't require a major workaround. It is a simple matter of reverting to the Flash 4 method of targeting movie clips using the `Tell Target` command. In Flash 4 the command would be as follows:

```
Begin Tell Target ("years")
    Go to and Stop ("y"&¬
../:current_year)
End Tell Target
```

Whenever we target movie clips using `tellTarget`, it is important to remember that we are entering the scope of that movie clip. For example, in the preceding code the variable `current_year` exists on the main timeline, but when we target the movie clip "years" we can't make reference to the `current_year` variable directly. We can use the relative variable name `/:current_year` or `_parent.current_year` or the absolute variable name `/:current_year` or `_root.current_year` if the variable is on the main timeline.

When the preceding Flash 4–compatible command is written in Flash 5 it appears as follows:

```
tellTarget ("years")
{
    gotoAndStop ("y" add ¬
_parent.current_year);
}
```

The method that we used to call the `event_handler` function repeatedly also came up as an error.

Because the `onClipEvent` handler is new to Flash 5, we get an error if we try to export our project as a Flash 4 movie. The alternative is to use a common Flash 4 technique for an infinite loop using the timeline. In this project, all of the interactive elements are located in the frame that we labeled "start." At that frame we could replace the stop action with the following actions:

```
Call("event_handler");
Play();And the frame directly
following the "start" frame would then
contain the single action.prevFrame();
```

Assuming you moved all the code from the `event_handler` function to a new *frame* labeled `event_handler`, the preceding code would accomplish the same task as the original code. Remember, if any variables needed to be passed to the function as parameters, we would need to make sure those variables were available to the script that was run from the call command.

ADDING MAGNIFY AND ZOOM FUNCTIONALITY

Another feature that would make this a richer media application would be the ability to magnify the whole picture or zoom in (5.19) or out (5.20) from a specific area. The key to creating realistic magnification in Flash is to keep an enlarged image of the picture moving smoothly in tandem with the movement of the mouse cursor.

For this example we'll design the zoom feature in a separate Flash movie. Start with the basic layout for the first three frames. That is, functions go in the first frame, a test to check if the movie is loaded goes in the second frame (5.21), and a `prevFrame` action goes in the third frame (5.22).

The magnify feature described here does not work exactly like a traditional magnifying glass; instead, the photo album zoom utility creates a magnified image in the upper right-hand corner of the movie. However, you can use the basic principles described here to create more complex magnifying tools that do function like a standard magnifying glass.

The code for this feature was set up to be modular so that as many photos could be added to the project as required. This example only covers how to implement this kind of project with one picture, but it is certainly possible to increase the number of pictures to create a sort of magnifying slide show. This would be a good project to use Generator in the offline mode because you could create a robust, automated system to modify, add, or delete photos.

The zoom project is an example of how you can use the `_scale` property and the masking feature in Flash to create a magnifying-glass effect. The project has four elements:

- A movie clip of a picture centered on the stage of the movie
- A magnifying glass movie clip to be dragged by the mouse that we'll call "cursor" (5.23)
- A movie clip with buttons to turn the magnifying glass on or off (5.24)
- A magnifying glass movie clip called "magnify" that contains a masked copy of the current picture shown (5.25)

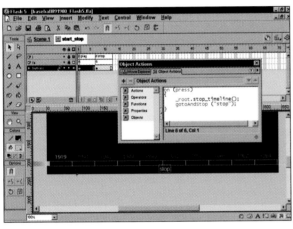

5.19

5.20

5.21

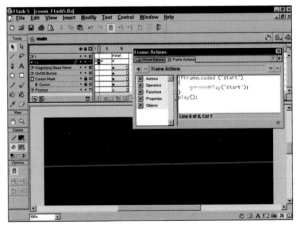

5.22

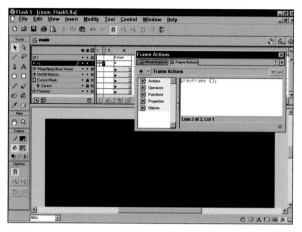

5.23

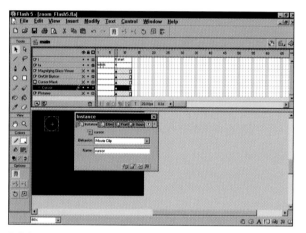

5.24

5.25

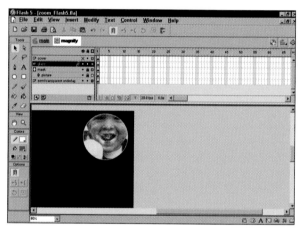

5.26

Follow these steps to create the zoom project:

1. Choose an image to magnify. Import the image you want to magnify and place it on the stage of your new movie. Select it and put it in a movie clip. Use the Instance panel to set the instance name of this movie clip to **pic1**. Make sure the center point of the movie clip is centered at the center of the stage. Because our movie is 640 × 480 (5.26) the center point is at 320, 240. You can find the coordinate information for the instance selected in the Info panel (Window ➤ Panels ➤ Info) (5.27).

Movie Properties

Frame Rate: 20 fps	OK
Dimensions: Width 640 px × Height 480 px	Cancel
Match: Printer Contents	Save Default
Background Color:	
Ruler Units: Pixels	Help

5.27

2. Create the magnifying glass. The magnifying glass that will be dragged by the mouse is just a simple graphic outline of a circle. Draw the outline of a circle that is about 50 pixels across and make it into a movie clip with the instance name **mag**. Place it under a mask that is the same size as the picture being viewed (5.28). If pictures change size, then this mask needs to change size as well. The reason for this mask is so that the cursor will only be visible over the picture we're viewing and won't show up over the rest of the screen.

3. Create an on/off button movie clip. The on/off button for the magnifying glass will be a movie clip with two instances of the button in an on state and an off state. Create a new movie clip called **b_mag**. It doesn't need to have an instance name.

4. Make a button. Make a button called **b_mag2** with the text "magnifying glass" and enough space to the right of that text for the words "on" and "off."

5. Edit the movie clip. Edit the b_mag movie clip. Add a labels layer, in this case called **l**, and create an **on** label in the first frame and an **off** label in the fourth frame. Add a button layer and drag an instance of the button into the first frame of the layer. Create a keyframe in the button layer under the **off** label in the fourth frame.

6. Create a new layer. Create a new layer for the text just above the layer the buttons are on. Under the label on place the text "on" to the right of the text "magnifying glass" in the button. Under the label off place the text "off" in a new key frame. Remember to place a stop command in the first frame of the movie clip so it doesn't continually repeat when it's shown.

We will place different code in the two instances of the button. When the button is in the off state, the code is fairly simple (5.29).

> **WARNING**
>
> Make sure you bring in the image at a higher resolution than you normally would. If you don't do this, then your image will look extremely pixilated upon magnification. As an example, if you want an image to be magnified 3× then you should bring the graphic in at around 3× the resolution of the display. On a standard 72 dpi monitor you would want to bring the image in at around 250 dpi.

5.28

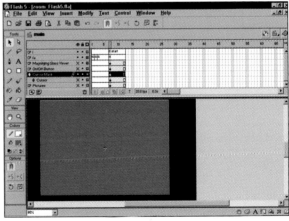

5.29

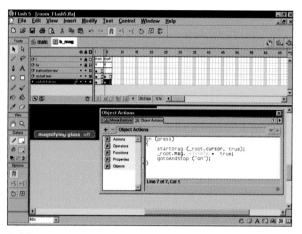

5.30

The code instructs the program to do the following when the button is clicked:

- Start dragging the magnifying glass outline
- Make the masked magnifying clip visible
- Change this button to the on state

The actual ActionScript code is as follows:

```
on (press)
{
  startDrag (_root.cursor, true);
  _root.mag._visible =  true;
  gotoAndStop ("on");
}
```

When the on button in the movie clip (5.30) is clicked to turn the magnifying glass off, we want the following to happen:

- Stop dragging the magnifying glass outline
- Hide it so we can't see the outline (5.31)
- Change this movie clip button to the off state

The ActionScript code is as follows:

```
on (press)
{
  stopDrag ();
  _root.mag._visible = false;
  gotoAndStop ("off");
}
```

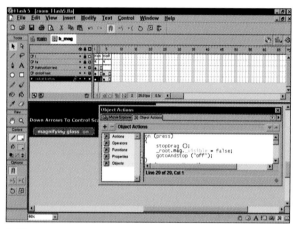

5.31

It is also nice to show the user what scale the magnifying glass is currently displaying. For this we can add a dynamic text field under the "on" frame that automatically updates every time the `current_scale` variable is changed (5.32). We'll name the field `_root.current_scale`. We need to reference the main timeline by using `_root` because the movie clip we are in is not in the same scope as the main timeline. In Flash 4 this would be equivalent to using `/:current_scale`.

Having a standard variable called `current_scale` makes the zoom feature easier to program. We'll only need to change the variable `current_scale` to change the zoom of the magnifying glass because we'll set up another function that continually updates the current scale based on that variable.

5.32

TABLE 5-7

CONDITION	ACTION
If the up arrow is clicked . . .	Then increase the current scale variable (5.35)
	And if the current scale variable is too high, then set it to the predefined maximum value
If the down arrow is clicked . . .	Then decrease the current scale variable
	And if the current scale is too low, then set it to the predefined minimum value

The optional code that can be placed in the on button to scale the picture (5.33) will accomplish the results listed in Table 5-7:

Here's the code to scale the picture:

```
on (keyPress "<Up>")
{
  with (_root)
  {
    current_scale = Int(current_scale /
SCALE);
    if (current_scale > MAX_SCALE)
    {
      current_scale = MAX_SCALE
    }
  }
}
on (keyPress "<Down>")
```

```
{
  with (_root)
  {
    current_scale = Int(current_scale *
SCALE);
    if (current_scale < MIN_SCALE)
    {
      current_scale = MIN_SCALE
    }
  }
}
```

Notice how we use `with(_root)` here to specify the main timeline. If we didn't use `with(_root)`, we would have to place `_root` in front of every variable because we are working within the scope of the on/off button movie timeline and not in the main timeline.

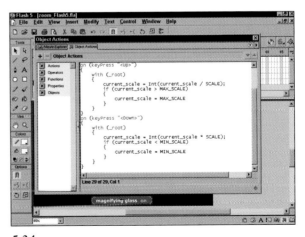

5·33

5·34

In the first frame of the main timeline we can define the constants we are using:

```
//
// CONSTANTS
//
// Maximum and Minimum percentage the
picture can be scaled to
MAX_SCALE   = 1500;
MIN_SCALE   = 5;
// Rate at which the picture is scaled
up or down
```

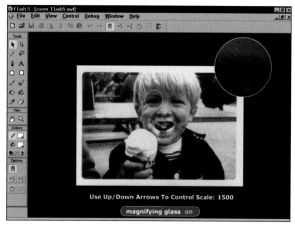

5.35

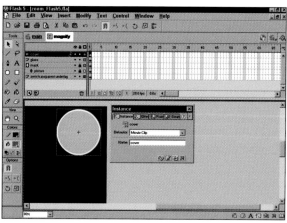

5.36

```
// Multiplied or Divided by the
current scale upon up or down keypress
to get the new scale
//  For example: If scale is
originally 100...
//  on down press it will be 100 * .8
= 80
//  and then on up press it will be 80
/ .8 = 100
SCALE  = .8;
```

We'll also initialize the center coordinates:

```
// Coordinates of the center of the
movie
// Used to determine how far the mouse
is offset from the current picture
// i.e. When the mouse goes down, the
movie under the magnifying glass goes
up
// and when the mouse goes up, the
movie under the magnifying glass goes
down
CENTER_X  = 320;
CENTER_Y  = 240;
```

The most complicated element in this project is the magnifying glass that contains a masked copy of the image currently shown on the main timeline. This movie clip consists of five layers.

- **Cover Layer.** A cover that acts as a lens cap (5.35).
- **Graphics Layer.** An outline around the magnifying circle.
- **Mask Layer.** The circle mask that defines what we can see (5.36).
- **Sub Mask Layer.** A copy of the image in a movie clip to move and scale — it doesn't matter where it's placed on the stage because we'll move it immediately when the masked magnifying lens movie is shown (5.37).
- **Background Layer.** A gray background that shows if the picture just above is moved out of view.

The only layer that will be interacted with is layer 4, the Sub Mask Layer. In this example, the movie clip that resides there will be called **pic1** (5.38). Via a repeated function call, the movie clip on the Sub Mask Layer will be moved and scaled. The function that takes care of the constant scaling and zooming of the picture we'll name **zoom**.

The zoom function will do the following if the mouse is within the coordinates of the picture on the main timeline:

- Make sure the lens is hidden
- Move the movie clip under the mask to the *x* and *y* coordinates that correspond to where the actual cursor is over the picture on the main timeline
- Scale the movie clip under the mask to the current scale
- Otherwise, put the cover on the magnifying glass by unhiding the lens

The code for the zoom function, placed along with the constants in the first frame, is as follows:

```
// Called repeatedly to scale and
reposition the picture under
// the magnifying glass
function zoom()
{
  if (_xmouse > pic_startx and _xmouse
< (pic_startx + pic_width) and
    _ymouse > pic_starty and _ymouse <
(pic_starty + pic_height))
  {
    // If the mouse is inside the
boundary of the picture
    // Then show the magnifying glass,
    // Move the picture to the correct
location
    // And scale it to the current
scale
    mag.cover._visible       = false;
    mag["pic" + current_pic]._x    =
(START_X - _xmouse) * (current_scale /
100);
```

```
    mag["pic" + current_pic]._y    =
(START_Y - _ymouse) * (current_scale /
100);
    mag["pic" + current_pic]._xscale
  = current_scale;
    mag["pic" + current_pic]._yscale
  = current_scale;
  }
  else
  {
    mag.cover._visible = true;
  }
}
```

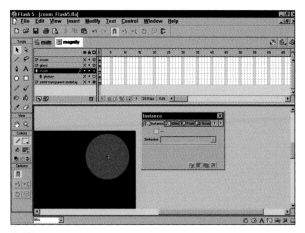

3.37

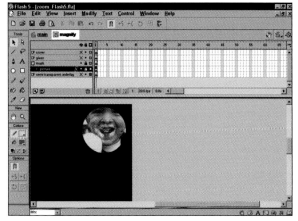

5.38

The variables that are used here are first initialized along with the constants in frame 1 of the main timeline, as follows:

```
//
// VARIABLES
//
// The default picture and scale (in
percent) at which it will be shown
current_pic = 1;
current_scale = 200;
// These variables will be set once
the image is opened
// We declare these variables here to
put them in the global scope
pic_width = 0;
pic_height = 0;
pic_startx = 0;
pic_starty = 0;
```

If this project involved multiple images, each image would have a different width and height. Therefore, to accommodate for this, we'll create a function called `init_pic` (5.39). This function would be called once for each image when it is shown so that we know its size. We will use that data to determine whether or not the user moved the mouse over the picture. In the preceding code, we see that only when

the mouse if over the image will we want to show the movie clip that contains the magnifying glass with the scaled picture. Here's the code for `init_pic`:

```
// Called only once when a picture is
shown
// to set global variables: width,
height, start x and y
// These variables are used to
determine if the mouse has rolled over
the image.
function init_pic()
{
  startDrag (_root.cursor, true);
   pic_width = _root["pic" +
current_pic]._width;
   pic_height = _root["pic" +
current_pic]._height;
   pic_startx = _root["pic" +
current_pic]._x - (pic_width / 2);
   pic_starty = _root["pic" +
current_pic]._y - (pic_height / 2);
   //mag.gotoAndStop("1" +
current_pic);
}
```

In this project, we only need to call the `init_pic` function once. So, under the frame labeled "start," we put in a call to that function.

After the function declarations in the first frame of the movie and the next two frames for the loader, we jump to the "start" frame where only two commands are inserted (5.40):

```
init_pic();
stop();
```

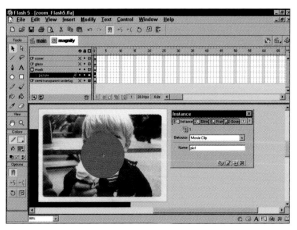

5.39

We'll use the new command for Flash 5 `onClip Event` to repeatedly call the zoom function. We can place the code directly on the masked magnifying movie clip:

```
onClipEvent(enterFrame)
{
   // Loop here indefinitely so the
magnifying
   // glass is continually updated.
   _root.zoom();
}
```

Test the movie. The magnify/zoom functionality should function properly. You could add even more value to this feature by modifying it to enable the magnifying glass to be dragged over the photo. If you want to push the edges of what Flash can do, you can even create code that enables a user to move a magnifying glass "in and out" of a picture in 3D and mimic a real magnifying glass's sense of depth.

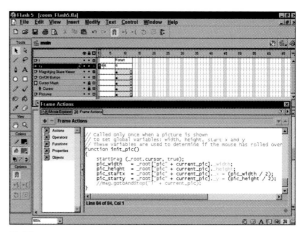

5.40

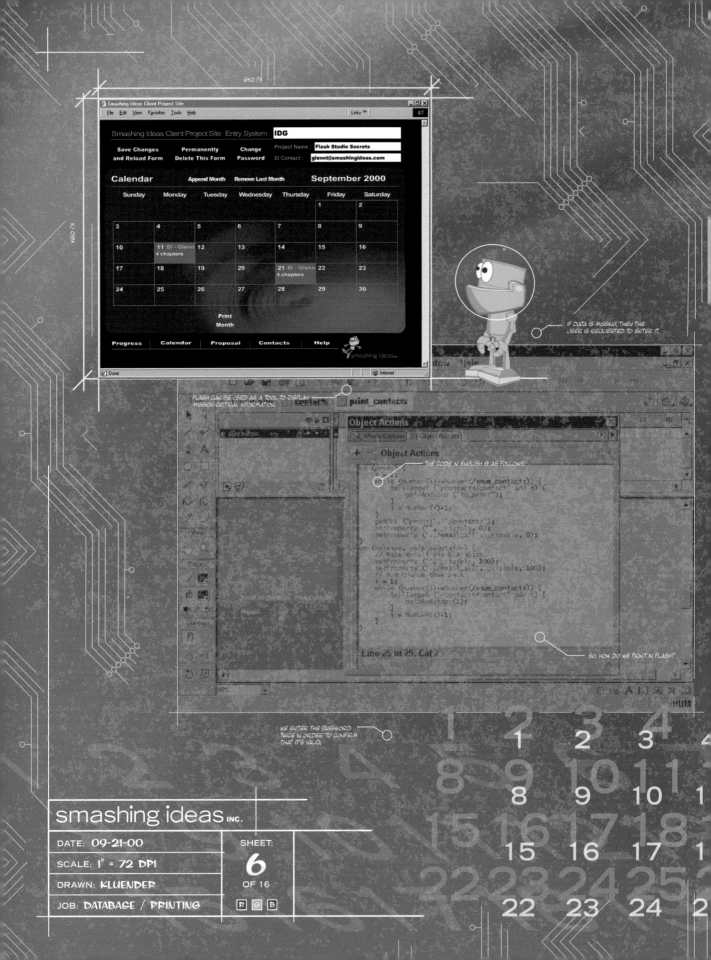

CHAPTER 6
INTEGRATING DATABASE CONNECTIVITY AND PRINTING

BY RUSS TARLETON AND GLENN THOMAS

Designers and developers can use Flash to create dynamic business intranets and extranets that are easily updatable and have efficient, user-friendly interfaces. By using its dynamic data-transfer capabilities, Flash can be used to display mission-critical business information in a structured, easily accessible manner.

This chapter focuses on a variety of aspects important to this kind of a project, such as creating unique user IDs, sending data to server-side programs from Flash, returning data from the server side to Flash, checking the Flash Player version that the user is running, and printing from within Flash. Developers can usefully integrate these features into their work for this type of project or any other.

This chapter covers both Flash 4 and Flash 5 techniques. It's important to understand the differences between the two versions because many clients will still require Flash 4 for their projects. Also, some of the newer programming approaches in Flash 5 don't work in Flash 4, so it's necessary that developers be able to work in either version.

By using its dynamic data-transfer capabilities, Flash can be used to display mission-critical business information in a structured, easily accessible manner.

CREATING A CLIENT PROJECT SITE

Smashing Ideas needed to create a way for producers to communicate project status and deadlines with our clients. We decided to have our producers build mini-sites for each of their projects and to display the mini-sites on our client-based Flash site. Clients were able to use the Web at any time to review a project's progress. In this way, we explored the possibilities of

125

using Flash to create data-driven extranets for mission-critical business applications.

The complete project included a Flash site where clients could review their project and an administrative site for producers to enter the data used to create the project site. The data that a producer entered was sent to a CGI script that saved it to a text file that could then be accessed by the client-side Flash movie. When a client or producer pulled up the calendar or contact sections of the client project site, they could also print out that information.

Each of Smashing Ideas' clients is sent a URL to the Smashing Ideas' studio site. This URL links to an HTML page that loads a single Flash movie that contains information about a client's project. This information includes a description of the project, the project schedule, a list of deliverables and meetings notes, a set of project contacts, and a brief help page (6.1).

The Progress section uses entries organized by date to communicate details about a given project (6.2). The Progress section is frequently updated with new meeting notes and project comps. Each date and detail can contain text summarizing a step in the project or a URL link that pulls up an HTML or Flash movie comp.

> **NOTE**
>
> When new versions of the Flash plug-in come out, it's always difficult to decide which version you should use to satisfy the goals of a client's project. Smashing Ideas hasn't updated its client project site to Flash 5 because it functions properly as is, so it doesn't need to be changed. The version choice for client projects has to be based on the current distribution of the new plug-in, the intended audience of the client, and the technical needs of the project. Some projects must be done in Flash 5 because of programmatic needs, while others can still be created for the Flash 4 plug-in or even the Flash 3 Player depending on client requirements. The important point to keep in mind is to weigh the options and choose the appropriate version that will make the project a success for the client.

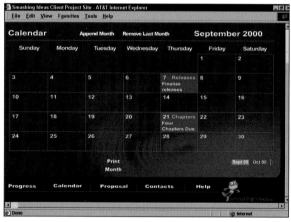

6.1

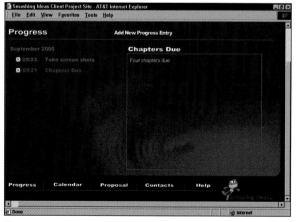

6.2

6.3

The Calendar section contains a printable calendar that shows the deadlines for the project as a whole. Deadlines are split into client deliverable deadlines and Smashing Ideas' deliverable dates. Each day of the month has two sections, a title and a body. The title area contains the name of the company or person responsible for this particular deadline and the body of the date's entry contains a short description of the nature of the deadline.

The Proposal section contains a written description of the project (6.3). The Contacts section contains the names of all of the people involved with the project from both the client's company and from Smashing Ideas, as well as their titles and contact information (6.4). Contacts can be e-mailed individually or as a group directly from the client project site. The last section, the Help area, contains a URL link to the client's project site and contact information for technical staff at Smashing Ideas. The business goal with this project extranet is to help communicate more clearly with clients and to give them a place to independently review the progress of projects.

INTRODUCING THE ADMINISTRATIVE SITE

On the administrative side, Smashing Ideas' client site provides a Web-based Flash interface so producers can enter the relevant information for each area of the client site. This information is then collected within the application and sent to a CGI script on the Smashing Ideas' server. The CGI script saves the data

into a text file in a format that Flash understands. When a client pulls up the client-side interface to their project site, Flash imports this data and displays it.

When a producer goes to the administrative area of the client site, the first screen he or she encounters enables him or her to either edit an existing client's information or add a new client (6.5). When we began writing this book, we added Hungry Minds, our publisher, to the site (6.6), using HMI as the client name, the title of the book as the project name, and then we entered a password. The password is used by the producer to gain access to the administrative site so that nobody else can accidentally change project details.

Notice that the producer has two fields to use for entering the password when setting up the project account. This is done to ensure that the password

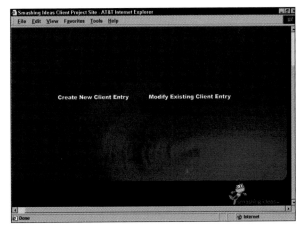

6.5

6.4

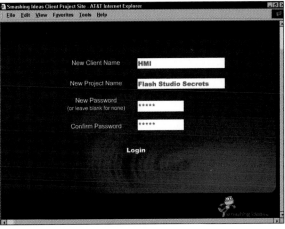

6.6

hasn't been mistyped. This is a useful approach to password creation because a mistyped password is difficult for a producer to figure out and would require the intervention of the server administrator to recover.

Inside Flash, the password confirmation capability is created with an If statement that compares the value entered in the first password text field to the value in the second text field when the producer tries to enter the site after creating the project account (6.7, 6.8).

The Flash 4 code exists at a label called `password Check` and is called when the producer logs in for the first time. The code at the label looks like this:

```
If (password1 = password2)
    Set Variable: "response" =
"Successful"
Else
    Set Variable: "response" = "Enter
password again."
End If
```

The Flash 5 code to do this would be a function instead of a call and would look like this:

```
function passwordCheck () {
if (password1 == password2) {
    response = "Successful";
} else {
    response = "Enter password again";
}
}
```

USING CALLS

The client administration site uses Flash 4, so it requires dozens of different calls. Calls are Flash 4's answer to functions. A call looks for a frame with a specific label and then runs the actions in the frames under that label. Flash 5 would make this a much simpler application to build because all of those calls could be turned into functions that can easily be used anywhere in the application. It would be easier to program and less memory-intensive for the user's computer. This is because we create many variables during actions that don't need to exist after that action has finished. These local variables stay around in Flash 4, but in Flash 5 they can be programmed so that they are removed when the function finishes running.

With the project account created, the Flash movie then creates a unique identification number based on a randomly generated series of alphanumeric characters for the project account. This unique ID is transmitted from Flash to the server to distinguish this project from all the other client projects in the system.

Generating a unique ID

Unique ID numbers are extremely important for many server-side projects. For example, a company's employees will be assigned a unique ID number so they can access a corporate HR intranet, or a supplier can be given a unique ID to track purchase needs on a

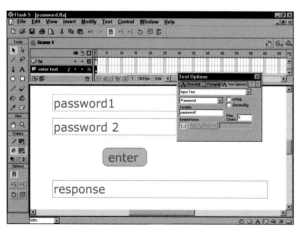

6.7

6.8

supply chain extranet. Unique IDs for individual users are used to locate information specific to the user.

You have several ways to create unique ID numbers for Flash server-side projects. One way is to have the numbers created by a program on the server side using CGI or some other language and return them to the Flash movie. This is the safest way to create ID numbers because the server script can ensure that numbers are always unique by checking against the current ID database.

Another way is to create the ID numbers randomly within Flash as we've done with our client project administration site. If the number of digits is large enough, then it's unlikely that any ID would ever match any other ID. As an example, the following number would create a one-in-a-billion chance that ID numbers would match.

```
client_id = random(1000000000)
```

The ID can be a large string of numbers and digits randomly generated and placed together. As an example, the following Flash 5 code snippet would create a 20-digit random ID with numbers at all the odd digits and alphabetic characters at all the even digits.

```
// Make Random ID Number
// of 20 Digits w/num & chars
client_id = "";
i = 1;
while (Number(i)<=20) {
  if (Number(i-(int(i/2)*2)) == 1) {
    random_char = random(10);
  } else {
    random_num = random(26);
// random(x) gives 0..(x-1)
// ASCII = CHR = (random)
// 97-122 = "a..z" = (0-25)
// Make it Lowercase
random_char =
chr(Number(random_num)+97);
}
client_id = client_id add random_char;
i = Number(i)+1;
    }
```

An ID could also be based on the user's clock. When carried to the millisecond, it's highly unlikely that IDs would ever match. The following Flash 5 code would create an ID based on the current time on the producer's computer:

```
date = new Date();
client_id = date.getDate() add
date.getHours() add
date.getMilliseconds()
```

Creating ID numbers randomly on the client side does mean that there's a possibility that duplicate IDs could be created. This would cause serious data integrity issues so it's important to double-check any Flash-created ID against the current ID numbers located on the server. This would be done in a server-side script before a new ID is saved to a server-side database. In this case, if the ID happens to be a duplicate of an existing ID, the server-side script would return an invalid ID parameter to Flash and ask that a new ID be generated. In general, it's the best practice to create unique IDs on the server side except in the case of projects that will contain limited number of IDs.

Recording project data

After the unique client project ID has been established, our producers have access to a series of forms that enable them to enter all of the information relevant to the project. The first place to enter information is in the Proposal area. We click the title area to enter a title, or click the text area to enter information (6.9).

Inside the Flash movie, recording project data is done by creating a movie clip called `proposal_text` and then adding two Input text boxes. The text fields are named `proposal_title` and

---

TIP

Use the `chr` action to create random IDs by getting the ASCII character set in Flash. Numbers 97–122 relate to the lowercase a–z characters. Use random (26) to get 0–25 and then add 97. By using `chr` with this number you'll return a lowercase character from a to z.

proposal_text (6.10). When the producer enters information, these variables get set inside the movie clip.

All of the information in the Flash movie is entered in a similar manner. Each section has a distinct movie clip where data is stored in Input text boxes (6.11–6.13). Although sections such as the calendar area are significantly more complicated, the basic principle is the same. Once all the information has been entered in each section, the producer saves to transfer the information to the server.

SENDING DATA FROM FLASH

The main steps in transferring data out of the client project site to the back-end CGI script are to create a blank movie clip, transfer the necessary data into that movie clip, send it to the back end using Get or Post, and then wait for the CGI script to return a success or error message. Whether done in Flash 4 or Flash 5, this is the standard way of transferring information to the server.

In a Flash 4 movie, when the producer clicks Save, the button tells Flash to go to a label called save and begins playing through a series of movie actions. The difference between Flash 4 and Flash 5 with this kind of application is that all of the calls would be unnecessary and would be changed into functions.

The first action calls to a label called hide_all with a series of actions that hides any of the administrative forms that might currently be open. This is so a user doesn't add data during the saving process

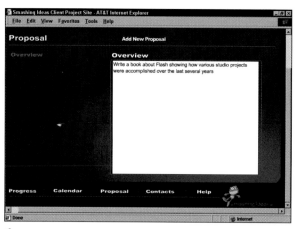

6.9

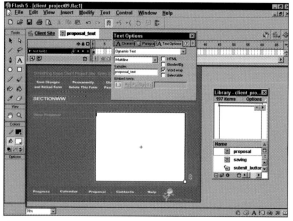

6.10

6.11

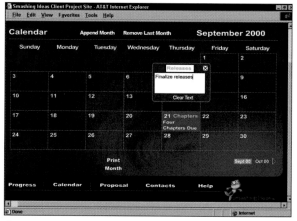

6.12

because this new information would not be saved to the server. Here's the code for `hide_all`:

```
call ("/progress_items/:off_admin");
/:section = "";
call ("/:hide_progress");
call ("/:hide_calendar");
call ("/:hide_proposals");
call ("/:hide_contacts");
call ("/:hide_help");
setProperty ("/dataentry", _visible, 0);
/:off_buttons = true;
```

Each specific series of hide actions then sets the visibility property of each movie clip to false so it becomes invisible (6.14).

The next set of actions check to see that specific information exists (6.15). There must be a client name, project name, and Smashing Ideas contact for the project to be saved. If this information doesn't exist, then the user is alerted to add it. If this information exists, then the client and project names are tested against all other projects to make sure this project doesn't already exist.

Because all of the project names were loaded into the Flash movie in the beginning when we asked the user to select a current project to edit, it's a simple matter of comparing names.

```
if ((/:client eq "") or (/:project eq
"") or (/data:contact eq "")) {
    message = "Client name, project
name and SI contact must exist.";
```

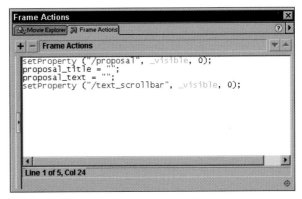

6.14

6.13

6.15

```
  call ("show_message");
  stop ();
} else {
  // Test the client/project names
against all other current projects.
  call ("/:check_names");
  if (/:message eq "") {
      play ();
  } else {
      call ("show_message");
      stop ();
  }
}
```

The next set of actions checks each of the client project site's sections and reviews whether all required data has been entered. If data is missing, then the user is requested to enter it.

Once we've checked to make sure that the user has entered all the necessary information, then we can prepare to send that information. The easiest way to do this is to transfer all of the information we want to send out of the movie to the server into one single movie clip and then use the Load Variables action to send it.

The client project Flash movie contains a movie clip called "empty" that contains one blank empty frame. It's a dumb movie clip that can be duplicated to create movie clips that contain data. The data in these data movie clips can then be sent out discretely.

If we don't transfer the data we want to send to the server into movie clips, then we would end up sending all the variable data that's on the main timeline.

TIP

It's possible to copy from and paste into editable text fields in Flash movies. On a PC, right-click the mouse to access a menu that enables you to copy and paste. On a Mac, Command-click the mouse (⌘+click). This is very useful when a Flash application returns data that you'll need to put into spreadsheet or document applications.

This would be inefficient because so many variables on the main timeline aren't relevant to the information that needs to be saved. Using discrete data movie clips to gather and send data is extremely important in Flash 4 programming for this reason.

In the case of the Flash 4 client administration site, we call a label called `copy_variables`, as follows.

```
// This is done in a separate frame
// to allow all var fields to update.
// Copy new data in to /outdata
call ("/:copy_variables");
```

The code at this label creates a duplicate movie clip called "outdata" from the empty movie clip. We create two variables within the outdata movie clip called "success" and "error." These variables are set to 0 and whichever one is reset to 1 when confirmation comes back from the server-side program will be used to let the producer know whether the information has been saved or not. The client name, project name, and unique ID are also created in the outdata movie clip. Here's the code:

```
duplicateMovieClip ("/empty",
"outdata", 100);
/outdata:success = 0;
/outdata:error = 0;
/outdata:client = /:client;
/outdata:project = /:project;
/outdata:contact = /data:contact;
/outdata:id = /data:id;
```

Once this is done we copy the variables we want to send to the server into the outdata movie clip, as follows:

```
call ("/:copy_progress");
call ("/:copy_calendars");
call ("/:copy_proposals");
call ("/:copy_contacts");
```

Once the actions have copied all of the data into the outdata movie clip, it is then sent out to the server using the `Post` method. Flash 4 sends and receives data using `Get` or `Post` with name/value pairs sent as URL encoded strings. A secure connection using `shttp:` can also be made with either `Get` or `Post`. We have to use `Post` with this project because so much data is being transferred. `Post` doesn't work with Internet Explorer 4 or earlier on the Mac, so it's not a universal solution. In the case of this project, we send the data to a CGI script on the server that saves the data.

```
tellTarget ("/outdata") {
  loadVariables ("http:/
/www.yourservername.com/cgi-
bin/client_project /request_data.cgi",
"", "POST");
}
```

The CGI script located on the server takes the data that Flash sends to it and then outputs a text file in a format that Flash can read. The text file's name is based on the unique ID number that has been generated inside Flash. The CGI script then sends a response back to the Flash movie showing that the file has been created successfully. If the administrative Flash movie doesn't receive this response, then a message alerts the user that the information hasn't been saved.

BRINGING DATA INTO FLASH

The client project site uses only one dynamically generated HTML page and one Flash movie for all of the different projects. Each project is viewed by sending a unique ID number to a CGI script. The script appends the ID number to the SWF file name in the dynamically generated HTML, thereby creating a unique HTML page. Flash then knows how to load the correct text file from the server from the ID that was appended to the SWF in the dynamically generated HTML page.

As an example, a particular project would be accessed at `www.yourservername.com/cgi-bin/client_project_site/project.cgi?id=11v5e6b9r4`. The `project.cgi` script would generate an HTML file from a template that has the code to embed the SWF: `client.swf?ID=#id#`.

To generate the HTML file, the CGI script replaces all occurrences of the text `#id#` on the fly with the ID that was passed in—in this example, `11v5e6b9r4`. The CGI script then prints the newly generated HTML with the ID number to the browser. When the Flash movie starts, it can use the ID variable to query the server, as follows:

```
tellTarget ("/data") {
  loadVariables
("http://www.yourservername.com/cgi-
bin/client_project/send_data.cgi?id="
add id, "");
}
```

The `send_data` CGI script on the server uses the ID number to locate the correct text file and send the variables in the text file to the Flash movie. Once the data is received in the Flash movie, a series of actions populate the information throughout the movie clips for each section. A more powerful way to bring in information and structured data in Flash 5 is to use XML. An example of how to get XML data into Flash 5 is located in Chapter 10.

ENABLING PRINTING

In some Flash applications, it might be useful to include the ability to print. For example, if you were designing a Flash-based calendar, you might want to add a button that could print the current month.

CHECKING THE VERSION

The ability to print is supported only in Version 4.0.25 (Windows) or 4.0.20 (Macintosh) or later of the Flash Player. This is an important factor to consider if your target audience will primarily be Flash 3 or early Flash 4 Player users because they'll have to upgrade their version of Flash Player to use the printing feature. Fortunately, you have a way to check which version of the Flash Player the user has from within Flash. In Flash 4, the following code tests the version number of the Player and directs the user to the appropriate place:

```
Set Variable: "ver" = eval("$version")
Set Variable: "release" = substring
(ver, (Length(ver) - 3), 2)
If ((release eq "" ) or (release <
20))
  Go to and Stop ("need_upgrade")
Else
  // The user has passed version
testing. Load the site!
```

```
Go to and Play ("start")
End If
```

If the user has release 20 or greater of the Flash Player, he or she will be taken to the `start` frame where the movie will start playing. If not, the user will arrive at the `need_upgrade` frame where a button can be placed with a `GetURL` command directing the user to download the latest version of the Flash Player. More information on how to check for the `$version` variable in Flash 4 can be found on Macromedia's Web site at `www.macromedia.com/support/flash/ts/documents/version.htm`.

PRINTING FUNCTIONS

Two actions are used to print in Flash 4 and 5. One is `print` and the other is `printAsBitmap`. Each action performs the same basic task, that is, printing

TIP

Macromedia has released a deployment kit that enables you to detect whether or not the version of the Flash plug-in you require is installed in the visitor's browser. You can find the Macromedia Flash Deployment Kit at `www.macromedia.com/software/flash/download/deployment_kit`.

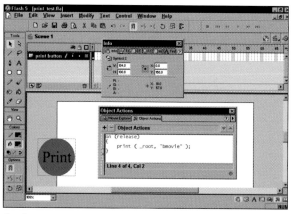

6.16

the specified frames to your printer. The difference between the two actions is that the `print` function uses vector-based printing, resulting in a higher quality print, whereas `printAsBitmap` renders the print as a bitmap. The `printAsBitmap` action should be used anytime you are printing frames that contain objects using transparency or color effects. Although the `printAsBitmap` function isn't as precise as the vector-based `print` function, it still prints at the highest printer resolution possible to attempt to maintain the highest quality print.

The following are all the variations of the `print` and `printAsBitmap` actions:

- `print (target, "bmovie");`
- `print (target, "bmax");`
- `print (target, "bframe");`
- `printAsBitmap (target, "bmovie");`
- `printAsBitmap (target, "bmax");`
- `printAsBitmap (target, "bframe");`

Each function has two parameters. The first, `target`, refers to the movie that contains the frames you want to print. The second, `bmovie`, `bmax`, or `bframe`, specifies how the size of the print will be determined.

The `bmovie` parameter is used to specify that the size of the print will be in proportion to the size of the movie's stage. Thus, if your movie size is 640×480, then your print will be scaled in proportion to those original dimensions. This enables you to print movies at smaller or larger than original movie sizes. When you do this, any graphic outside of the movie's stage will be cut. For example, if you used the command `print(_root, "bmovie");`, only the right half of the circle would be printed in the example shown in 6.16.

You don't have to settle for the print area size being the movie stage or always being in proportion to the size of your movie; instead, you can make specific parts of your movie printable. The `bmovie` parameter can also be used in conjunction with the frame label #b to specify your own custom print area for the target movie clip. Just label a frame as #b that contains an object that will define the bounding size of your custom print area.

We'll call this object the *bounding box* and whatever contents of the movie fall within the boundaries of the bounding box will be printed. It doesn't matter what shape the object is; it can be a rectangle, a circle, or any kind of shape. The bounding box won't ever be printed; it's just there to specify the new size and shape of the print area.

You can use the `bmax` parameter if you want the size of the print area to be the maximum of all the printable frames combined. This parameter is generally used when you are printing many frames that contain objects that vary in size. When printed, all the objects will be visible and in proportion with one another. Any frames labeled as #b are not considered when this parameter is used.

When you use the `bframe` parameter, the print area for each frame is based on the size of the objects in those frames. In other words, each printable frame is scaled to its maximum to fit on the printed page. The stage size is not considered; if you have printable frames that contain objects off the stage they will be scaled to fit on the page. Any frames labeled as #b are not considered when this parameter is used.

You don't have to print all of the frames in the `target` movie clip. In addition to the #b frame label, used with the `bmovie` parameter, you can label one or more keyframes as #p to specify that frame for printing. This label can be used in conjunction with the `bmovie`, `bmax`, or `bframe` parameters. This frame label can be particularly useful if you want to print content that will be within the bounds of the movie but not be shown on the screen to the user. The accompanying pictures are a good example of how this feature can be used. The first frame of the contacts movie is what the user will see (6.17) and the #p frame is what will be printed (6.18). To print a frame that the user does not see, it needs to be labeled as #p.

The #p label is optional, however, and if it is not found anywhere, then all the frames in the target movie will be printed. It's important to note that if you have labeled more than one frame as #p for printing, you will see a warning when you export the movie. This warning can be safely ignored. For example, if I label frames 2 and 8 of my movie as #p, I will receive the following message warning me that frame 8 contains the label #p that I used elsewhere:

```
WARNING: Duplicate label, Scene=Scene
1, Layer=Layer 5, Frame=8, Label=#p
```

> **TIP**
>
> An advantage to using the #b frame label is that you aren't limited to the boundaries of the stage when deciding where to place your printable objects. You can place the bounding graphic outside the stage if, for example, you wanted to print images that won't be shown to the user. This technique is often used to take information from a Flash movie and place it in a more printer-friendly layout.

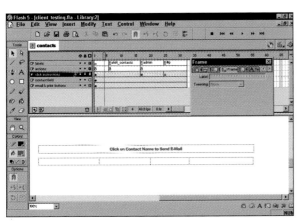

6.17

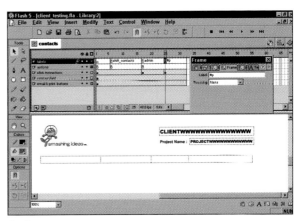

6.18

PRINTING DESIGN IN FLASH

While it is possible to put a print command in a frame that would automatically pull up the printing dialog box on the user's computer, it is much more common and courteous to design a button that gives the user control over the printing (6.19).

Keep in mind that the target movie should be completely loaded before the printing option appears. In the example movie we've been using, we didn't put a loader in because we were only using the movie as a standalone player. If your project will be a standalone movie, then you won't need to worry about a loader because the movie will load immediately when you double-click it. But if your project will be seen over the Web, you can use three different methods to make sure a movie is completely loaded before you let the print action be performed. All three approaches involve a method of repeating to continually check if a specific frame or bytes are loaded. When the condition is met, we move to a frame labeled `start_movie`. Frame 1 on the main timeline could contain one of the following methods:

```
// Method 1 - Checking if a particular
frame labeled end_movie is loaded yet
ifFrameLoaded("end_movie") {
  gotoAndPlay("start_movie");
}
play();

// Method 2 - Checking if all the
bytes of the movie are loaded yet
```

```
if (getBytesLoaded() ==
getBytesTotal()) {
   gotoAndPlay("start_movie");
}
else {
   play();
}

// Method 3 - Checking if all the
frames of the movie are loaded yet
// Essentially the same as checking if
all the bytes are loaded
if (_framesloaded == _totalframes) {
   gotoAndPlay("start_movie");
}
else {
   play();
}
```

And Frame 2 would contain `prevFrame();`.

When deciding the way in which to add printing capability to your Flash movie, it is important to first determine the objects that will be allowed to be printed and those that will be restricted. This decision helps you decide where to put the #p frame labels and whether it is necessary to have a custom bounding box. Often all the printable frames are placed in a separate movie clip.

First, do we want to prevent the user from seeing what will be printed? If so, we could place the printable material outside the stage of the movie, into its own movie clip called `printable_movie`. The command `print (printable_movie, "bmovie");` could then be used to print the material. With the #b label in the `printable_movie` movie clip we could further specify the size we would like the material to scale to upon printing.

Are you developing your project in Flash 4? Although the print and `printAsBitmap` actions aren't directly available in Flash 4, you can use the `GetURL` action to achieve the same results. Table 6-1 lists a couple of examples in Flash 5 and their equivalent action in Flash 4.

PRINTING CONTACTS

For the Smashing Ideas client site we wanted to give the client the ability to print out the list of contacts

6.19

TABLE 6-1

IN FLASH 5 THE ACTION . . .	. . . IS THE SAME AS THE FLASH 4 ACTION
print(printable_movie, "bmovie");	Get URL ("print:", window="printable_movie")
printAsBitmap(printable_movie, "bmax");	Get URL ("printAsBitmap:#bmax", window="printable_movie")

associated with its project. Because all of the contacts names reside inside a movie clip (6.20), we decided that it would be easiest if the target movie clip for printing was the "contacts" movie clip.

No bounding box was needed because we wanted all of the objects scaled to fit the page. Because all of the contact names fit on the movie stage, we had no reason to use the #b label. The #b label could have been used to specify a print area different than the stage size. Finally, a button was created with the "print" command. Because this project was developed in Flash 4, the code shown is Flash 4 compatible (6.21). Notice that the `print` action is in the `GetURL` action.

Most of the text in the "contacts clients" movie clip is a light blue (6.22). Were we to print the text as is, it would appear as a light gray on a noncolor printer. All of the text on the stage appears black when the print button is pressed (6.23). To make sure the black background isn't printed, the target movie clip does not contain a background graphic and the movie background in the movie properties box is set to white (6.24). These settings give us a legible black on white printout.

PRINTING YOUR CALENDAR EXAMPLE

In addition to providing the ability to print contacts, we wanted to be able to print the calendar itself. I'll briefly go through the steps I used to add printing capability to the calendar section of the Smashing Ideas client site.

We determined that we wanted to print the calendar as it is displayed on the screen with its column headings of Sunday through Saturday (6.25). Because the

6.21

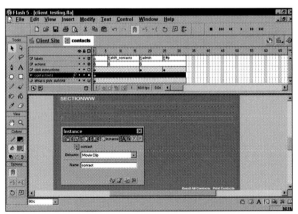

6.20

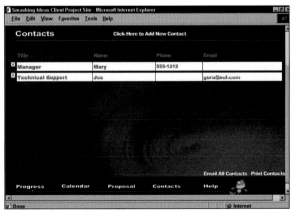

6.22

viewable text space in the calendar is so small, we also wanted any text entered in the calendar to appear in full below the printout of the calendar numbered sequentially by its date as a reference to the calendar above. Another movie clip was used as a template that could be duplicated and used for all the day entries

below the calendar. The template is called `print_calendar_text` and it contains a copy of the date, the title of the day, and the text entered for that day. Shown in figure 6.26 is the `print_calendar_text` template. The day, title, and text fields in the `print_calendar_text` movie are copied from the day movie clip where they were originally entered. Figure 6.27 shows the day movie clip template that will be used to contain the text for each day.

Because the text below the calendar would extend below the movie stage, we decided to set a bounding box, named "box," for the printout (6.28). We also could have used the `bframe` parameter to print and scale objects that lie outside of the movie stage. Because we wanted custom margins, we decided to use a bounding box that could be scaled to the height of all the text during the print procedure. Yes, you can have a dynamically sized bounding box. Because the box was to be changing size, it was important for it to be in the same frame as the text that was to be printed. To hide it from the visitor, we immediately set its alpha property to 0. Because we were using the alpha property and we didn't want the bounding box to show up in the print-outs, we used the `printAsBitmap` command.

To make the experience as seamless as possible for the user, we wanted the text below the calendar not to be shown on the screen while the calendar was printing. The text was hidden by assuring that the background behind the dynamic black text was always black.

Because all the information to be printed was to be generated dynamically, we were limited to printing it all on one page. If all days contain entries, the printout

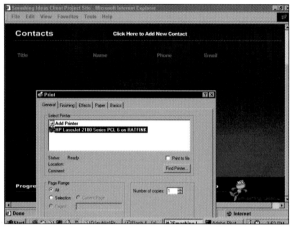

6.23

6.25

6.24

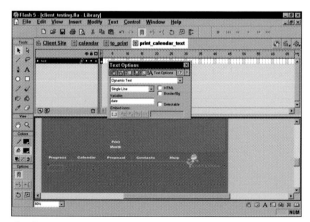

6.26

would appear very small because it would be scaled down to fit all the entries on one page. If we wanted to print on multiple pages, that would have required duplicating a movie clip that was a page template and then sequentially printing each of those movies. Hitting the print OK button multiple times would have been somewhat awkward for the user. The process of determining the printing area is a very important first step because it can result in a completely new design.

As with the contact section, all the text that appears on the screen in the calendar section is light blue on a black background. If we were to print the movie as it is, the light text would be hard to read on white paper. As long as the background color for the movie is set to white in the frame properties box (6.29) and no background exists in the target movie clip, the printout will also have a white background. To print the text as black instead of light blue, an additional frame was added in each day of the calendar that contains the text fields in the color black. When the "print" button is clicked, each of the days is set to this frame in the movie clip so all the text momentarily appears as black (6.30).

The Flash 4 printing command contained in the button for this section is as follows:

```
getURL ("printAsBitmap:#b",
"/calendar" add /:current_calendar);
```

By following these steps, we're able to give clients the ability to print out all of the information they need about a project from our client project site.

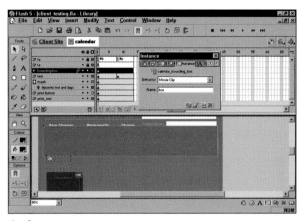

6.28

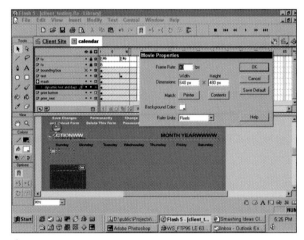

6.29

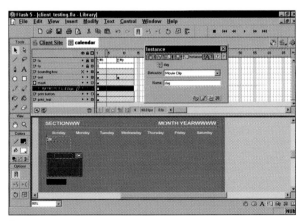

6.27

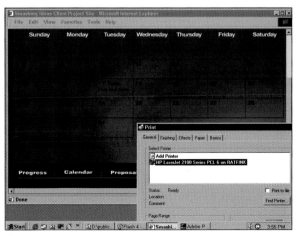

6.30

VBNM +1.25   HJK -0.125   UIOP+2.50   ASDF-0.375   RTYU

GENERATOR'S MAIN PURPOSE: TO SERVE UP DYNAMIC CONTENT THROUGH FLASH.

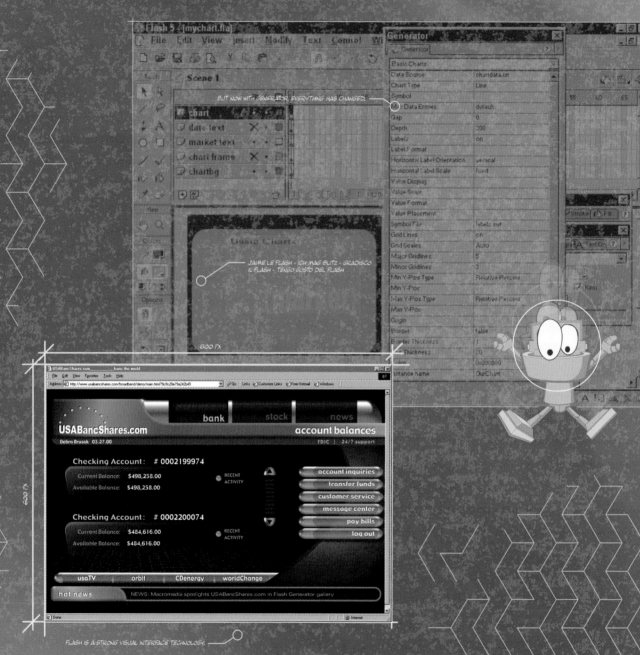

BUT NOW WITH GENERATOR, EVERYTHING HAS CHANGED.

JAIME LE FLASH - ICH MAG BLITZ - GRADISCO IL FLASH - TENGO GUSTO DEL FLASH

FLASH IS A STRONG VISUAL INTERFACE TECHNOLOGY.

DATE: 10-02-00	SHEET:
SCALE: 1" = 72 DPI	**7**
DRAWN: TORRONE / SCOTT	OF 16
JOB: FLASH & GENERATOR	

CHAPTER 7
MAKING SITES DYNAMIC USING GENERATOR

BY PHILLIP M. TORRONE

WITH CONTRIBUTIONS FROM PHIL SCOTT

I f you are a professional designer or developer who uses Macromedia Flash, chances are you'll want to make the server component of Flash, Macromedia Generator, a regular part of your toolkit. Generator, in comparison to the Flash product history, is a relatively recent data-driven solution from Macromedia designed to boost the capabilities of Flash. While Flash is great for delivering sophisticated vector-based animations and interactive movies over the Web, it is not powerful enough to create the type of on-demand, automated, and manageable content so often required for large corporate sites and applications. Also, Generator can integrate content such as JPEGs, GIFs, PNGs, and MP3s in your Flash movies. What if you want to redesign a financial site and include beautiful vector-based stock charts, calculated and drawn on the fly? Or what if you need to deploy data-driven graphics to the next generation of devices and Web appliances that don't yet support Flash? Or lower version of Flash? Until Generator, projects such as these had to be completed using traditional HTML with teams of designers or even Java applets; they couldn't take advantage of all Flash's well-known advantages. Here's my bank account in the first Generator-driven, 100 percent Flash-based online bank on which I led the development. All the text items are Generator variables from a legacy banking system and the scrolling lists and news tickers are Generator objects (7.1).

Some artists use paint, pastels, and clay to convey a message; others use charts, graphs, and numbers.

PHILLIP M. TORRONE

7.1

But now, with Generator, everything has changed. Because Generator can process dynamic content in Flash movies and in batch processes, you can take advantage of Flash's capability to deliver compelling low-bandwidth interfaces, even for projects that are data-driven or require a high degree of personalization. You can automate daily news updates and accompanying graphics for a very large Flash site or deliver secure, personalized bank-account information within an engaging Flash interface. You can also use Generator to dynamically create other, non-Flash types of assets such as GIFs, JPEGs, and PNGs. You can use it to deliver content on the fly to Palm devices or Web-based phones. Imagine a portal site created entirely within Flash that serves up personalized data such as finance news and stock prices that users can download to their PDAs each time they synchronize with their PCs.

While high-end developers responsible for big-budget corporate projects undoubtedly lick their lips as they contemplate all that Generator can do, creators of smaller-scale projects also have reason to get excited. Just because you're not creating an all-Flash interface for a *Fortune*-500 intranet doesn't mean you won't want to take advantage of Generator's capability to separate content from design. For example, Generator makes it much easier to incorporate those dreaded last-minute content changes from the client. It also enables you to frequently update data-driven assets such as charts and scrolling lists. And no matter how fast you are at editing Flash files, with Generator you can be even faster, because Generator enables you to edit the data source — and once you nail down the design of your template you don't even need to open up Flash.

SETTING UP GENERATOR

Make sure you have the Generator authoring templates installed. One of the best things about the authoring templates is that you can download a fully functional version for free from Macromedia's Web site at `www.macromedia.com/software/ generator/download`.

If you're using the newest version of Flash, you probably have the Authoring Extensions because they are included on most of the versions of Flash since Flash 5. If they're not part of your version of Flash, go to the Macromedia site to download and then install the templates. Once you've installed the templates, your Flash interface will have the extensions required for authoring Generator templates. These extensions include the Generator panel and the Generator Objects palette (7.2).

By themselves the Generator extensions don't come very close to fulfilling Generator's main purpose: to serve up dynamic content through Flash. So if your goal is to use Generator to present dynamic content and not merely as an aid in the manual updating of Flash files, then you'll need one of the two full-fledged flavors of Generator, Developer or Enterprise Edition.

AUTHOR PROFILE
Phillip M. Torrone

Coauthor of two forthcoming books on Flash and Generator, Phillip Torrone is a designer, developer, and inventor at Fallon Worldwide. From developing applications and hardware for the first PDA, the Apple Newton, to creating the first 100 percent Macromedia Flash-based, Generator-driven online bank, to creating Flash- and Generator-driven content for cell phones, devices, and automobiles, Phillip applies his diverse skills to push the boundaries of Flash and Generator. Recently featured in *Wired* magazine, Phillip currently sits on the Macromedia Flash Advisory Board, a Generator Premiere Partner, and regularly speaks at industry conferences and events. Fallon's clients include BMW of North America, Citi, drugstore.com, EDS, Holiday Inn, International Truck and Engine Corp., Lee Company, Nikon, Nordstrom, Nuveen Investments, PBS, Ralston Purina, Starbucks Coffee Company, Timex, and United Airlines.

CHOOSING A FLAVOR

The first of the two Generator flavors is the Developer Edition, a data-driven solution for automatically updating Flash and graphical content. It is designed primarily for use on projects that require scheduled, periodically updated content with low transaction volumes. The Generator Developer Edition includes a limited version of the Generator server component, as well as the Generator authoring templates. For coders who want to create their own custom Generator objects, it also includes a Software Development Kit (SDK) and an open API.

You can download a free trial edition of the Generator Developer Edition at `www.macromedia.com/software/generator/trial`. It is also included on the Flash 5 CD-ROM.

A popular way to use this flavor is with a common scheduling application to kick off offline Generator sessions, such as the Windows Task Manager (7.3) or Cron for Unix systems, which updates content automatically.

Offline mode relies on the executable component of Generator, called Generate. For PC users, this is basically a DOS application (generate.exe) that can run directly from the MS-DOS command line or from a

batch or scripting environment such as an MS-DOS batch file (7.4). For Unix folks, you can invoke the Offline Generator from the command line in a shell or from a Perl script.

With Online Generator, the Flash movie that is delivered to the user doesn't even exist until it is requested. Once it is requested, Generator cooks up the custom Flash movie on the fly and delivers it.

7.3

7.2

7.4

It's important to remember that, in Online mode, an .swt file is always being called in real time and used to produce an output that the developer has specified, or that the user has determined on request.

When Online Generator is given a request for a custom Flash file, it *marries* the data from the data source with the .swt by passing the request along to an instance of a Java servlet. Java servlets are objects used to process server-side requests and generate responses for the application, or for the client who made the request.

The Developer Edition does have some limitations. Because it processes only one request at a time, it is not useful for projects that require real-time generation of dynamic content. For example, you couldn't use this flavor on a site that serves up real-time data for a high-traffic personalized site. It also doesn't scale across multiple processors and is designed for low-volume Web sites that don't need up-to-the-minute content inside Flash. But though this flavor won't be able to handle Enterprise-class loads, lots of projects don't require that kind of performance.

Generator 2 Enterprise Edition is the heavy-hitter of the Generator flavors. It enables mission-critical, real-time information to be displayed to very large numbers of users, and it can still scale based on your needs. It can do everything the Developer Edition can do, and it also includes much more powerful features such as caching and a browser-based administration servlet. Generator 2 Enterprise Edition also supports multiprocessor systems, which are a prerequisite on sites with very high-volume traffic.

This flavor is the most expensive, but for deploying enterprise-class Generator projects, there is no substitute. How expensive? That depends on your usage, because it's transaction-based. The type of client that needs that type of mission-critical solution is the same client that spends millions on data centers, and software licenses, so the price of Generator Enterprise Edition has never been a deal breaker for those types of clients.

Perhaps you need real-time display of information based on data that changes frequently, or you're updating graphics that need to be part of a Flash interface. Real-time financial information such as charts and tickers needs to take advantage of real-time serving of content. Table 7-1 lists the platforms and Web servers both flavors of Generator will run on.

JRUNNING AROUND

When you install Generator Developer or Enterprise Edition, you also install the JRun application server from Allaire. JRun is the servlet engine and enables Generator to pass information to and from the Web server via the Java servlet protocol. The JRun servlet engine is preconfigured, and most users will never need to do more than start or restart the service. Macromedia goes through an intense certification process for these systems, and while advanced developers can dig in deep and get Generator to run in different environments, it's best to leave that up to the experts if you're not an expert on that sort of thing.

For our example, as well as all Generator templates (.swt), we can deploy our chart on either Developer or Enterprise Edition. One of the other benefits of using Generator is that the same template works on either version of Generator on any platform that Generator runs on. You can also just use the authoring templates for the chart example and use the Generator authoring templates as a free production automation tool.

GETTING TO KNOW GENERATOR VARIABLES

Generator variables, like Flash variables, are placeholders for values that you pass in later. Generator variable names must be surrounded by curly braces { } so Generator will recognize them. Generator variable data is passed in when the Generator template is processed. You supply the values for the variables in data sources that you create or use from a database, text file, or Java class.

NOTE

For a comprehensive guide to Generator check out *Flash and Generator Demystified: Building Advanced Web Applications* by Phillip M. Torrone and Chris Wiggins (Berkeley, CA: Peachpit Press: 2001).

TABLE 7-1   WHERE GENERATOR WORKS

PLATFORMS	WINDOWS WEB SERVERS	SOLARIS AND RED HAT WEB SERVERS
Windows NT 4.0 (with Service Pack 5.0 or higher installed) or Windows 2000	Internet Information Server 4.0	Apache HTTP server 1.3 or later (Solaris)
Windows 95, 98, or 2000	Internet Information Server 5.0 (Windows 2000 only)	Apache HTTP server 1.3.9 or greater (Red Hat)
Sun Solaris 2.6 or 2.7 (SPARC Processor (Intel version of Solaris is not supported)	Personal Web Server 4.0	Netscape Enterprise Server 3.5 and 3.6
Red Hat 6.1 Linux	iPlanet Web Server, Enterprise Edition 4.0 Dual processor server recommended for Enterprise Edition	iPlanet Web Server, Enterprise Edition 4.0

Generator variables can hold positions where you later insert any string of text. This includes not just visible text but also text inside ActionScript.

You can define Generator variables in the following places:

- Text boxes on the stage
- Parameters for Generator objects
- Parameters and arguments for Flash actions
- Frame labels
- Instance names

When using Generator variables with Flash 5 ActionScript, ActionScript treats Generator variables as strings. Generator variables must be enclosed in double quotes, as in "{myVariable}". For the actions and functions that accept string values for arguments, double quotes are supplied by Flash if the Expression checkbox is not selected. If the Expression checkbox is selected, or you are using Expert mode, you need to enter the double quotes around the Generator variable. For the actions and functions that do not accept strings as arguments, use one of the ActionScript functions to convert the string value inserted by Generator to the required type.

CHARTING

For our example we'll create a data-driven stock chart that displays the name of the stock market, the market values of the day, the date based on the server's system and also a complementary GIF for PDA/cell phone/device deployment. Here are the steps:

1. Start a new Flash movie (File ➤ New).

2. Choose Modify ➤ Movie to open the Movie Properties dialog box. Set the frame rate to 12 fps, dimensions to 400 × 280, and the background color to Black.

3. Create five new layers. Starting at the bottom and going up, name them **chartbg**, **chart frame**, **market text**, **date text**, and **chart**.

4. Select the Rectangle tool in the Drawing toolbar. Set the Corner Radius to 40 and draw a blue (#508CC8) filled rectangle in the "chartbg" layer.

5. Select the rectangle and use the Info panel (Window ➤ Panels ➤ Info) to modify the following settings: W: 380, H: 248, X: 10, Y: 29 (7.5).

6. In the chart text layer, specify a Generator variable. Use the Text tool to create a text box containing {market} in the market text layer (7.6). Make sure you stretch the text box as large as the area you wish the text to fill. Anytime you have different amounts of text coming in you should use a fixed-width text box so that the text wraps automatically.

> **NOTE**
>
> The names of the Generator variables can consist of any alphanumeric characters that are not case-sensitive. The variable name can contain spaces or any other nonalphanumeric characters, but shouldn't.

USING THE MANY CHART PARAMETERS

Select the chart layer and drag a Basic Chart Object onto the stage. You'll notice a ton of parameters (7.7). Set yours to the following values:

1. Enter **chartdata.txt** in the **Data Source** field. This is the text file we're going to create later to feed Generator the data. Data Source specifies the file name, relative or absolute URL, database connection URL, or Java class URL Generator uses to marry the data with the template. If we create a multiple line chart or a scatter chart, we could specify multiple data sources by entering a semicolon-delimited list of data sources.

2. **Chart Type** specifies the type of chart to create. Select Line.

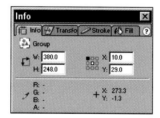

7.5

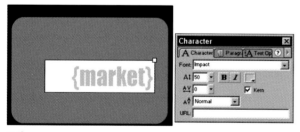

7.6

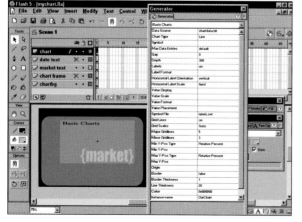

7.7

3. **Symbol** is the name of the symbol in the library to use for plotting points in scatter charts. Leave this blank because we're creating a line chart.

4. Set **Max Data Entries** to default. When set to Default or left blank, Max Data Entries has no effect on the chart; the number of values in the data source is displayed in the full width of the chart. This applies to all chart types except scatter. Max Data Entries controls the number of values displayed in the chart (both the maximum permitted and the minimum number for which space is allotted). For example, if Max Data Entries is set to 10, no more than the first ten values from the data source are plotted in the chart, and the remaining values in the data source are ignored. If Max Data Entries is set to 10 and only five values are provided, Generator renders those five values provided in the first half of the chart only.

5. Set the **Gap** to 0. This sets the amount of space to appear between objects plotted in the chart. Each unit is equal to 1/20 of a pixel. Set Gap applies to bar and stacked bar charts only.

6. Set the **3D Depth** to 300. This specifies the amount of depth to render in the chart (how deeply data is plotted along the Z axis). Each unit equals 1/20 of a pixel. Because we specified 300, our Line will be 15 pixels thick. The 3D Depth property applies to all chart types except scatter.

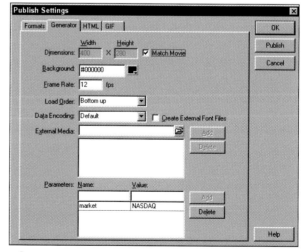

7.8

7. We want our chart to display the range of the market along with the time intervals; the range is on the Y axis so set the **Labels** property to on. This specifies whether labels should appear along the Y axis of the chart.

8. Leave the **Label Format** blank. Sounds crazy right? Not at all, because we're going to specify our own font labels for our chart. This is not a well know feature, hence a studio secret. Usually you specify one of the fonts available in the drop-down menu for this setting to set the font to use for the chart labels along the X and Y axes. Arial, Times are Courier are okay, but most of us want far more design control than that. After all, it's why we use Flash.

9. Set the **Horizontal Label Orientation** to Vertical. Label Orientation specifies whether the orientation of labels along the X axis. For our chart that will be the time interval and we want to display time intervals in a way that we can see them. This property requires the `hlabel` column in the data source that we'll specify as the time of day when we create the data source.

10. Set **Horizontal Label Scale** to fixed. This specifies the size of the label. The label can be scaled to fit the chart element (scale to fit) or displayed at the symbol size (fixed). Half and Double display the symbol at half or double its original size. You can also enter a numerical scale factor to apply to the symbol. For example, entering **0.50** scales the label to half the symbol size.

11. Value Display can be set to blank. This specifies whether the numeric value data should appear in the chart (always or never), or whether it is visible only when the pointer is over the chart area (rollover). This property only applies to bar, stacked bar, and scatter charts.

12. Set the **Value Scale** to blank. This indicates whether or not the text that displays the value data, when Value Display is set to Always or Roll-over, should scale to fit within the chart element's area or within a fixed size. This property only applies to bar, stacked bar, and scatter charts.

13. Set the **Value Format** to blank. This sets the font to use for the chart value labels appearing within the body of the chart. This property only applies to bar, stacked bar, and scatter charts.

14. Set the **Value Placement** to blank. This specifies where value labels should be positioned within a bar chart. This property only applies to bar, stacked bar, and scatter charts.

15. For the **External Symbol File**, type in **labels.swt**. This specifies the path to an external Generator template containing the symbols to use for chart labels and values. Because we set Labels to on, we're going to create a file that has a symbol named `chartLabel1` containing the variable `{label}`, and a symbol named `chartValue1` with the variable `{value}` for values in the font we want to use. If you're creating a scatter chart and use position labels, you must specify a symbol file. These labels are available to all chart types; values are available to bar, stacked bar, and scatter charts only.

16. Set **Grid Lines** to on. This specifies whether or not grid lines are displayed behind the chart.

17. Often you don't know how many grid lines may come from your data source so set the **Grid Scales** to Auto. Generator can calculate the number and position of grid lines automatically (auto) or calculate the position for the number of grid lines specified by the Major and Minor Grid Lines properties (manual).

18. For the **Major Grid Lines** property type in **5**. This specifies that five of the bolder grid lines will be drawn in the chart.

19. Set the **Minor Grid Lines** to **3**. This specifies the number of lines between the bolder grid lines will be drawn in the chart.

20. Set the **Min Y-Pos Type** to Relative Percent. This adjusts the chart's minimum value to the data by calculating a minimum value as a function of the range that the data spans. With Relative Percent, the minimum value on the chart is the minimum data value minus the difference between the data's maximum and minimum values multiplied by the percentage specified for Min Y-Pos. This calculation is made according to the following formula:

```
Minimum chart value = Minimum value -
(Maximum value - Minimum value) * Min
Y-Pos
```

When set to Absolute, Min Y-Pos Type is the lowest value represented in the chart.

21. Leave **Min Y-Pos** blank because we set Min Y-Pos Type to Relative Percent.

22. Also set **Max Y-Pos Type** to Relative Percent. This adjusts the chart's minimum value to the data by calculating a minimum value as a function of the range that the data spans. With Relative Percent, the minimum value on the chart is the minimum data value minus the difference between the data's maximum and minimum values multiplied by the percentage specified for Max Y-Pos. This calculation is according to the following formula:

$$\text{Maximum chart value} = \text{Maximum value} + (\text{Maximum value} - \text{Minimum value}) \times \text{Max Y-Pos}$$

When set to Absolute, Max-Y Pos is the highest value represented in the chart.

23. Set the **Origin** to blank. This specifies the positioning of the values equaling zero in the chart. Because we're viewing a range of data over time, this doesn't apply to our chart.

24. Set **Border** to false. This toggles a bounding rectangle around the chart object and displays the color value specified in the Color property.

> **NOTE**
>
> You may wonder why we purposely made some default fields blank. Although they don't "hurt" anything, when you pass a complicated file such as a stock chart to other members of the team, it is best not have extraneous information that can cause confusion in the workflow. Generator charts are much like playing Jenga; if you pull one piece out, your little chart will completely fall apart.
>
> Something else worth noting is *every value* we specified inside the chart can be a Generator variable in the curly braces and we could manage all the properties of the chart as well as the data externally via any number of data sources from a Java class to ODBC/JDBC.

Although it's a nice feature for quick prototyping, we're going to create our own frame for the chart.

25. We turned **Border Thickness** off but this property still controls width of the major grid lines. Because we want a very thin line, type in **1**. If wanted to make a thicker line, each unit equals ¹⁄₂₀ of a pixel.

26. Set the **Line Thickness** to **20**. This specifies the width of lines that display data in the chart. In this property each unit also equals ¹⁄₂₀ of a pixel.

27. Set the **Color** to black. Color sets the Web-safe color name (for our example, black), Web hexadecimal value (#000000), or regular hexadecimal value (0x000000) of the color for the chart. For bar, stacked bar, stacked area, stacked line, and scatter chart types, this value applies only to the grid lines and borders of the chart. For line and area charts, this value is also used to render the chart line or filled area of the chart.

28. Set the **Instance name** to **OurChart**. Just like a movie clip, Instance name identifies the instance of the object so that it can be used with actions such as `setProperty`. In our example, we'll use `loadMovie` to refresh the chart.

29. Now is a good time to save your work. Call the file **mychart.fla** and place it in a new folder. This is where we'll be keeping many of the assets.

For a detailed description of each parameter and all Generator charts, consult the Generator documentation or the *Flash 5 Bible* (from Hungry Minds, Inc., 2001).

CREATING THE DATA SOURCE

Now on to the data source. Usually, for financial information you'll be querying a database using a Java servlet or getting the feeds via a middleware source. For this example we'll create our own data source in a text file, as follows:

1. Open a text editor such as Notepad or SimpleText and type **value,color,hlabel**.

  - **value** is the value of the stock market for that particular row of data, or interval.

■ **color** is the column that we'll specify a value for just once in the first line. We're going to call it green in the first row. If we do not specify a new color, Generator makes our chart color the same as the chart lines — black. You can specify any Web-safe color name, Web hexadecimal, or regular hexadecimal value.

■ **hlabel** is the label that appears on the Y axis. These values will be times and start and close times of the market.

2. For the values, type the following text after the first line in your text file:

```
3240.54,green,Open
3144.81,,
3168.05,,
3199.30,,10:00am
3199.07,,
3186.85,,
3167.15,,
3173.22,,
3150.87,,
3127.17,,11:00am
3129.78,,
3105.26,,
3134.47,,
3144.51,,
3172.86,,
3161.83,,12:00pm
3197.24,,
3193.17,,
3227.67,,
3252.79,,
3225.35,,
3218.37,,1:00pm
3228.12,,
3218.34,,
3212.12,,
3225.66,,
3238.47,,
3249.55,,2:00pm
3254.19,,
3234.40,,
3239.08,,
3218.43,,
```

```
3216.73,,
3226.47,,3:00pm
3186.30,,
3180.80,,
3181.60,,
3200.87,,
3190.40,,
3168.38,,4:00pm
3168.17,,
3168.51,,
3168.49,,Close
```

These are the approximate NASDAQ values for a sample day. You can find many stock feeds out there; most are delayed 20 minutes. If you're on a project that requires this type of feed, the client most likely has a relationship in place and you'll just need to specify the format to the feed vendor.

3. Save the text file as **chartdata.txt**. Make sure this text file is in the same directory as any .fla files for this project.

We have five intervals in our data source, between each `hlabel`, so our chart has some activity between the labels. If this chart was going to be used for a purpose such as an annual report or a weekly chart that was updated, then managing this text file and using Flash to recompile the file or using Generator to periodically create a new updated .swf file would be the most efficient way to do it.

The following are additional steps for creating a data source file:

1. Go to the publish settings (File ➤ Publish Settings).

2. Under Type, check the boxes for Flash (.swf) and Generator Template (.swt).

3. Click the Generator tab in the Publish Settings dialog box and add parameters, which will be used to define variables (7.8). Type **market** into the Name field, and **NASDAQ** into the Value text field. Click the Add button to add these parameters. These parameters are actually not part of the final Generator template (.swt). But use them as a convenient way to test templates locally as part of development.

4. Finally, choose Control ➤ Test Movie. The Output window should appear. This is normal; this is your "window" into seeing what Generator is passing in as data and also where you'll see errors if they occur.

If you don't see any information in the window, under the Options menu of the Output window, set the Debug Level to Verbose (7.9). With this setting you can do the following:

- Examine the output of database queries or URL results using the Output window to ensure that the expected result is returned.
- Verify that the templates work as expected using static data before attempting to integrate dynamic data. This also ensures a thorough knowledge of the template's data source requirements.
- Create text file data sources to stand in for database or URL data sources.

Now back to our movie. You'll notice a few things you're probably not expecting. The labels defaulted to Arial because we haven't made our Symbol File yet (labels.swt). Also, the chart needs a frame to make it look like it's sitting in some 3D type space (7.10).

FRAME THAT CHART

Let's address the lack of a border on the chart first. We didn't specify a border in the chart settings so we'll

create one now. But how can we see the chart? It's just a box on the stage. Here's how to frame the chart:

1. Revisit the Publish Settings and in the Formats tab in the Type: settings panel, select PNG Image (.png) and then Publish the movie.

2. Now add one more layer to your movie and call it **chart guide**. Make the chart guide layer a Guide layer by selecting the layer, choosing Modify ➤ Layer to open the Layer Properties panel, and setting Type to Guide. Click OK to close the Layer Properties panel. Select the first frame in the chart guide layer and import the PNG we just published (select File ➤ Import, and then choose mychart.png). Now we can see the chart.

3. Using the Line Tool, the Paint Bucket, and other usual tools create a frame on the chart frame layer (refer to the picture here to match it to the example) or feel free to create your own. Keep testing your movie to get it exactly the way you want (7.11).

Now is a good time to save your work again before we create the custom labels in a Symbol file.

CREATING THE SYMBOL FILE

Start a new Flash movie. This is just a holder file for a couple of symbols so all the default settings are acceptable.

We're going to insert two movie clips that contain the fonts for the chart labels. First, create a new movie clip

7.9

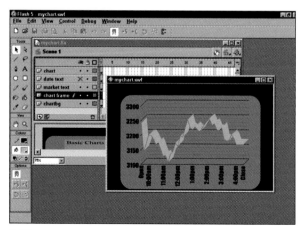

7.10

symbol named **chartLabel1**. This must be the name, so don't use anything else. Inside the `chartLabel1` movie clip, create a text box containing the following text: `{label}`.

Enter the font and size you want to use for the chart labels, and make the text block fixed—large enough to contain eight characters. For our example, use Impact with a font height of 16. If you don't have this font, feel free to use another one; you can always change it if it doesn't look good inside the chart. It actually doesn't matter where you place the text in the movie clip, but being good Flash developers means placing it somewhere near the center of the stage so others can find it.

Add one more movie clip symbol, named **chart Value1**. This must be the name, so don't use anything else. Inside the `chartValue1` movie clip, create a text box containing the following text: `{value}`.

Enter the font and size you want to use for the chart values (7.12). For this example, again use Impact with a font height of 16. As with the other movie clip, it doesn't matter where we place this on the stage, and the font choice is up to you.

If you're an advanced developer, you may notice the similarities of using a symbol file and external media files with Generator and using embedded fonts and shared libraries with Flash 5 and above. The fact is, Generator makes the smallest possible .swf without having to load in a new library and tacking on an embedded font. When you process a Flash Template (.swt), Generator uses only the characters and the symbols needed in the movie, thus making the smallest possible file. Generator also enables you to publish to the multiple formats, including earlier versions of Flash, all at once. For some projects this is a requirement and for others Flash 5 and above may be better suited after you become accustomed to working with both Flash and Generator together you'll start to see how they actually compliment each other quite well.

Now is a good time to save your work before you publish this file. Save this file in the same directory as the mychart.fla file, and call this file **labels.fla**. Open the Publish Settings dialog box (File ➣ Publish Settings) and select the Generator template. Make sure the file name is labels.swt; as you may recall, that's the name of the symbol file we specified in our chart (7.13).

Click the Publish button and close the Publish Settings dialog box. Go back and test your stock chart. Switch back over to the mychart.fla file and choose Control ➣ Test Movie. Voilà! That's a pretty nice-looking stock chart (7.14). To quote Eric Wittman's oft-used phrase about Flash, "But wait, there's more!" We're not quite finished yet. Let's delete the guide layer and the PNG in the library for tidiness.

GIF IT UP

In mychart.fla, go to the publish settings (File ➣ Publish Settings) and select GIF Image (.gif) Type in the Formats tab, and also deselect the PNG Image

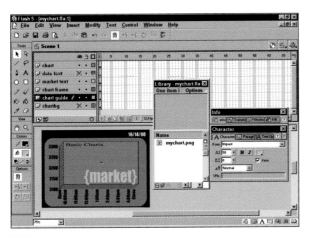

7.11

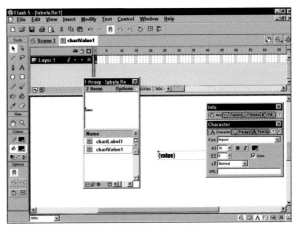

7.12

NOTE

If you don't have Developer or Enterprise Edition, this is where you can stop, install the Developer Edition, purchase Enterprise Edition, or just follow along. As you most likely have observed, once the chart is created, all you need to do is modify one text file and republish the Flash movie. This is something almost any person with even the most basic skill level can accomplish. If you're following along, we're going to do a few more things to make our chart ready for prime time.

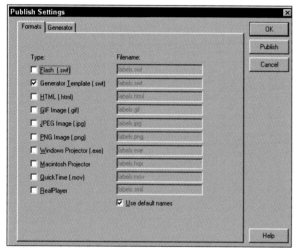

7.13

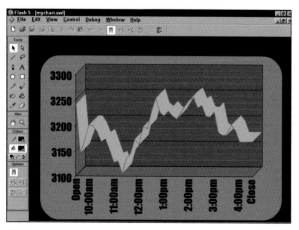

7.14

(.png) type. Click the GIF tab and set the Playback to Static (7.15). If this were an animated Flash chart or if the movie had multiple frames, we would have labels inside the Flash movie that indicated where Generator would go to grab the image or series of images.

To specify a single frame, other than the first frame in the movie, for a static GIF, place a frame label called **#static** on the frame of the Flash movie timeline to be included in the static GIF.

To specify a range of frames to be included in an animated GIF, place a frame label called **#first** on the first frame of the range of frames in the timeline to be included in the animated GIF and place a frame label called **#last** on the last frame of that frame range.

Next, click Publish. Open the folder where you're saving all your work and open the mychart.gif. If you're not happy with the palette or any of the settings, always modify the Publish settings.

IT'S A DATE FOR JAVA

In the date text layer, add {**short_date**}. Make the text and font whatever you choose, but make sure you make the text block large enough to contain a shortened date format of eight characters.

We just happen to have a Java class that returns the date based on the server's time. Why is this important? For mission-critical applications such as building online banks in Flash or trading stocks through Flash, the client's machine time is irrelevant; instead, we

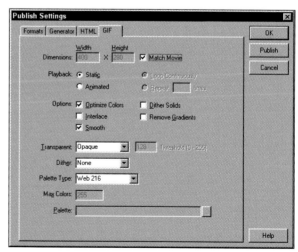

7.15

need to present an accurate data and timestamp that reflects the business from the server side.

In the Generator Environment Variable button above the timeline, you specify the name of the Java class. In our case it's `fgjava:///DateData Source` (7.16).

If this Java Class accepted parameters, you could also specify them here. You could also use a Generator variable here, but let's not get too carried away.

The start of the line, `fgjava:///`, tells Generator the data source is a Java class. It's important to remember if you're going to use Java classes for just authoring to make sure the Java class is on your hard drive in your Flash\Generator\Classes folder for Macs, and in the Generator\Classes folder on PCs. If you're using Generator Developer Edition or Enterprise Edition, this class needs to be in your Generator Classes folder, unless you modify the **generator.properties** file in the Generator\Properties folder. Most of the time the default setting is as follows:

```
com.macromedia.generator.userclasspath
=C\:\\Program\ Files\\Macromedia\\
Generator\ 2\\classes
```

You can also modify this setting in the Generator Administration servlet with Generator Enterprise Edition, along with many other settings (7.17). The User Class Path field specifies the folder where your Java data source classes are stored. If left blank, Generator defaults to the classes folder at the root level of the Generator application folder. You can also specify the labels.swt symbol file as the default symbol file for all charts and tables. If left blank, Generator uses the DefaultSymbolFile.swt in the bin folder at the root level of the Generator program folder.

Now test the movie (Control ➤ Test Movie). This time, a date appears (7.18).

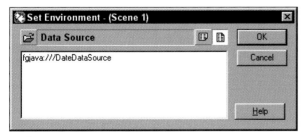

7.16

DEPLOYING THE TEMPLATE

If we were to deploy our template on a live Generator Server for real-time use, our HTML would need to look like this:

```
<HTML>
<HEAD>
<TITLE>mychart</TITLE>
</HEAD>
<BODY bgcolor="#000000">
<!-- URL's used in the movie-->
<!-- text used in the movie-->
<OBJECT classid="clsid:D27CDB6E-AE6D-
11cf-96B8-444553540000"
codebase="http://download.macromedia.
```

7.17

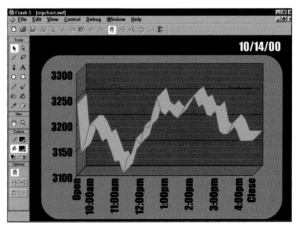

7.18

```
com/pub/shockwave/cabs/flash/swflash.
cab#version=5,0,0,0"
 WIDTH=400 HEIGHT=280>
 <PARAM NAME=movie VALUE="mychart.swt?
market=NASDAQ"> <PARAM NAME=quality
VALUE=autohigh> <PARAM NAME=bgcolor
VALUE=#000000> <EMBED src="mychart.
swt?market=NASDAQ" quality=autohigh
bgcolor=#000000 WIDTH=400 HEIGHT=280
TYPE="application/x-shockwave-flash"
PLUGINSPAGE="http://www.macromedia.com
/shockwave/download/index.cgi?P1_Prod_
Version=ShockwaveFlash"></EMBED>
</OBJECT>
</BODY>
</HTML>
```

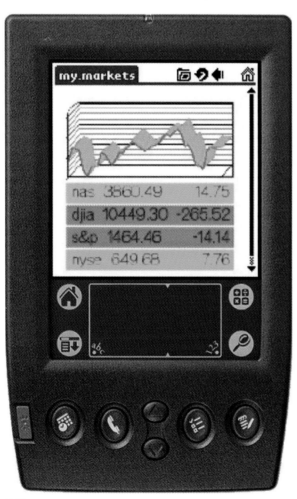

7.19

In the OBJECT and EMBED tags we specify the template (mychart.swt) and we pass the name of the market. Remember, it's only set in the Publish Settings for testing; it's not actually part of the template. By passing it in via the URL we can always change the name without opening Flash.

You can specify any media type that Generator supports via the URL. If we wanted this to be a GIF, we'd place an image tag in our HTML that looked like this:

```
<IMG SRC="mychart.swt?type=gif&market
=NASDAQ" WIDTH=400 HEIGHT=280 BORDER=0>
```

The only other graphic file format that's more supported than Flash is GIF. We can use the same template for Web browsers, print, PDAs, phones, appliances, television graphics, and anywhere a graphic can go (7.19).

ENGLISH IS SPOKEN IN ONLY 18 PERCENT OF THE WORLD

One last thing before we call this a chart.

J'aime le Flash — Ich mag Blitz — Gradisco il Flash — Tengo gusto del Flash

That's your author using babelfish. altavista.digital.com to illustrate that there's more than one way to present your message besides English. With Generator, you can publish multiple language versions of your charts with just one template. If you take a close look at the Publish Settings in the Generator tab, you'll also see the various encoding options available for other operating systems (7.20).

DECIDING ON A GENERATOR APPLICATION

The goal of our next project is to deliver several phases of a Web-based application that provide information to consumers about floor plans offered in new housing tracts built by SheaHomes.

The first phase of the project was to display drawings of all standard floor plans for each model (home) in every active community built by SheaHomes. The solution to this problem was to create static GIF files for each floor plan, catalog them in a database, and dynamically serve them to an HTML page using ColdFusion. It was also necessary to provide an online style guide to define image dimensions and style for use by external agencies (7.21).

The second phase of the project involved developing and implementing a Web-based user interface to enable SheaHomes.com visitors to visually change floor plans by selecting from a menu of predefined options. Visitors needed to be able to print the customized floor plans and application administration needed to be kept to a minimum. The goal was to create a highly functional user experience that more effectively communicates the options available for each home while engaging the customer in the product.

The solution was to create interactive Flash movies with a vector drawing of the floor plan and menus of predefined floor plan options. To keep the number of options reasonably limited, "floor plan options" were defined as any option that changes the walls or foundation of the home (7.22). This eliminated the possibility for confusion with the myriad other options available for a home.

Juxt designers then designed the user interface to provide easy and intuitive access to floor plan options. Next, Flash developers constructed a sample floor plan as a Flash 4 movie.

To print the floor plan (as configured by the user), a print button was included to use the following Flash

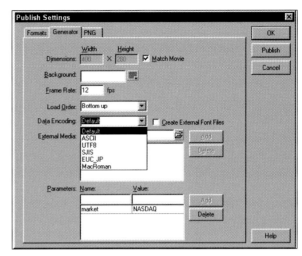

7.21

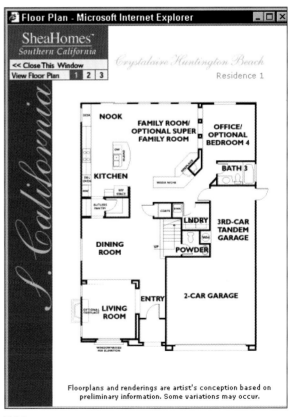

7.22

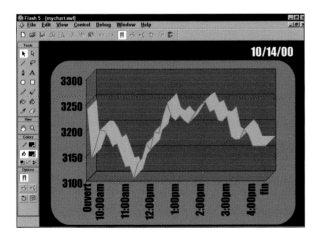

7.20

4 ActionScript: `Get URL ("print:", window=
"/floorplan")`. The sample Flash source (.fla)
was given to SheaHomes to be used as a guideline for
agencies to which Shea could outsource for mass production.

The online style guide was updated to include the
footprint and style for Flash floor plans. Finally, Juxt
updated Shea's content management and public Web
sites to handle Flash floor plans. The core solution
used pure Flash. There really wasn't a need to employ
Generator here, because the floor plan drawings had
to be custom-drawn or converted for each model
home. When the project objectives were examined,
Flash was a perfect solution all by itself.

The third phase of the SheaHomes project integrated Generator deeply into the application. The
goal was to develop a solution to enable real-time
price updates driven by a database and enable
SheaHomes administrators to disable home options
that are no longer available (7.23). It was also important to use technology to expand maintainability and
contain the cost of employing Flash floor plans while
leveraging floor plan renderings for use in future
planned visual interfaces (for example, furniture
placement and electrical/plumbing selections).

Juxt's first Flash-based floor plan solution involved
creating a single, self-contained Flash movie for each
home model. While this was a simple solution (and
simple solutions are almost always better than complex

ones) it had a few caveats. First, a lot of content was
duplicated because the user-interface design
and standard elements were exactly the same for every
Flash movie. Each movie contained four core components:

- User-interface (UI) design (branding, look, and
  feel)
- Standard UI elements (controls and help)
- Custom UI elements (floor plan options)
- Custom floor plan renderings

Second, because the UI design and UI elements
were duplicated into each movie, it would be costly to
make changes to the design or UI features. All of the
movies would have to be manually changed and
republished. While Juxt could have specified a movie
structure that would have solved this, it would have
required an unacceptable level of complexity for the
goals at the time. Basically, it would have blown the
budget, and over-engineered the solution. What
SheaHomes really wanted was a quick solution to
show interactive, printable floor plans on the Web.

Third, because the renderings were built into the
same movie as the floor plan user interface, they were
useless to any future applications.

In phase two of the project, there was no need
to involve a database to drive the list of options.
Because phase three required a database-driven list of
option pricing and availability, it made sense to also

SECTION AUTHOR

Phil Scott

Todd Purgason (left), Phil Scott (right)
and the rest of the team at Juxt Interactive recently created a Flash home-
builder Web application for SheaHomes
(www.sheahomes.com). The project
uses Flash 4 and Generator to deliver a
robust program that enables home buy-
ers to configure the home they want
SheaHomes to build for them. Phil Scott
discusses the way the project was developed and the thought process behind
using Generator.

Phil Scott is the chief technology officer
of Juxt Interactive, a Web design-technol-
ogy company aimed at participating in
the definition of interactive media while
meeting real world objectives for its
clients. His background is in traditional
and Web-based applications, programming, and project management.

dynamically build the menu of options from the database. It was clear that this would involve some programming that should somehow be developed once and reused for every floor plan. The solution was to separate the user interface from the floor plan rendering (7.24). This strategy eliminated the duplication problem by consolidating the user interface into a single application movie. It also enabled the renderings to be easily repurposed into other Flash applications using Flash's Load Movie action. So far, the solution still fell within the realm of pure Flash.

Juxt converted the custom menu of floor plan options into a database-driven menu (7.25). This enabled the custom menus to be built into a single application movie. Because we would already need to employ a database to tie pricing and availability to each floor plan option, why not add the names of each option and let the database provide the options menu? This could be done in a number of different ways.

SERVER-SIDE ASSEMBLY (THE GENERATOR WAY)

Generator could assemble the menu items with the List object. This would require designing a movie clip to encapsulate the look and behavior of the desired buttons. The clip would be supplied with eight frames, each representing one mode of the option

(for example, Den, Optional Study, and Optional Play Room use the first three frames). This allows for up to eight variations on one floor plan option. The list object populates itself from a JDBC or URL data

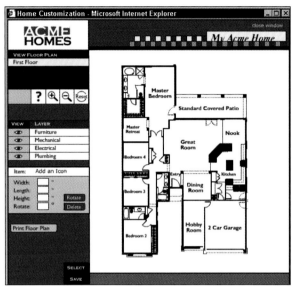

7.24

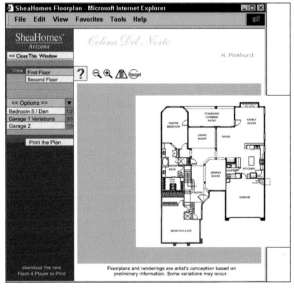

7.25

7.23

source. For most cases URLs are the best Generator data sources because they enable the flexibility of using middleware such as ColdFusion to format the data the way Generator needs it. As a result, we would code a ColdFusion script to query the database for a list of available options and prices. It would spew forth a familiar CSV data stream with the following column names:

```
clip, optioncode,
caption1, price1,
caption2, price2,
caption3, price3,
caption4, price4,
caption5, price5,
caption6, price6,
caption7, price7,
caption8, price8
```

Example data values for the Den option are as follows:

```
clipFPOption, den,
Den, 0,
Optional Study, 750.00,
Optional Play Room, 400.00,
, ,
, ,
, ,
, ,
, ,
```

The List object would place these data values into each button in the list. The result would be a list of buttons (resembling a menu), assembled on the server.

Another possible solution would be to handcraft a Generator menu object in Java using the Generator Extensions API. The reason to do this would be to simplify the data format needed for the List object to do its job, cutting out the middleware (ColdFusion), thus gaining a slight improvement in performance. For the effort required to build and debug the custom Generator object, the folks at Juxt decided to work within the confines of the prebuilt List object. "It's convenient, it's debugged, and it's familiar to all Generator developers. I would need a stronger reason than a slight performance gain and a simplified data format to build a custom Generator object," observes Phil.

Generator could also do the dirty work of joining the application movie with the floor plan movie. This could be done offline (see the generate.exe command), or it could be served on-demand (serving the movies directly from an .swt file). Either way, the Generator template would use a simple Insert SWF object to merge the floor plan movie into the application movie before serving it to the user.

CLIENT-SIDE ASSEMBLY (THE FLASH ACTIONSCRIPT WAY)

It would be possible to bypass Generator, and stick with a pure Flash approach. It's amazing what a Flasher can do with Load Movie and Load Variables in ActionScript.

The Load Variables action retrieves data from a URL, and uses the data as normal everyday Flash variables. Yes, Flash talks to the database. It just requires a script to be inserted in the middle. The trick is to point the URL to a server script (ASP, ColdFusion, JSP, CGI . . .), which formats the data into a *URL-encoded query string*—the kind you see on the end of the URL: userid=1&username=Joe+User. This technique is extremely enabling. (Fred Sharples of Orange Design first introduced Phil Scott to this technique.)

Consequently, Juxt could dynamically build a menu with Flash ActionScript. They would use the Load Variables command to get all of the data about the floor plan options. Using a single movie clip with eight frames (for up to eight variations on a floor plan option), they would use the Duplicate Movie Clip command to create several menu items. Then, the script would use the Set Property action to position the X and Y coordinates of each menu item. All of this would be done in a Loop so that it only has to

> **NOTE**
>
> While it can be tempting to use the Load Variables action any number of times in a Flash movie, for performance reasons, we prefer only to dip into the server once for the variables. This is purely an optimization of HTTP traffic; not a deficiency in Flash.

be programmed once, no matter how many floor plan options are found in the database.

The result would be a menu of movie clips that behave like buttons, all dynamically assembled by Flash with a little help from a ColdFusion server script and a database.

Using Flash's Load Movie action from the application movie (the one with all the ActionScript programming and UI design), the external floor plan movie could be brought into the intended area of the user interface. Flash would perform this action as soon as the first frame of the movie starts playing. This means that a little motion graphics are in order (at a minimum show a "Loading . . ." indicator) to keep the user occupied while the second movie streams in.

COMPARING THE SOLUTIONS

With a Generator-based solution, the Flash plug-in would not have to assemble the menu or talk to any middleware. All this work is done on the server. This reduces the work that the user's computer has to do before the user can use the application; this is an important factor when one considers that some users still use sub-300 MHz computers.

Here, bandwidth is not the only consideration. Processing power is. Not every consumer is going to choke down the applications that we develop on our megagigahertz development stations, especially if the application is competing for the user's time while attempting to solve a real business problem digitally. If the user has an alternative, not to mention universally accepted, method of getting floor plans and pricing (say, using the telephone or, heaven forbid, driving to the model home site), the digital designer had better not provide an excuse for him or her to be frustrated with the online method. The floor plans had better load and assemble quickly. Yes, even on a Pentium 233.

NOTE

The Flash floor plans seen in this chapter can be found in various states of implementation at `www.sheahomes.com`, the Arizona division of the SheaHomes Web site.

We know what solution Juxt chose (and you probably do too). Ignore the soapbox for a moment and decide which solution you would choose. With your intended audience, would it matter so much if the user's computer had to work harder to pull the dynamic pieces together? Would the user even recognize the difference? Would the benefits of server-side assembly of data-driven Flash be significant enough for your project to choose Generator? How about the cost of maintaining your solution?

Compare the Generator plus Flash versus pure Flash decision to the traditional client versus server question faced in HTML-based programming. With a sufficiently powerful (albeit browser-challenged) JavaScript language built into Web browsers, Web programmers have the choice of building intelligence into Web pages on the client side or the server side. So far, most have chosen the server side. (Admittedly, this statistic is skewed a bit because of the pain involved in developing JavaScript that works across browser versions and platforms.) But, advantages weigh heavily toward server-side intelligence:

- **Less bandwidth consumption.** Sending all that programming code to the client along with all the data needed by the programming to make its decisions does occupy bytes across the wire.
- **Secure code.** The logic is safely on the server, not floating around on the browser where someone else can deconstruct it.
- **Controlled processing environment.** The server provides the processing power and environment for program execution, thus controlling and guaranteeing the reliability and performance of the application.

We hope to have shown some of the thought put into visual interface technology decisions. Every project will tend to have different objectives. For the more advanced visual interface needs of the Shea-Homes project, Juxt selected Flash, and subsequently Generator to construct a solution.

Flash is a strong visual interface technology all by itself. Yes, Flash can be data-driven without Generator. However, with the addition of Generator, wisely applied, the process of developing real-world visual solutions in Flash becomes cheaper, easier, and faster.

SSOfX

Flash

File View Control Help

_ □ ✕

Scene 1

Sound Effects3
SoundEffects2
SoundEffects1
Intro/Outro Tunes

27   12.0 fps   2.2s

BE SURE TO KEEP IT LEGAL.

GENERALLY WORK WITH 44.1 KHZ 16 BIT AUDIO.

HER ONE SPOKEN LINE, "I KNOW KUNG FU."

BETH AM R-WBETH I-YFED GYNTA?

2:00

ADJUST THE LOOP POINTS TO HIT ON A "ZERO CROSSING" WHERE THE WAVEFORM CROSSES THE HORIZONTAL AXIS.

DATE: 3-17-01

SCALE: 1" = 72 DPI

DRAWN: PERKINS

JOB: FLASH & SOUND

SHEET:
8
OF 16

F C B

CHAPTER 8
GETTING GREAT SOUND IN FLASH

BY HEATHER PERKINS

M usic and sound are integral parts of any multimedia design project. Sound has the power to impart a message, set a mood, or make an impression. The sonic palette available to the Flash designer includes music, character voices, voice-overs, sound effects, aural feedback on rollover states or mouse-click, and more. Virtually anything is possible.

When working in Web-based multimedia, it is vital for the designer to consider the medium. The goal is to use the strengths of the available tools, work within the limitations of the medium, and, whenever possible, try to expand the capabilities of the medium. This is especially true with music and sound design.

The bottom line: plan your music and audio production, design for the medium, know your material, be creative, and experiment. And have fun.

HEATHER PERKINS

PLANNING YOUR PROJECT

A designer must know his or her medium, understand the intended impact and audience of the piece, and plan ahead. Just as the visual and sonic elements should compliment each other, file size and sound quality need to be balanced as well.

In short, plan your music and audio production, design for the medium, know your material, be creative, and experiment. Every project will be different.

KEEPING IT LEGAL

Many people have misconceptions about which sounds and music are legal to use. Some people think that just because you can find a sound file online, and download it, that it is legal to use that sound in whatever way they choose. However, the notion that it is legal to use even just a small portion of a copyrighted work is a myth. It is not legal to use even a few seconds of any copyrighted material.

When creating or contracting Flash soundtracks, know your sources. Check the legal rights of whatever music and sound you use. Ideally, you will work with a professional sound designer or composer, create the music and sound yourself, or get your music and sound from a legal buy-out library. But be sure to keep it legal.

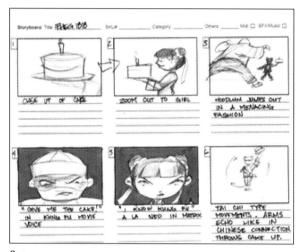

8.1

PREPRODUCTION PLANNING

I was asked to do sound design for a character animation (a cartoon with characters and a storyline). The project, titled *Kung Fu Birthday*, was to be an animated Flash greeting card for the Egreetings site.

Preproduction planning is an essential element of good sound and music design. In the case of this project, I worked with a storyboard from Flash artist Marc Aure to help determine which sonic elements would be needed (8.1).

Marc also kept me informed about changes to the action. In this case, three scenes were eventually deleted from the storyboard to tighten up the action and save file size. Egreetings animations are delivered in their final form as .swf files, and need to be kept to around 200–250K in size, so I took that into account as part of my design. This enabled me to design to the medium from the start, instead of making sacrifices at the end of the development cycle.

Looking at the storyboard, I knew I needed three pieces of music, several sound effects, and voices for the two characters. To save file size, I decided to create a looping track for the intro music and the fight scene intro, and to create a continuous music track for the end of the animation.

I usually like to get any spoken lines recorded ahead of time, so that the animator can synchronize the character's mouth movements to the audio. In this case, however, we wanted the mouth movements to be

AUTHOR PROFILE
Heather Perkins

Heather Perkins creates music and sound for Flash, new media, video, and dance at WaterDog Studio (www.waterdogstudio.com), and is currently accepting contract work.

THE STUDIO
I am the sound director for Egreetings Network in San Francisco, but I do all of my music and sound work at WaterDog Studio in Portland, Oregon. This is made possible through the miracle of a fast DSL connection. Egreetings Network is the premiere creator of animated Flash greetings, and my work has to cover many moods and musical genres.

I have a fully equipped music and sound studio, with three Macintosh computers, "real" musical instruments such as guitars and a Celtic harp, and a full MIDI (musical instrument digital interface) and digital audio studio to create, record and digitize original music for use in Flash. I also have a small recording booth for recording voices and custom sound effects, and several royalty-free music and sound-effects libraries.

out of synch, to imitate the effect of a badly dubbed Kung Fu movie so I was able to record the voices at my leisure.

At this point, I did a little research. I knew from talking with Marc that we wanted the girl to say "I know Kung Fu," imitating a line from the movie *The Matrix* (Warner Studios, 1999). I rented *The Matrix* so I could get the line reading correctly, and also rented a couple of Kung Fu movies, to see what kind of music was appropriate. During this time, Marc was creating the animation on Flash. The plan was for him to deliver the Flash file to me when nearly complete, I would add the audio, and send it back to him for final polishing. I began planning with the storyboard, but waited until I had a Flash file to actually begin the work.

First, I sat down and watched the animation a few times. I then plotted the action out on a timeline grid with pencil and paper, planning exactly how many seconds of audio I needed, and where the sounds would occur (8.2).

I also exported the silent animation as an .swf to see how much room would be left for audio. I'd already estimated how much sound I would need, and it looked as if I would have plenty of room for all the sound required. So I got to work on the sound itself.

DIGITAL AUDIO BASICS

This is a good time to cover some basics about digital audio. Sound in Flash is imported as digital audio. Digital audio is analog sound that has been converted into digital information. When you digitize analog sound, the analog sound is sampled at discrete intervals by the computer, and stored as digital information called a sound file or audio file. Macs generally use the .aiff file format for audio, while Windows computers generally use the .wav file format. (Flash 5 enables you to import other kinds of audio, such as MP3 audio, but I always work with standard audio files.)

The *sampling rate* of a sound refers to the number of samples per second used to digitally represent the sound. Sampling rates are expressed as a frequency, in hertz or kilohertz per second. This tells you how many times per second the computer "took a picture" of the sound. The higher the sampling rate, the better the sound quality. So if you sample audio at 44.1 kHz/sec,

it will sound much better than if you sample it at 11.025 kHz/sec.

Bit-rate is also an important factor in digital audio quality. The higher the bit-rate, the better the resolution of the digitized sound. The more bits used to describe the sound, the more accurate the digital representation of that sound will be. Audio bit-rate can be compared to the resolution of film. The visual quality of a film increases with film size. A 35mm film looks much better than an 8mm film, and 16-bit audio sounds much better than 8-bit audio.

For Egreetings, I generally work with 44.1 kHz 16-bit audio. Flash will only let you correctly import audio at standard sampling rates of 11.025 kHz, 22.050 kHz or 44.1 kHz. (Other rates cause pitch and speed problems.) Flash 4 only lets you import uncompressed .wav files for the PC and .aiff files for the Mac. Flash 5 enables you to import other kind of audio files, but Egreetings does not currently support Flash 5, due to the fact that, at the time this chapter was written, many consumers had not yet downloaded the latest Flash plug-in.

PICTURES OF SOUND

I use a variety of tools and resources in my work. As described before, I do sound recording, MIDI sequencing, and sound effects editing, among other tasks. A lot of my work is done in an audio editor. I use Peak, a Mac editor made by BIAS Inc., but many good editors are available for the Windows and NT platforms as well. I trim, edit, add effects, and create and test music loops in the editor. While Flash does have a few rudimentary built-in audio editing tools,

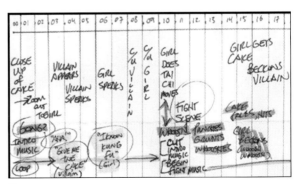

8.2

to do any real editing you need to use an external audio editor.

The visual representation of sound in an audio editor is called a waveform, and is a sort of picture of the digitized sound. In this example, you can see the entire sound at the top of the screen, and a single cycle of the sound below (8.3).

This is a waveform view of the sound of a gong, a sound I used at the very beginning of the Kung Fu animation. You can see in the view at the top of the screen that this waveform has a loud beginning, or *attack* to the sound, which represents the gong being struck, and then a long tapering fade-out as the sound dies away.

The sound is expressed visually along the horizontal axis from left to right in seconds, and the vertical axis shows amplitude, or loudness, measured in decibels. The louder the sound is, the "taller" the waveform will be in the window.

BASIC AUDIO TECHNIQUES

Although sound design is a complex discipline, some basic rules apply. As long as we're discussing audio editors, Let me cover some of the basic audio techniques that I'll be talking about later on in this chapter.

The waveform window of the editor is where I do all of my work. I can cut, copy, paste, mix, reverse, fade, and loop sounds. I can also use a variety of audio add-ons, or plug-ins, for processing and special effects, in the same way that graphic designers use special effects plug-ins in Photoshop. I use BIAS SFX Machine,

Cycling 74, Hyperprism's Ionizer and RayGun, and a complete suite of WAVES plug-ins, although these only represent a sampling of the plug-ins available for both the Mac and Windows platforms.

I take care when recording and editing to make sure the sound is free of clicks and pops, and is not distorted (8.4). I try to get as loud a level as I can without distortion, and start with the highest quality sound possible (8.5).

In preparing sound for Flash, one of the most important ways to save file size later on is to trim any unnecessary audio, such as silence, from the waveform. Although you can accomplish this later on in Flash, I prefer to do my trimming in the editor, where I have more control over the process. In this example, I trimmed the silences at the beginning and end of the gong sound by simply selecting the silent portions with my mouse, and using the Delete command.

I frequently use a few other basic audio processes in my work. The top four are equalization, compression, gain, and normalization. I don't always use all of these processes, and sometimes I don't need to use any of them. But they are some of the most important processes to know in order to produce audio for Flash.

Using equalization

Equalization, or EQ, is basically a complex version of the bass and treble controls on a stereo. High frequencies are treble, low frequencies are bass. You can use EQ to reduce or enhance selected frequencies of any sound, just as you use the bass and treble controls on your home stereo. With EQ you can bring out the

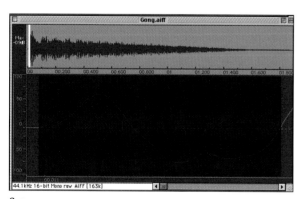

8.3

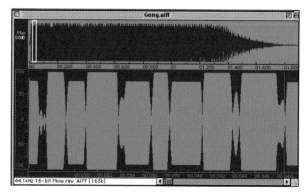

8.4

midrange of an instrument or voice to give it more "punch," reduce the bass frequencies of a sound to remove a low-level rumble, or nip off the high frequencies of a sound to reduce high-level hiss.

Because Flash audio compression can sometimes distort at the highest and lowest frequencies, I often use EQ to subtly remove some of these frequencies to make the audio sound better when compressed and played over a home computer audio system. (Many home computer audio systems won't reproduce these frequencies accurately.) This is not an exact science, so I use a little experimentation to make sure I am getting the best results in the final product.

I sometimes use what is called a "brickwall" EQ filter to remove just the highest or lowest frequencies. I usually set this brickwall filter somewhere between 60–100 Hz on the low end, and/or 6,000 Hz–20 kHz on the high end, so that all frequencies above those values (for the low end) or above those frequencies (for the high end) are cut off, or attenuated. (To help you understand these numbers, an electric guitar's fundamental frequencies range from 82 to 300 Hz, and a piano's fundamental frequencies range from 28 to 4,196 Hz.) I try to make sure to keep the sound as intact as possible, while removing frequencies that may not compress well in Flash, or sound good on a home computer's tiny speakers (8.6).

Using compression

Up until now, we've been talking about audio compression in Flash, such as MP3 or ADPCM. This kind of compression is the technology that compresses the file size of a sound for delivery on the Web. But another kind of compression is used when recording and editing sound outside of Flash.

Compression, in this context, is basically a way to even out volume levels, like an automatic hand on the volume knob. This enables you to even out the dynamic range of audio, reducing the loudest sections and bringing up the volume on quieter sections. I sometimes use compression to make voices more understandable, or to make sure that the louder parts of a musical track don't distort when exported as part of a Shockwave movie. I use compression plug-ins from WAVES to compress audio in my editor. The compression is then applied to the sound file permanently (8.7–8.9).

Using gain

Gain is basically volume, and is expressed in dbs, or decibels. Adjusting the gain of a sound is like turning the volume up or down. I use Gain Change a lot to increase the level of sounds to add more punch, or to decrease the overall level of a sound to avoid distortion. It is a very basic tool, and a very important one.

Using normalization

Normalization enables you to optimize the overall level, or volume, of an audio file. I almost always normalize audio in my editor before importing into Flash, using a setting of 70–90 percent to get a good

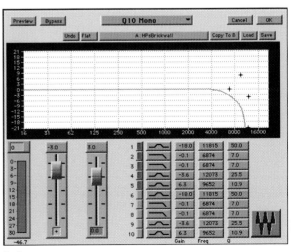

8.5

8.6

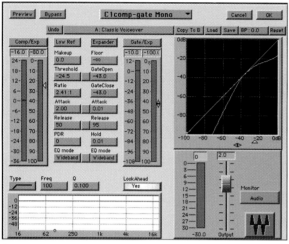

8.7

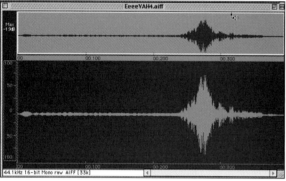

8.8

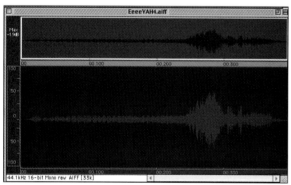

8.9

NOTE

If you set a five-second loop to Event, it will only take up five seconds' worth of file-size no matter how many times you loop it.

---

level. I can always use the volume controls in Flash to change the levels inside the project later, if I have to.

WORKING WITH THE SOUND

Now, back to the project. For the Kung Fu animation, I needed the following sounds and musical elements:

- Intro music for the introduction of the Kung Fu girl character
- Voices for both the villain and the girl
- Sound and music for the first fight scene
- Musical sting for the girl frozen midjump, *Matrix*-style
- Music, vocal effects, and sounds for the second fight scene and ending "punchline"

CREATING THE MUSIC

For the *Kung Fu Birthday* project, I decided to create the music first. Music and sound should fit the animation, and ideally will be created specifically for the animation. So I generally create all the music for Egreetings projects from scratch. I also have a few royalty-free music libraries on hand. For the intro music, I found a perfect Asian-sounding instrumental in one of my royalty-free libraries. So rather than reinvent the wheel, I decided to use it. Because file-size was tight, and I wanted to save my precious allotment for the rest of the music and sound, I decided to create the intro music as a loop to save room.

LOOPING

As long as the loop is musical sounding, and you don't overdo it, looping musical tracks in Flash is a great way to save file size. It is also a good way to save file size on background sound effects such as wind, rain, and crowd noises. If I need 15 seconds of music, I will often make a five-second loop and loop it three times in Flash. This enables me to cover 15 seconds at a "cost" of only five seconds' worth of audio.

It's important to note here that you can easily overdo looping tracks. Some Flash sound designers feel that it is sufficient to set an infinitely repeating three-second techno loop under their animations, and call it a done deal. But any music, no matter how well done, will begin to wear on the ear after a few repetitions. Looping audio, poorly used, can ruin an otherwise fine design. So use looping sparingly, and be creative. Layer in accent sounds occasionally, or use volumes and panning to vary the sound a bit.

To do my loop, I opened up the raw intro music file in my audio editing program and selected a musical section that I thought would make a good loop. I then set the loop points for the beginning and end of the loop and played it back to see how the intro music loop would sound when set to loop in Flash (8.10).

Once I had a good loop roughed out, I carefully adjusted the loop points to hit on a "zero crossing" of the waveform by zooming into the audio at the sample level (8.11). Here you see where I have set the beginning and end of the loop at a *zero crossing*, a spot where the waveform crosses the horizontal axis. If you don't loop on a zero crossing, your loop will probably have an audible "pop" or click in it.

I listened to the audio playback to make sure the loop was musical and clean, and then saved the selected section of music out as a mono 44.1 kHz 16-bit .aiff audio file.

I created a percussion loop for the introduction to the first fight scene in the same way. For the ending music, I decided to start from scratch and create a musical composition to fit the ending fight scene, and carry the animation into the text sentiment, or "punchline," ("Have a Kick-@$$ Birthday") at the end.

MAKING MUSIC

To compose the music, I used my MIDI studio. MIDI (musical instrument digital interface) is a musical computer language that enables musicians to create and edit elaborate musical compositions with many parts and multiple instruments. A MIDIfile is a lot like a player piano roll, consisting of data that tells MIDI synthesizers what notes to play when, and what instrument sound to use. With MIDI synthesizers, composers can have entire orchestras at their fingertips, enabling them to imitate drums, bass, violins, oboes, and the like. Synthesizers also produce sounds that could never be made by "real" instruments.

The heart of my MIDI studio is a piano-style keyboard, a couple of synthesizer modules, and a Macintosh MIDI and digital audio program called

Digital Performer. This setup gives me a lot of flexibility in writing, orchestrating, and recording music in a variety of styles. It also makes it easy to create "modular" compositions, enabling me to make changes to the music when required. The MIDI parts are like layers in a Photoshop program, and I can individually create and edit each part to my liking.

For this tune, I wanted to create a dynamic "slam-bang-pow" sequence with an Asian flavor. Using my paper timeline grid, I plotted out the places where I needed to create musical "hit" points, and also decided how long in seconds the piece would be (8.12). I then began to build the song as a MIDI composition, or

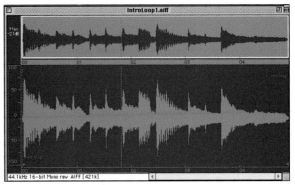

8.10

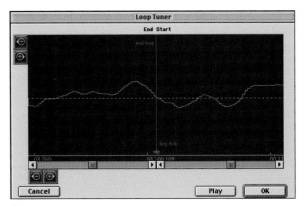

8.11

8.12

"sequence," by playing each part one by one into the computer using the keyboard to play the notes using the synthesizer's different instrument sounds. I started with the drum part, and then added horns one by one, and then played an Asian-flavored plucked-string sound to round out the composition.

Because Flash does not let users import MIDI files, I played back the finished sequence through my synthesizers, recording the output as a digital audio file for use in Flash. I then gathered the sound effects and other audio needed for the introduction of the characters, the conflict, and the ensuing fight scenes (8.13).

CREATING SOUND EFFECTS

As you can imagine, for a Kung Fu fight scene you need a lot of impact sounds, such as punches and kicks. Because Hong Kong action movies are over the top, I wanted the sounds to be over the top, too. So I went to my library of sound effects CDs and gathered whip cracks, body blows, wood snapping sounds, and the like to use as raw materials for the fight scene. Often, I will create sound effects from scratch by recording effects myself, but in this case, I found what I needed.

To make the punches and kicks sound bigger, I lowered the pitch of some of the sounds in my editor and increased the volume to the maximum so the sounds would have a real impact to them. I also needed some "whooshes" for some of the body movements, to

make them sound really heroic. My model was the Universal Studios' TV show *Xena, Warrior Princess*, where the sound designers underscore almost every movement of the lead character with a dramatic *whoosh*, (another technique borrowed from Hong Kong cinema). So I gathered some airy whoosh sounds, such as the sound of a whip right before it cracks, from my library, and edited them until they sounded right. I used these in the fight scenes and when the girl beckons to the villain — a whoosh for each motion of her hand.

HEARING VOICES

The next step was to record the voices I needed for the characters. My colleague Chip Harris played the character of the villain. After we discussed what was needed and how the voices should sound, Chip did the voices and provided me with digital audio files of the villain's voice parts via e-mail.

I did the Kung Fu girl's one line of dialog myself. I recorded it in my vocal booth, which is literally a closet outfitted with a small portable recording setup consisting of a good condenser microphone, a compressor, a mixer, and a digital audio recorder. I then transferred the girl's voice into the computer, and edited all of the voice parts in Peak. I raised the pitch of the girl's voice to make it sound a bit more girly, as my speaking voice is rather low (8.14). I also lowered the sound of Chip's voice to make it sound more guttural and "cartoony."

MAKING SOME FINAL EDITS

Now I had all of the music I needed, and more than enough sound effects and voices to choose from. I opened up all of the sounds for the project in my editor, and listened to them one by one, picking out the best versions of each kind of sound. I made final edits and tweaks to these sounds using some of the techniques described previously, and saved the selected sounds into a separate folder. I still had more sounds than I would end up actually using, but I prefer having a few versions of each sound when I get to the point of actually adding the sounds to the animation. Sometimes the results turn out differently than you

8.13

expect when you actually put the animation and sound together, so I allow for that by having more than one choice for each sound needed.

BRINGING SOUND INTO FLASH

Finally, it was time for the actual scoring of the animation. I opened up the animation in Flash, and used the File ➤ Import command to get all of the sounds into the Flash library, along with all of the visual elements used in the piece (8.15). In the library, you can easily see all the sounds in the movie, and audition them quickly by option-clicking (Mac) or right-clicking (PC) on each sound in the Library and selecting Play.

BRINGING THE PROJECT TOGETHER

The Flash timeline is where all the action is. Here's where I place the sounds to synchronize them to the animation. The Flash timeline offers a good visual way to synchronize sounds. If movie clips are used within the main animation, I will often need to open them up individually and place the sounds into the timeline of each individual clip, when needed.

In the Kung Fu animation, I added eight layers to the main timeline for the sounds, and placed them at the bottom of the timeline. I also named the layers so I could find them at a glance, to make it easier for anyone else working with the Flash file down the line. I prefer to work with the sounds at the bottom of the

SOUND RESOURCES

Here are some great places to get started on your sound libraries. As always, be careful of copyright infringement, though some of these sources provide sounds files for free. Sound Dogs, at www.sounddogs.com, offers more than 52,000 sound effects and production music tracks for online audition and purchase, as well as top Hollywood music and sound effects libraries on CD-ROM. Muinar offers subscription-based access to its online sound effects library at www.muinar.com. MeanRabbit Interactive, at www.meanrabbit.com, promises more than 5,000 new sound effects online. You can also find hundreds of royalty-free music loops for the beginner at www.were-here.com.

NOTE

The Flash manual recommends that you have each sound on a separate layer. But for a project such as this, I would be filling the screen with layers if I did that. So I just add enough layers to make sure the sounds are not all jammed together, and have never seen any problems with this method.

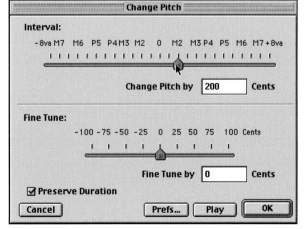

8.14

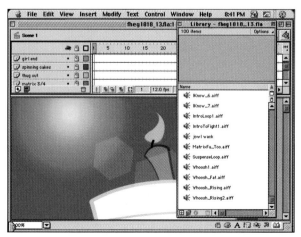

8.15

timeline, so that I can easily see both the sound layers and the animation.

To place a sound in the timeline, I locate the frame where the action I wish to add sound to begins, and create a keyframe in the sound layer on that frame (8.16). I then double-click that keyframe to open the Sound panel window. In the Sound panel, I select which sound I want for that keyframe, and also set many properties and do a bit of simple editing by using the sound Edit window.

Here you see the beginning of the animation already scored, with the gong sound and intro music loop in the timeline. To make the sound loop in Flash, I had to go into Sound panel to set the loop (8.17).

Because the mouth movements for the confrontation between the villain and the Kung Fu Girl were created as separate movie clips, I had to open up those clips separately to add in the sounds. But before I talk about lip-synching, I need to cover Event, Stream, Start, and Stop.

You will notice that four Sync settings are available to you in the Sound Panel. These are Event, Stream, Start, and Stop. The most misunderstood—and useful—settings are Event and Stream.

Event

The Event setting synchronizes the sound to a specific event in the timeline. An Event sound starts playing whenever the keyframe it is placed in comes up, and the sound plays from start to finish, even if the Flash movie should stop. The Event setting is best for short sound effects, and for any continuous music or background tracks that don't need to be tightly synchronized to the action. Sound effects will almost always need to be set to Event. Most music can be set to Event.

To save file size, you will almost always want to set looping sounds to Event. As previously mentioned, if you set a five-second loop to Event, it will only take up five seconds worth of file size no matter how many times you use the loop. If you set that same five-second looping sound to Stream, it will take up five seconds' worth of file size *each* time the loop is used.

To clarify, a five-second sound, set to Stream, increases in file size with each repetition. So if you loop it five times, it takes up the same amount of space on Export as would a 25-second piece of audio.

Stream

The Stream setting forces the animation to keep up with the sound, and Stream sounds will stop if the movie stops or runs out of frames in the timeline. In general, if you need tight synchronization, set the sound to Stream. This is especially important for character voices, and also for continuous music tracks that have been created with "hit" points that match specific actions in the animation time-line.

It is important to remember, however, that streaming causes the animation to drop frames in order to keep up with the sound, so use this feature only when necessary. Whenever possible, provide sounds that will be streamed to the animator ahead of time, so that the animation can be created with the sound in it, and so that they can work around the limitation of dropped frames. It is also important to give any voices that need to be synchronized to mouth movements to

8.16

8.17

the animator ahead of time so that the animator can create the animation to the voice track.

Setting the sound to Stream also enables you to "scrub" the sound in the timeline, which is to grab the red cursor at the top of the Flash timeline and drag it back and forth across the sound. This enables you to slow down and isolate parts of the sound file. In this way, you can easily hear the individual syllables of a voice track, and figure out which mouth movements go with that syllable, or to make sure that the musical crescendo that you timed to a visual cue is lining up correctly.

Start and stop

The other two synchronization settings available for sound in Flash are Start and Stop.

Start is just like Event except that, if the sound is already playing, a later instance of the same sound, set to Start, will play independently of the first.

Stop does just what it sounds like. It is a very handy way of stopping a sound cold (8.18). Most often, I use the Stop setting to halt a loop for a scene change. (You will rarely want a looped music track playing throughout an entire animation.) Because the Stop function is very abrupt, I usually like to cover it by placing another sound on top of the place where I stop a sound, thus making the audio transition smoother.

I used the Stop setting twice in the Kung Fu Girl animation. You already know that the intro music was constructed as a loop, and looped in Flash. To stop the loop, I created a keyframe in the layer that the loop was in, went to the Sound panel, and selected the Intro Music sound. I then selected a sync setting of Stop, and that was that. I covered the transition by placing a gong, and then a whoosh, over the ending of the Intro Music loop to lead into the next scene. I treated the music loop for the first fight sequence in a similar way.

LIP-SYNCHING

Now that we've covered the sync settings in Flash, let's move to lip-synching, and a prime example of when it is great to use the Stream setting (8.19). Because we were going for the look of a poorly dubbed foreign-language film for this movie, it was fine for me to do

the lip-sync (or lack thereof) after the fact, without using the animator's talents. But the technique I used is very similar to the way an animator would work with sounds when doing tight lip-sync.

First, I located and opened up the movie clip of the Kung Fu Girl's mouth movements for her one spoken line, "I know Kung Fu." I created a new sound layer in the clip's timeline. I then created a keyframe a few frames after her mouth began to move, and placed the sound file of the spoken line there (obviously I would have placed it more carefully in any other kind of movie)! I set the sound to Stream. I then grabbed the cursor and scrubbed back and forth to make sure the sound was perfectly *out* of sync with the mouth animation. (Obviously, you would use the same technique to make sure the sound was *in* sync!)

These are some of the basic techniques I used to place and treat all of the sounds in the movie. I used the Event setting for the sound effects and music loops, Stop to halt playback of the loops, and Stream for the voices and final music track.

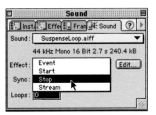

8.18

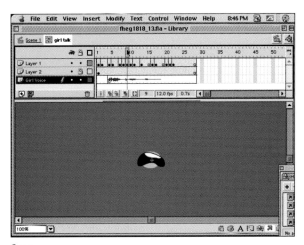

8.19

PANNING AND FADING

Once the sounds are placed in the timeline, and their sync settings selected, it's time for a bit of editing in Flash. Although Flash does not have the audio editing capabilities of a dedicated audio program, you have quite a few ways to manipulate audio in Flash. In Flash 5, these capabilities have been greatly expanded with the addition of ActionScript support, but this project did not require that kind of programming power.

Here, for the first fight scene, I started with the second music loop, a fast-paced percussion track. I then layered in multiple punches and a few whooshes and guttural grunts to give the feeling of a real Hong Kong action-movie sequence. I carefully placed a punch sound in each frame of the animation that showed the girl's fist connecting with the villain's face.

Panning

In the Edit Envelope window, you can fade a sound in or out, pan a sound, or truncate the beginning or end of a sound. You can also use the tools at the bottom of the window to zoom the waveform view in or out, and toggle between a timeline view incremented in seconds, or in frames. Even a mono sound will show up with both a Left and a Right channel in Flash, and this enables you to create simple stereo effects such as panning, even for mono sounds. Placing a sound to the left or right is called *panning*, and it has basically the same affect as adjusting the Left and Right balance on a home stereo system.

Because the close-up of the girls fist hitting the villain's face was placed on the right side of the screen, I wanted to make the punch sounds come from that direction as well. So, I went to the Sound panel and clicked the Edit button. This brought up the Edit Envelope window (8.20). For the hit sound, I dragged the left (top) volume handle down, so the sound would appear to come from the right side.

Panning is a great way to create a dynamic "soundscape," and gives a lot more realism and dimension to any Flash piece. In the following example, I took a whoosh sound and panned it so that it would appear to move from left to right.

Fading in, fading out

To fade a sound, you can use the preset fades available in the Effects menu at the top of the Edit window, but I like to create my own fade-in and fade-out curves (8.21). To do this, you just click in the waveform window with your mouse. This creates a box, or "handle," that you can drag around. Again, the top waveform is the "left" audio channel, the bottom waveform is the "right" channel. Drag down to the bottom to fade out on that side, and up to have full volume on that side. In this example, I used the volume handles to fade the sound out. You can create up to eight handles in each sound. This may seem like a lot, but for a complex sound, it sometimes isn't enough!

In the next example, you can see the way I set the volume handles to make a whoosh sound move rapidly

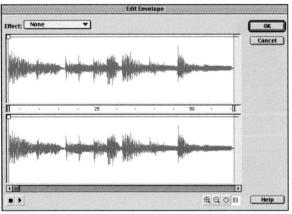

8.20

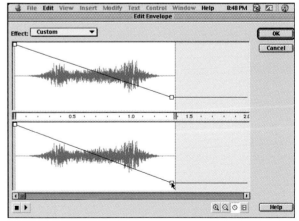

8.21

from the left speaker to the right, and back again (8.22). I didn't end up liking the way it sounded, but it is a good example of how to use the volume handles to do special stereo panning effects.

Once I did the volume and panning tweaks to all the sounds in the animation, it was time to set the compression levels.

COMPRESSION

An important part of optimizing sound for the Web involves setting the audio compression levels, to balance audio quality with file size. Flash has three basic audio compression settings for reducing file size on Export as an .swf file. I like to set the compression settings individually for each sound, using the Sound Properties dialog box.

The three kinds of audio compression available in Flash for .swf file export are ADPCM, MP3, and Raw. ADPCM is an older compression technology that does not compress as well or as much as MP3, and to my ears ADPCM sounds much inferior to MP3 compression. Raw really means "none," that is, no compression, but does enable you to change the sampling rate of sound on Export.

I start by going to the library and double-clicking the icon to the left of each sound to open up its Properties dialog box (8.23, 8.24). I select MP3 for the Compression setting. I then pick a Bit Rate, usually between 8 Kbps and 24 Kbps for effects, and

between 20 Kpbs and 48 Kbps for music, although nothing is ever set in stone.

For each sound, I click the Test button, wait a bit (or quite a while, for longer sounds), and eventually I will get an audio preview of what the compressed audio will sound like. I usually experiment for a while to get the best sound for the smallest k-size. Below the Compression pop-up list is a text file that shows the original and compressed file size of the sound file. This information updates every time you change the compression setting, and is a useful way to calculate

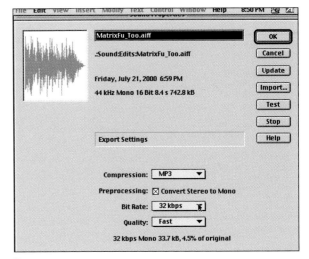

8.23

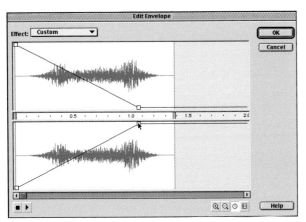

8.22

8.24

final file size as you test the different compression rates.

This process can be a bit tedious, but this is where you balance sound quality and file size. You can sacrifice a bit of quality on a sound effect to leave you more room to improve the compression quality for a music track. It's well worth the time spent here, especially if file size is tight.

I often set the compressions as high as I think I can get away with, and then Export the movie as an .swf file to see what the file size is. If it's still too high, I can go back in and tinker with the settings until I am under the file size limit.

EXPORT

Now it's time to export the finished movie with sound. Although you can just set a global compression rate for Stream and Event sounds in the Export Flash Player or Publish Settings dialog boxes, I like to set individual compression rates, as stated in the previous section.

TIP

You can also leave the sounds set to Default in the Properties dialog box, but because doing so means that all sounds will be set the same on Export, I don't use this setting.

Consequently, I usually leave the Override Sound Settings box unchecked, because my levels have been individually set. I like to set the Load Order to Bottom Up, so my sounds, placed at the bottom of the timeline, will load first. I now just have to Export or Publish my movie. That's it! Now I just ship off the finished .swf and .fla files for review, and hope that it's love at first sight/sound. In this case, it was.

THE BOTTOM LINE

I feel lucky to be doing what I love for a living. I work with great people in a new and interesting branch of animation. I encourage all Flash animators to work with someone like me if you can. It's vital to have professional custom audio as part of any multimedia design, whether it's character animation as described here, a motion graphics piece, or a simple Web interface.

Although I encourage people to hire professionals when they need sound or music, I also like to encourage people who want a career in creating sound and music to take up this noble field. With talent and perseverance, you can carve out a niche for yourself. A good ear, experience, and creativity are the most important tools I use in my work. Each project has its own needs. Each sound and each piece of music has its own characteristics, and will be used in a different context. The bottom line: plan your music and audio production, design for the medium, know your material, be creative, and experiment. And have fun.

PART II
FLASH EVERYWHERE

USE OF ONION SKIN MODE ALLOWS FULL VIEW
OF CHARACTER 'PUPPET' COMPONENTS

USE PHONEMES 2,3, 4 & 7 FOR SCOTTS
SCREAM REACTION BEGINNING KEYFRAME 43

TEST AS EVENT AND STREAMING SOUND
TO DETERMINE OPTIMAL PLAYBACK ON
CONNECTIONS FROM 56K TO T3

PER MATT: SET ALL PALETTE COLORS FOR SCOTT'S
OUTFITS IN EPISODE 1 TO CO-ORDINATE WITH
(#FFCC00) GOLDENROD JERSEY (REG. SCENE 3)

smashing ideas INC.

DATE: 2-15-99

SCALE: 1" = 72 DPI

DRAWN: RODRIGUEZ

JOB: CHARACTER ANIMATION

SHEET:

9

OF 16

CHAPTER 9
BROADCAST QUALITY ANIMATION

BY MATT RODRIGUEZ AND GLENN THOMAS

Flash is the worldwide standard for 2D character animation on the Web. Currently you have absolutely no alternative for creating high-impact, low-file-size animation for the Internet. Because Web-based vector animation is the original purpose for which Flash was created, it has a long record of success in this area and is the obvious choice to create great animation that is accessible to the largest possible Web audience.

Smashing Ideas has always been at the forefront of bringing great character animation to the Web and has had the pleasure of creating Web cartoons for established entertainment properties such as *Dilbert*, *Peanuts*, *South Park*, *Casper*, and *CatDog*, while also bringing Smashing Ideas' original cartoons such as *Lou's Deli Dayze*, *Say Uncle*, and *Bad Luck Boy* to Internet audiences (9.1–9.3).

...all the world's a stage.

WILLIAM SHAKESPEARE

9.2

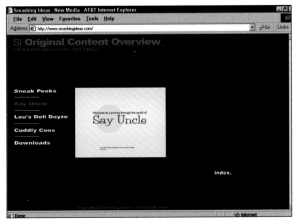

9.1

9.3

Ever since Macromedia added sound with Flash 2, Smashing Ideas has contended that the program enables broadcast-quality animation to be created for the Web. Although considerable planning has to be done to create a great cartoon that meets the medium's technical restraints such as limited bandwidth and varied playback speeds, we've always believed that the Web has to aspire to the quality and production values of other media if entertainment is to succeed on the Internet.

Smashing Ideas has worked with various broadcast networks in the past and created cartoons for television using Flash, but not until recently did Smashing Ideas have the opportunity to prove that a top-quality cartoon could be done solely for the Web.

We were lucky enough to begin working with the entertainment site Icebox (`www.icebox.com`) recently and they allowed us to prove that this truly is the case with the new hit Web animation series *Zombie College* (9.4–9.6).

Icebox wanted to create the highest-quality two-dimensional character animation for a new Web cartoon called *Zombie College* by Eric Kaplan. When nice guy Scott gives up M.I.T. to follow his girlfriend to Arkford University, he discovers that fitting in at a college filled with zombies takes a lot of adjustment. However, he also finds that it can be well worth it when you find that special someone who will let you eat her brain (9.7, 9.8).

9.4

9.5

AUTHOR PROFILE

Matt Rodriguez

In 1990, Matt Rodriguez unexpectedly began his career while zapping out lines of text with an outmoded Amiga 500 that he picked up at a pawnshop for $25. With a lightning-fast 400 bps modem, he occasionally connected to one of the embryonic BBSs that would one day converge with each other to form the World Wide Web. This could be almost as cool as CB, he thought to himself.

He attended the California College of Arts and Crafts and participated in various ill-fated experimental music projects. While designing full-time at Tower Records' corporate headquarters, he continued to develop his skills in cartooning and traditional animation as a part-time freelance artist. After setting up a personal tour of the Pixar animation studio in Richmond, California, he moved to Seattle, Washington to formally study traditional character animation while interning at a digital animation studio.

9.6

9.7

9.8

As director of character animation at Smashing Ideas, he has helped develop the system the studio uses to successfully produce animated series for the Web and guides the character design and movement for many of the new projects coming out of the studio. He can usually be found near his home on Seattle's Capital Hill, drawing from life while slamming Single Tall Hazelnut Soy Lattes and listening to piles of Mini Discs.

CREATING TRADITIONAL CHARACTER ANIMATION WITH FLASH

The link between the founders of Smashing Ideas is character animation, so adherence to the highest standards of quality has always been the hallmark of the studio's work in Web animation. Smashing Ideas is able to create fluid, lifelike animation for the Web by employing the skills of traditional 2D character animation and adapting those skills to the new medium.

Smashing Ideas approaches character animation in Flash slightly differently than many other Web animation studios. While not instantly conducive to standard techniques used by traditional 2D animators, all it takes is a little creativity and technical savvy to create movement that is both fluid and expressive (9.9, 9.10).

The first difference between our work and the other animation we see on the Web is that every piece of artwork used in a cartoon created by Smashing Ideas is drawn directly into Flash. Smashing Ideas does not create drawings in pencil, scan them, and then use the Trace Bitmap tool in Flash to get vectors; instead, we either draw directly into Flash using rough pencil drawings as a reference (9.11, 9.12) or we draw directly into Flash without reference to pencil drawings.

9.9

9.10

While the Trace Bitmap tool can produce some very interesting effects and textures, it is not the best way to produce traditional character animation for the Web. Drawing directly into Flash may be laborious at times, but we believe that it creates the cleanest lines, smallest file sizes, and best playback experience in Flash.

The next main difference is that Smashing Ideas rarely, if ever, uses tweening when it comes to true character animation. If you want to emulate organic movement and dynamic animation, the best way to kill it is to use a mechanical means. We find tweening to be very useful for animating mechanical objects such as androids or camera moves such as pans, trucks, and cross dissolves, but for character animation every single movement is keyfamed (9.13–9.16) in the way that animation has been done because it was created as an entertainment and art form.

9.11

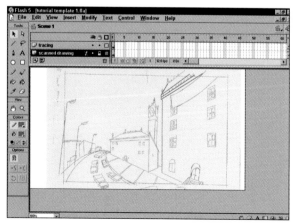

9.12

9.13

9.14

9.15

9.16

9.17

LEARNING HOW TO ANIMATE

A lot of what Smashing Ideas does is very similar, at least conceptually, to what has been done by animators in the past. The workflow in Flash is slightly different to what many professional television or film animators are used to, so the process does take a bit of getting used to.

The standard principles (9.17–9.21) such as squash and stretch, anticipation, staging, follow-through

9.18

9.19

9.20

9.21

RECOMMENDED READINGS

Smashing Ideas recommends that every budding animator read and reread a variety of traditional character animation books while working in Flash. These books include the classic *The Illusion of Life: Disney Animation* by Frank Thomas and Ollie Johnston (New York: Hyperion, 1995). The book details the Disney approach to creating lifelike characters. It's a treasure-trove of ideas about the process or creating an animated film as well as an explanation of animation technique.

Preston Blair's *Cartoon Animation* (Tustin, California: W. Foster Press, 1994) contains a lot of visual examples of character design and movement. It's a handy reference guide to keep around. Any books detailing the Hanna-Barbera method are worth reading because the process they have used is similar to the approach used in Flash. *Hanna-Barbera Cartoons* by Michael Mallory (Southport, Connecticut: Hugh Lauter Levin Associates, 1998) is a good introduction.

Any books by or about Chuck Jones are always worth reading because of his wonderful philosophy toward life and animation, such as Jones' *Chuck Amuck: The Life and Times of Chuck Jones* (New York, Farrar, Straus & Giroux, 1989), or *A Flurry of Drawings*, which Jones coauthored with Hugh Kenner (Berkeley: University of California Press, 1994) or the original Warner Bros. short cartoons featuring such beloved characters as Bugs Bunny, Marvin the Martian and all the rest are great places to learn both animation and a proven, successful approach to short-format cartoons.

Lifelike and cartoony animation are both built on some the principles of animation laid out by Disney. Some of the more important principles are as follows:

- Squash and stretch
- Anticipation
- Staging
- Straight-ahead action and pose-to-pose
- Follow-through and overlapping action
- Slow in, slow out
- Arcs
- Secondary action
- Timing
- Exaggeration
- Personality

One of the first places to start is a solid understanding of the principles of animation. Although this book can't begin to cover that field, many fine colleges and classes teach people animation.

THE DRAWING TABLET

It's nearly impossible for people to draw with a mouse in a natural way. Animators have to create many of the symbols and backgrounds used in Flash cartoons on the fly. The standard mouse interface has proven to be too cumbersome for this purpose.

Instead, Smashing Ideas uses Wacom's Intuos drawing tablets (www.wacom.com) throughout our production process. The tablet should immediately become your closest ally in drawing for Web animation. For now, it's the closest way to mimic traditional illustration and animation techniques digitally. While not quite as fluid as paper and pencil, it enables animators to draw directly into Flash and helps to maintain a familiar interface for people who come from a traditional animation background.

FLASH DRAWING TOOLS

Flash contains a number of natural vector drawing tools that may confound designers and illustrators raised on Bézier curves for vectors. Flash 4 had no Bézier curves. Instead, any line drawn in Flash 4 had to be grabbed at any point in order to shape it into a

action, character weight, personality, timing, exaggeration, arcs, easing in, easing out, and all the rest have not changed just because we are working in a new medium with specific technical constraints. If anything, they are more important to understand because the limitations of the medium make it so much more difficult to create great animation.

new curve (9.22). Although not very useful for illustrations that require precise control, this actually works quite well for animation.

The two main tools for drawing in Flash are the Pencil tool and the Paintbrush tool (9.23). However, the Line tool should be considered in order to minimize the amount of points it takes to create most drawings in Flash. The fewer points needed to map out a shape, the less data it takes to display and move that shape. Animation with fluid movement and smaller file size is easier to achieve when working with symbols that have been economically produced in Flash.

Flash 5 has added a Bézier curve tool so designers and illustrators will be more comfortable in the program. For people comfortable with pushing and pulling handles to render curves, this will be very useful. The Flash 5 interface has also been revamped

with the digital artist accustomed to palettes in mind. The transition from other digital art applications should prove easier than ever.

DRAWING AND OPTIMIZING IN FLASH

If the proactive approach isn't your forte, symbols that have been drawn with too many points (and you can't always tell just by looking at them) can be streamlined by optimizing them. The optimizing command (Modify ➤ Optimize) reduces the number of points it takes to display the symbol. By moving the Smoothing slider left or right, the artist can determine how many of these points should be deleted. The further right the slider is moved, the more points that will be deleted. The artist will need to determine how much of the symbol's quality can be lost before the result is no longer aesthetically acceptable (9.24).

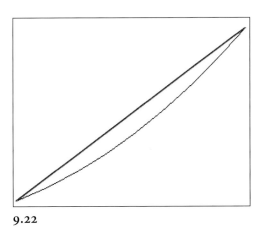

9.22

> **TIP**
>
> One of the biggest mistakes in drawing straight into Flash is to use the Paintbrush tool. The Paintbrush tool creates lines with many points, so they have a large file size and don't play back as smoothly. They are difficult to optimize, and when optimized to a reasonable file size, usually don't look very good.

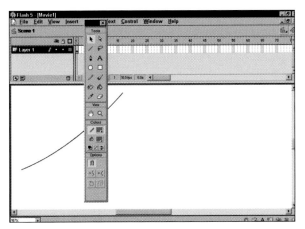

9.23

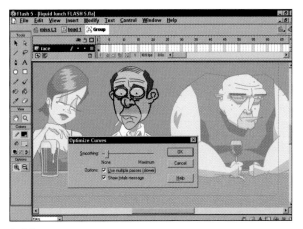

9.24

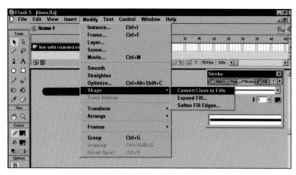

9.25

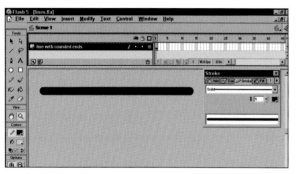

9.26

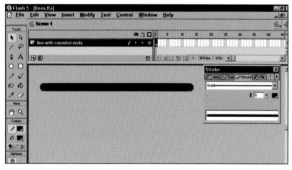

9.27

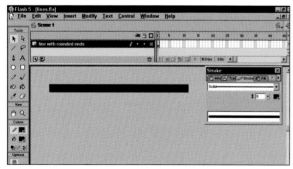

9.28

If for some reason you need to use a Paint (fill) line, it might be better to create a Pencil (stroke) line that is then turned into a fill line. You can do this by selecting the line and then choosing Modify ➢ Shape ➢ Convert Lines to Fills (9.25). One of the reasons to do this would be if you need to get straight ends on a line. Flash lines always have rounded ends (9.26) so the only way to get straight ends is to convert them to fills. Once the line is a fill, the rounded end can be selected (9.27) and erased (9.28).

Another reason to do this is because line widths sometimes resize at different widths when they're inside symbols. As an example, the lines in a character's hand symbol might resize to a different width or line weight than the lines in a character's arm symbol. The lines won't line up correctly and the character will begin to look pretty shabby. Hairlines do not change their weight when scaled up or down, thus making them more practical when used in symbols.

THE ANIMATION PROCESS

Animators first need to decide the basics of the movie — the frame rate and the movie size. With the current range of computer processors, we usually animate on ones at 10 frames per second and sometimes as high as 12 frames per second. The frame-per-second choice can become important later when the animation is transferred to video or film. A 12 fps movie translates fairly easily to the film rate of 24 fps.

SETTING UP THE MOVIE

The movie size affects both the playback and the aesthetic style of the film. If the movie size is too large, then playback might be slow. The movie size affects the aesthetic style of the film through the aspect ratio. The aspect ratio is the width compared to the height. The squarer the aspect ratio, the less interesting is the frame. More interesting compositional frames are rectangular. Follow these steps to set up your movie:

1. Choose Modify ➢ Movie from the main menu.
2. Change the frame rate by entering the number into the Frame Rate field. This should be 10 or 12 frames per second for animation (9.29).

3. Adjust the aspect ratio by entering the desired measurements in the Width and Height Fields. Standard measurements are 640 × 480 or a slightly more rectangular aspect ratio such as 1.65:1.

4. It's a good idea to make these Movie Properties a default so click Save Default and then click OK.

Zombie College was created at 12 frames per second to give us better lip-synching capabilities and smoother motion. The style of the show enabled this frame rate to play back well on the target computer.

Zombie College's movie size is 600 × 325. Because Flash uses resolution-independent vectors, scaling an animation up or down within an HTML page while still maintaining perfect line quality is possible. This makes the aspect ratio of the movie size as important as the precise dimensions. Aspect ratio is the width of the frame divided by the height of the frame.

Television aspect ratio is 1.33:1, which translates into a 640 × 480 movie size on the Web. This aspect ratio is very square and doesn't tend to provide the best size for staging visuals. Other standard aspect ratios are HDTV at 1.78:1 and the American theatrical film aspect ratio of 1.85:1.

Zombie College was created at the American theatrical release film aspect ratio while being storyboarded to play at the television aspect ratio of 1.33:1. At Smashing Ideas we've worked with a variety of different movie dimensions and definitely prefer the more rectangular and film-like aspect ratios.

GETTING DRAWINGS INTO FLASH

As mentioned earlier, we draw every piece of artwork directly into Flash. We tend to scan artwork and then trace over it with the Flash drawing tools rather than use Trace Bitmap. Although hand tracing is a longer, slower process, we believe the results look and perform better.

Icebox sent us paper character sheets for *Zombie College*, Photoshop files for the backgrounds, and a variety of different formats for the props. Each of these different formats was converted to a digital format that could be traced into Flash.

CREATING A TEMPLATE FOR TRACING

Smashing Ideas received artwork from Icebox via FTP or e-mail. The studio's director and Icebox's producer agreed on a format that these files should arrive in. The standard format that Smashing Ideas uses, as template for tracing artwork into Flash, is PSD. Other formats such as JPG, GIF, or PNG will do the job as well. Occasionally, Icebox delivered a piece of multi-layered artwork such as a background. The PSD format retains the artwork's layers created by Icebox's artists, enabling Smashing Ideas to easily and accurately turn these layers into individual symbols if need be.

Follow these steps to create a tracing template:

1. The PSD layers are exported as separate PNGs and are then imported into Flash. Once imported, the artwork may be found in the Flash library.

2. For the next step, create a layer in Flash dedicated to the artwork — or *template*, as it's known from this point on. It is important that this be the bottom-most layer because all of the tracing will be done on top of it.

3. From the library, simply drag and drop the artwork onto the timeline of the dedicated layer just created (9.30). To make movement and scaling of the template a little more manageable, it's not a bad idea to select all the elements and group them. Once the template is scaled and in position, lock this layer. It's no fun accidentally moving this layer later on when a lot of tracing has been done.

4. With the template scaled, positioned, and locked, the animator can begin tracing the artwork into Flash (9.31).

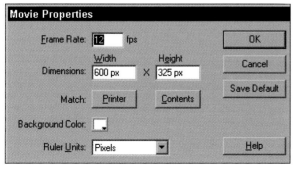

9.29

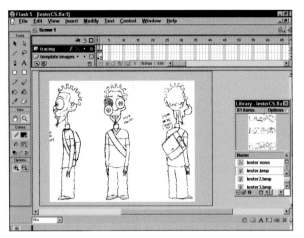

9.30

9.31

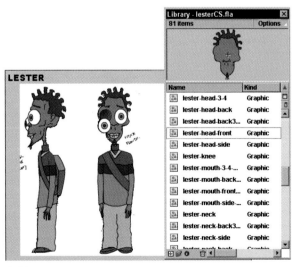

9.32

For *Zombie College*, the directors chose to trace all of the elements using the hairline weight for all line work. By choosing the hairline line weight, resizing symbols won't be an issue later.

To keep the overall file size of the animation to a minimum, the artwork is traced using only the Line tool. A line consists of only two points. Even the smoothest tracer will find rough points on a line if he or she were to trace an arc manually by hand. The line can then be adjusted to match the contour of the original artwork.

Generally speaking, as compared to simply using Flash's Pencil tool with the smooth option selected, this technique provides the artist with much more control over the final results of the tracing. The theory here is that the fewer points it takes to create a symbol, the smaller the overall size of the library will be. It's a technique that offers exponential savings over time considering the total number of symbols it takes to create a useable character library (9.32).

The way we look at it, absolutely anything can be converted into a format that can be brought into Flash and then recreated using Flash's tools. We believe that, at least for vector artwork, this is the way in which the best possible results can be gained.

BACKGROUNDS AND PROPS

Tracing semistatic objects such as props and backgrounds is a relatively straightforward process. By referring to the storyboards, the animator can determine a prop or background's role in the piece. If it's a nonanimated object that does not interact with a character, then it's usually combined and broken into the flat background (9.33). A background that does nothing more than serve as backdrop to the animation with no more than a simple truck or pan effect should be traced in as a flat symbol.

Occasionally, a little twist such as a multiplane camera effect is needed on a background and requires some special treatment. In cases such as this, it's nice to have the original artwork from Icebox drawn in a PSD format. As discussed earlier, the PSD artwork retains its layers and makes it that much easier for the animator to trace these individual template layers accurately.

After the individual layers of the background have been traced, it's very important to transform these layers into separate symbols, effectively creating a set of symbols that are independent of each other but together form the whole background. In a multiplane camera move, each of these symbols will be tweened on a separate layer to create the illusion of depth in movement (9.34–9.37).

CHARACTER SHEETS

Smashing Ideas starts by creating character sheets for each main character. The main parts of the character sheets are a front view, side view, back view, and a character rotation (9.38, 9.39). All of the standard mouth movements are also part of the character sheets (9.40). The character sheets that are developed enable all of the symbols for each character to be created. This main symbol library can then be shared among all the animators on a project.

MAKING SYMBOLS

It is crucial for an animator to keep in mind that the ability to recycle artwork as symbols is what essentially makes Flash a powerful Web animation tool. The main challenge facing all Flash character animators is the fact that they are forced to use very few assets to accomplish a great deal of movement for any given character. The fewer pieces, or in this case

9.34

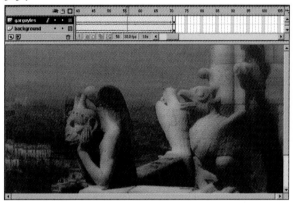

9.35

9.36

9.37

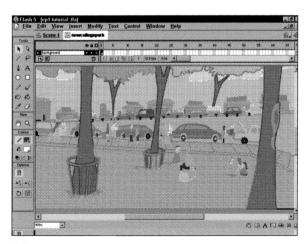

9.33

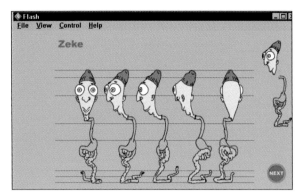

9.38

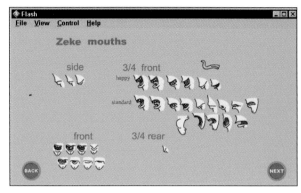

9.40

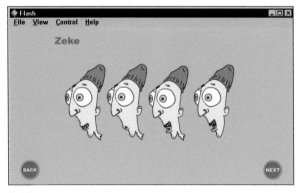

9.39

9.41

FLASH ANIMATION

Joel Trussell and Matt Rodriguez are two of the leading animators at Smashing Ideas. Between them they have directed the animation on some of the most groundbreaking original series for the Web including *Zombie College* and *Garbage Island* for Icebox and *Father's Day Fiasco* for Lycos (9.41). Studio work they've had a hand in includes *Liquid Lunch* (9.42), and *Helter Shelter* (9.43)

Q: What's your favorite part of animating in Flash?
MR: I like the fact that I can get instant feedback on character timing and motion.
JT: My favorite part of working in Flash is the easy edits you can make as you're working. It's easy to go into an individual frame and make minor adjustments, even in the final stages of a project.

Q: What's your least favorite part of animation in Flash?
JT: There's actually a few. If you're posting the final piece to the Web, monitor-

ing the file size is a burning pain. To make the download time reasonable for the viewer, you need to keep the size economical. This can really limit some of your original ideas, and cause some problem-solving.
MR: Until broadband truly takes hold, we have to animate for low bandwidth. This keeps me from being able to really go loose. It keeps me in the left brain a little more than I'd like to when animating.
JT: Another colossal gripe is programmatic difficulties. Flash has a hard time playing things back smoothly if too

symbols, the computer has to place, the more fluid the movement and smaller the file size. Period.

More complex or subtle movements require more symbols. Therefore, it's important to take into account the complexity of the characters in respect to the target file size and time budget. For Zombie College, the turnaround time per episode was as low as a few weeks and the maximum file size after loader, projector, credits, and sound was 1.8MB. The animators at Smashing Ideas broke the characters down as little as possible to stay within the target time and file size constraints while breaking the characters down as much as possible in order to make them as "pliable" as necessary. Only experience can guide animators in breaking up characters.

To design a character in Flash that is both "pliable" and "economical," the animator must think of all the potential positions in which the character may need to be posed. Getting away with creating as few new symbols as possible to achieve these poses is where a little creativity comes in handy. Some characters are simply more dynamic than others. As a rule of thumb, the more dynamic the character the larger the character's symbol library (pieces that make up the character). Too many dynamic characters could prove costly in terms of available file size and overall performance of the animation.

The animator should be thinking three-dimensionally. Keeping the basic principles of life drawing in mind is of utmost importance. The animator's best tools at this stage are a strong understanding of foreshortening, perspective, and accurate anatomy. The kinetics and physics of animation come into play later.

9.42

9.43

many details are animating at once. Sometimes what seems to be an easy scene to the creator turns into a Herculean task for Flash. This can cause animators to eliminate some action they feel is significant.

Q: How does the ability to continually review the playback of the animation you're working on affect how you animate?
JT: This is a noble feature of Flash. Being able to play back your piece as you work takes a lot of guessing out. It speeds up the entire process by assuring animators their section is shaping up.
MR: Reviewing the animation on the fly gives us the freedom to both fine-tune and experiment with scenes.

Q: What's the key to creating fluid and lifelike animation in Flash?
JT: Flash is the same as any other medium when it comes to lifelike animation. Paying attention to animation fundamentals such as cushion, stretch, bounce, and so on can add some weight to your characters. Also, adding sufficient in-betweens is something many (very many) Flash cartoons I've watched overlook. Another point to remember with Flash is to think of the character in three dimensions. It's easy to get carried away with trying to reuse your symbols, and not create new ones.

Q: What have you pulled off with Web animation that you thought was impossible?
MR: *Zombie College*, a series comparable to a television series. As animators we weren't sure if we could do it or not,

Again, it's very important to reuse as many symbols as possible from pose to pose. In effect, it's a game of sorts where the object is to achieve as many of these key poses using as few symbols as possible. Often times, a symbol that was initially intended to be a knee (which can also create a fine elbow) will be used as something as seemingly unrelated as a puffed up cheek or a shirtsleeve or even an entire torso for a character.

The key here is to remember that once a drawing, any drawing, is converted into a symbol, it can be distorted to create many other parts of a character's body. Once stretched, skewed, and scaled up or down, a seemingly limited library of symbols may surprise an animator with their flexibility. It's this type of resourcefulness that helps Flash do what it does best. Remember to always think about how you can recycle symbols.

Another element that is very important when converting a character drawing into a batch of poseable symbols is overlaps. These joining areas added to symbols are most useful when drawn as arcs to mimic the joints found in nature. The need to patch joining areas is decreased considerably when these arced overlaps are produced without any line work.

Once the character's main rotations have been traced and "broken" apart, the animators begin creating new symbols to bolster the character library. By referencing the storyboards, an animator can ascertain what symbols will be needed to convey subtle attitudes laid out by the storyboard artists. Key symbols such as hand gestures and mouths help build up the library.

Up to this point the main character library has been in the hands of only one production assistant or animator. This helps to establish a more uniform style to the overall design of the character and helps to reduce the possibility of doubling up on symbols. Now that the basic main character library has been created, the rest of the animation team can then reference it via computer network and begin placing the character symbols into each animator's individual timelines. Animators can make a copy of the main character library to their individual workstations but need to keep in mind that if they draw a new symbol, eventually it will need to end up back on the main character library.

When multiple animators begin accessing and adding to the main character library, it is very important to establish a strict naming convention for all the symbols within the library. An easy-to-understand naming convention helps to make all the symbols in the library easy to locate. A standard naming convention could include the character's name, body part, position, and number. The chances of different animators using the same names can be further avoided by having the individual animator add his or her initials to the naming formula.

Once all the main symbols are created for a character, one animator should go through the entire symbol

---

quite frankly. A one-off is one thing; a series is quite a different story. Just like any big animation, we had to get a lot of great people to work in concert with one another to make it come together.

JT: I haven't pulled anything off with Flash that I would have otherwise considered impossible. I think of all the animation I have seen and try to make my Flash animation live up to or surpass those standards. Keeping in mind that you are limited in Flash can be dangerous. Try thinking of the way you would like to see something, and work around the limitations.

Q: What animation books would you recommend people read in order to animate better in Flash?
JT: I did (partially) read a Flash 3 book when I was trying to learn the program, but beyond that I don't read animation books. I would recommend trying to work on your own skill through experience. I've seen people own libraries on subjects such as animation or film making; however, they have nothing to show for it. Get your hands dirty, and finish some animation goals you set for yourself.

Q: What movies or videos would you recommend watching?
MR: I recommend checking out the character designs by Mr. Ed Benedict. His work for Hanna-Barbera was brilliantly economical and slickly designed. Created decades ago, his style lends itself perfectly to Flash at the turn of the new century. Director Hayao Miyazaki's films are visually and contextually phenomenal from beginning to end. If you want to see the right way to set up a truly moving scene, look to him.

library and optimizes each symbol. Depending on the complexity of the drawings, this can save anywhere from 10 to 25 percent of the file size of the symbols.

One of the standard animation cycles for any character is a walk cycle. The walk cycle is also a good way to test the character library to see if all the pieces fit seamlessly together once applied to an animation.

CREATING A BASIC WALK CYCLE

One of the first movement studies for a character is a walk cycle. Walk cycles can vary greatly from one character to the next. The style established by the character designer can often inspire the overall movement of the character. The following steps outline a basic walk cycle:

1. Set up your timeline. If your movie has been set up to run at 12 frames a second, create a timeline that is 12 frames long. Make sure all the frames contain keyframes. Save the movie.

2. To simplify the process of producing walk cycles in Flash, pose the character in two extreme states or key poses. For a walk cycle, the two extremes can be considered *trace backs*, a term used in traditional animation houses. The only real difference between the two would be that, on the first extreme, the character's right foot is in front and, on the second extreme, the character's right foot is behind. To save time, it's a good idea to pose the first extreme into frame 1 of the time-line and then copy it into the other relevant frames.

3. Paste the pose from frame 1 onto frame 7 (9.44).

4. On frame 7, Select the foreground leg, foot, arm, and hand (9.45) and send them to the back (Modify ➢ Arrange ➢ Send to Back) (9.46).

5. Next, Select what was the background leg, foot, arm, and hand and bring them to the front (Modify ➢ Arrange ➢ Bring to Front) (9.47).

6. Create the crossover in the walk cycle. Copy the pose from frame 1 and paste the pose into frame 4. Repose the symbols to reflect the midway, or crossover position of the character's feet. It is important to note that the body and head of the character are at their highest point in the walk cycle during the crossover position.

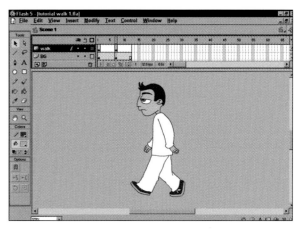

9.44

JT: *Twice Upon a Time* directed by John Korty is a staple piece — innovative, and a good story. Naturally, Nick Park's and Bill Plympton's animation is pure, raw talent at work. Movies such as *Akira*, *The Hobbit*, *Ninja Scroll*, and *Nightmare Before Christmas* are all very inspiring. John Kricfalusi, despite his reputation, harnesses a scary amount of talent. *Stimpy's Invention* and *Space Madness* are pieces that make me frequently angry at how good they are.

MR: The first, and some of the second season of *Ren and Stimpy* still serve as a tremendous inspiration for me. I watch these in slow motion on my VCR and I swear they still slay me every time — a georgous mix of dynamic and economical animation.

For some of the very best in classic cartoon animation, look to the work of Rod Scribner with director Bob Clampett while at the Warner Bros. studio in the '40s. Scribner takes squash and stretch to the limit and draws with skilled reckless abandon.

Q: Do you ever tween character movement?

MR: Other than moving an animated graphic like a walk cycle, tweening has no real place in character animation. A clever mix of key poses and "straight-ahead" animation is more my preference. I really enjoy going on autopilot for a while and animating "straight-ahead"; the results are almost always more rewarding than keyframing.

JT: Tweening, in most cases, is best when left to a minimum. Tweens can be good for mechanical movements, but make

The legs are parallel to the center point of the character to create the top of the walking arc. Natural movement is achieved by paying careful attention to the arcs and applying cushions throughout the animation. Just about every aspect of the walk cycle is based on an arc of some sort. Both arcs and cushions come into play even with the most subtle movements.

7. Time for another trace back. Copy the midway pose from frame 4 and paste it into frame 10. Repeat Step 4 (9.48). The main in-betweens of the walk cycle are now in place.

8. Copy the pose from frame 1 and paste it into frame 2. Adjust character movements accordingly, easing the transition to the next frame (9.49), and copy the pose.

9. Paste the pose from frame 2 into frame 8. Repeat Step 4 (9.50).

10. Copy the pose from frame 4 and paste it into frame 5. Adjust character movements accordingly (9.51) and copy the pose.

11. Paste the pose from frame 5 into frame 11. Repeat Step 4 (9.52).

12. Copy the pose from frame 2 and paste it into frame 3. Adjust character movements accordingly (9.53) and copy the pose.

13. Paste the pose from frame 3 into frame 9. Repeat Step 4 (9.54).

14. Copy the pose from frame 5 and paste it into frame 6. Adjust character movements accordingly (9.55) and copy the pose.

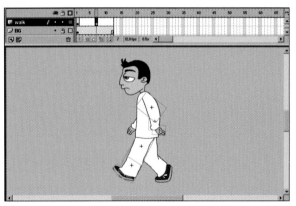

9.45

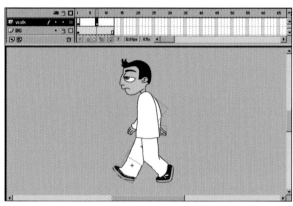

9.46

most character movement look unnatural. On the other hand, it can be useful in some physical gags when used properly. I've tried to refrain from tweening to keep my own in-betweening skills intact. Usually if I see a piece that is mostly animated by tweens, an instant "hack" alarm goes off.

Q: Tips and tricks . . . ?
JT: One big tip is to learn how to draw the human figure. This is an obvious point for any animator. If you don't have a good understanding of the human body, you'll run into a wealth of problems. Draw all the time. Don't stop. If it's not your passion, why do you want to animate?

9.47

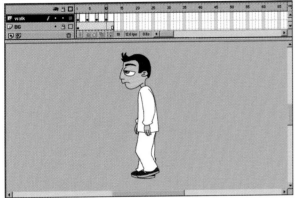

9.48

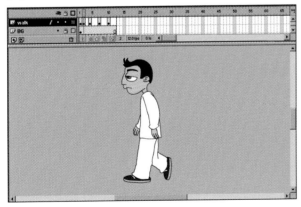

9.49

9.50

9.51

9.52

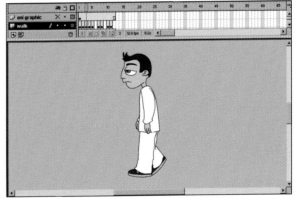

9.53

9.54

15. Paste the pose from frame 6 into frame 11. Repeat Step 4 (9.56).

To make the basic walk cycle easy to scale and tween across a background, turn it into an animated graphic. Here are the steps:

1. Select frames 2 through 12 (9.57) and copy all the keyframes of the walk cycle (Edit ➢ Copy Frames).

2. Go to frame 1 and select the entire pose (Edit ➢ Select All) (9.58).

3. Press F8 or choose Insert ➢ Convert to Symbol to turn the selected pose into one symbol. Give it a name and set the Behavior to Graphic (9.59). Click OK.

4. Double-click the symbol on the Stage in frame 1.

5. Within the symbol, select frame 2 and paste in the frames (Edit ➢ Paste Frames). Make sure frame 1 lines up with the following frames (9.60).

6. Go back into scene 1 in the main movie timeline and copy the symbol (Edit ➢ Copy).

7. Create a layer dedicated to the symbol (Insert ➢ Layer).

8. Select the new layer and paste the symbol in the frame. Make sure the timeline has been extended to include all of the walk cycle (at least 12 frames).

The new walk cycle animated graphic can now be manipulated to fit any part of the storyboard for the cartoon. It can be scaled, flipped (9.61), or tweened to enable the character to move about the scene as needed while keeping the file size extremely small.

9.55

9.57

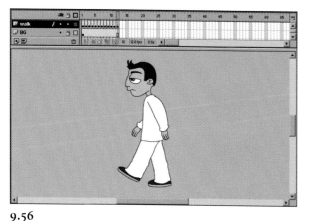

9.56

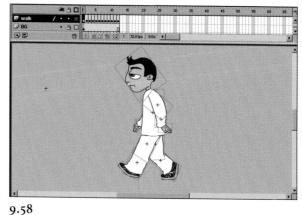

9.58

LAYING OUT SCENES

Animation requires a significant numbers of scenes for each cartoon. These are normally laid out in a storyboard. At Smashing Ideas, we still use rough paper storyboards to conceptualize the flow of the cartoon. We've found that paper storyboards currently give artists more freedom to sketch and play with ideas.

In the case of *Zombie College*, we received a paper storyboard from Icebox (9.62) and used these to inspire and guide the keyfames we produced in Flash. It's at this stage that the scenes (9.63) for the entire cartoon are laid out in Flash and distributed to the animation team. It's important to split everything up well so that problems don't occur in the future when the scenes come back from each individual animator to be compiled.

MUSIC, F/X, AND DIALOG

In working with larger cartoons, music, F/X, and dialog play a huge role in enhancing the overall piece. In the case of *Zombie College*, the soundtrack really picks up the pace of the cartoon and creates the right zombie atmosphere.

Unfortunately, lots of sound also results in huge file sizes. As a matter of fact, sound is usually the bulkiest portion of a cartoon. Even though MP3 compression has aided in reducing file sizes tremendously, animators still have to wrestle with ballooning file sizes caused by soundtracks.

For *Zombie College*, Smashing Ideas received all dialog and music as .wav or .aiff files. Much of the music consisted of short hits or stingers to punctuate key events in the show. Using more of these stingers to establish a mood and fewer long soundscapes aids in controlling the overall file size. The first step Smashing Ideas took to get a stinger into a piece was to manipulate it in a sound-editing program such as Cool Edit Pro.

When the studio brings a sound file into a sound-editing program, the first step is to ensure that the sound levels are optimal for Flash. All sound dropped onto a timeline should be as loud as it can be without any distortion and then fine-tuned in Flash. The theory is that Flash can only make the sound so loud, but can make any sound as quiet as it as needs to be.

9.59

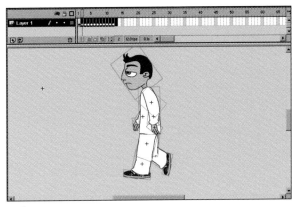

9.60

9.61

ANIMATING — OUCH, DON'T DO THAT!

Full-screen pans, zooms, and trucks with complex foregrounds and backgrounds are difficult to pull off in Flash because screen redraw is so dependent on the processor speed and graphics card. As an animator you can never be sure a pan or zoom will look right on the user's machine, so use them with caution.

Other playback problems come from intense action scenes or having multiple characters animating quickly at the same time. Frame rates don't usually remain high enough to enable these kinds of scenes to play back correctly.

Often times a sound effect or piece of dialog can become buried in the mix. When all the tracks are imported into Flash at maximum volume, it becomes much easier to control the mix (9.64, 9.65).

The next important step is to make sure that any extra data (dead air) has been permanently trimmed away from the sound file (9.66, 9.67). These inaudible fragments at the beginning and end of an audio track take their toll by adding slightly to the file size.

In Flash cartoons, the general approach is to add all dialog as streamed sound so it can be properly synched to the mouth movements (9.68). Sound effects are usually event sounds, so they can be reused without adding to the file size. Music can be either event or stream, depending on whether the music loops (9.69), needs to synch to a scene, or needs to be reused many different times.

LIP-SYNCHING

Animators need to use a standard set of mouth movements to properly mimic human speech. The main mouth positions that need to be developed for a Flash cartoon are those that correspond with the following sounds:

- A (ah) and I (ah-ee) are similar and can be swapped for each other
- E (ee)
- O (oh), U (oo), and W all have similar shapes and are swappable
- L and TH
- M, B, and P
- And one mouth shape for the rest of the consonants

After experimenting with a variety of ways to name mouth symbols and then synch to dialog, we have settled on naming all of our mouth shapes starting with the character's **initial**, followed by the word **mouth**, the sound the mouth is making, a number or letter set, and finally the initials of the animator who drew the symbol, as in **s mouth cc SS sa** (9.70).

At Smashing Ideas, we tend to do all of our lip-synching after the rest of the animation is completed. Animation will be done with a standard mouth symbol in place on the character's head and then that

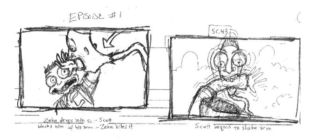

9.62

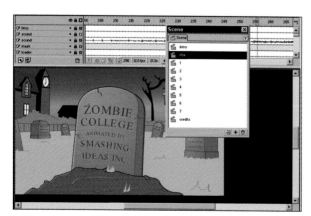

9.63

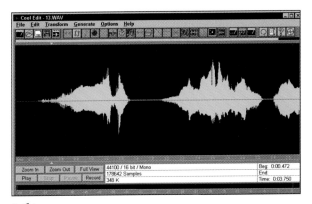

9.64

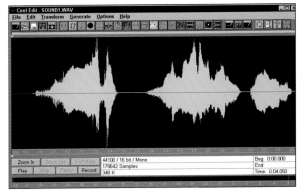

9.65

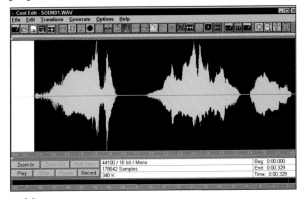

9.66

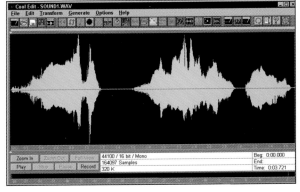

9.67

symbol is changed in order to synch to the dialog. It's important to dedicate a layer in Flash exclusively for lip-synching. Traditionally known as an *overlay cel*, this separate layer permits the underlying layers to be animated on twos (changed every other frame) while the mouth is running on ones (changed every frame).

In a script-driven animation, most speaking dialog needs to be on ones. By keeping the mouth animation on the same layer as the rest of the character, the animator is forcing the computer to render the entire character on ones. The results are usually dropped frames and awkward pacing. The best way to ensure smooth playback during dialog-heavy scenes is to have the mouth on a separate layer (9.71).

Once the voice track has been converted to stream, it can be "scrubbed" for easy reference. The

9.68

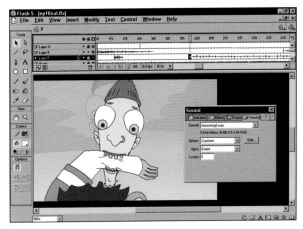

9.69

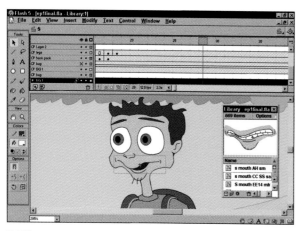

9.70

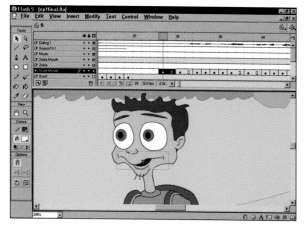

9.71

9.72

traditional step of creating exposure sheets for the purpose of lip-synching is skipped thanks to Flash's sound integration. The animator begins by playing portions of the streamed dialog over and over and phonetically breaking down the dialog into key mouth positions. The key positions are usually vowels, with the consonants serving as in-between states.

This technique very much mimics the traditional method of breaking down key mouth movements using magnetic tape with an editing sound head. It's not a bad idea for the animator to keep a small table mirror handy to actually see the positions the mouth contorts into when actually speaking a part of the dialog. Once the key mouth positions are established, the animator can go back and fill in the remaining frames between with the character's appropriate mouth symbols. In Flash, or any animation, it's always a good idea to have the mouth animation appearing at least one or two frames before the actual sound occurs (9.72).

With the mouth symbols all in place, the animator can now concentrate on further accentuating key parts of the dialog with the character's head, body, and hands. Fleshing out the subtleties includes punctuating words with the character's eyes. The amount of subtlety is usually determined by how "cartoony" the style of animation is, but small head movements usually aid in breathing life into any otherwise flat animation.

We've experimented with programmatic lip-synching in Flash and have found that, as mentioned, it's too dependent on the processor speed of the computer to give satisfactory results. Script-based lip-synching makes it harder to access and place the correct mouth, so it's easier to go out of synch or drop mouth movements.

WHY *ZOMBIE COLLEGE* WORKS ON THE WEB

In the end, *Zombie College* works on the Web not only because it contains great Flash animation but also because it is a well-written cartoon with engaging characters. Because it is character-driven, it requires few intense action scenes. The backgrounds are highly stylized and the lack of line complexity enables them to be used for pans. All of the technical and animation aspects of *Zombie College* are held to the highest quality, but in the end the cartoon engages the audience because it has good characters telling a funny story.

After all, animation is only acting out a story, so if the fundamental story isn't interesting the greatest animation in the world won't get people to watch the cartoon. Bad animation can kill a good story, but great animation can't save a bad one. In *Zombie College*, we've been lucky enough to meld our animation cre-ativity and skill with a great writer, phenomenal music, and standout voice acting to create a cartoon that can hold its own with any other cartoon on the Web as well as most cartoons on television.

At Smashing Ideas, we really try to take animation on the Web to the next level of quality. We believe in getting great movement and acting to tell a story. If you focus on those elements and strive to create engaging cartoons, you'll be successful with your Flash animation projects.

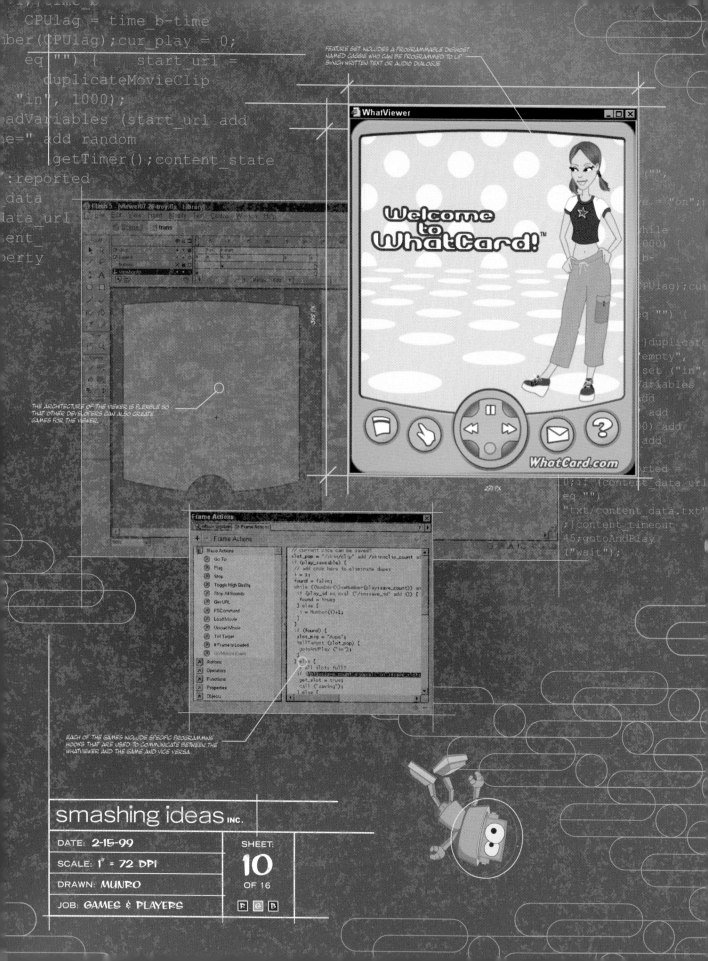

```
CPUlag = time_b-time
ber(CPUlag);cur_play = 0;
eq "") {     start_url =
    duplicateMovieClip
"in", 1000);
adVariables (start_url add
e=" add random
getTimer();content_state
:reported
data
ta_url
t
erty
```

FEATURE SET INCLUDES A PROGRAMMABLE DIGIHOST
NAMED CASSIE WHO CAN BE PROGRAMMED TO LIP
SYNCH WRITTEN TEXT OR AUDIO DIALOGUE

WhatViewer

Welcome to WhatCard!™

WhatCard.com

THE ARCHITECTURE OF THE VIEWER IS FLEXIBLE SO
THAT OTHER DEVELOPERS CAN ALSO CREATE
GAMES FOR THE VIEWER.

Frame Actions

Frame Actions

Basic Actions
- Go To
- Play
- Stop
- Toggle High Quality
- Stop All Sounds
- Get URL
- FSCommand
- Load Movie
- Unload Movie
- Tell Target
- If Frame Is Loaded
- On Mouse Event

Actions
Operators
Functions
Properties
Objects

EACH OF THE GAMES INCLUDE SPECIFIC PROGRAMMING
HOOKS THAT ARE USED TO COMMUNICATE BETWEEN THE
WHATVIEWER AND THE GAME AND VICE VERSA.

```
while
000) {
b-
PUlag);cur
eq "")
}duplicate
"empty",
set ("in",
ariables
dd
add
0) add
add
rted =
0;if (content_data_url
eq "")
"txt/content_data.txt"
;}content_timeout =
45;gotoAndPlay
("wait");
```

smashing ideas INC.

DATE: 2-15-99

SCALE: 1" = 72 DPI

DRAWN: MUNRO

JOB: GAMES & PLAYERS

SHEET:
10
OF 16

F G B

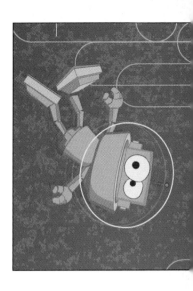

CHAPTER 10
CREATING ENTERTAINMENT PLAYERS

W eb designers and developers can use Flash to create entertainment players that users can personalize. The look and feel of entertainment players can be customized, as can the entertainment that the viewer receives. Based on a user's selections, different games, music, animation, or information can be sent to the user. Using Flash, companies can develop pure one-to-one entertainment players for the Web.

Smashing Ideas used Flash to create two distinct entertainment players for the Web. We worked with Launch Media (`www.launch.com`) to create the LAUNCHcast Player, a personalized streaming radio player (10.1). The service provides radio quality or better music at a 56K modem connection and near CD quality sound at broadband levels.

We also developed an entertainment player targeted at teens for the Web company WhatCard.com. The WhatViewer (10.2) combines an animated virtual host with games, trivia, and information about music celebrities.

Both of these entertainment players use Flash 4 and work extremely well. However, Flash 5 would have let us add significant features to either of the players. An XML (Extensible Markup Language) data structure would enable information to be transferred into the players more easily, and the capability to create an XML socket connection with the server would enable dynamic information to be sent to each player. We could create any kind of push application using the XML socket feature such as continually updated sports scores or stock quotes. Applications such as

Give the people what they want.

10.1   *LAUNCH®cast, printed with permission*

201

chat would also be easy to add. Programming either player in Flash 5 would also be cleaner, with fewer programming workarounds. We could also create a shared asset library for all of the different movies that make up the player, in order to significantly reduce the project's overall file size.

INTRODUCING THE LAUNCHCAST PLAYER

The features available in the LAUNCHcast Player are extremely rich. The player uses Flash to request, organize, and display a significant amount of data about the user and the song that is being played. All of this data is stored within a series of backend databases. The databases use a technique called *collaborative filtering* to return new song selections based on the material that a user likes as well as some selections based on the music favored by fans similar to that user. The idea behind this is that members will be more likely to enjoy new music that people with similar tastes like.

In addition to the extensive functionality developed inside of Flash, JavaScript on the HTML page extends Flash's functionality. JavaScript enables Flash to interact extensively with the corresponding audio or video stream carried over the Windows Media Player.

JavaScript also helps to trigger actions within the Flash movie (10.3). Flash provides the rich media front-end that enables the LAUNCHcast Player to function properly as it interacts with JavaScript, the Windows Media Player, and numerous databases to make the LAUNCHcast service function properly.

When users go to the Launch.com Web site, they can sign up for the LAUNCHcast Player service. The sign-up process checks for Flash 4 and the Windows Media Player on a new member's computer. Each new user enters a unique user name and password. The user name enables each person to customize the player. All of the data that will be subsequently submitted and organized will be based on this user name. Once a person has registered, the full functionality of the service becomes available.

New members set up their first personalized station by rating different genres and choosing personal DJs. These choices immediately begin influencing the songs that members receive. New members can set the amount of influence these outside factors have on the music they hear — the music can range from being highly influenced by the factors to not being influenced by them at all.

As members begin to use the LAUNCHcast Player, they rate songs, artists, and albums (10.4). These ratings are the heart of the personalized radio service because members receive a stream of music based mostly on the ratings they have entered themselves. As an example, if a member rates a particular artist's

10.2

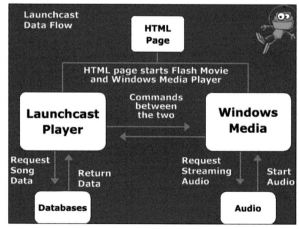

10.3

music highly, then that music will appear in the player frequently. It's a personal high rotation system that can be changed at any time. If a user gives a song a low rating, then that song will not play back very often. Members can also exclude songs, albums, or artists from their player entirely by rating anything an "x," which is the equivalent of zero and means never play again.

Rating are made in the player through the rating interface on the right side of the player. The first rating that is shown is always the song rating (10.5). A member can drag the slider up and down to set a specific numeric rating or click the buttons to the left of the slider to rate based on the nearest ten. Ratings appear in gray unless the song is rated over 90, which means that it's a personal favorite. The ratings of favorites appear in blue. Members can click the artist or album tabs and rate those as well.

Ratings are passed down based on a hierarchy of artist (10.6), album, and then song. If a member has rated an artist or an album, but not a song, then the song will carry the rating of the artist or the album

(10.7). The passed-down rating is shown in light gray to differentiate it visually from the case where a member has actually rated the song individually. In the LAUNCHcast databases, all of the rating information is saved to a database and then sent back by a set of Java servlets when requested by the Flash movie.

The listener can pause a song by using a Flash button that sends a JavaScript command using Flash's `FSCommand` action to the Windows Media Player audio stream. The Flash movie also communicates with the Windows Media Player to enable a user to control the volume or even mute the song. Members can skip songs they don't want to listen to or, even better, they can skip a song and set the player to never play it again (10.8). This sends a special rating back to the databases that excludes the song from ever appearing in a user's playlist again.

Members can share their ratings by sending their station to friends. A friend can actually choose to listen to a station based on another member's ratings. If both members are listening at the same time, they won't hear the exact same songs. Instead, both listeners will

10.4 *LAUNCH®cast, printed with permission*

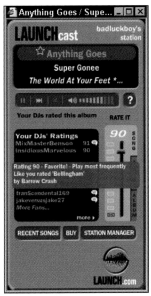

10.5 *LAUNCH®cast, printed with permission*

10.6 *LAUNCH®cast, printed with permission*

draw from the same set of ratings and hear a similar group of songs. Members can also select other rating sets based on musical artists, genres, popular DJs, featured DJs, and DJs whom LAUNCHcast recommends.

To establish a sense of community around the LAUNCHcast Player, members can also interact with any other member who shows up in the player as a fan or DJ. If a member, whether DJ or fan, is online, then a Whisper symbol (10.9) appears next to his or her member name. When a user clicks the Whisper symbol, a pop-up browser window appears with an HTML-based messaging service.

Although messaging could have been accomplished in Flash 4, it would have been more server-intensive than the HTML equivalent. With an application such as the LAUNCHcast Player that needs to scale the number of users quickly, it makes more sense to create a messaging system outside of Flash. In a Flash 5 player, it would make more sense to include this feature within the Flash movie because the feature could be done with an XML socket.

The player also collects and displays the average rating for a song based on all of the rating that have been entered into the database for that particular song (10.10). This enables members see how their chosen music goes over with the rest of the LAUNCHcast audience.

Songs are also classified by genre. This information is shown in the viewer because it's another attribute of the music that members can use to define which types of music they want to listen to. If a member loves surf music then he or she can choose to listen to that specific genre most of the time. Members can also choose to exclude all music from a genre in a player. If a member hates surf music, then he or she can get rid of it.

This deep personalization from a song to a genre level, combined with the community aspect of the player, makes for a powerful music platform. Members can even personalize more than one station (10.11). Users can create distinct moods that they choose to play at different times. Each mood can contain different genres, DJs, and ratings.

Even more information must come into the player, though, because a member can also go directly from the player to the Web pages of the song, artist, album,

10.7 *LAUNCH®cast, printed with permission*

10.8 *LAUNCH®cast, printed with permission*

10.9 *LAUNCH®cast, printed with permission*

fan, or DJ in order to rate songs in those places. Each URL link must be brought into the player. The goal is to enable members to rate as many songs as possible as quickly as possible because the more a member rates, the more personalized the player becomes.

Users are only one click away from being able to edit and update their information, review their song history, share their song ratings with friends, or buy the CD associated with the song they're listening to at any given moment.

HOW THE LAUNCHCAST PLAYER WORKS

Windows Media Player is the chosen streaming audio format for the LAUNCHcast Player. The project requirements included a Flash 4 player version as well as the capability for Flash to talk to Windows Media Player in order to control both the volume and pausing. As an example, in Flash the `FSCommand` action on the pause button would be something like the following:

```
fscommand ("pause_now");
```

This would send an FSCommand from the Flash movie to the HTML page where it would be mapped to trigger a specific JavaScript command. The code would look like this:

```
function swfmovie_DoFSCommand(command,
args)
{
if (command == "pause_now")
  {
    on_JS_Pause();
  }
}
```

The `on_JS_Pause()` command would then tell the Windows Media Player to pause.

```
function on_JS_Pause()
{
document.MediaPlayer1.Pause();
}
```

Besides these functional controls between Flash and the Windows Media Player, an enormous amount of information is passed into the Flash movie from the

10.10 *LAUNCH®cast, printed with permission*

10.11 *LAUNCH®cast, printed with permission*

databases. You'll find information based on the individual songs, the artists, the ratings, as well as data about fans, DJs, comparison ratings, and URL links to Web pages with more information about everything already mentioned.

A certain amount of the information is passed into the Flash movie when the HTML page opens based on variables dynamically placed in the Web page from server-side programs such as `flash_movie. swf?user_id=badluckboy&song_rating_ url=song_rating.html`. Based on this information, Flash calls out to a set of Java servlets located at those URLs to get more information for that user.

As an example, when the user "badluckboy" opens his LAUNCHcast Player, the Flash movie asks the Java servlets to query the databases. This is done with a standard `loadVariables` action. We tend to make our `loadVariables` calls from within movie clips and then put the transferred data into a specific place within Flash. This makes it much easier to manage which data is requested and returned. Instead of sending and receiving all variable data that is in the movie from the main movie timeline, it's possible to create discrete data sets that are sent and returned. This then makes parsing and displaying data a much quicker and easier process.

As an example, a call might look like the following piece of code in Flash 4:

```
tellTarget ("data_out") {
  member_id = /:member_id
  loadVariables
("http://www.yourserver.com/cgi-
bin/data_lookup.pl", "/data", "GET");
  }
```

In this example, Flash would request ask a `data_ lookup` CGI script from within the `data_out` movie clip to return information into the data movie clip on the main timeline. The `member_id` variable would be added to the end of the query to the CGI script and would be used to gather the data. This query uses `GET`, which returns a limited number of characters as a URL-encoded string. The limit is around 2K and can cause serious problems if that data limit is reached. If you reach the data limit, then the response will be truncated, omitting any names

and values that exceed the limit. This will probably cause your Flash movie to function improperly. Developers can also use `POST` when more data needs to be returned, but this functionality does not work properly in Internet Explorer 4 and earlier on Macs.

In the LAUNCHcast Player, badluckboy's user ID is passed to the servlets, which then request all of the relevant information. The Flash movie waits for data to be returned and then places it. If the data does not return after a certain amount of time, the Flash movie requests it again.

XML DATA IN FLASH 5

Flash 5 enables developers to bring XML data into a Flash movie. For most Flash developers, using XML is a new endeavor, and they may find themselves asking what exactly XML is. The World Wide Web Consortium (W3C) calls XML "a common syntax for expressing structure in data." XML lets you define tags that describe words and the structural relationship between them.

In contrast to the fixed set of HTML tags that specify layout presentation, XML tags identify the category of information and the relationships between the information. For example, in an XML document on an e-tailer's Web site there might be a `<PRODUCT_ID>` tag, a `<PRODUCT_NAME>` tag, and a `<PRICE>` tag. Each tag would define a specific type of information and, in this example, the `<PRODUCT_NAME>` and `<PRICE>` tags would be based on the `<PRODUCT_ ID>` tag.

XML therefore separates structure and content from presentation. This enables XML documents to be displayed on any XML-capable platform, whether it's computer monitors, cell phones, or PDAs. The buzz about XML is that it enables you to make documents intelligent, powerful, and portable.

In the following Flash example, we ask for and receive several names and associated e-mail addresses from an XML file. We take that data into the Flash movie and display the data based on the XML tags (10.12).

We're first going to create our XML data source. We want to display names that a viewer can click in order to send e-mail to that person. An XML document looks similar to an HTML document, but instead of the familiar layout tags such as `<font>` or `<h1>`, words are enclosed by tags such as `<person>` or `<name>`. In our case we are creating a list of names and e-mail addresses related to a company, so we start the document with `<company>` and end it with `</company>`. We then want to create a set of data tied to a specific set of people. To access the information, we'll give each person an ID number so the first tag of the data definition is `<person id="1">`.

Inside this tag we are going to include name and e-mail information, so the next tag should read `<name>` with a person's name inside of it, in this case "Glenn Thomas," followed by the end tag (`</name>`). Next we'll add the e-mail information inside of the `<email>` tag. We'll add another name with e-mail information before we save the document with the name **xmltest.xml** (10.13). This document could grow to contain thousands of name and e-mail records.

Now that we've created our data source, we need to create a Flash movie that can display the information. We'll create a new Flash movie called **xml_data_test.fla** and save it in the same folder where we created our XML document. We then have several steps to take to show the XML data inside the Flash movie.

The Flash movie needs to request the document. In this example, we will hardcode the document's name, but the document's name could just as easily be a dynamic variable. In the first frame of the movie, the following code loads the movie:

```
xmltest = new XML();
xmltest.load( "xmltest.xml" );
```

The first line creates a new, empty XML object, and the second line gets the XML document xmltest.xml and places the XML document structure inside the previously defined XML object.

Once we've got the XML data into Flash, we need a place to put it. We add a layer to our movie and place a Dynamic Text box on it. In the Text Options panel, set the Variable for this dynamic text box to output and select the HTML option to give the field HTML formatting. We also deselect the Selectable option and select Multiline (10.14).

We now need to create a function that will parse and place the XML data (10.15). We'll call it **get_xml_doc**() and put it in the first frame. The first step is to clear the output field and then define the objects that will hold the XML data. We write the following code at the start of the function:

```
Function get_xml_doc(){
output = "";
maintag = new XML();
```

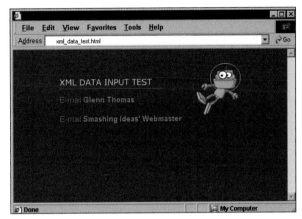

10.12

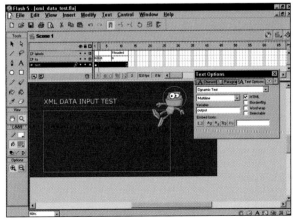

10.13

10.14

```
person_tag = new XML();
item_tag = new XML();
person_list = new Array();
item_list = new Array();
```

After this part of the function where we've defined the objects, we then must populate the new objects with the XML data. First we put the XML data from our XML document into our `maintag` XML object within Flash. In XML parlance, this data is set at different levels of nodes that relate to the tags. Because the person is what our data is based around, we take all the information and put it in the `person_list` array we just created. We can then trace this to see what data came into our Flash movie.

```
maintag = xmltest.firstChild;
person_list = maintag.childNodes;
trace (maintag.childNodes);
```

TIP

Flash 5 enables you to preserve HTML formatting in editable text boxes. Supported tags are <A>, <B>, <FONT COLOR>, <FONT FACE>, <FONT SIZE>, <I>, <P>, and <U>. This enables you to do tasks such as create HTML style links from within your editable text boxes.

10.15

Now that we've put all of the XML data into an array, we need to parse it and place it in the output data field. The next part of the function loops through all of the names in the list and then formats the name and e-mail information for the output text field (10.15).

```
for (i=0; i<person_list.length; i++) {
  person_tag = person_list[i];
  if
(person_list[i].nodeName.toLowerCase()
== "person")
{
    item_list = person_tag.childNodes;
      for (j=0; j<item_list.length; j++)
{
      item_tag = item_list[j];
      if (item_tag.nodeName.toLowerCase()
== "name")
{
    name =
item_tag.firstChild.nodeValue;
      }
  if (item_tag.nodeName.toLowerCase()
== "email") {
      email = item_tag.attributes.href;
      }
  }
  output = output+"E-mail <a
href=\"mailto:"+email+"\">"+"<b>"+name+"
</b>"+"</a>\n\n";
  }
}
```

We're almost finished, but first we need to make sure that the XML data has arrived inside Flash before we try to parse it. To do this, we create a simple routine that checks whether the data has been loaded and, if it has been loaded, then sends it to a new label where the function is called. We put this code in frame 2 of the movie and then just loop over that frame by putting a `gotoAndPlay` frame 2 action in frame 3 (10.16). We then place a label called `loaded` a few frames later in our movie. When the data has been loaded, the action in frame 2 sends us to this label where we tell our parsing function to start (10.17). We then easily create the Flash movie and associated HTML document by publishing it.

Place the XML file on your Web server in the same folder as your Flash movie and HTML page. The XML document and the Flash movie must be in the same domain or this will not work properly. When you open your HTML page, the Flash movie will request the data and display it.

WHATCARD.COM'S WHATVIEWER

The WhatViewer entertainment player that Smashing Ideas developed for WhatCard.com combines teen-targeted games, trivia, and tips with a virtual host (10.18). The entire WhatViewer, including the games, animated host, and viewer, was built in Flash 4. The device's feature set includes a programmable digihost named Cassie that can be programmed to lip-synch written text or audio dialog (10.19, 10.20).

Cassie can be told by an editor to sing, to talk, dance, walk, jump, or any number of other physical actions. It's as simple as selecting an action from a list and synchronizing that action to a specific time in the movie. Cassie runs through all of the actions in sequence as she talks to the entertainment player's users about viewer features such as the different player skins that site members can choose from (10.21, 10.22), the resize feature of the viewer, and the volume control attribute.

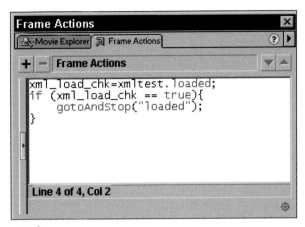

10.16

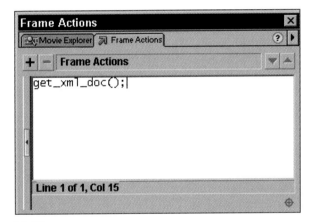

10.17

WARNING

The first version of the Flash 5 player did not include a way to disregard white space in XML documents. Because of this, Flash parsed all of the white space as if it was information nodes. This created a serious performance issue for parsing and displaying any XML documents inside Flash. Version releases 5,0,41 and 5,0,42 of the Flash 5 player include a code change to ignore the white space between tags, although white space within a true text node will still be counted as significant. As an example of this, the code `ignoreWhite = true` would be added to the XML document object within Flash prior to loading the XML data from the external XML file.

10.18

One of the strengths of the WhatViewer is that members can see recent programming (10.23) and build a playlist of favorites (10.24). If a member loves a particular game or information section, then that member can save it and easily return to it later. Members can also skip programming they're not interested in watching as well as rewind to previous content.

The WhatViewer also includes the capability to dynamically change and target rich media advertising. If a certain member saves all of the programming and content based on music, then music ads can be sent to the viewer. If a member saves all of the programming about movies or sports, then advertising based on those interests can be sent to that member.

GAMES IN THE WHATVIEWER

Games are the centerpiece of the WhatViewer's programming. We wanted a variety of games so we created teen trivia games, arcade-style action games, word puzzle games, random chance games, and many others. Conceptualizing and creating games is always a lot of fun for a creative group of designers, developers, and game producers.

With the WhatViewer, our team came up with dozens of ideas that would interest a teenage, and predominantly female, audience. After brainstorming the game ideas, we categorized them into distinct game genres because we wanted representative games

in areas such as memory, action, and trivia. We rated the games based on their level of fun, their playability, and their stickiness (the amount of time a teenager would stick around to play the game). We then produced the top ranked games in each category (10.25–10.28).

Each of the games included specific programming hooks that are used to communicate between the WhatViewer and the game and vice versa. This enabled, among other things, the games to be paused and saved. The architecture of the viewer is flexible so that other developers can also create games for the viewer.

We've already looked at Flash programming by creating a checkers game, so let's take a look at a completely different type of game, in this case, a memory game (10.29). In this kind of game, a player must match a specific pair of tiles or cards.

As tiles are selected during the game, Flash has to check to see whether they match. If they match then they remain face up, while if they don't match they're turned over (10.30). Once all of the cards are matched, a player wins. Because card games normally require some kind of comparison, the basic functions used in this memory game can be expanded for use in most kinds of card games.

We already know the standard rules of this game, but we want to add a few twists. We want to time the game. If a player has not matched all the cards before

10.19

10.20

10.21

the time counts down to zero, then the game ends. We also want to create three stages where additional cards and time are added at each successive stage. We also want to enable players to print out the tiles used in the game. With these additions in mind, we'll want to make the code as modular as possible to allow for these additions.

Our first step is to define the symbol set. In this case, we need to create a specific number of cards that will be used to build the game layout. The last stage of this game contains a 5×6 grid of cards so at the maximum we need 15 different matching pairs of tiles.

We create 15 different tiles and turn them into graphic symbols. We'll then duplicate each of these symbols once and make them into separate movie clips. We'll need to choose a naming convention for the tiles so we can set them and then check them easily. We'll want to use a number based on which tile set it is, from 1 through 15, and then whether it's the first or second tile of the matched pair so we'll name the tiles **t1_1, t1_2, t2_1**, and so on.

We also need a tile cover symbol and an invisible button that is inside a movie clip symbol. The button movie clip will match the number of the tile it's

10.22

10.23

10.24

10.25

10.26

10.27

underneath, so we only need one button for the entire gameplay. We'll name the button symbols **s_1**, **s_2**, **s_3**, and so on, while the tile covers will be called **t_1**, **t_2**, **t_3**, and so on.

Modular programming uses the name of the symbols within all of the actions to create powerful sets of actions and buttons. If we did not do it this way, then a different button with separate, but completely identical except for the name, programming would be needed for each tile. The last thing we do is create a tile cover symbol. We need a button and a tile cover symbol that are related to each specific set of tile pairs so we duplicate and name button and tile cover symbols for each tile.

These tasks could all be done programmatically by dynamically creating, naming, and placing each tile cover and button into new levels based on using a looping action with a changing *i* number. This *i* number would be used to create the tile cover and buttons related to the tile sets. Unfortunately, we have button navigation elsewhere in the game that would be covered by the tile buttons if we did this. Although we could dynamically place those buttons into levels or programmatically turn all of the button movie clips off, it turns out to be less complex to do it physically by dragging the movie clips onto the stage and naming them individually. If we needed to create a

highly flexible game structure, it would be best to create and name the button movie clips dynamically through programming.

Next, we need to define the functions that will make the game work. Because this fairly simple game is for Flash 4, all of the actions for each "function" will be *in a frame with a label*. These actions are called when they are needed by other parts of the game. The first function we need is one that sets the game layout with the correct number of cards.

Eight pairs of matched tiles are in the first stage. We need to initialize the game by defining what stage we're in and describing how many tiles appear in that stage. Here's the code to do so:

```
stage = "1";

if (Number(stage) == 1) {
    tiles = "16";
}
```

Next we'll place the pairs of tiles, along with the tile covers and the buttons that relate to the tiles. The logic is to use the number of tiles to randomly generate a tile number that is linked to a place in the layout. Each time a tile is chosen, it's put into a list of chosen tiles that the function checks. If that tile is randomly chosen again, then it's not placed. Once the

10.28

10.29

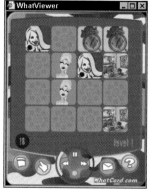

10.30

tile is placed, a button and tile cover with matching numbers in their names are put in the layout in the same place.

When a player clicks the first tile during a turn, the button needs to run through a certain set of actions. Some of these actions are contained within the button actions, while others are contained at a label in the main movie timeline.

The actions on the button remove the tile cover and then set a variable that tracks which tile has been selected. The variable is set based on the getting the number out of the button name using the `substring` action, specifically `substring ( _name, 3, 2 )`. Using `_name` returns the current symbol's name. That number is then used to build the tile cover name. Another action tells the correct tile cover symbol to go to a label and play an animation that shows the card flipping over. When a player clicks the second tile during a turn, the actions on the button need to remove the tile and set the variable that defines what tile has been selected. The following code is in Flash 4 because that was how the project was originally developed, but could be done with standard Flash 5 dot syntax without Tell Target and still be exported to Flash 4.

```
else if (Number(../:c_set) == 2)
{
  ../:sel2 = substring(_name, 3, 2);
  ../:chk2 = eval ( "../:tile" add
../:sel2 );
  if (../:sel2 ne ../:sel1) {
      ../:c_set = "3";
      tellTarget ("../t_" add
../:sel2) {
          gotoAndPlay ("on");
      }
```

The actions then check whether the two tiles match. If the tiles match, then we add a number to a match variable to signify that another pair has been found. If the tiles do not match, then we put the tile covers back on and let the game player continue trying to match tiles.

```
if (Number(chk1) == Number(chk2)) {
  set ("s_" add sel1 add "_g", "1");
  set ("s_" add sel2 add "_g", "1");
  match = Number(match)+1;
  s_match = "1";
} else {
  tellTarget ("t_" add sel1) {
    gotoAndStop ("off");
  }
  tellTarget ("t_" add sel2) {
    gotoAndStop ("off");
  }
}
```

Each time a player matches a pair of tiles we add a number to a match variable. When this variable matches half the number of tiles, then we know the game is over. The last action in the frame checks to see if that's happened.

```
if (Number(stage) == 1) {
  if (Number(match)< (tiles/2)) {
    gotoAndStop ("sel");
  }
  else {
    gotoAndStop ("win");
  }
}
```

When the player matches all of the tiles correctly, we send the player to an animation that tells the player that he or she has won this round and invites him or her to move on to the next level.

TIP

Flash 5 contains a method of the movie clip object called `hitTest` that enables a developer to test whether an object has hit another object or the mouse has rolled over an object. This is extremely useful for creating action games that require collisions or shooting. It's also useful in board games where you need to know where pieces have been dropped on a board. Using `hitTest` also gets rid of the hand that appears in the rollover state when you use buttons.

USE LOTS OF SOUND AND SOUND EFFECTS AS ENCOURAGEMENT WHEN GIVING FEEDBACK TO KIDS.

THE FLASH MOVIE WILL ASK FOR DATA FROM THE TEXT FILE AND THEN USE IT TO CREATE THE QUIZ.

INCORPORATE NON-VARIABLE 3-ANSWER SETS FOR SIMPLICITY / MAX. WRAP 2 LINES

TERRY AND CONNIE HOST GLOBAL ADVENTURE FOR THE KIDS IN ROOM 17 OF PS 1511

smashing ideas INC.

DATE: 2-15-99

SCALE: 1" = 72 DPI

DRAWN: MARKEY

JOB: EDUTAINMENT

SHEET:
11
OF 16

R C B

mashing idea

CHAPTER 11
FLASH FOR EDUTAINMENT

Kids love animation, interactivity, and games. When kids find a fun and challenging educational program that uses these three features, they'll spend hours and hours using it and learning from it. A well-designed Web site using educational Flash games can entertain children while establishing a solid educational foundation for subjects such as math, science, reading, and language (11.1).

Flash enables developers and educators to create CD-ROM-style edutainment for the Web containing animation, puzzles, and games. Quiz-based programs that follow traditional educational methods can be enhanced with characters and fun feedback to reinforce learning. Kids love a great learning adventure and concerned parents prefer edutainment to regular arcade-style games because of the rich educational value.

Three important elements in this type of project are creating a fun immersive environment with strong characters (11.2), maintaining a solid educational curriculum (11.3), and giving kids feedback (11.4) with an opportunity to learn and improve.

Imagination is more important than knowledge.

ALBERT EINSTEIN

TARGETING CHILDREN

Smashing Ideas' cofounder Evan Clarrissimeaux developed *Terry de Ferma and the Global Explorers* as a broadband interactive edutainment program for children aged six to ten. The show focuses on the trials of an adventurous Aussie globe named Terry de Ferma and his computer laptop sidekick Connie. The

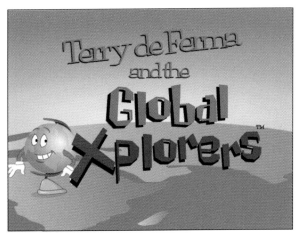

11.1

11.2

two take the children of Room 17 of PS 1511 (11.5) all around the world to explore different ecosystems and find out about animals, nature, and science.

Global Explorers uses Flash to create an immersive environment with strong storylines combined with interactive education. It's a program that kids love because its fun and parents enjoy because their kids learn from it. In the first program of the series, Terry and Connie take one of the schoolchildren to Antarctica (11.6) to learn about penguins (11.7). While they're in Antarctica, they also learn about icebergs, temperatures, and other animals. The program starts out with a ten-question geography quiz that helps cover the time it takes to download the photos, sound, and animation of the program.

CREATING LEARNING QUIZZES

Learning quizzes are an important part of any educational curriculum. They give children feedback about

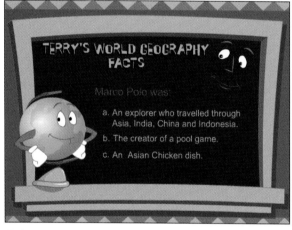

11.3

> **NOTE**
>
> *Terry de Ferma and the Global Explorers* can be found at www.flashstudiosecrets.com.

11.4

11.5

their knowledge of a subject and help teachers understand what kids need to study further. Learning quizzes in edutainment can go beyond standard quizzes by giving children different questions based on their level of ability as shown during the quiz.

It's extremely important to create a data structure for learning quizzes that is flexible, easily modifiable, and provides feedback to kids. You have a variety of ways to accomplish this in Flash, including making calls to a backend server database with all the quiz data stored in it (11.8), creating Generator templates (11.9) or pulling XML data into Flash 5. For this example, we will work with an easier way to get data into our quiz. The quiz data will be stored as name/value pairs in a text file (11.10) that sits in the same folder as the Flash movie on the Web site. The Flash movie will ask for the data from the text file and then use it to create the quiz.

The beneWts of creating a template in this way are that once the quiz has been built, someone who doesn't know Flash can maintain the site. An educator can simply create new quizzes by editing the text Wle. A Web-based entry form could even be created to make this task even easier. This is much more efficient than opening the Flash movie and going through the movie frame by frame to Wnd and replace all of the questions and answers.

11.7

11.8

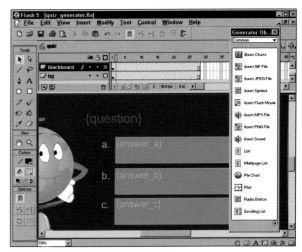

11.9

11.6

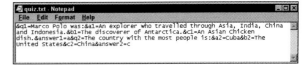

11.10

DEFINING YOUR QUIZ

The first step in planning a dynamic quiz structure is to define your question and answers set. Will the number of answers per question be variable or will it remain constant? The former adds to the amount of programming that needs to be done, but is much more flexible. How long will the questions and answers be? The answer affects the size of the textboxes and you may have to create a resizing function if any of the questions or answers are too long.

To remove this complexity, the *Terry de Ferma* geography quiz structure does not change. Each question has three answers. The questions can be eight to ten words long, as can the answers. Both the questions and the answers can wrap onto two lines.

Although it would be possible to create this as a ten-question quiz with multiple symbols for each question, that would not be very efficient. Any time you needed to change the style of a symbol, you would be forced to change ten question symbols and 30 answer symbols. That's not enjoyable work at all.

Instead, by creating a dynamic, flexible structure you enable the computer and Flash to take care of all of the repetitive work. The internal Flash structure that creates the quiz contains two main symbols, one for the question set and one for the answers (11.11), that are updated each time a new question needs to be displayed. To make a graphic change to all of the questions and answers, all you have to do is edit those

two symbols, whereas outside of Flash all you have to do is edit the text file to make the data change. It couldn't get much easier than that.

DEVELOPING YOUR QUIZ

We'll now take a step-by-step approach toward looking at the quiz that was created for the opening sequence of *Terry de Ferma* and see how these principles are applied. This quiz was created in Flash 4 for an interactive television system with Flash 4. The figures show the project as it was brought into Flash 5 with some conversion to the code, but with the slash syntax still prevalent. Code referenced in the book has been changed to the standard Flash 5 dot syntax. Here are the steps:

1. Create a new movie with layers for the quiz questions and the actions. The first step is to create a new Flash movie called **quiz.fla**. You'll want to export it to Flash 4 so be careful, because not all of the new Flash 5 ActionScript will be available.

2. Create symbols. Then create two movie clip symbols calling one **question** and the other **answer**. Place the question symbol on the main timeline in the questions layer. Give it an *instance* name of questions and edit it. Name the first layer **questions** and add a Dynamic Text box with the variable name **q** to it. Make sure Multiline and Word Wrap are selected (11.12). Switch to editing

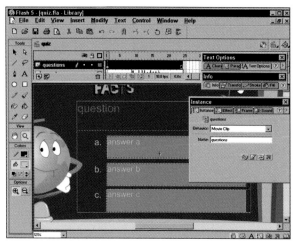

11.11

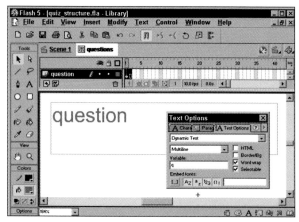

11.12

the answer symbol and create a Dynamic Text box with the variable name **answer**. Select Multiline and Word Wrap again. Switch back to the question symbol and add an answer layer. Take the answer symbol and add it three times into the answer layer (11.13). Make the instance names for the three answer symbols **a**, **b**, and **c**.

3. Create an invisible button that controls the answer symbols. Place it in a layer underneath the Dynamic Text box in the answer symbol and resize it so that it's as large as the text. You're now finished creating the structure (11.14) that you'll need for the quiz.

4. Now that the symbols are built, create a data file for the questions and answers. Create a .txt file called quiz.txt in any text editor. Define the names and values for the data. To keep it simple, call the questions **q1**, **q2**, **q3**, and so on, and the answers **a1**, **b1**, **c1**, **a2**, **b2**, **c2**, and so on. The correct answer for each question needs to go to the movie, so call those **answer1**, **answer2**, **answer3**, and so forth. With Flash's name/value pairs, the start of our text file reads &q1= Marco Polo was:&a1=An explorer who traveled through Asia, India, China and Indonesia.&b1=The discoverer of Antarctica.&c1=An Asian Chicken dish.&answer1=a.

5. The next step is to get the question data into the Flash movie. In the first frame of the movie, add a `loadVariables` action that references the quiz.txt file. We're going to load the data into the questions movie clip, so set the Location to Target and type questions in the text box. We also need to start a counter that can keep track of which question we're on, so set a variable i equal to 1 because the starting question is number 1 (11.15). The counter will be used to set the data for each new question and answer set.

6. Now you need to take the data you've received from the text file and put it in the dynamic text blocks in the symbols. To create a flexible, easily modified quiz structure, none of the variable names inside the Flash movie match the names of the data from the text file. As an example, the answers for the questions are a1, b1, and c1, but we only have a dynamic text block named answer in our symbol. We'll now take the data and rename it to match the names of the text blocks using the counter variable i.

7. The dynamic text field for the question is called q so we need to match it to the data that has been loaded into the questions symbol from the data file called **q1**. Add a label, named **set**,

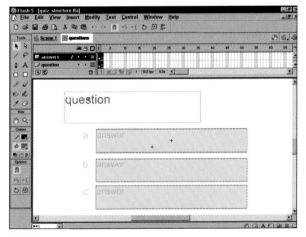

11.13

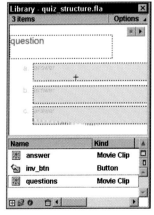

11.14

in the second frame of the movie and add an action that sets the variable q in the questions movie clip to equal the data that's returned from the expression returning a value of questions. q1. Remember that you set *i* to be equal to 1, so you should be able to create an expression that appends the value of *i* to the string questions. q. Variable q has now been successfully filled with value of q1 from the text file. The text blocks for the three answers are treated in a similar way as are the translations of the correct answers to the standard variable name answers (11.16). This approach is flexible because, as long as you continue to increase the value of *i*, it will work for any number of questions and answers.

8. It often takes time for data to get into the movie, so add a safety test to make sure you have data before you try to do something with it. If the data hasn't arrived before you try to set it, you'll end up with an empty quiz. Add an if statement that checks to see if a text string that corresponds to the first answer to the question has loaded into

the Flash movie (11.17). If no data exists yet, then Flash will let the movie play. Add another frame and place a "go to previous frame" action (11.18). Because there's a play action in the first frame if the data hasn't loaded, this creates a loop that keeps checking to see if data is loaded. Once data is loaded, the set actions place all of the data and the movie stops. Test the movie and see if the data loads into the question and answers.

Once you have the data structure created you have to create the structure of the answer movie clips. This enables the child to choose the correct answer, get positive feedback, and move on to the next question or, if the child's answer is incorrect, tells the child to try again. We are going to build an answer movie clip that contains frames with different responses depending on the child's answer choice. An invisible button sends the movie clip to a specific response based on a child's actions. Here are the steps:

1. We're going to control the response that is returned when a child chooses an answer with the underlying invisible button. Four layers exist in the answer movie clip — labels, fa, text, and button.

The first keyframe in the answer symbol is the default state of the symbol and contains a stop action.

Five different response states exist at five different labels (over, r, w, off_r, and off_w) that the invisible button can display based on what the child does. A rollover state is at the over label that shows text when the child rolls over the invisible button.

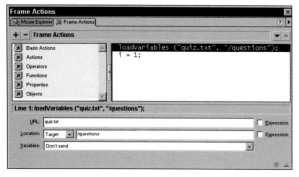

11.15

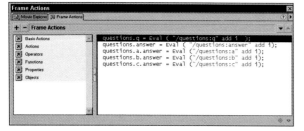

11.16

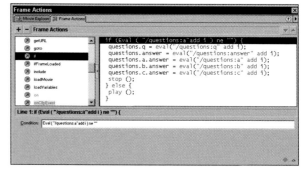

11.17

When a child chooses the answer by pressing the invisible button, two responses are possible. There's a correct response state at a keyframe labeled *r* for when the answer is the correct one "for the question. A wrong response state is at a keyframe labeled *w* for when the question is answered incorrectly.

Two states are also possible when the child releases the invisible button (`off_r` when right, `off_w` when wrong) to answer the question (11.19). This release state is so that, once the question is answered, kids can't accidentally hit the buttons again during the middle of Terry's animation payoff sequence.

In the answer layer, add a Dynamic Text box called **answer**. Underneath each of the labels, create a new keyframe in the text layer and change the color of the text. This will help tell kids that they've done something.

2. Add the code to the button for each state. Let's look at the rollover and rollout states first because they're the easiest (11.20). All you need to do is add a "go to" and "stop" action that goes to the over label. The actions on rollout are just as easy; add an action to go back to the first frame of the movie. Test the movie and play around to see what happens. The data for the question and answers should load. You should be able to change the color of the answer text by rolling over it, but nothing will happen when you press the answer.

3. The "on press" actions are more complicated. When a child presses the button, an action in the movie needs to check to see if the answer is correct

and then let the child know the result with feedback. Positive feedback occurs in two ways in this quiz — Terry does a congratulatory animation and the text changes to tell the child that the answer was correct. If the answer is incorrect, the child is asked to try again.

We check to see if the answer is correct by comparing the correct answer variable (`questions. answer`) to the name of the symbol instance (`_name`). Because the name of the symbol instance will always be the same as the answer in that symbol, it enables us to use the instance name as the value to check against the correct answer variable (11.21). When the answer is correct, add a "go to" and "play" action that sends the main timeline to a label called **correct**. This is where Terry will give his congratulations. Also add an action to go to the label r where the text tells kids they got the answer

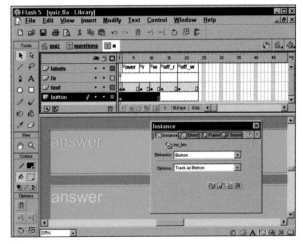

11.19

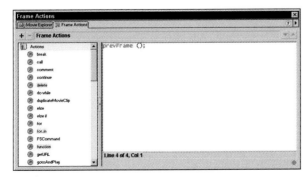

11.18

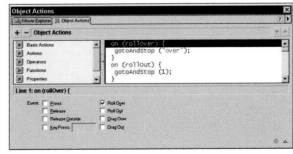

11.20

right. If the child answers incorrectly, then add a "go to the label w" action where the text tells the child to give it another shot. You'll need to change these text fields from Dynamic Text boxes to Static Text boxes or else your answer will continue to show up. Here's the code:

```
on (press) {
    if (_root.questions.answer ==
this._name) {
    _root.gotoAndPlay("correct");
    gotoAndStop("r");
    } else {
    gotoAndStop("w");
    }
}
```

4. Test the movie to make sure the answer-checking really works. If it works properly, then all you need to do is add the release actions to finish the button code.

5. The release state of the button has to do different things based on whether the answer is correct or incorrect. If the answer is incorrect, we go back to frame 1 and give the child another chance to

---

> **TIP**
>
> **Use lots of sound and sound effects as encouragement when giving feedback to kids. Children respond extremely well to positive audio support.**

choose the correct answer. If the answer is correct, then the buttons all need to be turned off so a child can't click them again before the next questions come up. The button is "turned off" by removing it from the frames that contain the labels off_r and off_w (11.22).

On release, we again need to find out whether the answer is right or wrong by comparing the correct answer variable to the symbol instance name. If these match, then this is the correct answer and a series of actions occurs that sends each answer symbol to the off state, whether right or wrong. This is done by comparing the correct answer variable (set to a, b, or c) to the name of each answer symbol (either a, b, or c). When they don't match, that symbol is sent to the off_w label because it's the wrong answer. If they match, then nothing happens because it's the correct answer and that's dealt with in the last action. This action tells the current symbol, which we know to be the correct answer, to go to the label off_r (11.23). Here's the code:

```
on (release, releaseOutside) {
    if (_root.questions.answer ==
this._name) {
        if (this._name != "a") {
        _root.questions.a.¬
gotoAndStop("off_w");
        }
        if (this._name != "b") {
```

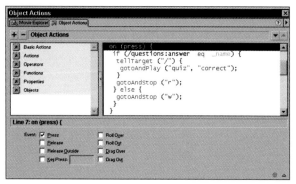

11.21

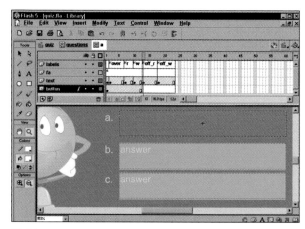

11.22

```
      _root.questions.b.¬
gotoAndStop("off_w");
    }
    if (this._name != "c") {
      _root.questions.c.¬
gotoAndStop("off_w");
    }
    this.gotoAndStop("off_r")
  } else {
      this.gotoAndStop(1);
  }
}
```

6. Test the movie again to make sure that everything works. If the movie functions properly, then go back into the main timeline and add the congratulatory animation in a frame labeled **correct**. Add animation and sound effects; in this case Terry jumps up and spins in happiness (11.24).

7. Add a way to get to the next question. At the end of the animation, add a stop action and, in a new keyframe, add a next button (11.25). The ActionScript on this button does two things—first it adds 1 to the counter variable *i* and then it sends the movie back to the set label. The new *i* value enables the next group of question and answers to be loaded into the question symbol when the set actions occur (11.26).

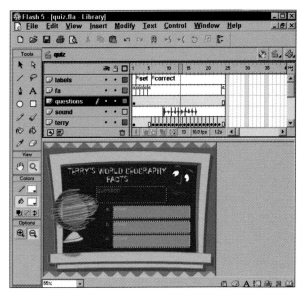

11.24

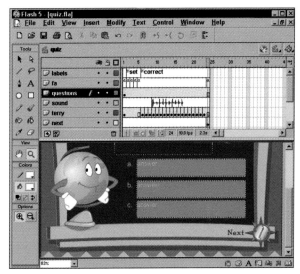

11.25

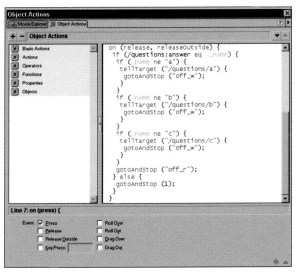

11.23

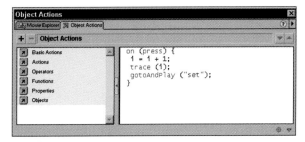

11.26

ADJUSTING DIFFICULTY LEVELS

The preceding discussion completes how to create a Xexible, modular quiz template in Flash based on an external text Wle. Using this as a start, many other features could be added to this template. Different sets of questions and answers, from easy to hard, could be loaded into the movie and, depending on a child's success with a question, a harder or easier question can be delivered to the child. This would enable kids who have trouble with questions to receive easier questions in an attempt to give them more success, while kids who Wnd the questions easy continually get more difficult questions in an attempt to challenge them.

A child's ratio of correct and incorrect answers could be saved and calculated so a child would receive a score at the end of the quiz. A score such as this helps kids to learn and improve. This score could then be sent back to a server database so parents could check in at any time to see how their children are doing. This kind of structured quiz offers many useful ways to help kids learn.

ENCOURAGING EXPLORATION

After the geography quiz, *Terry de Ferma* displays the front of the school. This is a place for kids to explore. Kids are curious. They love to investigate rich digital environments. They'll click around a scene over and over again in order to find all the surprises. Click-point or rollover animations draw kids into the environment and feed their curiosity by returning new and different animations as they play around the scene (11.27).

> **TIP**
>
> In Flash 5, you can create a custom cursor by making the regular cursor invisible and then using a draggable symbol to replace the regular cursor. The code `onClipEvent (load)` is attached to the specific symbol you want to drag and then the code `Mouse.hide` is added followed by `startDrag ("the name of the symbol you are dragging," true)`. When a child goes over a button, the draggable symbol can be changed into a new graphic or animation. This adds to the fun quotient of a scene. Lots of fun click points exist in the scene — kids can turn streetlights on and off, there's a monster hidden under the sewer lid, a kid hidden in a window, and more (11.28). One favorite click-point is a paper airplane that flies out one window of the school and disappears into another window.

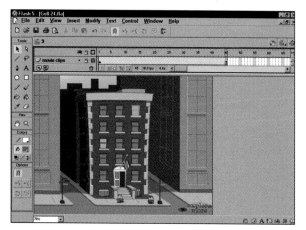

11.27

11.28

ESTABLISHING CLICK POINTS

Click points are easy and fun to create. They use invisible buttons to trigger animations. Sometimes the click points are linked and using one changes the animation of another click point. The first step in creating click points is to take a scene and brainstorm ideas. You should figure on brainstorming five to ten concepts for every click-point idea you keep. If you plan on coming up with this number of ideas, then you're certain to come up with enough great ideas to make a high-quality program.

DEVELOPING THE CLICK POINTS

The basic structure of all your click-point animation will always be the same — a `stop` action in the first frame with the animation at a specific label later in the timeline. There will always be an invisible button in the first frame that goes to the label and plays the animation either on mouse press or mouse rollover. Here are the steps to create click points:

1. The first step in the creating a click point is to open the scene you want to work with in Flash. Insert a new symbol and go into the symbol to edit it. Add layers called **labels**, **fa**, **sound**, **patches**, **plane**, and **button** to the symbol. Add a motion guide to the plane layer. Put a stop action in the first frame of the symbol on the fa layer.

2. Move a few frames into the timeline of the symbol and create the animation of the paper airplane flying through the scene on the plane layer (11.29). The paper airplane is a symbol that follows a curved motion guide to give the sense of fluid, flying movement (11.30). It's also good to add a few sound effects to click-point animations on the sound layer. The patches layer contains any objects from the main scene that the animation needs to go behind. In this case there's a patch of the side of the building at the left of the window so that it appears that the airplane is coming out of the window and not out of the wall.

3. Once you've created the animation, add a label to the frame that starts the animation; in this case the label's called **plane1**.

4. Go back to the first frame of the symbol and create a new button symbol on the button layer. In this case, the shape of the button is based on the window in the main scene, so add a graphic representation of the window shape to the hit area of the new button (11.31).

5. Add the correct code to the button — in this case, a simple "go to and play" action on rollover that goes to the label **play1**. In the last frame of the animation, add a keyframe with code that says "go to and stop" in frame 1. This will return you to the first frame of the movie clip.

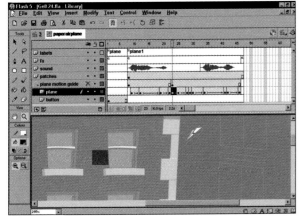

11.29

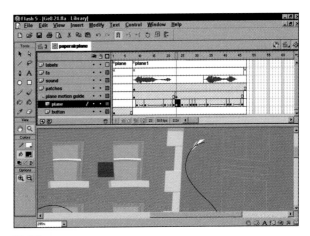

11.30

6. Test your movie and you should have your first click-point animation. You're well on your way to giving kids hours of fun and enjoyment.

CREATING STRONG CHARACTERS FOR EDUCATION

Another important aspect of creating edutainment for kids is creating animated characters that act as teachers and helpers. Terry and Connie are both strong characters that help children learn about the world. Terry focuses on animals and nature (11.32), and Connie focuses on science and technology (11.33). These role models show children how to behave as well as promote the idea that learning and intelligence are fun.

Terry has a gung-ho attitude that sometimes gets him into trouble, but his bravado and Connie's assistance invariably get him out of jams. Connie is a positive role model for girls interested in math and science. Connie loves those subjects and always has the latest technological gadgets (11.34).

After the geography quiz and click-point animation, kids go through an exploring adventure while sampling a variety of educational features. Connie directs information about technology and science. At the end of each bit of information, kids are asked a question about it. Words that are new to kids are highlighted so that when children roll over them a definition pops up, and the word is pronounced. Connie introduces all the information about these subjects and makes them her own.

11.32

11.33

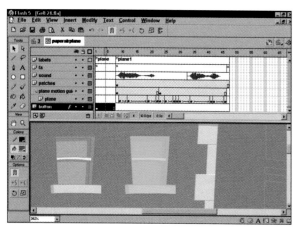

11.31

11.34

Terry gives kids information about the penguin and the animals of the Antarctic (11.35, 11.36), but doesn't ask too many questions. Terry's approach is very visual and shows lots of animal animation. His personal feeling is that it's a whole lot of fun to watch and learn about animals.

As Terry, Connie, and a student motor around the Antarctic on their ice floe, questions are scattered throughout the program that test kids on counting ability and vocabulary (11.37). Each time a child gets the correct answer, there's positive audio feedback and a payoff animation happens (11.38). Negative feedback is never given; instead, kids are asked to try again until they get the right answer. This gives kids an opportunity to learn and improve. The payoff animations are so much fun that lots of times kids will answer the same question several times, giving them even more educational reinforcement.

The goal throughout the project is to maintain a solid educational foundation while still creating a fun experience. It's easy enough to create edutainment that is more entertainment than education, so it's important to always keep the learning goals of the project in front of the development team.

One of the important aspects of the program is to leave kids with projects and printable materials that will extend the learning beyond the computer. These features also promote parental involvement in their

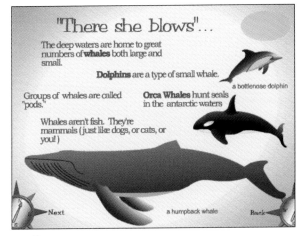

11.35

11.37

11.36

11.38

children's learning. All of the Global Explorers programs contain a Home Experiment that kids can do with their parents. In the Antarctica segment, the experiment teaches children about icebergs by having them make one. A Flash teaching movie shows kids all the steps necessary to freeze and then float their own kitchen-sink iceberg (11.39, 11.40). All of these steps are printable so kids and their parents don't have to be tied to the computer.

Terry de Ferma and the Global Explorers could add another useful feature that would enable a child's progress to be saved to a backend database. The database could store the right and wrong answers of the child as well as data that could show what parts of the program that child liked the most. This database could easily be hooked into a Web-based system that would give parents the ability to track a child's progress.

Parents could check in at anytime to see how their kids are doing and see where a child needed help. This would give parents more of a reason to be involved with their child's education. Because parental involvement is a strong signifier of a child's academic success, this is important to promote.

By using Flash to create educational programming for the Web, developers can create strong characters in an immersive environment while teaching kids in an entertaining way. Great-looking animation gives Flash edutainment an edge with kids. Click-point animations are always fun for curious children, while animation brings characters to life. Quizzes, questions, and games combine to create a winning educational experience for children, while positive feedback gives children an opportunity to learn and improve.

11.39

11.40

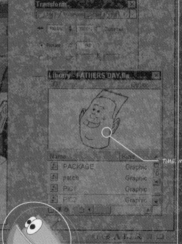

smashing ideas INC.

DATE: 6-10-00	SHEET:
SCALE: 1" = 72 DPI	**12**
DRAWN: TRUSSELL	OF 16
JOB: VIRAL MARKETING	

CHAPTER 12
BRANDING — ADVERTISING, VIRAL MARKETING, AND E-COMMERCE SITES

Flash is leading the Web in a new direction in the fields of branding, viral marketing, and advertising. As the Web matures, sites increasingly need to distinguish themselves from the competition (12.1). Companies can create an emotional reaction to the brand by telling a story that speaks to consumers. The use of animation and entertainment in both brand-building and advertising can be a strong competitive advantage for sites.

Branding, at its best, attempts to build an audience for a product over time by creating an emotional connection with the audience. The biggest and best brands create a loyal following because they have a good product, and they differentiate it in a way that people respond to positively.

Currently Web sites, as well as advertisers, rely on GIF banner ads to build both brand and site traffic, with Web sites attempting to survive based on banner ad revenue and advertisers attempting to gain customers through banners. Unfortunately, it's not working well for either group. Banner ads don't support the full cost of Web sites and, with an average click-through rate of under 1 percent, as shown in a variety of studies, banners aren't successful enough for advertisers.

With these problems in mind, advertisers and sites are turning to much richer immersive advertising and branding using Flash (12.2). Companies are creating full-screen advertisements using rich media and inter-activity. A growing field called *advertainment* focuses on developing self-branded cartoons and games for clients. These kinds of projects have generated from 15 to 20 percent click-through rates for companies we

Interactive media needs to enhance a brand. Flash helps us get a client's message across better.

NATALIE ZEE

12.1

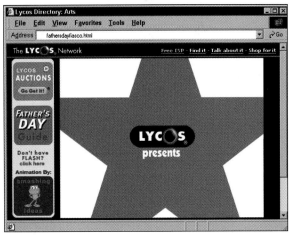

12.2

have worked with, even when the advertising isn't personalized to the consumer or targeted based on personal preferences. The advantages are obvious, so rich media advertising and branding using Flash is growing rapidly.

DIFFERENTIATING SITES

Lycos asked Smashing Ideas to create an entertaining cartoon for a Father's Day promotion revolving around a part of its site. As a portal, Lycos needs to differentiate its Web site from the competition. One way to do that is to give Lycos more of an attitude by using entertainment with humor and a bit of irreverence. Lycos's goals with the project were to keep visitors on the site longer, tell viewers about one of the site's services in an entertaining manner, and then drive those viewers to the chosen service.

Smashing Ideas came up with the idea to create a cartoon about how a family uses the Lycos auction site to get dad a Father's Day gift (12.3). The cartoon runs about two minutes long and tells the story of a family "heirloom" that is placed on the auction site and causes a family bidding war with unexpected results.

KNOWING THE BRAND

It's extremely important to understand the brand if you're going to create entertainment that carries a company's name. We researched the site and the Lycos marketing and advertising material to get a better feeling

for the Lycos brand. To some degree Lycos wanted to create entertainment that didn't entirely mirror the brand so we weren't confined to what we found. However, we did need to understand how the brand was being portrayed before we began brainstorming.

The Lycos brand currently revolves around the Lycos dog, a black retriever signifying the search and fetch roots of the site. Although we didn't have to focus on the dog for our cartoon, we did add it as a fun detail for eagle-eyed viewers to catch (12.4). The television ad spots featuring the Lycos dog are slightly irreverent and fun.

The Lycos site itself contains the normal set of portal tools such as search, mail, personalization, stocks and news. The site does distinguish itself from competitors through color and layout. When product features don't create great differentiation, the brand then becomes paramount to attracting consumers and creating audience loyalty. With this in mind, we went to work.

Smashing Ideas came up with a variety of concepts before we settled on the *Father's Day Fiasco* idea. The biggest problem with many of the ideas we brainstormed was that they didn't really fit the Lycos brand. Creative limits have to be accepted when it comes to creating entertainment specifically for brands. Because the entertainment is so closely affiliated with the brand, it has to fit the brand's audience and can't create a negative reaction toward the brand among viewers.

We came up with ideas about volcano disaster victims checking for maps to help escape lava flows, the band on the Titanic downloading MP3s to get just

12.3

12.4

the right final song, pygmies that loved Lycos, and so on. In each case there was a problem with the idea as it related to the brand. Many of the ideas were funny and irreverent, but they didn't adequately promote a Lycos service or reach a wide enough audience.

The idea that finally worked showed a family, a major part of the Lycos audience, using a Lycos site service in a humorous way. In *Father's Day Fiasco*, two teenage boys need to buy their dad a gift for Father's Day. One of the few items dad really loves is a curvaceous bookend. Although he lost the other one years ago, he won't give up his spectacular collectable. While the boys are moaning about how hard it is to get dad a

gift, their mother takes the bookend and loads it onto the Lycos auction service (12.5–12.7).

When dad logs onto the auction site, he discovers the long-lost matching bookend (12.8, 12.9). At the same time his two sons stumble upon the auction (12.10, 12.11). Without realizing it, they begin bidding against each other and, as the seconds tick down, become increasingly nervous (12.12, 12.13). As the price mounts, mom is all smiles (12.14). The boys win the bidding war and all involved show the emotions of a completed auction — celebration at success, happiness at a profit turned, and sadness at an object lost (12.15–12.17).

You can imagine the surprise when the mailman delivers the Father's Day gift from the two boys and dad realizes he's got his old bookend back. The story

12.5

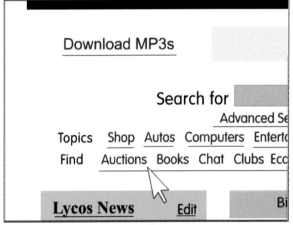

12.7

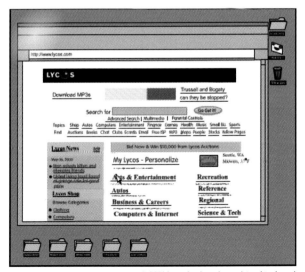

12.6

12.8

12.9

12.12

12.10

12.13

12.11

12.14

12.15

12.16

12.17

uses humor to show how easy it is for the whole family to use the Lycos auction service. The cartoon, as directed by Smashing Ideas' Joel Trussell, achieves the Lycos goals and promotes the brand through storytelling. The story that is told captures the drama and excitement of the auction while showcasing the service as an easy way to buy or sell items.

The technical requirements we had to consider when we thought about the cartoon are no different than any other form of entertainment on the Web, namely the target computer platform and the proper bandwidth. The audience for the cartoon was any Lycos site visitor with a 56K modem connection. This meant we had to do our utmost to keep the cartoon file small in size, but rich in detail and production quality.

The cartoon starts out with a short title sequence to help cover the download of the cartoon. The title sequence begins almost instantaneously and then turns into a short loading sequence for lower-speed connections (12.18). There's a one and a half minute wait on a 56K connection and a wait of around two and a half minutes on a 28.8K connection. Although this is a longer wait than we would have preferred, it's due to the music and dialog, which we couldn't shorten without taking away from the cartoon.

Father's Day Fiasco debuted as a graphic link on the front page of the Lycos site and was also sent out as a URL link in an e-mail to the Lycos mailing list. Hundreds of thousands of viewers were exposed to the cartoon and it was successful because it added to the stickiness of the Lycos site, improved click-through to the auction service, and put Lycos in an entertaining context.

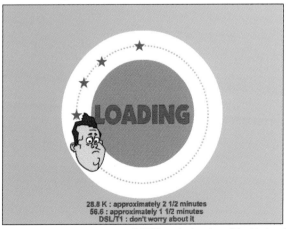

12.18

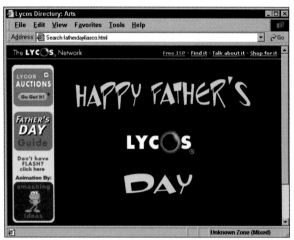

12.19

RAISING CLICK-THROUGH RATES

One of Lycos's goals with the cartoon was to get viewers to click through once they watched the whole cartoon. The cartoon's Web page contained persistent links to related content or services. The cartoon was embedded in a page with prominent graphic links to the auction site and a special Father's Day Guide section of the Lycos site (12.19). Click-through to the auction service occurs through the persistent navigation in the Web page or a "call to action" at the end of the cartoon telling the viewer to click through to the auction site.

Internet research firms have shown that providing simple calls to action such as Click Here or Click Now significantly increase the number of click-throughs on a banner ad. The same is true of rich media ads, so the end of *Father's Day Fiasco* contains a button telling viewers to click through to the auction site (12.20, 12.21). Because we want to make this choice as easy for people as possible, the button hit area occupies the entire screen (12.22). In the end, the Lycos *Father's Day Fiasco* cartoon contributed a higher than average click-through while keeping viewers on the site longer and giving them a strong brand impression.

12.20

12.21

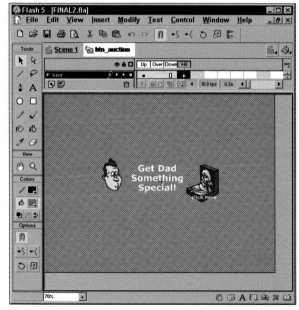

12.22

BUILDING BRAND IDENTITY

Flash provides e-commerce sites a way to build a brand identity through engaging multimedia content. The Crab Broker is a seafood site that ships fresh seafood from Alaska, the Pacific Northwest, and Australia to Web consumers around the world. The company makes a commitment to providing the finest quality seafood and the best service to every customer while providing recipes and seafood-related information through the *Hook, Line and Sinker* newsletter. The company's brand focuses on putting a fun, fresh face on seafood (12.23).

The Crab Broker approached Smashing Ideas to animate the site's mascot, a lovable crab named Louie. The goal was to give the crab a personality that shoppers would associate with the site in order to make consumers more loyal (12.24, 12.25). The crab

12.24

12.25

12.23

ZEE ON FLASH FOR BRANDS

Natalie Zee is the interactive design director of rich media at marchFIRST, a global digital services company where she's involved with bringing many high-profile brands into the digital media space. She has also coauthored books about the Web, including *HTML Artistry: More Than Code* (Indianapolis, IN: Hayden Books, 1998)and *The Last Mile: Broadband and the Next Internet Revolution* (New York: McGraw-Hill, 2000).

Q: You work on projects for major consumer brands. Do you approach these clients' Flash Web projects any differently than HTML projects?

A: There is a difference in the way we approach Flash projects. Where HTML is limiting in some aspects of interactivity, we try to make the most of it with Flash — full-screen, audio, motion, and interactivity. It helps us get a client's message across better. Take harman/ kardon for instance (`www.harman-multimedia.com`). Our concept was to show off its new product line, which are speakers and subwoofers for computer desktops. We needed Flash to create an mascot appears consistently throughout the site as well as in other marketing materials and in site merchandise (12.26). The crab is used in a consistent way throughout the branding material (12.27) and, as Rob George, the founder of the Crab Broker, points out, "I figured visitors would easily remember him, which in turn, would make them remember the site. My customers and first-time visitors just love him."

Using a mascot can also bind consumers more closely to the site by generating fun contests and content. The Crab Broker recently ran a Name the Crab contest. In a short time, thousands of entries had been received from site fans. The contest gave consumers another reason to get involved with the site. The winning name, Louie, will help shape the future personality of the mascot and enable him to become an even more integral part of the site.

Louie can now be a helper throughout the site. He can recommend different seafood packages or introduce recipes. The benefits of the Louie character are hard to quantify, but Rob George puts it best when he says "Louie makes it a site that people will tell their friends about, which you can't put a price on, but it's

12.26

12.27

interactive environment for users so they could really experience the product. With Flash, they can get a 360-degree view of the product or see and hear the animated sound comparison chart.

Q: How do you approach creating interactive media that fits the brand?
A: It's all about balance and cohesiveness. Some people think interactive media is making things move and be "flashy." We all know how much harder it is because you don't want to misrepresent a brand by the kind of animation

that is going on. I approach it this way. Interactive media needs to enhance a brand. For a brand such as harman/kardon the interactive design team used the product box designs (also designed by marchFIRST) as an inspiration for the Flash site. How can you best translate these beautiful transparent speakers and subwoofers online? We decided we needed to really show the product with full-screen images and product spins, as well as having music to enhance the whole user experience. Because we work on brands for offline as well as online

work, we can make sure the brand message is clear throughout.

Q: With such factors as consumer communication and instant feedback, do brands need to change the way they are defined to fit the strengths of interactive media?
A: Definitely. For a brand such as Barbie, I was really pleased that the client was so open to new and different ideas on how to redesign Barbie.com. The site really enhances the brand, but it also takes advantage of the medium, enabling rich,

exactly what we're striving for." In retail sales, word of mouth is a powerful force.

Because the Crab Broker site is focused on retail sales, the animation could not interfere with the site's primary retail sales mission. With Flash, we were able to create animations of the mascot with extremely small file sizes that easily integrated into the HTML pages of the site. The small file sizes mean that consumers don't have to wait a long time for animation to load, even when they're using low-speed connections. If consumers don't have Flash, then the animations can easily be changed into static GIFs.

ADDING AN IMAGE IF FLASH ISN'T INSTALLED

Flash has a Publishing Template feature that enables developers to select predefined HTML templates or create their own (12.28). The standard templates will create an HTML file that either places the Flash movie or adds JavaScript code that checks for and prompts the Web user to install Flash 3, 4, or 5 (12.29, 12.30). One template lets a viewer choose whether he or she wants to download the Flash Player and, if they don't, sets a cookie so the viewer always sees static images in the future. Specialized templates exist to create pages for Generator, QuickTime, or static image display.

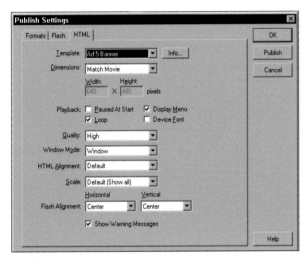

12.28

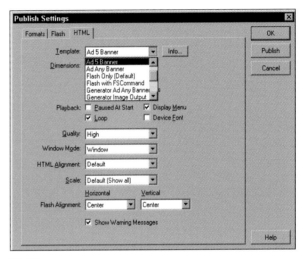

12.29

interactive activities that appeals to little girls. The concepts behind the games were well thought out to help girls have fun, express themselves, and at the same time better prepares them for the digital future. We worked closely with Mattel and their team of little girls who gave us feedback on their likes and dislikes. The end result is offline and online brands that support each other and make the overall brand stronger.

Q: Is it more of a challenge to create interactive media for a new brand or established brands?
A: Creating interactive media for both new as well as established brands is definitely a challenge because the medium is so new and most clients have a directive to be successful in the digital realm of their business. That said, though, it is slightly more difficult to work with new brands because what you establish for them on the Web could be one of the first impressions or experiences consumers have.

Q: What are the challenges you face in designing interactive media for clients?
A: Part of the challenge and frustration is having to support multiple browsers and platforms. We are all in this great exciting time trying to move things forward and it gets difficult because you can get bogged down on the intricacies of platforms and browsers that are so two years ago.

Q: How important is it to understand the technical limitations of the medium and the possibilities of the technology

Although multiple templates come with Flash, you often need to create your own specific templates. If you know how to create a regular HTML page, it's as easy as creating your HTML code and then replacing any of the values relating to the Flash movie with variables that begin with a dollar sign ($). An easy way to see some of these variables is to open one of the standard templates that comes with Flash. These are located in the Flash 5\HTML folder.

As an example of how to create variables in an HTML template for Flash, the following HTML code would be customized so that flashmovie.swf would be changed to $MO, while 440 would be changed to $WI, and 330 would be changed to $HE.

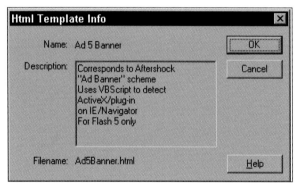

12.30

```
<embed src="flashmovie.swf"
width="440" height="330"> </embed>

<embed src=$MO width=$WI
height=$HE></embed>
```

When the modified code is saved in an HTML page and placed in the Flash 5\HTML folder, a developer can choose that template and publish to it. This becomes incredibly useful when complex HTML code needs to be developed. It can be created by one person and then shared with the rest of a development team to be used at the click of a button.

This more complex code can include the ability to swap out an HTML image if Flash is not present. Although some of Flash's default templates will do this, more complex JavaScript routines are usually necessary to ensure that the swap occurs on every machine. The following JavaScript routine is used on the Crab Broker site to replace the Flash logo with a GIF image if Flash is not installed.

```
<SCRIPT LANGUAGE="JavaScript">
<!--hiding contents from old browsers
//If this browser understands the
mimeTypes property and recognizes the
MIME Type
//"application/x-shockwave-flash"...
```

---

in order to create compelling interactive media?

A: It's very important for a designer to be both visually and technically creative. Because we are designing for a medium that is constantly evolving, technology plays an important role. As designers, we are shaping the way in which this technology is being used and perceived. I'm amazed sometimes at how much stuff we have to balance, but it's such an integral part of life on the Web.

Q: Describe your approach to a project. How do you begin?

A: A client usually comes to us with certain needs and requirements. We take that information and do additional research on our own to take ideas further. For instance, while designing games for Barbie.com, we did research by looking at all the Barbie toys on the market and combined that with real games kids are playing. We translated these physical activities to the online world with games that little girls could have fun with and understand, while

getting familiar with a computer at the same time.

Storyboards and prototypes help us visualize and test out whether or not our ideas will work. Then we do a lot of organizing, designing, and programming to put the final pieces together. Finally, it's testing, testing, and more testing to make sure that everything works.

Q: What is your guiding philosophy toward interactive media?

A: The key word in interactive media is *interact*. My goal is to try to connect the

```
if (navigator.mimeTypes &&
navigator.mimeTypes["application/
x-shockwave-flash"]){
    //...write out the following
<EMBED> tag into the document.
    document.write('<embed src="
images/logo.swf" swLiveConnect=
"FALSE" WIDTH="550" HEIGHT="225"
LOOP="true" QUALITY="autohigh"
BGCOLOR="#FFFFFF" TYPE="application/
x-shockwave-flash" PLUGINSPAGE=
"http://www.macromedia.com/shockwave/
download/index.cgi?P1_Prod_Version=
ShockwaveFlash">');
    }
    //Otherwise,...
else {
    //...write out the following <IMG>
tag into the document. The image need
    //not be the same size as the
Flash Player movie, but it may help
you lay out the
    //page if you can predict the size
of the object reliably.
    document.write('<IMG
SRC="images/home_logo.gif" WIDTH="400"
HEIGHT="140" BORDER="0" ALT="The Crab
Broker">');
```

```
}
//Done hiding from old browsers.-->
</SCRIPT>
```

Using these techniques helps the Crab Broker site succeed. Users don't have any barriers to buying seafood from the site because they don't have to download the Flash Player if they don't want to. If they do have the Flash Player, then they get a more entertaining experience with no added download times.

USING VIRAL ENTERTAINMENT AND ADVERTISING

Wakmail, a service of Smashing Ideas' subsidiary MediaBlink, creates pass-along e-mail entertainment programming for clients (12.31). Wakmail content can be created specifically for a sponsor, or advertisers can place rich media advertising into a stable of Wakmail programming. With an 18- to 35-year-old male demographic, the programming is edgy, irreverent, and outrageous.

Wakmail focuses on creating short interactive animated content that can be downloaded from the Wakmail site or a client's site. Wakmails can be integrated into Web pages or attached to rich media e-mail. The goal is to get short, funny entertainment

---

user to the site so that he or she is engaged, entertained, and informed.

Q: What influences your work?
A: Everything influences me as a designer — observing everyday life. I like that spark of inspiration sometimes if I see a shape in a building and that becomes the beginnings of a project. It's all about seeing what's going on at the moment, forecasting, and translating that into my work. And I get a lot of inspiration from magazines. I'm addicted to magazines.

In terms of other designers, Paul Rand, Tibor Kalman, and Kyle Cooper have definitely been major influences on me both for work and life. Each of them has done phenomenal work in design while balancing such admirable traits such as teaching (Rand), social responsibility (Kalman), and humbleness (Cooper).

Q: What's a dream project?
A: A dream project is no budget, no deadlines, and no client feedback. Impossible!

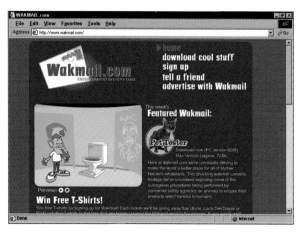

12.31

12.32

12.33

content to as many people as possible in as short a time as possible.

As an example of the content, the viewer can get eight different jokes in the Wakmail piece "Kev Needs a Job, Damnit." All of the jokes are based on the premise that Kev is practicing for a job interview. As viewers click each choice they get to view a surprising new tactic Kev is rehearsing (12.32).

If a viewer is online, then a rich media ad is delivered from the Wakmail ad server at the start of the entertainment. If a viewer is offline, then a Wakmail self-branding promotion plays. When the viewer clicks the last choice, an animation segment plays and then the viewer is moved into an end screen containing navigation, information about Wakmail, and another sponsor or self-branding ad (12.33).

Current click-through rates for these ads are in the 18 to 20 percent range for products targeted at the demographic. Although this rate will undoubtedly decline, it shows how much more effective large rich media ads are in creating both click-throughs and a branding experience. Banner ads barely make an impression anymore, but rich media advertising delivers results.

FLASH PROJECTORS

Most of the Wakmails are created to be viewed as projectors. A Flash projector enables a Flash movie to be viewed on a Windows or Mac computer where the Flash Player isn't installed. Projectors also enable people to view Flash movies outside of the browser. When Flash movies are turned into projectors, the Flash standalone player is "wrapped" into the file and plays the movie back directly.

It's a straightforward process to turn Flash movies into projectors for Windows and the Macintosh. The easiest way to create projectors is to open the Publish preferences in the File menu when you have a movie open in Flash (12.34). Select the Windows Projector (.exe) and the Macintosh Projector types in the Formats tab. When you publish the Flash movie by choosing File ➢ Publish, two projectors will be created — a Windows Projector (EXE) and a Macintosh Projector. These can easily be sent to people who don't have the Flash Player.

CREATING PASS-ALONG MEDIA

The goal with Wakmail is to create entertaining programming that can carry rich media advertising that increases an advertiser's brand awareness and improves click-through rates. To do this, Wakmail creates pass-along media. Pass-along media uses the viral nature of the Web by providing entertainment that people want to share with their friends. Because e-mail is instantaneous, pass-along media can lead to rapid and immense viewership.

As an example of this, one of the original Wakmail-style programs we created was sent to a mailing list of approximately 100,000 people. Around 30,000 of those people received the entertainment as a projector attached to an e-mail while the other 70,000 received it as a URL link in a marketing newsletter e-mail to a download page. Out of that original group of people who had access to the entertainment, over 1,000,000 views of the program were logged in the first month alone.

The challenge, then, is to create entertainment that viewers truly want to share with friends. Our experience with this format shows that it's extremely important to create entertainment targeted at your audience. You have to know if your audience is old or young, male or female, irreverent or stodgy. If the audience that receives the entertainment really likes it, it'll immediately send it along to friends; if it's the wrong audience then it'll promptly delete it and probably send you hate mail as well.

We've found that humor and small games are the most passed-along form of Web entertainment. Although glad tidings and feel-good messages are successful for some audiences, humor and games consistently work.

It's difficult to predict how viewers will react to entertainment before they actually see it, but one of the standard ways to get media passed along is to tap into an issue of the moment. Whether it's about drivers using cell phones or some kind of hot-button political topic, people love humor about current issues and pass it along.

Besides trying to make entertainment that's truly engaging in order to get it passed along, you need to be aware of a few other rules with this kind of media. First, don't spam! If you're going to send messages to people, make sure the group of people you're targeting want to get your message. Make sure you have an opt-in e-mail list, meaning that the people who are on the list signed up for it, and that people can be removed from this list upon request.

With these thoughts in mind, create a Flash movie that everybody you know will pass around. If people like it and send it to their friends, you're sure to gain—if nothing else—fame and notoriety. Combine that with rich media advertising and there's even the opportunity to make some money at it because rich media advertising offers significant opportunities for companies to create powerful marketing and branding messages. That's what the Web is currently lacking and, when a personalized rich media advertising vehicle is finally created, much larger amounts of advertising money will certainly pour into the Web.

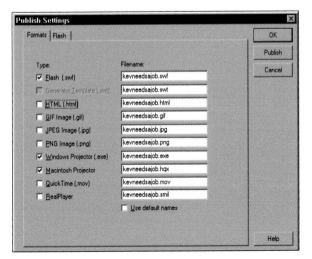

12.34

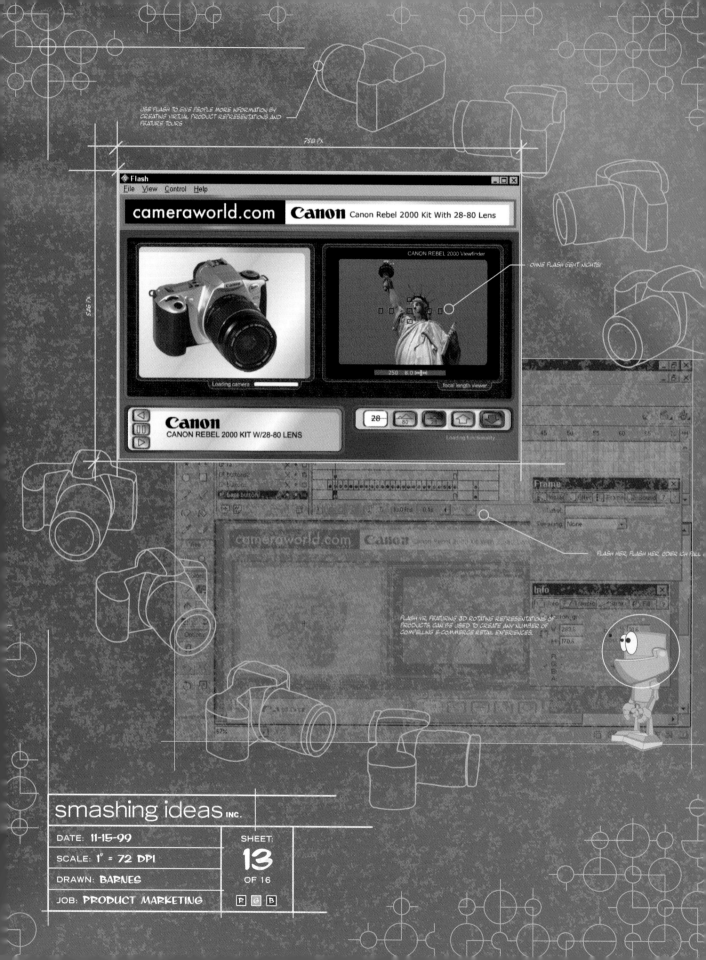

CHAPTER 13
DISPLAYING AND MARKETING PRODUCTS

Internet retailers often struggle to find a way to show their customers a realistic representation of their product that will impress people enough to buy. Often a single photograph cannot show enough of a product to convince people that they should buy it. Web sites can use Flash to give people more information by creating virtual product representations and feature tours. Flash Virtual Reality (VR), featuring 3D rotating representations of products (13.1–13.3), can be used to create any number of compelling e-commerce retail experiences, while adding information about features provides users with a better understanding of the product.

CREATING FLASH VIRTUAL REALITY

Cameraworld, a noted photo and video retailer, runs an e-commerce site targeting average Web consumers at www.cameraworld.com (13.4). The company wanted to create a Web experience where customers could play with the zoom strength of cameras while seeing a virtual representation of that camera combined with text information (13.5). Flash VR (virtual reality) enables developers to create 360-degree product rotations packed with information that viewers can control.

One of the keys to product display in Internet retail is to make it easy for everybody to see the product. If consumers can't see it and want it, then they won't buy it. Because the client wanted the largest number of possible consumers to see the experience, it was determined that Flash 3 would be the player choice for

If you show them, they will buy.

13.1

13.2

the project. Although Flash 3 put significant limitation on the programming side, this project deconstruction is an important case of the client knowing best about its business. As Flash developers, we have to create a successful project within our client's needs.

Because more than 90 percent of the Web can currently see Flash 3 content, the following manner of creating Flash VR is a great solution for consumer-oriented retail Web sites. It does, however, push the program to its limits. This project is possible in Flash 3, but just barely.

LOADING THE EXPERIENCE

The piece requires 63K to load prior to a viewer getting an experience (13.6). Because the site was aimed at higher bandwidth Web users, this size was reasonable. Any wait that occurs is covered by streaming in the interface with text information and a spinning wireframe of the camera (13.7). Once this has loaded, the zoom photos in the camera viewfinder appear (13.8) to give the user a new image to look at while the wireframe of the camera spins. Once all of the camera photos used in the VR experience have downloaded, then the VR camera fades in while the wireframe fades out.

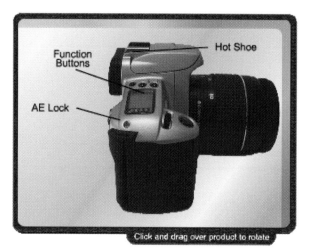

13.3

13.4

13.5

13.6

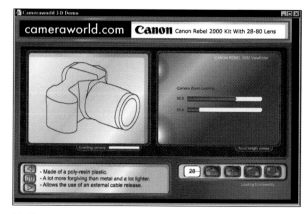

13.7

TAKING THE PHOTOS

To create a VR experience, a developer needs to take a series of 24 photos of a product on a turntable set at 15-degree intervals. This is best done on a turntable that lets a product be locked down onto it. Although a variety of expensive turntables have been created specifically for this process, a regular turntable can be modified to do this.

The lens angle you choose to use will also change the look and feel of the spin. Telephoto lenses compress the plane of the picture, while wide-angle lenses emphasize it. A fish-eye lens could be used to make the product really pop out of the background. The photos were taken against a neutral background that made it easy to remove the background.

We also took a second series of photos showing how the zoom lens moved in and out as it was focused. This complete set of photos provided the rough assets that were manipulated and then imported into Flash to create the 360-degree VR experience.

WORKING WITH THE PHOTOS

Although developers can bring photo assets into Flash, break them apart, and crop them, we don't recommend it. Flash isn't a great photo editing tool. If you're in dire straits, you can use it to crop photos and delete areas of the photo, but it should never be your flrst choice. Instead, use a specialty tool such as Adobe Photoshop or Macromedia Fireworks to edit your photos.

Flash supports the importation of PNG files with alpha channels. This is useful because PNG files with alpha channels create smaller files and enable developers to use more fully featured photo editing tools to work with assets prior to bringing them into Flash. To make the background of an image transparent prior to import into Flash, we'll use Fireworks to create a PNG Xle with an alpha channel. Here are the steps:

1. Open the image in Fireworks (13.9).
2. Click the background with the Magic Wand tool (13.10). You may need to zoom into each photo and select around the edges of the product to get all parts of the background. Once the entire background has been selected, delete it (13.11). This will make the background an alpha channel when you save the image.
3. Save the image. The standard Fireworks file format is PNG so there's no way to go wrong here.

> **NOTE**
>
> **Several books on both Photoshop and Fireworks are available from IDG Books Worldwide (now known as Hungry Minds, Inc.). We recommend either the *Photoshop 6 Bible* by Deke McClelland or the *Fireworks 3 Bible* by Joe Lowery. Visit** `www.hungryminds.com` **for more book ideas.**

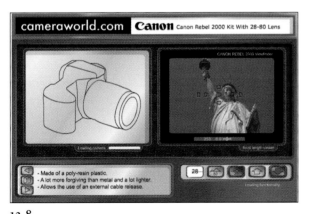

13.8

13.9

4. Repeat these steps for each photo in the series. Make sure to save them as a series of sequentially numbered images such as **img001.png**, **img002. png**, and so on (13.12).

5. Import the first PNG in the series into Flash (13.13). Flash will ask you how you want the PNG file imported. Leave the defaults checked. Flash will also ask whether you want to bring the entire sequential series into the program (13.14). You want to agree to this because Flash will then import all of the Xles and put them in their own frames. Even better, the sequence will be in the right order and, if your graphics were all the same size, then they'll be aligned properly.

6. If the photography has been done correctly, then you're now finished with your image rotation. Each camera image has a transparent background and the animation sequence shows the spin exactly the way the photographer shot it. If the spin was shot a bit oV, then you might need to adjust the location of the photos frame by frame.

Your next step of the process is to create a wireframe of the camera spinning. Although the easiest way to do this would be to have 3D model made of each camera and export a series of vector images based on a 3D rotation, we didn't have that luxury. Instead, we drew vector outlines over the top of the imported photos. The one key to doing this is to put the line drawings and photos on different layers and make sure you lock the photo layer. The last thing you want to do is accidentally move your photos out of alignment.

DEMONSTRATING FLASH VR

The Flash VR product experience as demonstrated in the following example is a Flash 3 movie. Given the limitations of that version of Flash, it's amazing that it even works. You have a variety of reasons to use Flash 3, chief among them being that, as previously mentioned, more than 90 percent of Web users can see Flash 3 movies. For e-retailers and other sites wanting to provide users with a VR experience with the lowest barrier to view it, this is the best possible solution.

Although Flash 3 offers the most extensive user base, it offers the least amount of features and programmability. Sites that currently require Flash 4

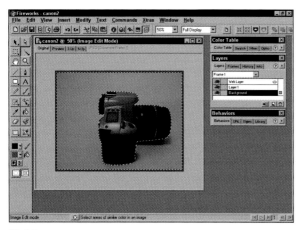

13.10

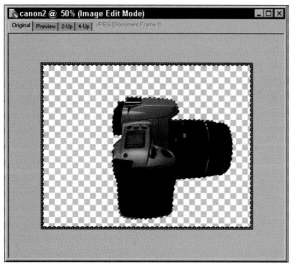

13.11

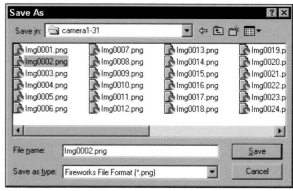

13.12

should deflnitely use it to create a more sophisticated VR experience. A better product spin or VR experience could be achieved in Flash 4 by tracking the mouse cursor at all times using a draggable movie clip. By dragging an invisible movie clip, the Flash movie can always calculate the direction and speed the mouse cursor is moving. Based on that information, ActionScript can be written that moves smoothly through your series of images.

This would provide a better user experience because the buttons used in the camera spin in Flash 3 sometimes lose contact with the mouse cursor. At those times the spin stops working and the user has to click the image to begin the drag again. By creating a Flash ActionScript code module, this VR experience would also enable multiple versions of product spins to be built more quickly.

Other reasons to do this in Flash 4 would be to extend the capabilities of the experience to provide customized information through variables and server-side calls. An order form could be integrated directly into the user experience or sales information could be passed into the movie.

As sites begin to use Flash 5, it will allow for even greater functionality with the new capability to access XML data, create an XML socket, and add the power of the new ActionScript language. Much smoother VR could be created in Flash 5 by using mathematical functions to track the mouse cursor and swap the photos. Integrated customer service features could enable consumers to contact store representatives immediately with questions about products. Flash 5 would add signiflcant value to a VR experience like this one.

BUILDING A VR EXPERIENCE

Programming for Flash 3 is much different than what we've learned about so far. It's extremely limited when compared with programming in Flash 5. In Flash 3, the only way to create interactivity was to create symbols and use `Tell Target` to communicate with them. Buttons and frames could talk to a symbol and tell it to go to a speciflc label and frames. There were no variables or calls, so it was almost impossible to create dynamic events.

The example that follows shows the steps to create a Flash VR experience for Flash 3. If this same experience were to be created in Flash 5, then the steps to make it would be quite different. The reason for understanding how to do this kind of project in Flash 3 is that the approach to programming in Flash 5 is so different that projects in Flash 5 won't work with the Flash 3 player. This is completely unacceptable to many consumer retail sites so the project must be done for the Flash 3 player and can then contain additional features that only work with more recent players.

In this project, the products rotate based on the interaction of two movie clips, one containing the photos showing the VR product experience and the other containing the buttons that make the camera spin.

Before you begin anything else, start a new Flash movie. Open the Publish Settings and select Export to Flash 3. When you are working in Flash with this option checked, all of the ActionScript that won't work in Flash 3 is highlighted in yellow. This is incredibly useful because it makes it harder to make mistakes by using ActionScript that's not allowed.

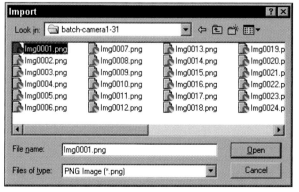

13.13

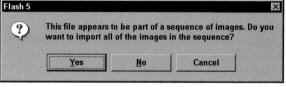

13.14

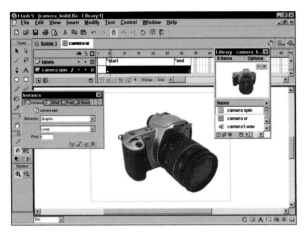

13.15

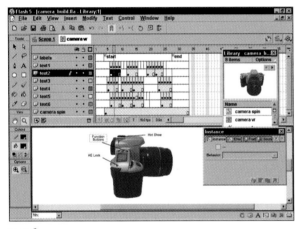

13.16

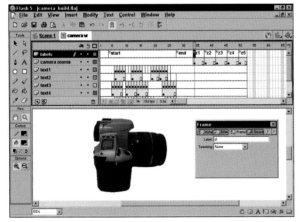

13.17

Once that's done, you're ready to get started. Follow these steps:

1. Create a graphic symbol called **camera spin**.

2. Import the series of images, in this case a total of 24, into this symbol.

3. Once the images are imported they may need to be moved around slightly to get the smoothest possible product animation. This can occur if the product gets slightly off axis on the turntable during the photography session.

4. Create a movie clip symbol called **camera vr** and edit it.

5. Add a layer, name it labels, and place a start label in frame 4. Add the camera spin symbol to a new layer called **camera spin** in frame 4. Place an end label in frame 28 where the camera's spin ends (13.15).

6. Add text describing the various features of the camera in layers above the camera spin (13.16). Make sure short text lasts for 5–10 frames so that viewers can read it. Longer text should last for 15–20 frames.

7. At the end of the movie clip, add in all the zoom photos. Add labels defining the parts of the zoom from *z1* to *z5* (13.17).

8. Add empty frames at the beginning of the movie clip. In the first frame, add a "go to and stop" action in the frame labeled start (13.18).

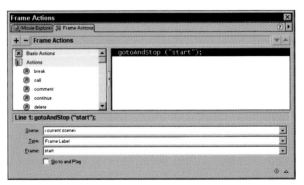

13.18

9. Now that the camera spin movie clip is ready, it's time to place it on the main timeline. When you place it in the main timeline, a small white circle is the only thing that shows up. This is because the first frame of the movie clip does not contain any graphics. Name the symbol instance **camera** (13.19).

CREATING THE INTERACTIVITY

Our next step is to add the interactivity to the camera spin. We want the user to be able to spin the camera, move the cursor away from it, and then be able to come back and spin the camera again from the last position. Because this is Flash 3, it's not an easy thing to do.

The interactivity is done through another movie clip called camera vr buttons. This symbol contains a series of buttons that communicate directly with the frames in the camera vr movie clip. The buttons dictate which frame the camera vr movie clip goes to as the user moves the mouse cursor around.

To do this, there has to be a different set of buttons in the camera vr buttons movie clip that relate to each different frame of the VR experience in the camera vr movie clip. This is because Flash 3 does not support variables. In Flash 4, the spin could be controlled by an expression that sequentially changed which label number the camera vr was sent to.

We tried many different ways to combine the two movie clips in Flash 3, from exotic labeling schemes to tricky mouse cursor tracking, but, after considerable testing, we eventually found a solution that provided the best possible results on all computers (13.20). Here are the steps to combine the two movie clips:

1. Create another movie clip called **camera vr buttons**. The layout of this movie clip is similar to the layout of the camera vr movie clip.

2. You'll see start and end labels as well as a new set of labels *1* to *24* in between. The first frame contains an action that sends the movie to the start label (13.21).

13.20

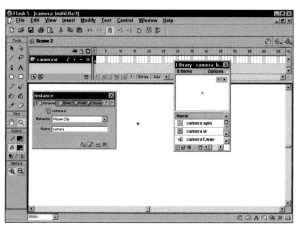

13.19

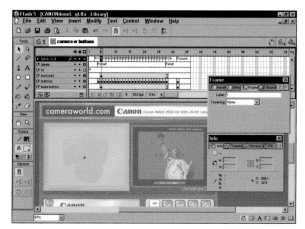

13.21

3. The next part of creating the interactivity is the hard work of adding all the buttons, coding them, and ensuring that they work. The first button that is added is a large rectangular button on the bottom layer (13.22). This is a safety valve button that, on release, always sends the button movie clip back to the start label (13.23).

4. The next layer up contains a set of 24 invisible buttons, one for each frame of the camera spin.

5. Each button in the start frame contains an action to "go to and stop" at one of these specific frames on press (13.24). The movie clip is always sent back to this frame when a viewer releases the button. The 24 buttons in the start frame correspond to labels *1* through *24* sequentially from left to right. For example, if a user clicks the fourth button from the left the movie would go to and stop at label *4*.

6. The button series in label 4 is indicative of all the other series so lets examine it more closely. After pressing the button and going to label 4, the viewer is now pressing on an anchor button that does only one thing — it returns the movie clip to the start label when the button is released (13.25).

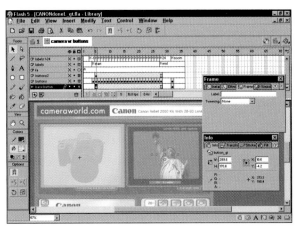

13.22

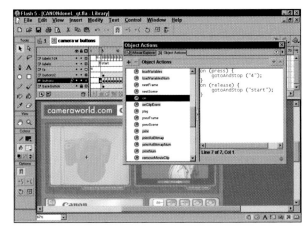

13.24

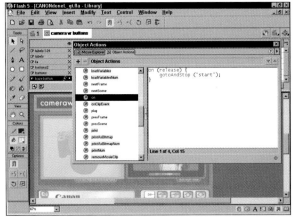

13.23

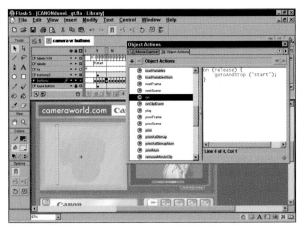

13.25

7. If the viewer drags the mouse cursor, then the cursor moves over the next button in the series in that frame. The button to the right of the anchor button always contains code that tells the camera target to go to the next frame and then tells itself to go to the next frame in the timeline (13.26). The button to the left contains code that tells the camera target to move to the previous frame and then tells itself to go to the previous frame in the timeline (13.27). Both of the buttons contain code that returns the movie clip to the start label on release.

8. All of the buttons to the right of the anchor button contain exactly the same code as the button just described. They move the camera vr target and the movie clip's timeline to the next frame. All of the buttons to the left contain code that sends the camera vr target and the movie clip's timeline to the previous frame. The reason for this redundant setup is that, in our testing, the frame movements and button capture of the mouse cursor were often delayed. By making all of the buttons in the frame map to the next frame in both the camera vr target and the movie clip's timeline, we ensured that the spin didn't lose any frames. Even if the viewer moved the mouse quickly, all of the frames would be played back smoothly because the only command that would be sent would go to the next frame of the camera vr movie clip.

9. The last buttons to add are a picture frame of buttons around the main set of buttons. These buttons contain code that sends the movie clip back to the start label whether they are rolled over, rolled out of, dragged over, dragged out of, or released (13.28). These buttons ensure that the button movie clip always returns to the start label so the user can once again begin using the Flash VR experience.

This kind of product spin could be automated using Generator. Each of the photos could be inserted using a Generator Insert PNG object that would pull a PNG file name from a database or text file to create a Flash VR model. Generator could also add the product marketing text quite easily. By doing this, a template could

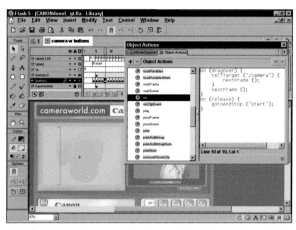

13.26

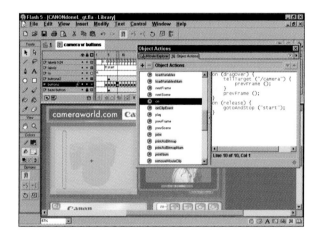

13.27

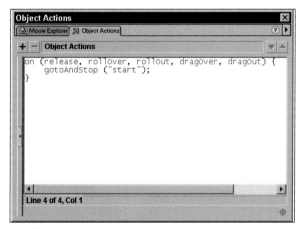

13.28

be created that would enable a non-Flash developer to gather the photographic assets, enter them into a database along with marketing text, and hit a button to create the entire Flash VR experience. This would drastically reduce the expense of creating multiple Flash VR products as well as accelerate the process.

FLASH ZOOM

The second main part of the Cameraworld project was to show what a photographer would see through the zoom lens of any given camera. Because one of the key selling points for many photographers is getting a decent zoom lens, this was extremely important to the Web retail client. The Flash VR needed to hook into a zoom showcase.

The zoom buttons that make the camera and the zoom interact contain a complicated series of actions because they have to communicate with multiple movie clips (13.29). They have to change the camera image, show the zoom lens moving in and out, show the zoom in/out of the lens, and show the focal length as it relates to the image in the viewfinder.

The camera vr movie clip contains a series of images of the camera lens extending and retracting. Each image has a specific label from z1 to z5. The focal length of the viewfinder picture relates directly to one of the zoom labels to show the proper camera image. At each of the zoom label frames, an action tells the camera vr buttons movie clip to "go to and stop" at a zoom label (13.30). This label contains a

button that, when pressed, sends the camera vr movie clip to a specific frame of the spin and sends itself to a similar place in the timeline. This enables the viewer to jump out of the zoom experience and into the Flash VR experience with ease.

The next important movie clip is the picture movie clip. It contains a motion tween on a photo from the 28mm focal length to the 80mm focal length. In each frame of the movie clip is an action that tells the camera spin movie clip to go to a specific label that shows the extension of the camera lens (13.31).

The Zoom In movie clip contains a button that causes a controlled zoom all the way into the picture in the picture movie clip (13.32). This was done quite simply by telling the picture movie clip to begin playing through the tween on the press of the zoom-in button. The button also tells the viewfinder movie clip to begin playing. The two movie clips play back in tandem. The viewfinder movie clip tracks the focal length of the lens as the viewer zooms in and out of the photo (13.33).

For the viewfinder movie clip and the picture movie clip to synchronize properly, the number of frames in the dial in the viewfinder movie clip and the motion tween in the picture movie clip have to be exactly the same. Although it might appear to be more precise to link these two movie clips with labels and ActionScript, this is actually the most effective way to synch them in Flash 3. Using labels and ActionScript makes the linking too dependent on the processor speed of the computer. If frames are dropped, then you miss out on going to the right label and begin to go out of synch.

13.29

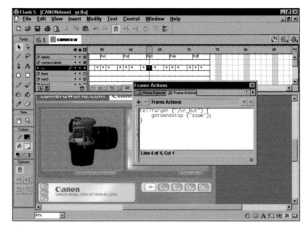

13.30

13.31

13.32

On the release of the button, all of the movie clips are told to stop. The code on the button is as follows:

```
on (press) {
  tellTarget ("/picture1") {
    nextFrame ();
    play ();
  }
  tellTarget ("/view mc") {
    nextFrame ();
    play ();
  }
  tellTarget ("/zoom_out_gt") {
    gotoAndStop (1);
  }
  tellTarget ("/28gt") {
    gotoAndStop (1);
  }
}
on (release, releaseOutside) {
  tellTarget ("/picture1") {
    stop ();
  }
  tellTarget ("/view mc") {
    stop ();
  }
}
```

The zoom-out button was a bit trickier to do because it's impossible to tell Flash to play backward, so you can't just reverse the direction of the picture movie clip. Instead, the zoom-out button tells a movie clip called previous to begin playing (13.34,

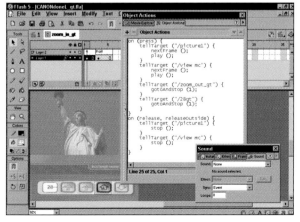

13.33

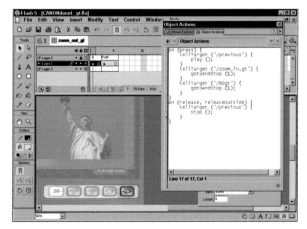

13.34

13.35). This movie clip runs in a continual loop that keeps telling the picture and viewfinder movie clips to go to the previous frame (13.36).

The focal length controls (13.37) do the same basic functions as the zoom-in and zoom-out movie clip buttons, but with one twist. Instead of actually zooming in or out of the picture, they jump straight to the beginning or ending focal length of the picture. They also tell the camera vr to go to the proper label, move the focal length viewfinder to the right place, move the picture to the correct frame, and set the zoom-in and zoom-out buttons (13.38).

One of the last key points in this project is to turn the focal length buttons off or on depending on whether a user is already at that focal length. The viewfinder

movie clip contains a dial that shows the starting and stopping focal lengths (13.39). The other movie clips tell it where to go. The only thing the viewfinder movie clip can do is turn the focal length buttons off or on when it reaches the beginning or end of the zoom. As an example, at the start of the zoom when the camera

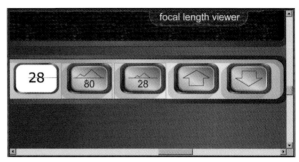

13.37

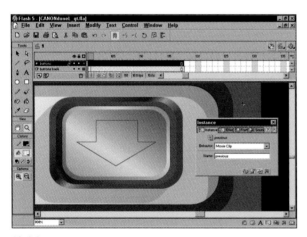

13.35

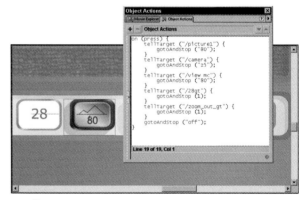

13.38

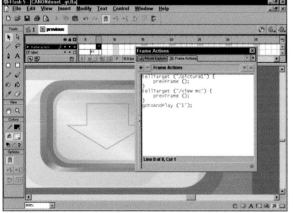

13.36

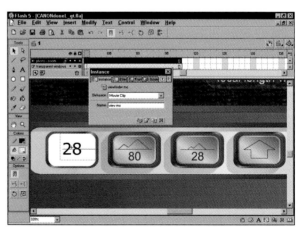

13.39

zoom lens focal length is set to 28mm, the zoom-out and 28mm buttons are not active because they can't cause any further changes (13.40).

This is an often overlooked aspect of interface design, but it's crucial to turn buttons off when they don't do anything anymore. It's incredibly frustrating as a user to be presented with buttons that are active when they don't do anything. It's even worse in the case of many Web sites, where active buttons often just refresh the current page. This is sloppy design.

OTHER EFFECTS

One of the trickier effects created for this project was for a set of binoculars. Rather than zoom into the scene, binoculars focus on the foreground and then move the focus to the background while throwing the foreground out of focus.

To achieve an effect such as this, cut your picture into distinct elements based on the foreground, mid scene, and background in a photo-editing program such as Fireworks. A picture with strong elements in each of these planes is necessary for this effect to work. Save two copies of your new pictures. One copy will stay the same, while you'll manipulate your other copy.

Let's work on the foreground copy first. Before you begin your blurring work on the photo, select everything outside of the foreground and make it transparent. Now select the foreground and use a blur filter on it (13.41). You'll probably need to blur it multiple times to give it the proper sense of being out of focus. Bring all of the blurred and nonblurred copies of the photo into Flash.

Make each of the photo elements into a symbol and rebuild the photo by placing the blurred and non-blurred elements on top of each other. Start out by making the foreground come into focus by making the blurred foreground symbol transparent and leaving the blurred background symbol completely visible. Make the middle ground blurred symbol partially transparent.

You'll need to play with the levels of transparency in the symbols, but this will give the user the effect of the binoculars focusing on the foreground of the scene with the background completely out of focus and the middle ground partially out of focus. To create the sense of focusing, you create motion tweens that shift the blurred symbols on each plane from being completely transparent to being completely opaque.

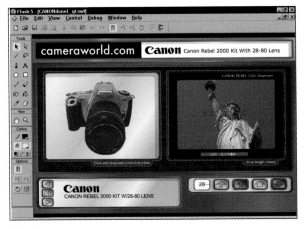

13.40

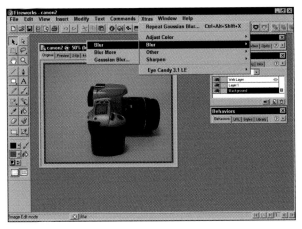

13.41

ORIGINALLY THERE WERE VERY FEW WAYS
TO CREATE 3D VISUALS WITH FLASH.

FLASH BEGINT MET HET IN KAART BRENGEN
VAN DE STRUKTUUR VAN EEN OBJEKT.

ONCE THE Z DEPTH IS CALCULATED, THE
MOVIE CLIP CAN BE SCALED APPROPRIATELY.

THE ANIMATED OBJECT IS THE CAMERA.

A DARK-ORCHESTRAL
VISUAL AND MUSICAL
EXPERIENCE

THREE DIMENSIONS (X, Y, Z) ARE
AVAILABLE INSTEAD OF JUST TWO.

DATE: 07-28-00

SCALE: 1" = 72 DPI

DRAWN: CLEMENT

JOB: 3D IN FLASH

SHEET:

14
OF 16

CHAPTER 14
3D IN FLASH

BY MANUEL CLEMENT AND GLENN THOMAS

Because Flash is considered the premiere method of showcasing rich media on the Web, designers and developers have always wanted to use Flash to display 3D graphics and 3D worlds. Although Flash was a designed to be a 2D vector display program, since the program originally came out, creative designers have been using it to create 3D-like experiences including the illusion of depth and dimension.

Originally, there were very few ways to create 3D visuals with Flash. Designers could create 3D animations in other programs and export them as raster or vector graphic sequences. These sequences could then be brought into Flash. Raster graphics usually had to be redrawn as vector graphics, while vector graphics usually needed to be broken apart and optimized to control file size.

Since those early days, a number of companies have created solutions to this problem. Again, none of them are true 3D solutions for Flash because Flash is a 2D vector display program; nonetheless, all of the following solutions create the illusion of 3D graphics in Flash.

Ideaworks3D (`www.ideaworkds3d.com`) came out with Vecta3D (`www.vecta3d.com`), a stand-alone program to create 3D graphics for Flash. Ideaworks3D then came out with a plug-in for 3D Studio Max that made it possible to output 3D Max files and animations as Flash movies, Vecta3D MAX. This plug-in combines the power of the most common 3D creation program with the Web ubiquity of Flash.

Since Flash originally came out, creative designers have been using the program to create 3D-like experiences, including the illusion of depth and dimension.

USING VECTA3D MAX

This particular example is the trailer of The Dark Symphony Project (`www.thedarksymphony.com`) (14.1), a project related to music, arts, and life. The trailer consists of a 3D scene representing a chapel and is animated via a camera walkthrough. The simple aspect of the vectors, made of thin gray lines on a black background, creates an interesting mood and drives emotions. The ultimate goal of this project was not to try to render a variety of gradients or to attempt to create photorealistic video. Rather, the project goal was to recreate the intimidating feeling of the TheDarkSymphony.com project.

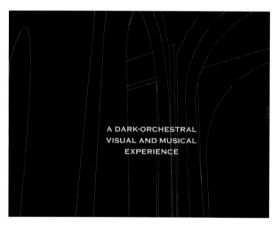

14.1

3D Studio MAX was used to model the scene. The vector rendering was accomplished using Vecta3D MAX to achieve the type of simple *edged-lines* rendering needed for this project. Finally, Flash 5 was used to put the animation together, arrange the graphics, and add in the text.

USING 3D STUDIO MAX

Flash is a two-dimensional program, so any depth or perspective you may achieve is an illusion originating from mathematical code or from a frame-by-frame animation. In the case of the TheDarkSymphony.com trailer, the illusion is created by inserting a sequence of keyframes (14.2). Each keyframe consists of vector lines, representing the geometry of the objects in our scenes. The targeted file size will be an average of 500 bytes (0.5KB) per keyframe.

The scene was modeled using several techniques including *lofted shapes* and different Boolean operations in 3D Studio Max (14.3). Most of the adjustments and sculpting was achieved using the Edit Mesh modifier and Boolean operations.

In this example, the camera is the animated object. Through 3D Studio MAX, the animation is built with keyframes on a timeline. The animation is created in a similar manner to animation creation in Flash, but here, three dimensions (x, y, z) are available instead of just two (14.4). When you select an object, its own

AUTHOR PROFILE

Manuel Clement

Manuel Clement is the designer behind Mano1.com. His clients range from GOOEY to Data Protect, from the Florida Department of Health to French President Jacques Chirac. With seven years of training in classical piano and music theory, he also runs OnlineDJ.com, an emerging site for the music industry. Winner of two Macromedia SSOD awards in 1999, Manuel is passionate about design and technology. He often speaks at conferences around the world.

He also contributed to such books as the *New Masters of Flash* (Friends of Ed: Birmingham, UK, 2000) and the *Flash 5 Bible* (from Hungry Minds, Inc., formerly known as IDG Books Worldwide).

timeline appears at the bottom of the interface. To recreate the 3D Max portion of The Dark Symphony Project, follow these steps:

1. Set the Vecta3D MAX plug-in as both the default and production renderer. Click Vecta3D, and select the Production Renderer and Draft Renderer (14.5).

2. Four views of the 3D landscape are shown in the interface — top, front, left, and perspective. Make sure the view you want to render is set to active by right-clicking it. This does not select an object, but instead selects the view that will be rendered by Vecta3D. Vecta3D also has a Properties toolbox on the right side (14.6). Select Hairline for the Outline style, which is best for creating really crisp lines.

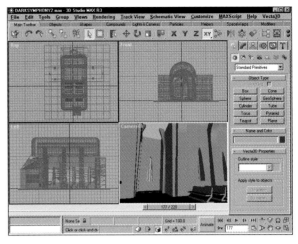

14.3

> **NOTE**
>
> Unfortunately, we can't cover all modeling functions in this tutorial. To learn how to use 3D Studio MAX, visit places such as `www.3Dcafe.com` and `www.extra3D.com`, where you will find tutorials, useful source files, and be able to ask questions of other 3D artists. Another great resource is the *3D Studio Max Bible* published by IDG Books Worldwide, now known as Hungry Minds, Inc.

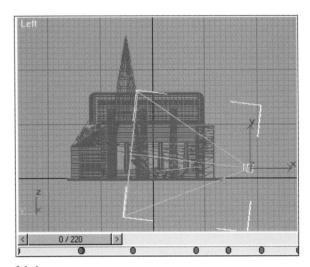

14.4

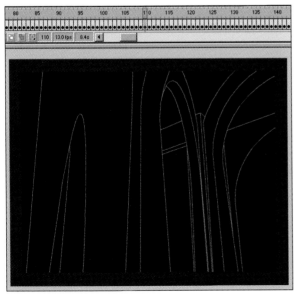

14.2

14.5

14.6

3. Click Render Scene (14.7) to access the rendering dialog box. For Output, you can choose to render the scene to the screen only, save it as an SWF, or save it as an AI sequence. In this case, we'll output to Macromedia Flash file (*.swf). Under Render style, select the checkboxes Highlights and Intersections (14.8).

4. Click Render to start the rendering process (14.9). When the rendering process is done, your vector-based animation is output as a SWF file, ready to import into Flash.

MANIPULATING IN FLASH

Now that you've rendered the animation as a SWF file, you can import it into Flash to manipulate the file and add in any additional effects you need.

1. Open Flash 5 and import the SWF animation you've just rendered (File ➢ Import). You should see the keyframes imported in Flash and displayed as black lines (14.10).

2. To change the color of all the lines of our animation, click the Edit Multiple Frames button on the Flash timeline, and move the Onion Skin

> **NOTE**
>
> The problem with exporting from Vecta3D is that it exported black lines on a white background. We want to make the background black and to change the line color of all the keyframes.

14.7

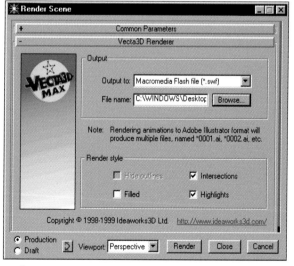

14.8

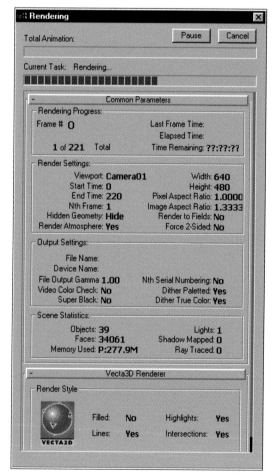

14.9

Markers so they encompass the entire animation (14.11).

3. Choose Edit ➢ Select All to select all of the lines on the screen. This step can take a long time to execute as well. Open the Color Mixer (Window ➢ Panels ➢ Mixer). Set the Stroke Color in the Mixer panel to white (14.12).

4. Deselect all the objects (Edit ➢ Deselect All), and then press the Edit Multiple Frames button once more to turn it off.

5. Now change the background color of the movie to black (Modify ➢ Movie).

NOTE

Always save your work before onionskinning a file. Your computer may hold for a few seconds before it displays all of the keyframes all at once on your screen. It can take up to a minute, or even longer, depending on your computer speed and the number of frames to be edited at once. Your computer may even crash Flash and you'll have to shut down the program. If this happens, then edit fewer frames at any one time or upgrade your computer.

TIP

Here are a few links to sites integrating 3D graphics in Flash: www.wholetruth.com, www.mtv2.co.uk, and www.mano1.com.

14.11

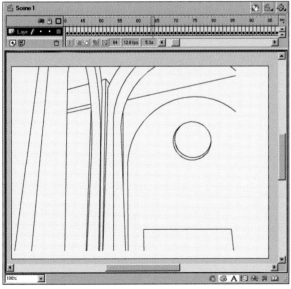

14.10

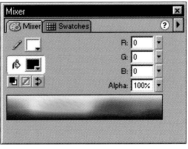

14.12

TABLE 14-1

BUTTON	FUNCTION
New	Creates a new movie.
Open	Opens a previously saved movie.
Save	Saves the current movie.
Create Text, Create Sphere, Create Cone, and Create Torus	Allow for text to be added to a scene or simple objects such as spheres, cones, and toruses (doughnuts) to be added into the scene.
Scaling Mode	Lets you resize selected objects.
Camera Pan Mode	Allows for panning movement left, right, up, and down in a scene.
Show Secondary Camera	Creates a second Viewport window next to the original Viewport. This enables two different views of the scene to be monitored at one time; for example the main Viewport can show the scene from the front while the secondary camera shows the same scene from the top. This enables designers to monitor the depth of objects in the scene more easily.
Zoom Camera Extents	Positions the camera in front of all of the objects in the Viewport and zooms in or out so that the objects fill the Viewport.
Reset Transformation	Removes all the sizing and location changes that have been applied to an object.
Help	Enables any feature in the interface to be directly explained by clicking the button and then clicking the interface feature.

6. At this point it is wise to import the 3D animation into a movie clip. This step enables you to build a library of animations that you can reuse in your project by dragging an instance of the symbol from the library to your stage.

WORKING WITH SWIFT 3D

Swift 3D from Electric Rain (`www.swfit3d.com` and `www.erain.com`) is a program with a rapidly growing audience of Flash developers. Swift 3D is a standalone 3D application with a more fully featured set of tools than the Vecta3D standalone program but a much smaller set of tools than 3D Studio Max. Designers can use Swift 3D to create fully animated 3D shapes and text, while also importing and manipulating more complex 3D Studio Max models or worlds to create richer 3D experiences. Swift 3D then exports to the SWF format with outlines, flat shading, area shading, or full polygon gradient shading, thus enabling designers to choose between file size constraints or graphical richness.

You can use Swift 3D to create rich 3D animation or smaller 3D elements that can be integrated into an overall design and layout within the Flash movie. Swift 3D is frequently used to create 3D icons that rotate or spin on button rollovers and for this feature alone is a valuable tool for the designer. At the time of publication, Swift 3D does not have a free demo of the program to test, but the company does offer a money-back guarantee if a user doesn't like the program.

GETTING TO KNOW THE SWIFT 3D INTERFACE

The first step in understanding Swift 3D is to become familiar with the interface (14.13). It's a fairly straightforward interface, but does have some quirks that can take some getting used to:

■ **Menu items.** The menus enable the user to manipulate files (File), edit the current scene or object (Edit), change the view of the interface (View), control the animation (Animation), arrange objects into groups (Arrange), control which document is currently displayed in the interface (Window), and provide a method to access help (Help).

- **Main toolbar.** The main toolbar (14.14) contains buttons that enable elements of the document, scene, or objects to be changed, as described in Table 14-1, from left to right.

Property toolbox

The Property toolbox (14.15) lets you change the elements of the 3D scene. The properties are listed in the Property list box. The default properties Layout and Environment, which are displayed if nothing is selected, control the size and display of the scene.

The Property list box is context-sensitive. For example, if a lighting effect has been selected in the scene, then the Lighting property will be selected in the Property list box. Similarly, if an object in the scene has been selected, then the name of the object will be shown in the properties toolbox. Each of these toolboxes contains properties relevant to the selected feature.

Animation Timeline toolbar

The Animation Timeline toolbar (14.16) enables the user to adjust how objects and lights are displayed over time within a scene. The Animation Timeline is based on keyframes and reflects the animation of the object the user has selected within the scene. The Animation Timeline toolbar also contains the playback controls and a counter that shows the current frame rate.

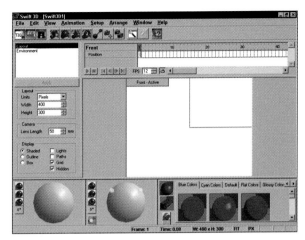

14.13

14.14

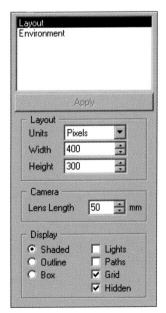

14.15

> **WARNING**
>
> When the Camera Pan button is selected it's impossible to select objects in the scene. It's better to avoid using this button and pan by left-clicking a part of the scene without objects and dragging. This accomplishes the same goal. Clicking and dragging with the right mouse button enables Camera Zoom.

14.16

Viewport

The Viewport shows what the actual action of the 3D movie looks like. The Camera View drop-down menu enables the view of the scene to change to or from Front, Back, Top, Bottom, Left, and Right. The

14.17

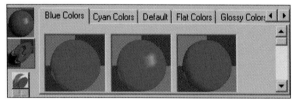

14.18

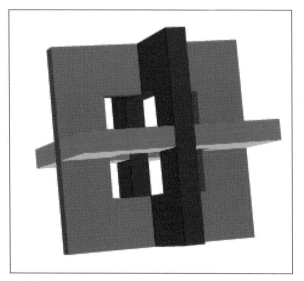

14.20

Rotating Camera View option enables a camera view to be animated during a scene or change the aim of the primary camera.

Also displayed in the Viewport is a 3D grid using the X, Y, and Z coordinate system. A red line represents the X or horizontal axis, a green line is the Y or vertical axis, and a blue line shows the Z or depth axis. The intersection of the three lines has the coordinates 0, 0, 0.

Crystal Trackballs

Swift 3D has interface elements called Crystal Trackballs that enable the position of objects and lights to be changed. The Crystal Trackballs act like virtual balls that can be spun by clicking and dragging with the mouse.

The Object trackball (14.17, left) lets selected objects in the scene be spun or rotated based on the position of the trackball. Buttons to the left of the trackball control the kind of rotation (horizontal, vertical, or spin) and the increment of the rotation.

The Lighting trackball (14.17, right) enables lights in the scene to be placed and controlled.

Gallery tools

The Gallery tools (14.18) contains two different tools, the Materials palette and the Animation palette.

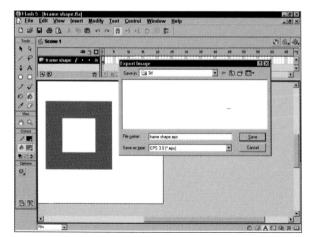

14.21

The Materials palette contains drag-and-drop materials that can be applied to objects. Each material contains an Ambient Light, a Diffuse Light, and a Highlight and are available for use on objects.

The Animation palette contains drag-and-drop animations that apply predefined movements to objects. Animations can be previewed by clicking the graphic in the Animation Display Window above the text description of the drag-and-drop animation.

Status bar

The status bar (14.19) shows information about the current frame number, the exact time in the movie, the dimensions of the document, and the way in which the Viewport is being shown.

ICON ANIMATION

By creating a rotating 3D icon (14.20) that can be imported into Flash, the user can learn about Swift 3D's interface through completing a simple project. Here are the steps:

1. Create the simple frame shape in Flash (14.21) and export it as an EPS file called **frame shape.eps.** Although you can create simple cubes, spheres, and toruses (doughnuts) in Swift 3D, it's usually easier to create your shapes in a different program and import them into Swift 3D.

2. Open Swift 3D and create a new, empty 3D document (File ➤ New) (14.22).

3. Import the frame shape.eps file into Swift 3D (File ➤ Import) (14.23). We'll next create the entire icon using this shape.

4. Select the object by clicking it. A wireframe box will appear around it (14.24).

5. Select Sizing from the Property list box in the Property toolbox. Set the Depth to 0.1 and click Apply.

The base 3D shape that will be used to create our final icon is now complete. The next phase of the project is to copy, paste, and manipulate the shape to create the icon. Follow these steps to do so:

1. Copy (Edit ➤ Copy) and paste (Edit ➤ Paste) the original object. Select the new object.

14.22

14.23

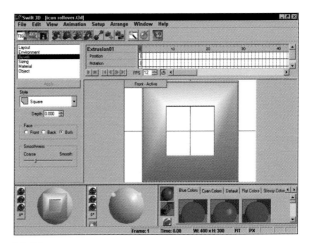

14.24

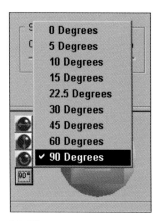

14.25

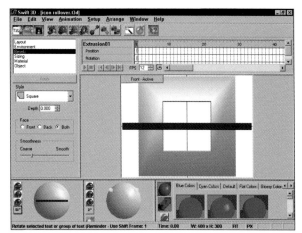

14.26

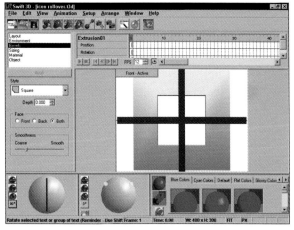

14.27

2. Click the Lock Vertical button next to the Object trackball to lock its axis so the object only moves in a specific direction.

3. Change the Rotation Increment to 90 degrees (14.25). Using the Object trackball, tilt the new object 90 degrees vertically (14.26).

4. Copy and paste this object.

5. Select the new object. Click the Lock Spin button. Use the Object trackball to spin the new object 90 degrees (14.27). The icon is now built.

6. Next we'll apply colors to one of the objects. Select the upright object and choose Material from the Property list box. This brings up three options — Faces, Bevels, and Edges — this is the Material Surface list box. Select Faces from the Material Surface list box.

7. Click the Show Materials button in the Gallery tools. Select a Flat Color from the Materials palette. Drag and drop the color onto the Material Sphere located under the Material Surface list box (14.28) in the Property toolbox. Optionally drag and drop the color onto the correct plane of the object in the Viewport.

8. To see the new color, click the Apply button to update the view.

9. Select another color and then select the same object again. Select Material from the Property list box, and then select Edges in the Material Surface list box. Drop a new color onto the Material ball and click the Apply button to update the view (14.29). You can repeat this with the Bevels if you so desire.

10. Add colors to the other two frame objects in the same manner.

The objects that make up the icon are now complete. The next goal is to animate the icon using one of Swift 3D's predefined drag-and-drop animations. Here's how:

1. Select all of the objects (Edit ➤ Select All) and group them (Arrange ➤ Group).

2. We'll next apply one of the predefined animations. Select the Show Animations button (14.30) in the Gallery Tools.

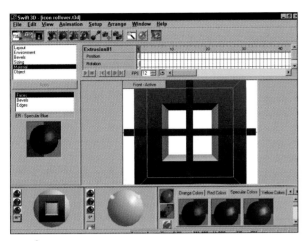

14.28

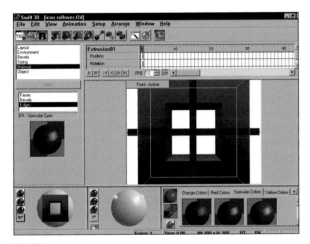

14.29

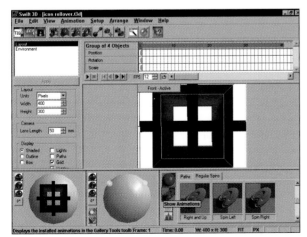

14.30

3. Go to Regular Spins. Click the Right and Up thumbnail image to preview the animation. Drag and drop the Right and Up animation onto the icon in the Viewport (14.31). The animation will now be attached to the icon.

4. We now need to make the group a bit smaller. Select the group and choose the Scaling Mode button from the main toolbar (14.32).

5. Scale the object down by dragging toward the center of the object (14.33).

6. Click the Play Animation button in the lower-right corner of the Animation toolbar to play the movie. Make sure that none of the animation goes out of the Viewport.

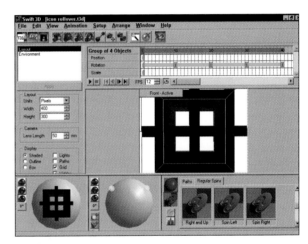

14.31

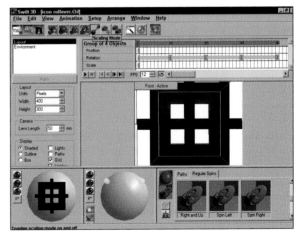

14.32

7. Export the animation (File ➤ Export) as **3d icon animation.swf** using Flat Fill (14.35). This removes all of the lighting highlights.

> **WARNING**
>
> Any part of an object that doesn't appear in the Viewport will not be a part of the exported .swf file. Review your animation carefully and make sure that everything you want in your final Flash movie is within the Viewport. If it's not, you'll have to redo the entire procedure.

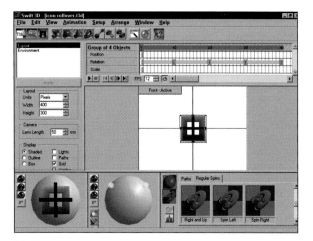

14.33

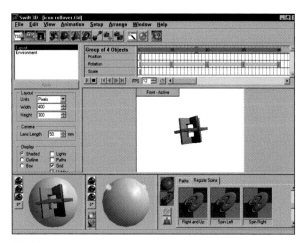

14.34

Swift 3D takes a lot of time to export because it has to generate each frame (14.36). All the information contained within each frame has to be changed into the Flash movie format. The final result is an unlocked .swf movie that can be imported back into Flash and used as an element in a larger Flash navigation or design project.

Swift 3D is a useful program for any Flash designer to learn because it affords so much flexibility when creating 3D elements for integration into Flash sites. Although the interface takes a bit of getting used to, the program has a lot of power and many features that enable Flash designers to create highly original Web sites and other rich media.

CREATING 3D DIRECTLY IN FLASH

Both of the previous examples are 2D representations of 3D objects created in other programs and then imported into Flash. However, with the release of Flash 5, developers can finally script true 3D engines in Flash.

The basis of this 3D work in Flash is the use of complex ActionScript to calculate a Z depth for Flash movie clips. Once the Z depth is calculated, the movie clip can be scaled appropriately to give the illusion of 3D depth.

Simple shapes such as cubes can be rotated using ActionScript to calculate the perspective and placement of lines between the corners. Although extremely complex shapes or 3D worlds cannot be created with this technique, many exciting opportunities still exist to use 3D code within Flash.

Suddenly such things as flight simulators (14.37) or deformable 3D shapes can be made directly in Flash. The objects that are created are true 3D objects rather than 2D objects creating the illusion of 3D and can be manipulated by the user or through scripts within the Flash movie.

The 3D that can be done with Flash is currently fairly limited so it's unlikely that Flash will ever challenge any of the programs built specifically to create 3D. For the most part, designers and developers will have to continue to use 3D outputs to 2D Flash files to create the illusion of complex 3D worlds and objects. However, it's still an interesting new aspect of Flash that designers and developers can use to push the boundaries of interactive media.

14.35

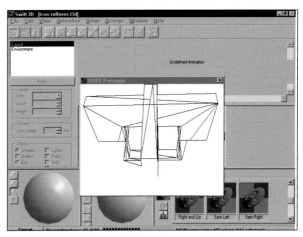

14.36

TIP

The imported .swf comes in as a series of keyframes on one layer. It's important to go through the imported animation to check for any static or duplicated images that can be turned into symbols. By doing this, it's possible to achieve a much smaller file size.

14.37

BITMAPS HAVE A SPECIFIC RESOLUTION AND
CAN'T BE SCALED WITHOUT IMAGE
DEGRADATION OR FUZZY INTERPOLATION

638 PX

Flash
File View Control Help

Flash 5 - [holidaycent
File Edit View

Tools   Scene 2

QUICKTIME MOVIES CAN BE IMPORTED INTO THE FLASH
AUTHORING ENVIRONMENT AND THEN CONTROLLED WITH A
FLASH INTERFACE OR SURROUNDED BY A FLASH MOVIE.

Eddie Bauer
Holiday Central

IT'S IMPORTANT TO MAKE VERY SMALL AND SUBTLE
CHANGES IN ORDER TO MAKE THE MOTION LOOK RIGHT

smashing ideas INC.

DATE: 11-23-99

SCALE: 1" = 72 DPI

DRAWN: BOUGHTON

JOB: FLASH & VIDEO

SHEET:
15
OF 16

R G B

CHAPTER 15
WORKING WITH VIDEO

D esigners can use Flash in several different ways to manipulate video or to create an experience for the viewer that has the look and feel of video. Designers can manipulate photos to achieve a documentary filmmaking "photos as video" effect. Short video loops created from sequences of raster images can be used to show video motion while keeping file sizes small. This technique can be taken a step further by posterizing the video frames to create a specifically vector style showing the video motion. Also, to varying degrees, Flash can be integrated with any of the Web video standards so Flash can be used for its strengths (vector graphics, interactivity, interfaces, animation) while the actual video is shown using a more robust video plug-in such as QuickTime, Real 8, or Windows Media Player.

TURNING PHOTOS INTO VIDEO

Eddie Bauer approached Smashing Ideas to create a rich media Christmas holiday gift guide for its online retail site at www.eddiebauer.com. The guide needed to have the right look and feel to best represent Eddie Bauer's outdoor brand and to create a sense of the holiday season (15.1).

 The target audience for the project was any consumer with a 33.6K modem. Because Eddie Bauer's site targets the average Web consumer, our project also had to work on slower modems. To capture the

Video killed the radio star

BUGGLES

15.1

© Eddie Bauer, Inc. 2000

right emotional feeling, we had to include both holi-day-themed music for the project as well as photos of Eddie Bauer's clothing, which took up most of our allotted file size, leaving us with very little for the other assets. Within these constraints, Smashing Ideas needed to give the project a richly cinematic feeling of winter and the holidays.

The solution to the design problem was to take a photo and move into it as if it were an actual winter landscape (15.2). The approach used in this project is similar to the methods of many documentary film-makers. Because documentary filmmakers don't always have access to live action of their subjects, these filmmakers rely on camera movement over still photos to create the illusion of cinematic motion. We used Flash to approximate the camera movement the same way to create the illusion of cinematic motion.

We use pans across a scene and zooms into or out of a scene to create a cinematic feeling. Although these techniques do give a sense of movement, the one technique that truly imparts a feeling of motion is a change in perspective in which objects change their positions (15.3). When this change in depth percep-tion occurs over a period of time, it's known as *motion parallax*. The foreground moves very quickly,

while the background moves slowly. This gives view-ers the feeling that they are being drawn deeply into the scene.

An example of motion parallax can be achieved by simply driving in your car. If you were to film out the side of the car window as you drove down the high-way, the telephone poles on the side of the road would move very quickly past you, while the shop-ping mall in the distance would move more slowly and the sky and clouds would barely move at all.

In the Eddie Bauer opening, we used two pictures to accomplish this movement. The background scene is a snow-covered meadow in front of a forest, while in the foreground beech tree trunks appear. As we begin to move forward in the scene, the tree trunks move forward and to the sides, while the background moves slowly forward to give a sense of depth and movement (15.4). The rectangular screen size com-bined with the verticality of the trunks adds to the sense of movement by allowing for a strong layout.

Combined with the winter music, the opening gave the viewer the sense that he or she was leaving the fringes of a forest to cross a meadow and enter a deeper forest. This natural setting matched the Eddie Bauer outdoor clothing brand.

15.2   *(c) Eddie Bauer, Inc. 2000*

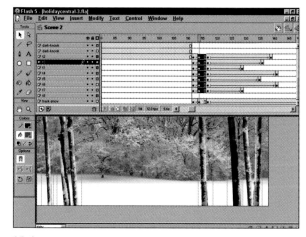

15.4

15.3

IMPORTING PHOTOS

When working with photos as integral parts of a Flash movie, it's important to understand the benefits and limitations of using raster images in a vector graphics world.

Bitmaps have a specific resolution and can't be scaled without image degradation or fuzzy interpolation. Standard monitor resolution is 72 dpi so, in general, import images at 72 dpi at the largest, static position that it will have. Images brought in at a slightly higher resolution can look grainy because simply too much pixel information exists to display and Flash will try to interpolate. If the image resizes or moves, weigh the cost of when it can look its worst — usually when the action holds on the image the shortest period of time.

A variety of raster file types exist and each has a particular use and function. The standard Web file types are JPEG and GIF, but they are not the best for using with Flash. JPEG is an adjustable compression scheme format for photographic images. JPEG compression is variable, loses information, and varies by programs.

Usually Flash will maintain the imported JPEG settings, but Flash will often recompress Progressive JPEG images and degrade the quality. Progressive JPEGs are the image files that load in waves, adding more detail to the entire image as more information downloads. Flash doesn't recognize these settings and will recompress the image based on the document settings. GIF files are lossless and limited to a palette of 256 colors or fewer.

In comparison to these two formats, BMP and PICT are raw native raster files for the PC and Mac, respectively. BMP or PICT files can have JPEG compression applied to them from within Flash. PNG files are like BMP files, but can also contain an alpha channel or mask layer.

Which file type to use depends on the purpose of the raster images in your project. In general, always start with BMP, PICT, or PNG files for importing photo images into Flash. PNG files tend to be the best format to start with because they are usually smaller in file size and supports transparency.

For nonphoto images, use GIF files for elements with limited colors or large areas of flat colors. JPEG is used for images not using the Flash JPEG compression scheme. Remember to set Flash JPEG compression quality to near 100 if you don't want the quality of an imported JPEG file to degrade significantly. JPEG is the file format of last resort when no other file type is supplied by the client.

Even though a file is optimized before importing it into Flash by sizing it properly and reducing any extraneous color information, the adjustments for correct quality and performance continue inside of Flash.

Although export settings for the entire movie are set in Publish Settings, it's important to test and change export settings for individual images in the Library to get the best ratio of quality to file size. Some images only need low export settings with JPEG compression to look good, while other images need to be set at a very high export setting. By testing images individually, designers get great quality and, if settings can be lowered, then they also get more file size to work with in a movie.

CREATING MOTION PARALLAX WITH PHOTOS

Let's take a look at the two photos that are used to create this opening. We have a background photo of a snow-covered forest. The foreground photo contains a number of snowy trees that will be cut out in a photo-editing software program and turned into individual tree images. The landscape behind the trees will be deleted and made transparent. The images will be turned into PNGs so this transparency can be maintained.

We import the background photo and the five individual tree images. First we make all the images into movie clip symbols and then place the background photo on the bottom layer. Next we place the tree trunks on seven separate layers so we can tween them at different rates (15.5). Four trees appear on the right and three on the left, with two tree images being used twice to help conserve file size.

The difficult part of creating motion parallax by using photos is that we have to work hard to get the movement right. It's easy to make objects move in Flash, but it's not as easy to make them look like they are moving in a realistic manner. To achieve the illusion of realistic-looking motion, we tween all of the different images at different speeds over different distances.

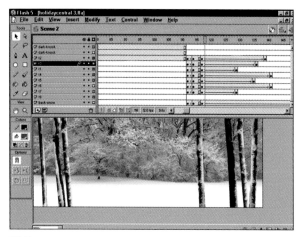

15.5

The background image will move more slowly toward the camera, while the trees will grow larger and move to the left and right more rapidly. The trees closest to the camera scale the most and move the most quickly off to the sides (15.6–15.9).

It's now important to make very small and subtle changes to make the motion look right. We have to play with the speed and distances that the individual trees move and then use our best judgment about whether this looks realistic.

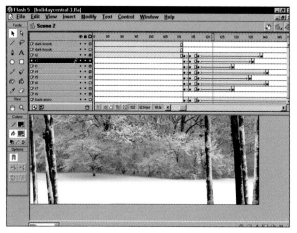

15.6

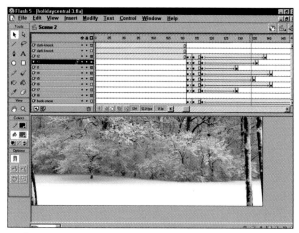

15.8

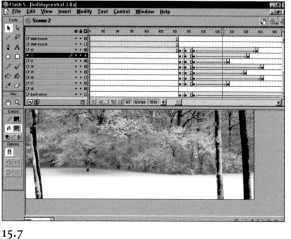

15.7

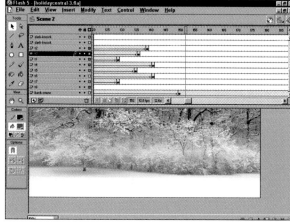

15.9

USING VIDEO LOOPS AND POSTERIZATION

One of the most striking effects that has emerged from using Flash to manipulate video images on the Web is the single or two-color posterized effect (15.10). This effect relies on importing sequences of still images taken from video footage and using the Trace Bitmap tool to turn the raster images into vector artwork. This vector artwork is then changed into one or two colors.

We will work with a video sequence of a pietà statue to explore how to achieve this effect. The video sequence we'll use is originally from black-and-white 16mm film that has been transferred to video. Once it's been digitized, we need to get a sequence of PICTs or BMPs out of the footage (15.11). Most video-editing software programs can do this and, at this stage, the main task is to make sure the sequence is sequentially numbered so that the images are easy to import into Flash.

In our case, we'll choose a video sequence that shows a camera tilt down the statue and go through the steps to make this sequence into stylized vector artwork in Flash. The easiest way to do this is to import all of the files into Flash directly (15.12, 15.13). When we import the sequence, we'll get a frame-by-frame insertion of the images aligned to the upper-left corner of the Flash movie stage (15.14).

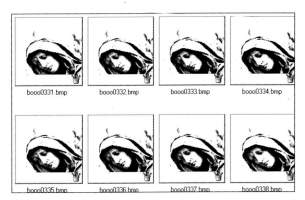

15.11

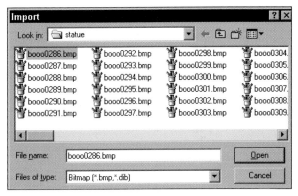

15.12

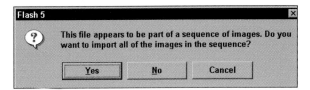

15.13

15.10

15.14

At this point, we select the image in the first frame and choose Modify ➤ Trace Bitmap. Trace Bitmap has settings that enable us to select a Color Threshold, a Minimum Area, Curve Fit, and Corner Threshold (15.15).

15.15

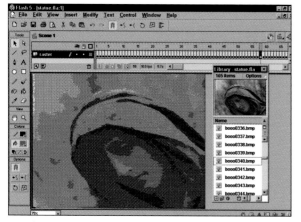

15.16

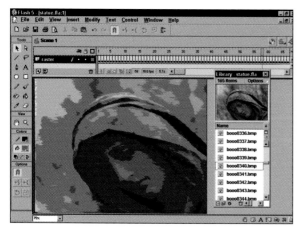

15.17

The Color Threshold value can be from 1 to 500. When two pixels are compared, if the difference in the RGB color values is less than the color threshold, the two pixels are considered the same color. As you increase the threshold value, you decrease the number of colors, so the higher the threshold value, the better the posterization effect.

The Minimum Area can be a value from 1 to 1000. This sets the number of surrounding pixels to consider when assigning a color to a pixel. Curve Fit gives options that determine how smoothly outlines are drawn. Corner Threshold defines whether sharp edges are retained or smoothed out.

To create a vector graphic that looks most like the original bitmap (with a very large file size, however), enter **10** for the Color Threshold and **1** pixel for the Minimum Area, and then choose Pixels for Curve Fit and Many Corners for Corner Threshold. To get the most posterized effect do the opposite: choose 500 for Color Threshold, a high number for Minimum Area, Very Smooth for Curve Fit, and Few Corners for Color Threshold.

Once we've chosen our values for the settings, we trace the bitmap (15.16). If we like the result, we use those same values and apply the Trace Bitmap command to each image one by one (15.17). After all of the images have been traced, it's then useful to optimize each frame to decrease the file size and streamline the vectors for playback.

Unfortunately, problems occur with this straightforward approach because the colors in the original image can make the file size of the traced image very large. This makes it difficult to get a good posterized effect and also causes slow playback because too many vector lines exist.

> **TIP**
>
> Once you've traced all your images, select all of the images in your library and delete them. Then save your Flash movie with a new file name. This makes the file size of your Flash movie much smaller and should improve movie editing performance on most computers.

You have a better way to get a strong vector image in Flash from our posterized video footage. Prior to importing the sequence of still images into Flash, we have to manipulate the images with a photo-editing program such as Adobe's Photoshop (15.18).

We open an image from our sequence and save it with a different name. This will be the image that we use to work out how we want to manipulate our video footage to make it easier to posterize.

First we de-interlace the image by choosing Filter ➢ Video ➢ De-Interlace. De-interlacing the video smoothes the moving video image and removes the lines. We then turn the image from a color graphic into a grayscale image by choosing Image ➢ Mode ➢ Grayscale. Because we're going to posterize the image down to a single color, all we really want are the contrasting values, so we can discard the colors.

We then adjust the curves (Image ➢ Adjust ➢ Curves) to bring out the values (5.19). The grays can be turned to either white or black. This will help us create a strong vector image when we apply Trace Bitmap. We save our curves values as an .acv file so that we can use the settings for all our other images.

Once we've figured out what we're going to do to our image, we record the procedure as a New Action by clicking the Create New Action button in the Actions palette. We then run that action on all of the images in our image folder. By automating this task, we decrease our workload enormously.

We open an image and begin recording our series of actions by clicking the Create New Action button in the Actions palette (15.20). When the New Action dialog box opens, we name the action **statue manipulation** and start our changes (15.21). We choose Filter ➢ Video ➢ De-Interlace. We change the mode to Grayscale (Image ➢ Mode ➢ Grayscale) and apply the previously saved curves file to the image (Image ➢ Adjust ➢ Curves). Because these are the three actions

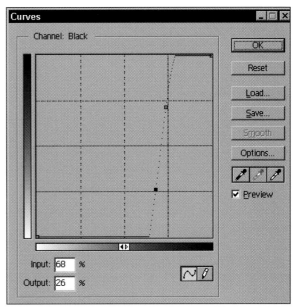

15.19

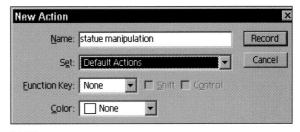

15.20

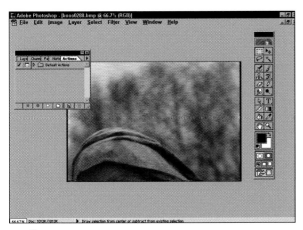

15.18

15.21

we want to apply to every video footage image, we then stop the action (15.22).

The next step is to batch-process the entire series of images with this saved action. To do this, we choose File ➤ Automate ➤ Batch. We choose the desired action (statue manipulation) from the Action drop-down list, set the Source to Folder, and choose the folder with all of the images. Save and Close from the Destination drop-down list, and click the OK button (15.23).

We run the batch process and then import this new sequence of images into Flash. We again go through our Trace Bitmap steps to vectorize our images. We then optimize those new vector frames. This provides for a better posterized style because the color has been removed and the contrasting values have been highlighted.

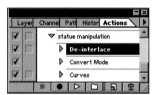

15.22

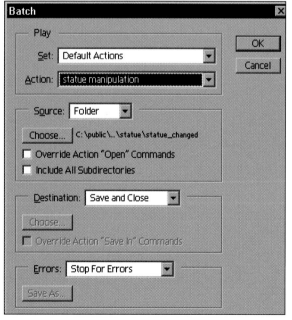

15.23

FLASH INTEGRATION WITH WEB VIDEO STANDARDS

Flash works most tightly with QuickTime. Quick Time movies can be imported into the Flash authoring environment and then controlled with a Flash interface or surrounded by a Flash movie. The resulting file is then exported as a QuickTime movie that includes a Flash layer. One limitation with this approach is that QuickTime 4, the most widely used version of the QuickTime player at this time, only supports Flash 3 authoring; none of the features of Flash 4 can currently be used. QuickTime 5 does support Flash 4 functionality so targeting QuickTime 5 provides the most flexibility and control in using QuickTime video with Flash navigation or dynamic data capabilities.

Real Networks supports Flash 4 as a part of the Synchronized Media Integration Language (SMIL) architecture in the current RealPlayer 8 release. This enables Flash 4 files to be included as a part of the SMIL that plays back within RealPlayer. Flash 5 also writes directly to SMIL by creating a Flash 4 movie, a RealAudio soundtrack, and the controlling SMIL file (15.24). Flash movies enable forms within RealPlayer, so they are a great way to create e-commerce or user communication from within the RealPlayer. This is an exciting new feature for the RealPlayer.

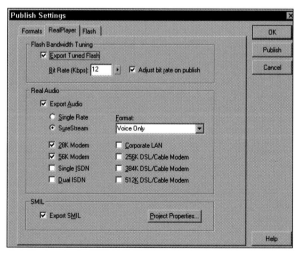

15.24

Windows Media Player has the loosest integration with Flash, but does enable Flash 5 movies to integrate with Windows Media Video. In Windows Media Player, Flash exists as a separate file (similar to the Real integration) that can be controlled by the video file or, in turn, control the video file by using JavaScript. This programmatic bridge facilitates powerful data exchange between the file formats as well as extensive control.

WRAPPING FLASH'S INTERFACE AROUND A VIDEO STREAM

Smashing Ideas worked with the Game Show Network and ICTV, leaders in the broadband cable revolution, to create a broadband content demo for the Game Show Network's popular television program *Inquizition* (15.25, 15.26).

The game show pits four contestants against each other. Each contestant tries to answer the same series of questions posed by the host of the show. The host, Inquizitor, whose face is never shown, does not refrain from putting down contestants who are having difficulty answering questions. At the end of each round, the contestant with the lowest score must leave the competition. The game concludes when only one contestant remains.

The goal of the project was to show how a Flash interface could interact with the game show's video stream to enable people accessing the Web through broadband cable systems to play the game at home in real time with the real contestants (15.27).

> **NOTE**
>
> **Flash can work with all three of the major Web video standards (Real, Windows Media Player, and QuickTime) to create Flash and video experiences.**

15.25   © 2000 The Game Show Network, L.P.

15.26   © 2000 The Game Show Network, L.P.

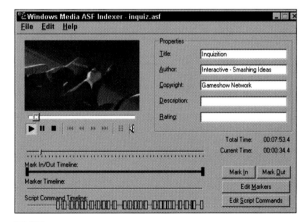

15.27

This project was created for the Flash 4 player. Although ICTV's technology allows for the quick-and-easy update of new media players, most television-based interactive technology relies on set top boxes for interactive television that might be one, two, or even three versions behind the most recent media players. This is a significant limitation and presents a real challenge to rich media developers.

Due to the data interchange capabilities of Windows Media Player, this technology was chosen for the video stream. The project consisted of creating a Flash movie interface containing the game play controls for the home user, a video stream of the game show encoded with the answer information, and the JavaScript code to let the two files talk to each other.

COMBINING FLASH AND WINDOWS MEDIA PLAYER VIDEO

To combine Flash with the Windows Media Player we must create a Flash movie that can accept values passed to it from the Windows Media Player from an .asf file (Advanced Streaming File). The .asf file is the encoded video and contains a set of script commands with the correct answers to each question embedded in the video at the appropriate moment. In this case, the Flash movie needs a set of buttons for the user to choose the correct answer, whether a, b or c. The answer value for each question is passed into the Flash movie from the video stream.

The Flash movie also needs a timer that disables the buttons after a player has three seconds to answer the question. The Flash movie needs to be triggered from the video stream to start the counter countdown. The Flash movie also needs to keep score of the game player's correct answers. In this project, the Flash

> **NOTE**
>
> A *set top box* is a box used for interactive television, such as for WebTV.

movie does not need to display the question, which makes for less data to pass back and forth between the video stream and Flash.

On the other hand, the video stream needs to send the answers to the Flash movie at the right time in the show. The video file also needs to tell Flash when to start the three-second countdown. The JavaScript on the HTML page needs to transfer the information sent from the video stream into the Flash movie.

To build and integrate these three elements, we first start by defining what scripts we need to have in order to transfer data and manipulate the Flash movie from the video stream. As a standard command, we'll want to be able to move about the Flash movie, so we create a `gotoLabel` JavaScript command. The JavaScript code then uses the Flash `FSCommand` called `TgotoLabel` to pass the argument (in this case `bstrParam`) to the main timeline. This can be triggered from the video stream to send the Flash movie to a specific label. The main JavaScript command that will be used to pass all of the values to the Flash movie is `sendCommand`. This command can have the arguments `countdown` or the answer `a`, `b`, or `c`. Depending on the argument, different variables are set in the Flash movie.

The JavaScript code for these two commands is as follows:

```
<SCRIPT LANGUAGE="javascript"¬
FOR="MediaPlayer1" ¬
EVENT="ScriptCommand(bstrType,
bstrParam)">
//ALL COMMANDS THAT COME FROM THE
MEDIA PLAYER
if (bstrType == "gotoLabel")
{
  flash.TGotoLabel("/", bstrParam);
}
else if (bstrType == "sendCommand"){
  if (bstrParam == "countdown"){
//Time to start the 3 second timer.
  flash.setVariable ("/:startTimer",¬
bstrParam);
  }
```

```
   else if (bstrParam == "a" ||¬
bstrParam == "b" || bstrParam == "c"){
//We will send to flash the correct¬
Answer for the question.
flash.setVariable("/:¬
correctAnswer", bstrParam);
   }
}
</SCRIPT>
```

Once we have the JavaScript commands we can use them in the video timeline to send information to Flash. The Windows Media Player has a script editor called the Windows Media ASF Indexer that has a visual interface to scrub along the video to find the correct time to insert commands (15.28). It's also possible to create text documents full of times and commands that can be imported directly into the script editor and saved with the video file. Scripts can be saved out from the ASF Indexer to a text file so you can work on them more easily.

We open the video file in the ASF Indexer and find the place in the video where the Inquizitor starts asking questions. We select the Edit Script Commands button to pop up a dialog box to review scripts. We click the New button to enter our new command.

It shows the time we've chosen and then enables us to change the Type to the name of our command — in this case, `gotoLabel` — and set a parameter — in this case, `beginQuestions`, the name of our label in Flash (15.29). This tells the Flash movie to get ready to start the question and answer sequence.

We then move through the rest of the video timeline and add all of our other commands. The main command used throughout the rest of the movie is called `sendCommand`. The argument that is passed with `sendCommand` is either to begin the countdown or set the answer to a, b, or c (15.30). These arguments are then passed to the Flash movie by the JavaScript code as specific variables.

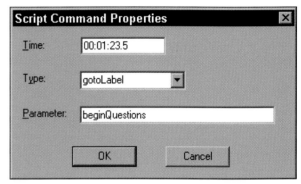

15.29

15.28

15.30

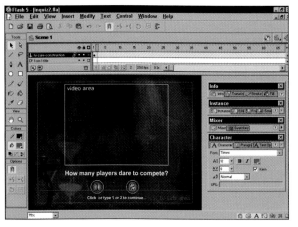

15.31

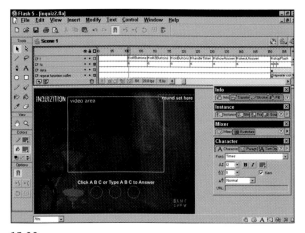

15.32

```
Frame Actions                                                    [x]
[Movie Explorer] [Frame Actions]                              (?)[▶]
[+] [−]  Frame Actions                                        [▼][▲]
//   INITIALIZATIONS
//   error checking to test if
//   the user entered data in time
//   because the show will go on!
if (Number(/:numPlayers) == 0) {
    /:numPlayers = 1;
    /:name = "Player 1";
} else if (Number(/:numPlayers) == 1 and /:name eq "") {
    /:name = "Player 1";
} else if (Number(/:numPlayers) == 2 and /:name eq "") {
    /:name = "Player 1";
    /:name2 = "Player 2";
} else if (Number(/:numPlayers) == 2 and /:name2 eq "") {
    /:name2 = "Player 2";
}
/:score = 0;
/:score2 = 0;
/:answerSet = false;
/:correctAnswer = "none";
/:userAnswer = "none";
/:user2Answer = "none";
/:TIME_LIMIT = 3000;
/:CHECK_TIME = 2500;
/:one_on_one = false;
/:select_controls = "";
/:lastQuestion = false;
if (Number(numPlayers) == 1) {
    setProperty ("/2player_inst", _visible, 0);
} else {
    setProperty ("/1player_inst", _visible, 0);
}
play ();
                                                                [▶]
Line 22 of 33, Col 1
```

15.33

The Flash movie and associated video will be played back by cable users on their televisions. We have to create the project with this eventual playback environment in mind. The video and all of the answer buttons are all built within a TV-safe area so that the game is always playable on televisions (15.31).

The series of buttons (15.32), several other movie clips, and a variety of calls are what, taken together, make the Flash movie work with the commands from the video. When the first command from the video sends the Flash movie to the label `begin Questions`, the Flash movie runs through a series of actions to initialize the structure of the game. Flash sets whether the game will be one player or two. For this example, we'll be working solely with the one-player designation. We also set all of the variables used during the game to an empty or none state to show that they haven't received information yet. For example, the `correctAnswer` variable is set to none to show that the answer hasn't been received from the video. We also set the time limit that a player has to answer a question to three seconds, or 3,000 milliseconds in this case (15.33). Making this a variable enables us to programmatically change the amount of time a player has to answer a question.

The next command that comes in from the video is to start the `countdown`. The command sets the variable `startTimer` in the main movie timeline to countdown. Because this is a Flash 4 project, the movie contains a two-frame repeater movie clip that continually runs to check whether the `startTimer` variable has been changed to `countdown` (15.34). When this variable has been changed to `countdown` and the `correctAnswer` variable is none, then we call a set of actions at `handleTimer` that

```
Frame Actions                                                    [x]
[Movie Explorer] [Frame Actions]                              (?)[▶]
[+] [−]  Frame Actions                                        [▼][▲]
if ((/:startTimer eq "countdown") and (/:correctAnswer eq "none")) {
    call ("/:handleTimer");
} else if (/:correctAnswer ne "none") {
    call ("/:checkAnswer");
}
play ();
                                                                
Line 1 of 7, Col 68
```

15.34

track the counting down of the time that a player has to answer the question. Sand in an hourglass begins to run down when the countdown begins and then `handleTimer` continually checks the expiration of time to see if the game player has run out of time to answer (15.35).

```
if ((/:startTimer eq "countdown")¬
and (/:correctAnswer eq "none")) {
  call ("/:handleTimer");
} else if (/:correctAnswer ne "none")
{
  call ("/:checkAnswer");
}
play ();
```

During this time, the game player watches the video in which the Inquizitor reads the question and answers. The answers remain on the video stream and enable the player to select the button to choose answer A, B, or C. This sets a `userAnswer` variable to a, b, or c. When the time runs out, Flash turns the buttons off so a player can no longer select an answer.

About three seconds after the video stream begins the countdown, a `sendCommand` transfers the right answer to the question from the video to the Flash movie by setting the `correctAnswer` variable in the main movie timeline. When this has changed, the repeating movie clip then stops checking the time and instead checks to see if the answer the user selected is correct.

The actions at `checkAnswer` first call another set of actions called `showAnswer` that check whether the player-selected answer is the same as the correct answer:

```
// TEST USER1 ANSWER
if (/:userAnswer eq /:correctAnswer) {
    /:score = Number(/:score)+1;
  }
```

Once the answer has been checked, the `check Answer` actions then reset all of the variables to empty or none, the hourglass is reset to full and the buttons are turned back on ready for the next question. This series of actions, from countdown through answer checking, to the resetting of variables, continues throughout the game with the video sending in

the proper variables that give the Flash movie the necessary information to count down the time, check answers, and set the score.

Now that we have all three of the pieces for the broadband game experience, we need to put them together. The JavaScript goes in the HTML page and then we use the Z layer to place the video file on layer 100 on top of the Flash movie on layer 1.

```
<div id="Flash_layer"
style="position:absolute; ¬
left:0px; top:0px; width640px;¬
height:480px; z-index:1">
```

```
<div id="MediaPlayer_layer"¬
style="position:absolute;¬
left:132.7px; top:32px; width:384px;¬
height:288px; z-index:100">
```

The video can only play on top of the Flash movie; unfortunately it can't play underneath the Flash movie and appear through a transparent layer.

The Windows Media Player also has many attributes that can be set in the HTML document. The main ones we have to concern ourselves with are the attributes that turn off user control of the video. We also want to turn off the Windows Media Player animation that occurs when the video player starts because the Game Show Network and *Inquizition* logos were the only branding allowed in the project.

15.35

Setting the following parameters to false turns off the majority of the video controls and the animation at the start of the movie:

```
<OBJECT ID="MediaPlayer1"¬
WIDTH=384¬
HEIGHT=288
 type="application/x-oleobject"
 CLASSID="CLSID:22D6F312-B0F6-11D0-¬
94AB-0080C74C7E95">
<PARAM NAME="FileName"¬
VALUE="inquizition.asf">
//filename of source asf <PARAM¬
NAME="AnimationAtStart"¬
VALUE="false">
<PARAM NAME="AllowChangeDisplaySize"¬
VALUE="false">
//controls are disabled
```

```
<PARAM NAME="Enabled"¬
VALUE="false">
//disable right click menu
<PARAM NAME="EnableContextMenu"¬
    VALUE="false">
<PARAM NAME="ShowControls"¬
VALUE="false">
</OBJECT>
</div>
```

With all this in place, the game is ready to be played. The video integrity of the original *Inquizition* game show has been preserved by using the Windows Media Player's strength in video, while Flash's strengths in interactive media and interface design create a better user experience for the broadband cable Web audience by enabling people to play the *Inquizition* at home.

CHAPTER 16
EXPLORING THE LIMITS OF ART AND PERSONAL EXPRESSION

BY GLENN THOMAS

BASED ON CONVERSATIONS WITH JOSH ULM AND SHANNON RANKIN

T he quote to the right neatly sums up the belief of the influential French linguistic Roland Barthes that the reader creates the meaning of the text through the actual act of reading. In his conception, the author of a text is removed from a position of supreme importance because a text doesn't exist without the interaction of the reader. The position of the reader to the text changes in his philosophy, with the reader moving from being the consumer to becoming the producer of the text. This is done as the reader extracts meaning from the text by bringing to it "what has already been read, seen, done, lived, assuming many different, and possibly contradictory roles as a text is read"(New York: Noonday Press, 1991).

Barthes has had a profound theoretical influence on the conception and development of hypertext fiction, as well as influencing the direction of interactive art. In hypertext fiction this "death of the author" is represented by the ability of the reader to choose an individual path through a text with multiple narratives; in interactive art a similar tendency draws the designer to create work in which the viewer/user must explore the work in order to derive meaning.

Although this requirement for the audience to engage and explore is a fundamental direction of interactive art, we disagree with Barthes that it represents the death of the author. Instead, a more complex interaction exists between artist and audience in which the artist creates the environment and set of meanings that can be taken from an artwork. The author defines the context from which the viewer/user draws meaning. The artist is not dead, but removed.

The death of the author.

ROLAND BARTHES

This notion challenges the idea of what an artist is because many interactive artists explicitly accept that they are providing a framework within which the viewer is the collaborator in creating the final artwork.

This creation of artwork that requires viewer/user engagement is one of the fundamental differences between interactive art on the Web and other artforms. The user/viewer must act or interact with the artwork to fully experience and understand it. The artwork becomes whole through the individual experience of each viewer and each viewer's path through the artwork.

Artists have always challenged society's perceptions in the process of offering a personal vision to the world; now interactive artists enter into an unspoken compact with the audience that meaning is derived through the action of the audience. Today, on the Web, artists search for a new language of interactivity as they struggle to define interactive and Web art.

Interactive art, as a new medium, still searches for a universal language. What will that language look like? The language of interactive art is only beginning to take shape, but it is clear that a number of elements such as information, visuals, sound, time, communication, audience, collaboration, and interactions through the mouse and keyboard are extremely important. Defined interactions such as rollover, mouse press and release, and keyboard press and release combine with programmatic, time, or audience interactions to change the visual or audio information.

The global language that is developing is highly visual and less based on text. It's iconic, as befits an international artform. Individual artists have begun to create sites using Flash to define this new language

of interactivity and to stretch the limits of what interactive art can do. This is an exciting time as we witness the birth and development of this new medium.

The Web and Flash have changed the world of the digital artist significantly. As never before, artists can reach the entire world through the Internet. Artists can collaborate much more easily with each other to create new work. Artists can communicate more easily. Artists can also provide frameworks within which collaborative artwork is created by the audience as viewer. All of these new abilities are enabling interactive artists on the Web to create the vision they see inside themselves and challenge audiences to engage and explore the meaning of that vision.

CREATING MEANING THROUGH INTERACTION

The Remedi Project (16.1) focuses on showing interactive art that creates meaning through artwork/viewer interaction. At this site, digital art is explorative. Artists combine different facets of artistic expression such as poetry, painting, animation, drawing, video loops, sound, and text to create a vision that requires audience interaction to generate meaning.

The Remedi Project, as curated by Josh Ulm, has quickly become a showcase for digital media pushing the limits of interactive media on the Web. Josh became involved with Flash at a very early date and uses the remediproject.com to investigate the potential of digital media on the Web to develop a new interactive language that creates artwork out of the interplay through a viewer's exploration of an artist's work (16.2).

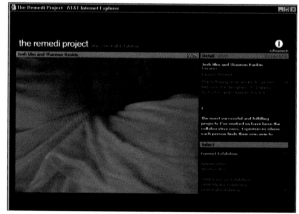

16.1　　　　16.2

BEHIND THE REMEDI PROJECT WITH JOSH ULM

Josh Ulm (16.3) is an extraordinarily talented interactive designer who has been involved with Flash from the beginning. He designed a number of enormous Flash projects at Quokka Sports that required interactive informational display.

16.3

Q: How did theremediproject.com start?
A: The name Remedi is definitely one of those cutsey things designers use to show off that they are crafting something, but yes, there was (and is) a problem to which this was (is) a remedy for. The name stands for Redesigning the Medium through Discovery.

Early on, I was involved with a community of designers through a site I did called Eye Candy. It was nothing more than a cool site of the day (when there were such things …), but it enabled me to open dialogs with designers who were, at the time, breaking new ground in a completely virgin medium. The sad thing was that these incredibly intelligent pioneers were being held back, very early on. The Remedi Project's primary mission was simply to enable the artists who were so closely connected to shaping the medium to have the control, even if only over their own work. These artists had never been empowered to simply let go, or explore where they thought the Web could go. These people knew the tools better than anyone else on the planet, and yet they were being held back by their short-sighted clients. That seemed very wrong. We all complained about it for a long time. One day I just decided that there was a very simple solution.

Q: theremediproject.com presents work focusing on interactive art. Does interactive media enable artists to do anything new in their approach to questions of personal expression?
A: Indeed, although interactivity is a misappropriated word. Right now, anything that the user can click is termed *interactive*. This might be legitimate in one vein, but a very different definition exists for the interactivity that Remedi explores.

True interactivity comes when the author and the audience come together to create something that neither of them could have envisioned on their own. As esoteric as it sounds, it has many similarities to biological evolution.

Your parents could never have predicted what you would look, act, or speak like. Nor could they have made you by themselves. Only together can two ideas combine to form a third unique concept. When the painter works his magic and presents it, I may very well interact with the work on a cognitive level. My breath may even affect the oils on the

canvas. But I have no substantial effect on the message being communicated. It does not change through my interaction with it. Interactive art does change substantially. In fact, the best interactive art does not even exist until the user participates. It is in this way that interactive art transcends its ancestors.

So to ask if interactivity enables artists to personally express themselves in different ways, I would suggest that it does by enabling them to express themselves through the actions of their audiences. It is a collaborative expression. It builds from the participants. Interactive art is fundamentally cumulative.

Q: How does technology affect personal expression?
A: It seems as if the most common answer in this new medium, regardless of the question, is "it depends." There are just so many variables. That fact answers the question as well. Of course, technology affects personal expression, but it depends on the technology and the expression being communicated. I don't believe that the technology is qualitatively a better artistic medium, any more than clay is better than watercolors. It is just different. Think of mediums as languages, and the subtleties of each as accents. You express the same messages, but you do it in different ways, and, in that language's way, it takes on characteristics and nuances of that language's nature and history.

If anything, the Web is behind technologically. Film and television have a much richer history and palette from which to create the most compelling narrative. If anything is different, it is the depth of interactivity. And yes, interactivity, true inter-activity, adds new words to the language's dictionary.

Q: In your own personal work, how did you get involved with Flash and the Web? What is your approach to interactive media?

A: I saw Flash first when it was FutureSplash. Then it was more or less just an animation tool. Not being a real animator, I realized, as a departure from the probably natural intention of the program's designers, that I could do film work using the program. My background is in film and anything that could take me closer to making films again was a step I knew I would be taking.

I had a great deal of experience in film titles and editing and, obviously from Web design, graphic design experience. The program fit my model of thinking, and I've kept up with it since.

The major breakthrough for me however, was the introduction of ActionScripting. The worlds I had created in Director until then were limited by the complexity of the program and my own shallow understanding of it. Flash quickly helped me to realize how I could author truly interactive designs — work that found its form, function, and character out of the user's participation, not simply from my own mind (16.4).

Q: Where does your inspiration come from?

A: Nature. I hear that a lot too, which makes me smile, though I wish it were more recognizable in the design work I see being done. Everything is pervaded by the same rhythms. I shouldn't have to clarify the word "everything," but from photography to music, urban planning to psychology, fashion trends to the stock market, the structure of inter-galactic nebulae to little puffy clouds over my head, there are threads that pass through it all. The answers are easy to find when you look for them in nature. They were answered eons ago. After that, everything just falls into place.

INTRODUCING SHANNON RANKIN AND SELF/FLESH

Shannon Rankin is one of the artists who has shown work at The Remedi Project as well as at other Web forums for interactive art. She is a traditional and interactive artist who runs her own personal site Self/Flesh at `www.selflesh.com` (16.5). She has fine-arts training but became interested in digital art during college. In 1997 she graduated from Maine College of Art, in Portland, Maine, with a BFA in graphic design. Since then she has been a self-employed freelance graphic designer, working in print and online with a variety of clients. During her free time she works on artistic projects

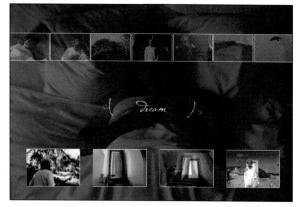

16.4

16.5

ranging from artist books to interactive experiences. She has been a contributing artist for The Remedi Project and has most recently collaborated with ioresearch on an experimental project titled *Dreams* specifically created for *Atlas* magazine.

Q: You pursue traditional artistic mediums such as drawing and painting. What attracted you to interactive media originally?

A: I studied both fine arts and graphic design. I majored in graphic design and while focusing my energies on my thesis, I met Josh Ulm. The majority of my work up to that point had been in print media but I was beginning to do more sound- and video-based projects. Slowly, I was beginning to be exposed to work on the Web. At that time, Josh was curating his own site called Eye Candy where he kept links to all of his favorite interactive work from all over the world. It just blew me away! I wanted to make lovely things that could move and make sounds. I wanted to reach a larger audience. It is still a new medium, which makes it that much more exciting because we still have so much to explore.

Moving from print media to multimedia I was able to explore the use of sound and motion, bringing the element of time and a sense of space to my work.

Q: How do you view your work?

A: Much of my work has focused around creating pieces that the viewer must come to and explore. The user is encouraged to participate. I provide the raw materials of words, images, and sound to help viewers discover something new for themselves.

Q: The rewards of viewing your work are based on how much a viewer/user interacts with it. Do you ever think of creating purely narrative experiences as part of the interactive experiences you create?

A: My work builds layers of images and meaning based on how much a viewer investigates the work. The layers create a sense of depth — windows and doors to new spaces. It is up to the viewer to enter those spaces. Much of my work contains layers of multiple meanings. The viewer is then able to bring his or her unique perspectives to the work, to find a significance for themselves.

I have thought about creating more purely narrative experiences. However, I think I would like to try to find a way to integrate the two approaches into one piece.

Q: How has Flash enabled you to follow your personal vision?

A: Flash is the one program that enables me to work in a variety of ways. I can produce work that has a variety of qualities and possibilities.

Q: What would you like to see made better in Flash?

A: I find that I have a difficult time learning some of the scripting aspects of Flash. Being a visual person I hope that scripting becomes easier to learn.

Q: What's kind of responses do you receive to your work?

A: The best experiences I have had with responses to my work have been those where people provide their own personal interpretation of the work. When this happens, my mind is opened to experience my own work in a new way with a new perspective. This is the most rewarding process because the work's meaning then seems to change over time.

Q: How do you start a project? Is it through writing, drawing, or some other method?

A: Writing, drawing, sketching, brainstorming. I tend to work in a variety of subjects or mediums on multiple projects simultaneously. While shifting from one project to another, I bring elements and perspectives from each area that can inform another. In most cases I work intuitively. I combine a synthesis of spontaneous chance actions with planned decisions.

Q: What is your process during a project?

A: My process is a process of addition and subtraction.

Q: How do you work in Flash?

A: Intuitively. I lay out all the information needed for the project on the first scene. I begin moving images and text around on the "page" until I find some relationships that somehow seem to make sense. I step away from the work and do something completely different, and then come back to the piece and edit out what doesn't make sense. It is an ongoing process of add and edit.

Q: Where do your ideas come from? What inspires you?

A: Books, writing, drawing, my dreams, life, seeing, experiences. After reading and being greatly influenced by Carl Jung's *Man and His Symbols*, I was inspired to focus my senior thesis project on the discovery of the "self" and the "process of individuation" where one finds one's own "inner center" through the investigation of one's own dreams.

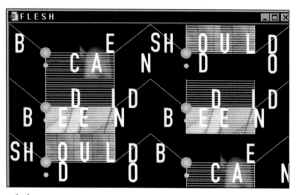

16.6

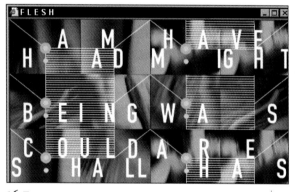

16.7

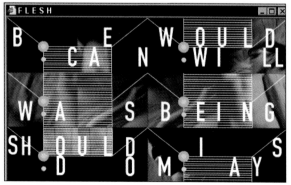

16.8

Since then I have found myself reflecting upon my life and my dreams. It has been this process of reflection, investigation, and analysis that has enabled me to decode parts of myself. I apply this same process to my work.

Q: Do you create projects to express personal experiences or are they more global artistic or political statements?
A: For now, my projects tend to be expressions of personal experience.

Q: It took years for a visual language to take root in film, but we're moving rapidly toward a visual language of the Web and interactivity. What do you feel are the key parts of this global visual language? Where do you see it going?
A: Globalization? Hopefully not in the hands of big business. Is that where it is going already? I imagine that the artists will still create; wedging their way into the mainstream, hoping listeners are still out there, making for the people.

Q: "Flesh" is intensely personal. What made you want to create it for the world to see?
A: "Flesh" (16.6–16.8) began as a video sketch, a performance using the body as the material. I had been thinking about the body as a landscape. I had also been thinking about conversation as a landscape and the way we connect words together with the use of the in-betweens such as *be*, *is*, *am*, *are*, and so on, to make sentences. So I merged the two subjects and created my first Flash piece.

I consider all of my artwork to be personal. The pieces are direct projections of my self. Perhaps you could call them self-portraits.

The Web lacks a true physical experience. I wanted to express the "idea" of physicality, and create a "sense" of presence. The viewer is able to move through a landscape of the visible body parts and sound elements.

I have been fascinated with voyeurism and surveillance for some time now and would like to continue to explore these topics in the future.

Q: In "Gardens," your visual essay exploring gardens, you juxtapose gardens where people create an idealized version of nature against natural, uncontrolled flowers. What do you hope people discover by asking them to explore this tension? What does "Gardens" mean to you?

A: "Gardens" (16.9–16.14) is a visual essay created specifically for artandculture.com. It is one piece in a series of visual essays on the experience of immersion. This piece was a collaboration between me and the art director of artandculture.com, Michael Chi Chi, along with scripting assistance from Josh Ulm.

"Gardens" is a meditative experience where viewers can create their own personal garden or composition.

Q: From the personal world of "Flesh" and your explorations of the garden, we move to the idea of the nomad, of movement and wandering, that infuses your work in "re_migrate." Describe your thought process when creating "re_migrate."

A: "re_migrate" (16.15–16.18) was a direct representation about what was going on in my life at that time. I had a few symbolic images that represented some of my feelings and seemed to communicate to me something specific. It is about moving through situations in your life even if that means swimming against the current or entering spaces that are unfamiliar.

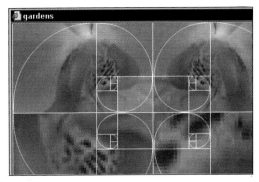

16.11

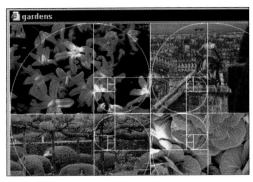

16.12

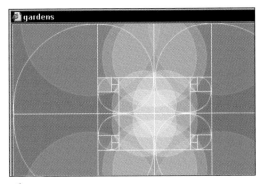

16.9

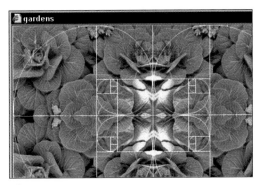

16.13

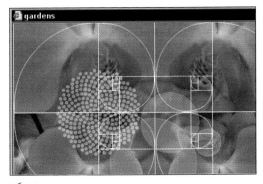

16.10

16.14

Q: "Dreams" is a collaboration with Josh Ulm. How did that work?

A: It was a great experience. I think we work very well together. At the time we were sharing the same studio space, so getting together when we had some free time was easy to do. We would take time to brainstorm, sketch, and simplify our ideas, and then we would go out and shoot. Josh works very hard at what he does, he was and still is an inspiration to me.

Q: How has the Web changed your artistic vision?

A: I believe art is for the people and should be available for everyone to experience. The Web has provided so many talented artists the opportunity to freely express themselves and let their voice and vision be heard and seen. In that sense I don't feel confined to my present living space. I am able to reach out to a wider audience, which is a great opportunity.

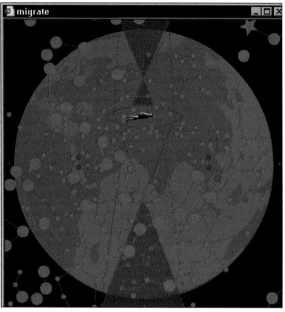

16.15

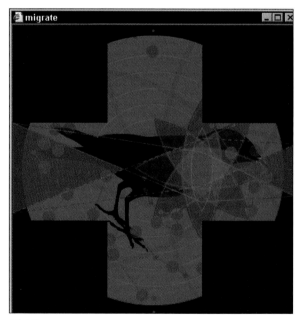

16.16

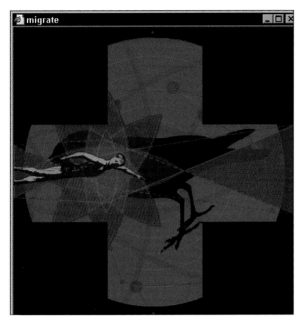

16.17

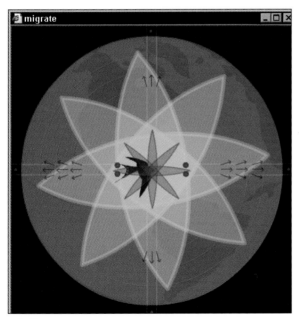

16.18

MANY MORE SITES

Beyond the work shown at The Remedi Project, many other fascinating individuals and groups are investigating the limits of interactive expression on the Web. One of the more intriguing academic groups to follow is the MIT media laboratory aesthetics + computation group (http://acg.media.mit.edu). The group combines the work of academics and theorists with actual working projects in order to explore the junctions of art and computers.

The magazine *Shift* at www.shift.jp.org shows a series of interactive experiences. *Shift* also creates the Gasbook Series that collects interactive art from an international group of contributors into a multimedia package. The Korean Web magazine *WebA* at www.weba.co.kr contains interactive experiments and experiences focused around specific themes. Submethod at www.submethod.com also uses interactivity to create intriguing digital media.

Numerous sites from individuals and companies explore a variety of directions with interactive artwork and design. Josh Davis keeps www.praystation.com fresh with experiments that combine art with physical forces such as friction and tension as created in code. He also puts personal work up at www.once-upon-a-forest.com. Matt Owen puts his individual design and expressive work at www.volumeone.com. The company vir2l at www.vir21.com explores different interactive directions in a series of experiments at their site. One of the acknowledged masters of interactive navigation design in Flash is Yugo Nakamura; he showcases his new thoughts and directions at www.yugop.com.

Great new artists and designers come out and showcase their interactive explorations using Flash all the time on the Web. There is always something new and innovative to find in the amazing global playground called the Web.

THE BIRTH OF THE INTERACTIVE ARTIST

As opposed to Barthe's suggestion that the author is dead, the growth of the Web and interactive media creates a world in which the role of the artist and the artist's engagement with a global audience is only beginning to be defined. We are still at the beginning of this new era where interactive artists take as fundamental the idea that the artwork only has meaning through a dialog with the audience.

As artists focus on making a personal artistic statement whose meaning is amplified by the audience, new and exciting ways of depicting and understanding the world are being developed. Digital interactive art will change our understanding of ourselves as fully as the camera changed the way the world looked at itself.

As the tool analogous to the camera, Flash facilitates the growth and development of interactive art over the Web because it is ubiquitous and flexible. With so many people finally having access to a simple, usable program for creating interactive art, an age full of boundless creativity and experimentation is happening around us.

We are lucky to be living at this time of creative ferment. In the years to come, we will look back and remember the experiments that resonated with the audience to create the global language of interactivity while still remembering the noble failures that pushed the boundaries without taking root. This is what it feels like at the birth of something new.

ABOUT THE AUTHOR

One of the founders of Smashing Ideas, **Glenn Thomas** discovered the first version of Flash and has never looked back. Since that time he's been involved with bringing numerous entertainment and media projects to the Web for clients such as Nickelodeon, Icebox.com, Intel, Shockwave.com, Eddie Bauer, Warner Bros., Universal, Launch Media, Popsicle, Real Networks, and others.

His goals are to encourage innovation on the Web and to push for the creation of compelling, rich media user experiences. Smashing Ideas' recent projects include partnering with WeMedia to create the Flash-enhanced Webcast of the Sydney 2000 Paralympic Games, producing the Madonna "Music" interactive music video, and creating games such as Email Chess. Smashing Ideas produced the Devo "Big Dirty Farmers" interactive music video, Blue's Clues Ford Safety Site, and also worked with Icebox to create *Zombie College*. Smashing Ideas is currently expanding beyond entertainment to focus on deploying Flash in the corporate world as well as getting Flash into both the wireless handheld market and interactive television.

Over the last several years, Smashing Ideas has won numerous awards for its work, including Shockwave Site of the Day, a Bandie for the LAUNCHcast streaming personalized radio player, several Emerald City Awards for the Devo interactive music video, a special jury award from FIFI for the CuddlyCoos Magical Music Maker, as well as being a semifinalist for the Global Internet Infrastructure award.

Glenn Thomas has spoken about using Flash and Generator for entertainment, advertising, and corporate applications at numerous conferences and symposiums. These engagements include FlashForward NYC 2000, the Macromedia User Conferences in 1997 and 1999, Macromedia Web World 2000, Web Design World 2000, Web 99 and Digital Sandbox 99.

Glenn has also written about Flash for *MacAddict* and the Macromedia Developer Center. He's taught people about Flash at Intel, Organic Online, Starwave, and the School of Visual Concepts.

COLOPHON

This book was produced electronically in Foster City, California and Indianapolis, Indiana. Microsoft Word 98 was used for word processing; design and layout were produced using QuarkXPress 4.11 and Abobe Photoshop 5.5 on Macintosh G3 and G4 computers. The typeface families used are Minion, Myriad Multiple Master, Prestige Elite, Symbol, Trajan, and Zapf Dingbats.

Acquisitions Editor: Michael Roney
Project Editor: Sharon Eames
Technical Editor: Chrissy Rey
Copy Editor: Michael D. Welch
Proof Editor: Patsy Owens
Project Coordinators: Louigene Santos, Nancee Reeves
Graphics and Production Specialists: Robert Bihlmayer, Rolly Delrosario, Jude Levinson, Michael Lewis, Victor Peréz-Varela, Ramses Ramirez, Kathie S. Schutte
Quality Control Technicians: Dina F. Quan, Rob Springer
Permissions Editor: Beth Kluender
Book Designers: Margery Cantor, Kurt Krames
Illustrators: Troy Parke and Steve D'Amico
Index: York Production Services, Inc.
Cover Image: Anthony Bunyan

INDEX

Continued

Continued